Sacred Spaces and Public Quarrels

Sacred Spaces and Public Quarrels:

African Cultural and Economic Landscapes

Edited by

Paul Tiyambe Zeleza & Ezekiel Kalipeni

Africa World Press, Inc.

P.O. Box 1892
Trenton, NJ 08607

P.O. Box 48
Asmara, ERITREA

Africa World Press, Inc.

P.O. Box 1892
Trenton, NJ 08607

P.O. Box 48
Asmara, ERITREA

Copyright © 1999 Paul Tiyambe Zeleza & Ezekiel Kalipeni

First printing 1999

Book design: Wanjiku Ngugi
Cover design: Jonathan Gullery

Figure 4.3. is reprinted with permission from the University of Chicago. Originally published in Robert A. Murdie's *Factorial Ecology of Metropolitan Chicago*, 1951-1961. Department of Geography Research paper, #6, 1969.

Library of Congress Cataloging-in-Publication Data

Sacred spaces and public quarrels : African cultual & economic
   landscapes / edited by Ezekiel Kalipeni & Paul T. Zeleza.
      p. cm.
   Includes bibliographical references (p.　) and index.
   ISBN 0-86543-706-8 (HB). -- ISBN 0-86543-707-6 (PB)
    1. Civil society --Africa. 2. Democratization--Africa. 3. Africa-
-Politics and government--1960- I. Kalipeni, Ezekiel, 1954-
II. Zeleza, Tiyambe, 1955-
JQ1879.A15S23　1998
320.96' 09'045--dc21　　　　　　　　　　　　　　　　98-41077
                                   CIP

CONTENTS

Preface vii

Rethinking Space, Politics, and Society in Africa 1
Paul Tiyambe Zeleza and Ezekiel Kalipeni

Part I: Changing Dynamics of Urban Spaces

Rethinking Cities, Sustainability, and Development in Africa 17
David Simon

The Spatial Economy of Structural Adjustment in African Cities 43
Paul Tiyambe Zeleza

The Spatial Context of Lilongwe's Growth and Development 73
Ezekiel Kalipeni

Part II: Landscapes as Ritual and Therapeutic Spaces

The Construction of Therapeutic Spaces 111
Wilbert Gesler

Ethnomedicine, Sacred Spaces, Ecosystem
Preservation and Conservation in Africa 127
Charles Anyinam

"Stray Women" and "Girls on the Move": Gender, Space,
and Disease in Colonial and Post-Colonial Zimbabwe 147
Lynette Jackson

Part III: Narrating and Imagining Spaces

Art as Time-Lines: Sacral Representation in Family Spaces 171
Nkiru Nzegwu

Self and Place in African and African-American
Autobiographical Prose: Equiano and Achebe, Soyinka and Gates 197
F. Odun Balogun

The Niger Delta, Nativity, and My Writing 233
Tanure Ojaide

Part IV: The Spatiality of Nations, Communities, and Identities

Crisis and Accounting: Towards a Spatial
History of the African Nation 251
Kwaku Larbi Korang

Community, Citizenship, and the Politics of
Ethnicity in Post-Colonial Africa 271
Dickson Eyoh

Southern Africa's Land Dilemma: Balancing Resource Inequities 301
Tiyanjana Maluwa

Land Restitution, Ethnicity, and Territoriality:
The Case of the Mmaboi Land Claim in
South Africa's Northern Province 323
Richard Levin

Contributors 357

Index 361

PREFACE

Space, Culture and Society in Africa was the theme of the 23rd Annual Spring Symposium organized by the Center for African Studies at the University of Illinois, Urbana-Champaign in 1996. Most of the papers in this collection were first presented at this symposium. The theme arose out of our conviction that the rapid and complex changes that Africa is undergoing cannot be adequately explained by the conventional and narrowly-focused disciplinary perspectives and approaches. The case for devising more complex and integrated inter-disciplinary paradigms becomes more compelling by the day.

Using the strategic concept of space as physical place, historical process, social reconstruction, and imaginative landscape, the symposium brought together scholars from different disciplines whose work on African societies, cultures, and political economies has largely remained unconnected. Among the social scientists the tendency has been to focus on the political economy of land ownership, production and struggle. In fact, in the past, the Center has organized conferences on questions of agrarian systems and land tenure, whose subsequent publications, such as Crummey and Stewart's *Modes of Production in Africa: The Pre-colonial Era* and Basset and Crummey's *Land in African Agrarian Systems*, have become influential texts in their respective fields.

In organizing this symposium we wanted to build on the theoretical insights and empirical findings of previous symposia, and to engage the emerging analytical perspectives in African Studies, in this case, the use of conceptions of spatiality as constructions and process, as context and states of social existence, being developed among cultural geographers, social historians, political ecologists, literary critics, cultural theorists and anthropologists, among others. These attempts to understand African social phenomena using new theoretical tools reflect growing dissatisfaction with the conventional paradigms in each discipline, and the increasingly apparent inability of positivist social science, often imported from elsewhere and uncritically imposed on Africa, as a whole to adequately explain the nature and dynamics of African societies and cultures. Progress has been hampered by the limited intellectual interactions and conversations among social scientists.

The aim of this collection, therefore, is to bring together streams of analysis, research and debate that focus on the spatial contexts of society and culture which have remained largely separated from each other, to cross disciplinary boundaries, as part of what must be our continuous collective efforts to devise paradigms and research methods that are better equipped to analyze and explain African histories, societies, and realities.

The symposium from which this book emanates would not have taken place without the financial support we received from the College of Liberal Arts and Sciences of the University of Illinois at Urbana-Champaign; the International Studies and Programs at the University of Illinois, then headed by Professor Roger Kanet, who graciously accepted to open the symposium; The John D. and Catherine T. McArthur Foundation; and the U.S. Department of Education, Title VI program. To all these organizations, we offer our deepest thanks. We are grateful to the Center for Advanced Study at the University of Illinois for the appointment of Ezekiel Kalipeni as Fellow which offered him release time from teaching to work on this and other projects during the Fall of 1996. We also thank the staff of the Center for African Studies —Sue Swisher, Mrs Gladys Robinson and Eric Custar and all the graduate school volunteers—for the work they did in making the symposium a success. We further extend out thanks to following colleagues who accepted to chair or act as discussants for the four panels: David Wilson, Bruce Newbold, Alma Gotlieb, Alice Deck, Kwaku Gyasi, and Joyce Bowen . We also owe our thanks to our colleague Merle Bowen who played an instrumental role as a member of the organizing committee. Finally, we would like to thank Professor John Jakle of the Department of Geography at the University of Illinois for his inspiring suggestions at the pre-planning stage of the symposium

Ezekiel Kalipeni and P. Tiyambe Zeleza

RETHINKING SPACE, POLITICS, AND SOCIETY IN AFRICA

PAUL TIYAMBE ZELEZA AND EZEKIEL KALIPENI

THE STUDY OF AFRICA IS EXPERIENCING FUNDAMENTAL transformations as African societies undergo rapid and complex changes that cannot be adequately explained by the conventional and narrowly-focused disciplinary perspectives and approaches. The disciplines themselves face increasing epistemological challenges, spawned by passionate internal debates and external institutional and intellectual pressures over what should be their concerns, content, and composition. This is also true of the field of African studies. The disciplines and the area studies programs are being pressed to become more interdisciplinary and comparativist in their analytical paradigms, methods, and research themes (*Daedalus* 1997; *Africa Today* 1997).

Organized with these issues in mind, the symposium sought to bring together scholars from different disciplines whose work on African societies, cultures, and political economies is often unconnected; to encourage an interdisciplinary conversation among them framed around the theme of space and spatiality. Together with historicity, spatiality is key to the formulation of social theory, to understanding social phenomena. Time and space are not isolated, separate entities, but inextricably interwoven and interactive dimensions that together constitute social relations. There are of courses many types of spaces: real spaces, architectural spaces, imaginary spaces, and symbolic spaces. Indeed the term "space" resists definition in either formulas or words and as Couclelis (1992) notes, it is appropriate to speak of a hierarchy of spaces: mathematical spaces, physical spaces, socioeconomic spaces, behavioral spaces and experiential spaces. As experiential spaces, to use Yi-Fu Tuan's (1977) term, all these spaces are socially produced and they produce the social, that is, in as much as space is socially constructed the social is spatially constructed, too, for, all social phenomena, activities and relations have a spatial form and a relative spatial location. "'Space' is created," argues Doreen Massey (1993:155-6), "out of the vast intricacies, the incredible complexities, of the interlocking and the non-interlocking, and the networks of relations at every scale from local to global." Space and the spatial stage and contextualize economies, politics, and cultures, and invent and inscribe places and landscapes with ethical, symbolic and aesthetic meanings. Space, then, is not a static and passive template of social exist- ence, but an active, constitutive force of the social's very composition and construction. Space and spatiality are complex and articulated material, cultural, symbolic, and discursive formations that structure and are simulta- neously structured by historical change (see, e.g., Liggett and Perry 1995; Simonsen 1996; Thrift 1996).

THE OVERARCHING CONCEPT OF SPATIALITY

We wanted the symposium's participants to excavate and examine notions of spatiality embedded in the conceptions and narratives of their disciplin- ary encounters with African social realities, processes, and data; to unravel the economies, politics and aesthetics of space from the vantage points of their disciplines and specializations in order to deepen our understanding of how Africans have and continue to organize and experience space. Our trepi- dation that the symposium might turn into a conversation of the deaf was quickly dispelled as the participants focused their minds on the social and discursive constructions of space and spatiality. The exchanges were ener- getic and engaging. By the end of it we all saw space everywhere; appreci- ating more keenly that the production and consumption of material and cre- ative cultures, of the city and the literary text, as well as the constitution and representation of bodies, communities, and nations, take place in both real and imagined geographical and social spaces; that social existence and re- flexive subjectivity are mapped and marked by space and time, and vice- versa.

Out of the many sub-themes that could have been chosen, we selected four that, in our view, best highlighted some of the emerging approaches that employ the overarching concept of spatiality and can fruitfully promote intellectual cross-fertilization among the various disciplines in the humani- ties and social sciences. The first sub-theme deals with the dynamics and morphology of urban spaces. The second sub-theme examines the con- structions of therapeutic and ritual places, cultural and medical geographies, ecological knowledge, and the spatial dynamics of social ecologies of gender and disease. The third sub-theme explores the question of spatiality and artistic production, specifically relations between texts and contexts, autobiography and space, narrative and nation. The last sub-theme discusses questions of territoriality as manifested in the land struggles in Southern Africa, at regional, national, local and domestic levels and the complex and shifting inscriptions of race, ethnicity, gender and class that mark them. The works in this collection, we hope, offer a singular opportunity for scholars to shed some of the analytical blinkers of their respective disciplines and to engage each other, so that we can begin to collectively see the African world in all its splendid complexity using the overarching concepts of space and spatiality. Below we summarize the content and context of each of the four sub-themes.

THE CHANGING MORPHOLOGY OF URBAN SPACES

As noted above, the first sub-theme deals with the dynamics and morphology of urban spaces. The three papers in this section seek to reconceptualize African cities, their sustainability and development, and interrogate especially the impact of economic crisis and structural adjustment programs on the organization and reproduction of urban life, including the social dynamics of gender roles and economic change in urban Africa. David Simon reopens the debate on African cities and urbanism by examining the legacies of colonialism and modernism and theorizing the postcolonial patterns and processes of urban change. He begins by critiquing the simplistic and superficial characterizations of African cities often made by academic tourists who have fixed Eurocentric views of what a "real" city should be. He argues that the central struggle for the postcolonial city has been between the different value systems, priorities, and mechanisms embodied in modernist conceptions and structures of the city and in the imaginations and needs of the popular classes, particularly those currently marginalized, as they seek to reclaim and reshape urban spaces in their own images. Sustainable urban development can only be achieved, he concludes, if issues of equity and democratic governance are directly confronted and resolved.

Ezekiel Kalipeni's chapter examines these questions in the context of Lilongwe. It traces the city's growth from its beginning; outlines its role in Malawi's political economy and the complex forces and calculations behind its development as a capital city; and shows how its internal spatial structure was conditioned by the changing fortunes of the country's authoritarian developmentalist model, which was bankrolled and inspired by South African capital and apartheid urban planning. The growing inadequacy of social services, including housing and wage employment, which were exacerbated by structural adjustment programs, led to the expansion of the informal sector. Eschewing popular idealistic accounts, Kalipeni does not see the informal sector simply as a benign reservoir of coping mechanisms or entrepreneurial skills, but also as a source of the social pathologies of corruption, crime, and disease. The spatial economy of structural adjustment in African cities is the subject of Paul Tiyambe Zeleza's chapter, in which he looks at the often hidden spatial metaphors in discourses about structural adjustment programs and their imputed consequences. Specifically, he examines the metaphors of urban-bias, globalization, and recolonization. He then proceeds to analyze the spatial reorganization of production brought about by structural adjustment and the remapping of the spaces and structures of employment and the development of coping strategies that altered the morphology of urban spaces, including their ruralization through farming. Also transformed was the temporal-spatial production and consumption of leisure and popular culture, and the patterns of migration and mobility. The chapter concludes by delineating the spatialization of struggles for democratization in the cities.

THE CONSTRUCTION OF LANDSCAPES AS RITUAL, THERAPEUTIC AND AESTHETIC SPACES

The three papers in the second sub-theme examine in various ways the constructions of therapeutic and ritual places, cultural and medical geographies, ecological knowledge, and the spatial dynamics of social ecologies of gender and disease. Wilbert Gesler offers a comprehensive overview of the paradigmatic shifts in medical geography, from the traditional approaches of cultural ecology and the spatial analytic approach of health care delivery, to the development of contextual and meaning-centered perspectives. Inspired by radical political economy, from the 1970s some medical geographers sought to incorporate the political and economic contexts in which disease or illness occur and treatment is organized and delivered. They paid greater attention to struggles for control in health care delivery systems. Others motivated by the humanistic perspective began focusing more closely on the meaning attached to illness as articulated through ritual and language, and to see healing places as settings where context and meaning are bound together. Concluding the chapter is a brief exploration of healing among the Kalahari Kung, which demonstrates the complex intersections of context, meaning, and healing. Charles Anyinam develops some of these insights further, noting the growing acknowledgment, even in scientific circles, of the strong interactions between religion and environmental management. His chapter explores the intricate links between ethnomedicine and ecology, arguing that ethnomedical practices, particularly the creation of sacred places, have played, and can continue to play, a strong role in the conservation and preservation of African ecosystems. He makes a compelling case of the therapeutic and ecological value of folk cultures and knowledges, rooted in their complex visions of nature and creation of sacred spaces, which are so often denigrated in the anthropocentric universal religions and the positivist and materialist convictions of modernism.

Closing this section is Lynette Jackson's fascinating exposition on the colonial and postcolonial constructions of gendered spatial and social boundaries. She shows that the convergence of colonial and indigenous patriarchal ideologies facilitated the feminization of sexually transmitted diseases, resulting in the pathologization of African women's bodies and the effective policing of their mobility and autonomy. Colonialism was a project not only of "geographical violence," as Jonathan Crush (1994:337) calls it, in that it sought to reconstruct, rename and control the spaces conquered by imperialism, but also of spatialized gender violence, which was effected through the medicalization and stigmatization of women's sexuality, independence, and movement between the strictly segregated spaces of the city and the countryside, wage work and unremunerated household labor, the visiblized male public world and the invisiblized private female world. The intersections of colonial and postcolonial discourses on gender, space and disease, despite changes in some specific regulatory practices and legislative rhetoric, points to, Jackson contends, the persistence of gender hierarchies and patriarchal power in Zimbabwe.

SPATIALIZED CONTEXTS OF LITERARY TEXTS, ARTS AND AESTHETICS

The third sub-theme is on "Narrating and Imagining Spaces" and contains three papers which explore the question of spatiality and artistic production, specifically relations between art and space, texts and contexts, autobiography and space. Nkiru Nzegwu's chapter investigates the intersecting categories of time, space and reality in the creative expressions of several prominent Nigerian artists. Using the notions of "body-space," "ideational space," and "spirit-space" as mutually permeable and interpenetrable spatial spheres and ontological states, she probes the complex idea of time-lines that family memorials and artists' representation of sacral objects reveal about how we inhabit spaces, inscribe value to such spaces, and carry the articulated systems within us. In an intriguing account of her journey to Nigeria to research on Yoruba arts and aesthetics, we see how the author's identity shifts through intricate spatial and temporal frames, in which the physical world or body space, the mental world or ideational space, and the pneumatic world or spirit-space connect and communicate in complex ways. The interspatial shifts and interactions are graphically enacted at her uncle's funeral through the *mmuo ogonogo* (the tall spirit of the threshold/crossroad) whose appearance and performance confirms the multiplicity of spatiotemporal states of reality and the possibilities of inter-spatial and inter-temporal travel, so that death turns into a natural extension of life, and the cycle of life is reaffirmed and family cohesion and lineage memory is reinforced. Nzegwu's argument is that we cannot fully understand African artists unless we comprehend their spatial and ontological frameworks. She compares two major Nigerian artists, Odinigiwe Ben Enwonwu, the ailing painter whom she goes to Nigeria to study, and Sokari Douglas Camp, an internationally renowned sculptor who lives in London. The analysis and appreciation of the two artists' work that we are offered is elegant, subtle, and insightful, so that the spirits, ideas and individuality inspiring and inscribing these works are evoked with dramatic intensity. Nzegwu's larger task it to validate the conceptual schemes of "traditional" African thought, often vilified by those immersed in the positivistic and physicalist imperatives of European and European American scientific knowledge. Specifically she takes to task the work of the Beninoise philosopher, Paulin Hountodji, who blames Africa's scientific and technological underdevelopment on the propensities of "traditional" thought to cover scientific knowledge in obfuscating layers of mythology.

Nzegwu's emphasis on the centrality of ontological and philosophical contexts in the creation and consumption of artistic products, is echoed in the two subsequent chapters in this section. Odun Balogun examines self and place in African and African American autobiographical prose, while Tanure Ojaide reflects on the impact of the Niger Delta on his poetry. Reading the two chapters makes it clear that the postmodernist reports of the death of the author have indeed been exaggerated. Poststructuralist criticism seeks to divorce books from the creative conceit of authors and the contamination of worldly contexts, and reduce them to texts, depersonalized constructs of linguistic and discursive forces. Literary texts become textual inscriptions of warring ideological representations. Lost in all this is the sheer pleasure of reading, of engaging our intellectual and emotional economy in the experiences the text represents, the worlds it evokes, which are bound to, and require, contextual and historical knowledge. The deeper the contextual and historical knowledge of the text and the author, and the more informed the reader is of their linguistic and literary conventions and of the prevailing beliefs, values, and morals, the more complex, nuanced, dense, and meaningful will be the reading (Abrams 1997; Gallagher 1997; Saldivar 1997).

Literary texts, therefore, are inextricably tied to contexts, which are themselves marked by spatial imperatives. Texts are inscribed with the context of space as much as they ascribe spaces with the meanings of context by naming places and defining a sense of place. For literature places provide imaginative spaces for playing out the texts of human drama and fantasies; they constitute texts upon which cultures, histories, and memories are registered and rendered. Balogun's and Ojaide's chapters chronicle the complex intersections of texts and contexts, imaginative space and real space, and the processes of transforming physical spaces into cultural places through imagining, historicizing, and remembering. Balogun compares the rendition of spatialized personal and collective identities in the works of Oluadah Equiano and Chinua Achebe, Wole Soyinka and Henry Louis Gates. Chosen for analysis is Achebe's *Things Fall Apart* and Equiano's *The Interesting Narrative of the Life of Oluadah Equiano*, Soyinka's *Ake: The Years of Childhood* and Gates's *Colored People: A Memoir*. He argues that apart from hailing from the same ethnic group, although separated by a couple of centuries, Achebe and Equiano adopted similar stylistic strategies to portray Igbo culture as a representative African culture and valorize it in the face of European racist condemnations. He also sees striking similarities in the narrative structures and politics of Soyinka's and Gates's autobiographies. Balogun's reading of these works conveys an unabashed aesthetic pleasure, and celebrates their subtle narrative strategies, evocative linguistic appeal, and the intimate interactions between space and self, in which place is more than a decorative geographical and temporal setting, but an active, animated presence that shapes and is reshaped by the human protagonists. The cleansing of the biographer's place of racist denigration in each of the four books, he argues, serves to undermine the racial definition and disempowerment of the biographical self, which facilitates the epistemic liberation of the collective geographies of identity in which the self is located.

Ojaide provides a riveting self-reflexive account of the meaning of his native Niger Delta to his artistic imagination, to the idioms and imagery of his poetry, to the language and grammar of his creativity. But the traffic is not one way: his poetry invests the Niger Delta with new meanings, which transforms it for the (outside) reader into a culturally defined landscape, into the recognizable homeland of the poet. The Niger Delta gives the poet an endless reservoir of memories and the vocabulary with which to craft his poetry in distant places and the imaginative capacity to domesticate those places. He writes: "The mystery of the large expanse of the sea instills a certain awe among the Urhobo to worship its spirit. This spirit is the goddess of beauty and wealth that lives in a skyscraper of needles underwater. Such is the impact of the native god/dess that at my first physical contact with the Pacific in the San Francisco-Sausalito Bay Area, I had to invoke *Umalokun* [goddess of the waters and wealth]." But it is not just the inspiration of myths that keeps the poet's creative juices flowing, but its histories of often tragic encounters with European imperialism and postcolonial tyranny. And so the poet laments the physical and psychic devastation of the Delta by the oil companies and authoritarian postcolonial state, which have robbed the native inhabitants of their lands, livelihoods, and landscapes. The poet's writing becomes a struggle against forgetting, a defiant affirmation of his nativity, an invocation of the memories of collective identity.

The theme of identity and identities has become one of the central questions of intellectual and political discourse. In North America its purveyors are to be found mostly among literary critics and cultural theorists. But it has invaded even political science with its scientific pretensions and idealization of democracy, thanks to the legacies of the social movements of the 1960s and 1970s for racial, gender and sexual reforms, reinforced by the epistemic challenges posed by feminist, poststructuralist, and ethnic studies (Smith 1997; Lindblom 1997). Similarly, African political science long committed to the nationalist and modernist projects of state construction and developmentalism has discovered the irrepressible energies of cultural pluralism. Debates on identity have centered on the constructions and the multiple intersections of race, class, gender, ethnicity, and nationalism, and their interrelations with globalization, postcoloniality and diasporic connections (Appiah and Gates 1995). Globalization intensifies the travel of cultures and commodities, ideas and institutions, signs and spaces, leading to the creation or consolidation of what Appadurai (1996) calls ethnoscapes: vast and complex landscapes of group identity, networks of transnational and diasporic solidarities. Thus the accelerated mobilities of global modernity are reshaping the economies of space and time, resulting in "time-space compression" that is redrawing the sites, dynamics, and effects of identity formation (Lash and Urry 1994).

THE POLITICAL ECONOMY OF TERRITORIALITY AND IDENTITY FORMATION

In African identity discourse pride of place has gone to the holy trinity of nationalism, ethnicity, and gender: how these identities are constituted, connected, and commemorated; how the collective memories of assumed identities are reconstructed and foundational myths instituted; what is forgotten and remembered in the construction of identities; and whose memories and imaginings prevail in the inventions of communities. The four chapters in the last section, on "The Spatiality of Nations, Communities, and Identities," grapple with these questions. Kwaku Korang's chapter makes a bold attempt to theorize a spatial history of the African nation. The architects of this project, he argues, were the middle class intelligentsia, a social strata spawned by colonialism and condemned to straddle the multiple and muddled spaces of nativity, coloniality, and modernity. It was their very mediating position in the spatial economy and cognitive structure of the colonial order that made them acutely aware of their historical agency, as redeemers of conquered native space and patrons of its genuine modernization. Despite their own organic affiliations to the varied ethnocultural spaces of nativitiy, the future nation imagined by the middle class intelligentsia was conterminous with the administrative cartography and bureaucratic fictions of the colonial state. Korang illustrates his thesis of the inherent ambivalences of the middle class nationalist imaginary by examining the political thought of Ghanaian nationalists, such as J. B. Danqua, Casely Hayford, and Kwame Nkrumah. The fatal flaw of this imaginary - a fatality imposed by objective circumstances not wilful myopia - was its singular preoccupation with politics, not culture, with the seductions of state power, not the negotiations of cultural diversity, as the critical domain of nation-formation. The massive investment of the dreams of independence in the state was a recipe for postcolonial authoritarianism and the eventual unraveling of the state itself. To be sure, there were alternative propositions from this etatist positivism, represented, for example, in the thought of Amilcar Cabral, the Guinean revolutionary leader. Cabral's challenge, Korang contends, remains: to identify and reconstruct the spatial frames in which African peoples derive their socio-historical significances as cultural subjects, where they can become a people.

The rediscovery of ethnicity in African intellectual discourse owes a lot to the stubbornness of ethnicity as a political reality and the failures of the political kingdom to create one people out of the many peoples enclosed in the spatial boundaries of the colonial state. This is the subject of Dickson Eyoh's splendid chapter. Once stigmatized in the neo-Marxist and modernization paradigms, ethnicity's rude intrusion as a serious analytical theme and political issue from the 1980s was facilitated by the proliferation of social movements and the growing popularity of political pluralism, as well as the persistence of ethnic conflicts. Embracing the social constructionist perspective, Eyoh sees ethnic identities as neither given nor static, inherently positive nor negative. As products of human agency, they are valorized and transformed in the context of struggles over structures of power and access to political, economic and symbolic resources. Almost invariably they intersect with the hierarchies of race, class, gender, and religion. Ethnicity acquired its potentially disruptive potency from the racialized imagination of colonialism, which inspired the rigid territorialization of ethnic identities, as well as from African adaptations, (re)inventions and manipulations of cultural identities. The salience of ethnic identities after independence partly arose from the fact that, notwithstanding their etatist modernist visions, the nationalists relied on ethnic networks and political brokers to mobilize the population, which ensured that ethnic affiliation would be inscribed in postcolonial claims to representation and the distribution of the fruits of *uhuru*. After independence ethnicity continued to play a critical role because these states had competing systems of power derived from the constitutional and community registers of citizenship. Also, Eyoh suggests, ethnicity offered a space of relative autonomy from the centralizing ambitions and bureaucratic exactions of the postcolonial state: it provided moral communities for cultural citizenship, accumulation, elite accountability, refuge from the failures of developmentalism, and resistance against authoritarianism. And in the context of rapid and often bewildering societal change ideologies of home underwrote the moral solidarities of ethnic attachment. Ethnic identities and conflicts are, he concludes, as modern as nationalism itself and raise fundamental questions about the meaning of citizenship, the basis of state power, and modes of representation.

Land remains central in the production of identities and power in most African societies, especially in the regions that were violently restructured and remapped by settler colonialism, such as Southern Africa. Settler colonialism was fundamentally a process of robbing, renaming, and racializing the land of the natives, emptying it of their presence and memories, and investing it with new memories and meanings (Darian-Smith et al. 1996). The last two chapters by Tiyanjana Maluwa and Richard Levin investigate the legacies of settler land appropriation in Southern Africa, the struggles they engendered, and the cultural identities and political imaginations they forged. Maluwa offers a broad overview of land inequities in the region, focusing on four major dilemmas. First, he examines the struggles over land restitution and land restoration following the end of colonial rule and especially the demise of apartheid in South Africa. Second, the chapter looks at the challenges of counterbalancing customary land rights and statutory land rights, a legal and structural tension introduced by colonialism and now exacerbated by pressures towards land privatization exerted by local bourgeois agrarian interests and external donor agencies wedded to the creed of neo-classical economics. Third, the persistence of women's inequitable access to land and other property rights is examined. Despite formal equality guaranteed by the constitutions of all the Southern African countries, including post-apartheid South Africa, which prohibit sex and gender discrimination, women continue to be denied equal access. It is one of the strengths of the chapter that it simply does not record these inequalities, it also proposes a gendered perspective of the land question in Southern Africa, and explores the struggles by women and other concerned interest groups for equality of access to, and control over, land and other property. Finally, Maluwa argues that in addition to race, class, and gender, ethnicity has also been a major factor in the struggles over land in the region; struggles that are tied to efforts of indigenous communities to reconstitute their spatial and cultural identities and protect their environments and livelihoods; in short, to safeguard their rights to autonomy and development.

The question of land restitution is discussed in detail by Levin, who presents an exhaustive analysis of a specific case, the Mmaboi land claim. The chapter traces the long history of Mmaboi land dispossession from the nineteenth century through the forced removals of the twentieth century and the apartheid years. Land restitution is only one of the three approaches to land reform adopted by the ANC-led government in South Africa. The other two are land redistribution through the market and land tenure reform. It is widely agreed that the restructuring of land relations is central to democratic transformation and development. Despite its good intentions, the land restitution program, Levin believes, has many pitfalls. In so far as the restitution claims are supposed to be lodged by homogeneous and identifiable communities, the process encourages the reinventions of primordial ethnic identities and affiliations which, in turn, revive or reinforce chieftaincy, for it is communities that can be represented by a single institution claiming "traditional" legitimacy that are favored. The resuscitation of chieftaincy as a key institution in the land claims process poses a threat to the democratization of land relations and stokes spatial conflicts in cases of overlapping claims between revitalized ethnic groups. Moreover, given the patriarchal ethos of chieftaincy, it also undermines political and constitutional commitments to restructuring gender relations.

CONCLUSION

It can be seen every chapter in this book has engaged, from different disciplinary and theoretical perspectives, the complex notions of space and spatiality as physically, socially, and imaginatively constituted settings and relations. Variously reacting to the perceived methodological and theoretical inadequacies of their own disciplines, especially the increasingly apparent inability of positivist social science to elucidate African social phenomena, and inspired by new critical spatial and cultural theories, these authors have attempted to map out a deeper understanding of African societies and cultures. The aim of the symposium and this book was to encourage interdisciplinary conversation, centered around, concepts of space and spatiality, as part of what must be an ongoing effort to develop research methodologies and theoretical frameworks that are better equipped to comprehend African realities. The fact that scholars from such diverse disciplines as geography, history, art history, literature, political science, and philosophy were able to sit together for a couple of days and exchange views and realize that they could not only understand each other, but also learn from each other about the changing morphology of urban spaces, the spatialized contexts of literary texts and art, the construction of landscapes as ritual, therapeutic, symbolic and aesthetic spaces, and the political economy of territoriality and identity formation, was quite encouraging. We hope some of the intellectual excitement of the symposium has been imparted in this book, which may encourage others to pursue the various issues raised.

REFERENCES

Abrams, M. H. "The Transformation of English Studies: 1930-1995." *Daedalus* 126, 1 (1997):105-131.

Africa Today. 44, 2 (1997). Special issue on The Future of Regional Studies.

Appadurai, Arjun. *Modernity at Large*. Minneapolis: University of Minnesota Press, 1996.

Appiah, Kwame Anthony and Henry Louis Gates. *Identities*. Chicago: University of Chicago Press, 1995.

Couclelis, Helen. "Location, Place, Region, and Space." In *Geography's Inner Worlds: Pervasive Themes in Contemporary American Geography*, eds. Ronald F. Abler, Melvin G. Marcus and Judy M. Olson. New Brunswick, N.J.: Rutgers University Press, 1992.

Crush, Jonathan. "Post-colonialism, Decolonization, and Geography." In *Geography and Empire*, eds. Anne Godlewska and Neil Smith. Oxford: Blackwell, 1994.

Daedalus. 126, 1 (1997). Special issue on the Disciplines.

Darian-Smith, Kate, Liz Gunner and Sara Nuttall. *Text, Theory, Space: Land, Literature and History in South Africa and Australia*. New York: Routledge, 1996.

Gallagher, Catherine. "The History of Literary Criticism." *Daedalus* 126, 1 (1997):133-153.

Lash, Scott and John Urry. *Economies of Signs and Space*. Thousand Oaks, CA: Sage, 1994.

Ligget, Helen and David C. Perry. *Spatial Practices*. London: Sage Publications, 1995.

Lindblom, Charles E. "Political Science in the 1940s and 1950s." *Daedalus* 126, 1 (1997):225-252.

Massey, Doreen. "Politics and Space/Time." In *Place and the Politics of Identity*, eds. Michael Keith and Steve Pile. London and New York: Routledge, 1993.

Saldivar, Jose David. "Tracking English and American Literary and Cultural Criticism." *Daedalus* 126, 1 (1997):155-174.

Simonsen, Kirsten. "What Kind of Space in What Kind of Theory." *Progress in Human Geography* 20, 4 (1996):494-512.

Smith, Rogers M. "Still Blowing in the Wind: The American Quest for a Democratic, Scientific Political Science." *Daedalus* 126, 1 (1997):253-287.

Thrift, Niger. *Spatial Formations*. London: Sage Publications, 1996.

I
THE CHANGING DYNAMICS
OF URBAN SPACES

Rethinking Cities, Sustainability, and Development in Africa

David Simon

INTRODUCTION: WHAT IS (IN) A CITY?

Lusaka is tiny and charmingly fails to project an urban image. Of course it tries; there are a few high-rise (but not very high) status symbols, several pretentious banks, the usual airline offices, embassies, shopping arcades and pseudo-supermarkets (their stock reminding me of Rumania), an international airport, a few of Zambia's seventeen cinemas, an elegant residential area (mainly occupied by expatriates) and the offices of the usual plethora of UN free-loaders. But none of this, somehow, adds up to a *city*. One is much more aware of the desperately impoverished shanty towns around the edges—known, for some obscure reason, as "compounds." These seem to be (and are, numerically) the real Lusaka, where tens of thousands endure poverty with fortitude. But of course that poverty breeds crime and in the city-center pickpocketing has been brought to a fine art.... However, when one compares the lifestyles of the expatriate colony and the compounds it is hard not to see White pockets as "legitimate economic targets." (Murphy 1994:250)

For the moment, the city works. However, as the pressures arising from population growth, inflexible and traditional administration and planning, and economic hardship and liberalization build up, it is becoming a little like a pressure cooker. If Harare is to continue to provide economic opportunities and a pleasant and healthy environment for its residents in future, more responsive urban administrations, implementing more realistic and innovative policies, are needed quickly. (Rakodi 1995:275)

THESE TWO RECENT REPRESENTATIONS OF LUSAKA AND Harare respectively, encapsulate many of the issues to be addressed in this chapter and I will indulge in a little textual analysis by way of illustration. First, a little context is necessary. In 1992, Dervla Murphy, the veteran Irish travel writer, undertook a marathon bicycle journey from Nairobi to Karoi in Zimbabwe. This was evidently her first visit to east and southern Africa. The title of her book reflects the dominant concern and issue encountered en route (*ukimwi* is kiSwahili for AIDS). Her brief encounter with Lusaka came near the end of her route, shortly before she suffered a serious attack of malaria. Conversely, Carole Rakodi's judgement represents the final few sentences of a monograph which draws on several years of research and writing on land and shelter issues, in particular, in Harare (and prior to that also Lusaka). Hence we are not really comparing like with like. Nevertheless, there are several points of similarity: both authors are Caucasian, English-speaking, female, and outsiders, yet sensitive to issues of cross-cultural comparison and the dangers of Eurocentrism.

Although both cities shared British colonial origins in the late nineteenth and early twentieth centuries, and lie in neighboring countries, their histories and economic trajectories have long been very different. Ironically, although Lusaka was laid out as a classic colonial garden city in tropical Africa and benefited from the copper boom in the 1950s and 1960s, it has suffered severely as a result of Zambia's postcolonial decline, bound up with the prolonged copper depression, lack of economic diversification, political and economic mismanagement, and a shadow effect from Salisbury/ Harare. The latter's fortunes have been far more buoyant, reflecting the more diversified and dynamic settler economy. It became the capital of the ill-fated Federation of Rhodesia and Nyasaland in the 1950s, a crucial event which gave it supranational functions and greater attractiveness to commercial, industrial and business service investors. Sanctions during the UDI years represented a setback but stimulated a rapid programme of import substituting industrialization centered on both Salisbury and Bulawayo. After Zimbabwean independence, conditions once again became favorable, especially given that country's role as the *de facto* economic leader of the Southern African Development Coordinating Conference (SADCC)[1] as a counterweight to South Africa. In the last few years, though, the impact of the Economic Structural Adjustment Programme (ESAP) has affected many residents severely, creating real hardship (Tevera 1995). In aggregate population terms, the cities are comparable. Lusaka had a population of 982,000 at the 1990 census (Potts 1995), compared with just under 1.5 million in Greater Harare (including Chitungwiza) at the 1992 census (Rakodi 1995:144).

Even thus contextualized, the quotes provide sharp contrasts. To Murphy, Lusaka barely merits the label *city*, despite being the capital and having such a large population. For her, the various components fail to hang together, to offer an integrated whole. She conceives of the low-income "compounds" as separate(d) in every sense, even to the point of apparently excluding them from her sense of the city. Poverty and crime, reflecting both reputation and her own experience, are widespread, making an urban landscape of contrasting iconographies: poverty-wracked compounds and well protected expatriate "colonies" (itself an evocative term suggesting that, even today, they remain alien implants) represent different and grossly unequal lifeworlds. The principal interaction between them occurs and finds expression in a crime-ridden CBD, with pampered international aid and development staff the prime targets.

By contrast, Rakodi—in very carefully chosen and dispassionate terms—depicts Harare as a well functioning city, albeit one in which the combined effects of growth, economic hardship and inappropriate urban policies will soon precipitate serious problems in the absence of change. As the rest of her book demonstrates, she is clearly well aware of the substantial inequalities and contrasts which characterize Harare, and indeed virtually all African cities regardless of whether indigenous or colonial in origin (Simon 1992).

Implicit in both quotations is the urgency of substantive change in the nature of African cities and urbanism. In particular, it is imperative to address the grave inequalities which threaten to destabilize urban life, and to promote more sustainable urban development. This chapter takes up the challenge, explaining how intimately linked the notions of equitability and sustainability are, and suggesting possible ways forward with respect particularly to urban morphology in the light of current theoretical debates. This task naturally implies a close interrelationship between theory and applied research. In this context, morphology is interpreted as constituting cultural spaces as much as purely physical spaces, since cities are socially produced cultural artefacts. However, a related task, of reconceptualizing cities and urbanism as cultural expressions (or as culturally produced social artefacts), in relation to the question of what is (in a) city, falls beyond the scope of this chapter. Similarly, I will make only brief mention of the politics of the built environment which are inevitably bound up with the nature of urban change being discussed here.

THE URBAN LEGACY OF COLONIALISM AND MODERNISM
Since decolonization, Africa's urban areas have experienced strong elements of continuity as well as change in respect of their morphology, social character, economic functions, planning, management, and politics. Towns and cities almost everywhere inherited a legacy of physically and socially structured inequality. The only partial exceptions to this were indigenous centers which had been ignored or bypassed by colonial settlers and their infrastructure and administrations. Here, as in Ife, Katsina, and Kumasi, for example, indigenous social structures, customs and land allocation mechanisms survived comparatively well, and inequality was less marked than in other previously indigenous cities like Kano or in those of colonial origin.

By way of generalization, the main postcolonial urban changes over the last 40 years can be characterized as follows. Some of them relate specifically to urban morphology, but all have clear—and sometimes dramatic—implications for city structures and the nature and quality of urban life for different groups of residents. Although evident almost everywhere, these processes of change may have been somewhat more pronounced and intense in cities and towns in settler colonies than in those where the colonial presence was numerically limited.

A. Generally rapid urban growth, finding expression principally in outward expansion of the built-up area, apart from vertical commercial development and the construction of apartment blocks in a few specific residential zones.

Although rapid urbanization was long held to be virtually irreversible, the impact of severe economic depression coupled with structural adjustment policies has shown otherwise: Accra experienced net outmigration during the worst of Ghana's crisis in the early 1980s while Kitwe and Ndola on the Zambian Copperbelt have been similarly affected more recently (Potts 1995; Simon 1996a). The relative fortunes of large, intermediate and small towns also change according to prevailing conditions; for example, intermediate centers in Tanzania offer rural migrants a range of basic needs and risk-spreading opportunities despite high levels of unemployment and a cost of living which exceeds that on their rural *shambas* (Holm 1995). It is worth noting that none of the centers just mentioned were predominantly colonial settler towns. Despite concerns about statistical accuracy and comparability, international data suggest that access to basic needs (e.g., potable water, sanitation services, basic health care and education) remains greater in urban than rural areas even after more than a decade of structural adjustment and economic recovery programmes (Simon 1996a, 1996b; UNDP 1995).

B. Population growth principally through high net inmigration, although the contribution of natural increase (i.e., births to existing urban residents) is gradually rising in both absolute and relative terms.

Most new migrants have been poor, from rural areas and from diverse ethnic and cultural backgrounds.

C. The inability of formal housing delivery systems, both official and private, to cater to the majority of new urban residents (Hardoy and Satterthwaite 1989).

Consequently, residential densities in existing housing units have increased through "doubling up" and subletting, while the proportion of urban residents living in informal/irregular shelter—either self-built or rented—has risen almost everywhere. In a substantial number of African cities they are in the majority, e.g., Lusaka 50%; Ouagadougou and Dar es Salaam 60%; Luanda 70%; Bangui 75%; Mogadishu 80% (even before the recent urban war); and Addis Ababa 85% (Simon 1992:107).

D. A modest degree of urban densification through plot subdivision and redevelopment in existing middle and upper income areas. However, there is still scope for considerably more.

E. Notwithstanding the above, relatively little change to the inherited physical fabric, as bricks and concrete are not amenable to rapid or large-scale restructuring short of massively expensive comprehensive redevelopment.

The extent of such redevelopment has generally been greatest in the CBDs of major commercial centers, and reflects the operation of essentially capitalist land markets rather than state-led restructuring for socio-political ends. This applies to towns and cities of both indigenous and colonial origins.

F. Rapid expansion of public sector and some categories of industrial and commercial employment during the 1960s and 1970s, with business and personal services representing the main growth category thereafter.

Overall formal sector employment has been generally static or in decline since the early to mid-1980s as a result principally of structural adjustment, liberalization and privatization policies. Almost without exception, African cities remain strongly multifunctional.

G. *Generally sustained growth in the range and relative importance of so-called informal or unregistered employment, despite efforts to suppress it.*
    In many parts of Africa, the numbers of people engaged in such income-earning strategies have mushroomed in inverse relation to formal sector employment trends since the mid-1980s.

H. *The persistence of inherited and generally inappropriate town planning mechanisms and procedures (Simon 1992).*
    The result is that land use zoning, development control, building standards and urban design more generally have usually failed to address the needs and aspirations of the majority of urban dwellers or to formulate more locally, culturally, economically and environmentally appropriate alternatives even for new developments.

I. *Cutbacks in social expenditure by the central and local state under structural adjustment, whether as part of formal IMF packages or self-imposed in an effort to avoid the invocation of aid conditionalities.*
    School enrolments and the coverage of primary health care services are therefore falling in both urban and rural areas of many countries. Maintenance levels of physical infrastructure (e.g. roads, street lighting, water and sewerage reticulation systems and public buildings) have also declined almost everywhere, and alarmingly in some cities.

J. *A marked increase in the number and significance of urban-based protest movements and civil/political conflicts during the 1980s and 1990s.*
    Some of these, such as the so-called "bread riots" in Tunis, Accra, Harare and Lusaka, for example, were triggered by the often harsh and inequitable impacts of subsidy cuts, wage freezes, and retrenchments under structural adjustment. In South Africa, a campaign to literally "make the townships ungovernable" formed a crucial element of resistance to apartheid in the mid-1980s. Unusually, recent years have witnessed several wider civil wars which had particularly devastating consequences for some towns and major cities and their inhabitants, most dramatically in Angola, Somalia, Liberia, Sierra Leone and Rwanda, although urban-focused conflicts are still raging in Algeria, Burundi and also intermittently in Burundi. In some cases, like Kigali, the cities were effectively emptied of people for a limited period but elsewhere, as in Mogadishu, Bardera and some smaller towns in Mozambique physical destruction was considerable. Many of Angola's inland cities and

towns, especially Huambo, Moxico and Malange, have been all but destroyed. Others, like Luanda, experienced substantial inflows of displaced people.

GENERALIZING AND THEORIZING URBAN CHANGE
The extent to which meaningful generalization about urban Africa is possible has been analyzed in empirical terms (O'Connor 1983), with respect to more theoretically informed concerns with underlying forces and processes of urban development during the colonial and postcolonial periods (Simon 1992) and in terms of contemporary urban management challenges (Stren and White 1989). At one level, there is substantial evidence that a process of convergence in urban morphology has been occurring, with the gradual "Westernization" of hitherto indigenous cities and the "Africanization" of colonial urban centers. On the one hand, this reflects the diversification of functions and the development of new residential urban areas outside indigenous quarters. On the other, it refers to socio-cultural change and the effects of the different priorities of the local inheritors of cities previously designed by Europeans essentially for Europeans.

However, I have elsewhere argued against assuming an all-embracing, uniform or unidirectional process of convergence and homogenization even under the influence of increasingly globalized production, distribution and consumption (Simon 1992, 1996a). Here I take issue with Roland Robertson's (1992) thesis that globalization, convergence and homogenization are virtual corollaries. Rather, on both intuitive and empirical grounds, it seems that convergence and globalization vary in impact and extent across both space and time, and even within and between social groups (defined in terms of ethnicity, class, culture, etc.) in a given locality. Political and cultural countermovements are also common, while new divergences and syncretic or pastiche forms constantly emerge. These find expression in social as well as physical urban terms, whether in postmodern architectural forms or distinctively new urban designs more in keeping with postcolonial and postmodern times.

This argument raises another way of seeing and interpreting the processes and features described in points A-J above. European colonialism in Africa was naturally motivated by a range of considerations and found expression in different ways according to local circumstances at a given time. However, driven by late nineteenth and early twentieth century industrial capitalism, the colonial impacts in terms of civilizing and Christianizing zeal, the nature of territorial administrations established, and the European-derived forms of urbanism and planning norms introduced, for example, were clearly modernist and modernizing in thrust and content. Eurocentric, supremacist, discriminatory and exploitative they frequently were, but they provided a comprehensive justification for suppressing, deprecating and/or ignoring the alien, the different, the "other" in the name of this presumed "greater good." Town planning and other administrative codes were—and often remain—concerned with creating and maintaining a narrowly conceived, formalistic and very procedural notion of urban order. This was clearest in settler colonies and cities in non-settler colonies designed by Europeans, but also strongly evident in settler components of previously indigenous cities.

After independence, the hegemony of this modernization paradigm persisted, despite often radical changes in personnel (through indigenization) and political/development ideology. After all, it is now widely recognized that the various strands of radical nationalism and socialism shared the modernist pedigree of modernization, namely being a universalizing "grand theory" or metanarrative concerned with defining and pursuing a single, "best" or "correct" path to a desired outcome. However, the ability to implement or continue implementing such agendas began to wane, as a result of sheer pressure of urban growth at one level but, more profoundly, also on account of their internal contradictions and their alienness and inappropriateness to local conditions and indigenous values, however these had been transformed by the colonial experience in any given context. Despite its obsession with neatness and order, modernist town planning, rooted as it was in a particular type of colonial and capitalist project in a specific period, has contributed directly to the current problems facing African and other excolonial cities.

Seen in this way, the "breakdown" of conventional urban planning, development and management becomes not so much a matter of inadequate skilled staff and resources (which is the conventional argument) but a struggle between different value systems, priorities and mechanisms. People have increasingly been bypassing the state and its formal procedures because these do not and cannot cater to their needs and aspirations. In other words, there is both necessity and defiance in popular actions. Local people, especially those currently marginalized, are claiming or reclaiming urban spaces and shaping them in their own images. The resultant conflicts and contradictions, the juxtapositions of radically different construction processes, built forms, identities, lifestyles and cultural expressions, have become almost the norm rather than the exception in Africa. Uniformity has given way to diversity, albeit often by default and grassroots action rather than by official design. In a very real sense, though, this is the essence of postmodernity. Whereas such pastiches, divergences and pluralities are still exceptional and very limited in physical extent in certain Northern cities (see Watson and Gibson 1995), they are widespread and have been manifest far longer in many parts of the South. One of the ideas explored below is how the promotion of more equitable and sustainable cities might embody or "design in" difference and diversity rather than designing them out as conventional urban planning has sought to do.

This ties up nicely with the implication of one less theoretical—but nevertheless essential—conclusion to be drawn from points A-J above. Although structural adjustment-type policies may have "balanced the books" of the state and local authorities to some extent and reduced excessive reliance on distortionary subsidies, few urban residents across the continent would agree that their situations have improved tangibly in recent years. Indeed, there is considerable evidence to the contrary, even in those cities not directly affected by war (cf., Commissao Nacional de Plano et al. 1993; Holm 1995; Tevera 1995).

Hence, whatever the particular issues and problems in individual towns and cities, it can be argued that most present forms of urbanism remain highly inequitable and inappropriate, and have now also become both economically and environmentally unsustainable. This applies to some or all of: urban structure; modes of design, organization and control (including planning and resourcing); rates of growth; the nature and patterns of energy consumption; the disproportionate consumption of other resources; and environmental quality in the broadest sense. There is therefore a widespread need for urban reconstruction, not merely in the narrow sense of rebuilding or repairing so as to reproduce past processes, structures and forms, but in very different ways with different intended outcomes. These should accord with prevailing conditions and promote more sustainable, equitable and diverse forms of urbanism. The remainder of this chapter explores how this objective might be promoted. This certainly implies a continued need for planning mechanisms and procedures, although of a different kind from those in use hitherto. These should not be conceived of as a simplistic panacea, since contestations and new/different inequalities, albeit hopefully less pronounced, will remain inherent to any such system. Some Northern interpretations of postmodernism involve an abandonment of institutionalized planning in what amounts to a virtual *laissez faire* situation of individual or collective self-expression (see some of the contributions in Watson and Gibson 1995). I do not share this conception, while the problems inherent in a totally unplanned situation are too well known to repeat here.

THE NATURE OF SUSTAINABILITY AND EQUITABILITY

I do not propose to engage in protracted definitional debates about sustainable development. For present purposes it is only necessary to point out the essential prerequisite that the environment in the broadest sense be utilized carefully so as not to degrade it (e.g., through the pollution of renewable resources) beyond local tolerance levels, deplete non-renewable resource endowments or otherwise compromise its long term viability and the ability of future generations to attain a comparable quality of life to ours. Interestingly, there is a strong resonance here with many traditional (but now generally transformed or lost) indigenous African cultural systems and mores, in terms of which the current generation were regarded as trustees of their land, environment and traditions for future generations.

A certain minimum acceptable level of equitability and quality of life (in having basic human needs met) in any given context is also essential. Otherwise, efforts to achieve sustainability will be undermined by the day-to-day struggles for survival by the poor and/or direct conflicts over control of and access to resources between rich and poor. Put more explicitly, general legitimacy, acceptability, participation and empowerment are necessary. This is a somewhat broader consideration than the need to contribute to poverty reduction identified in the Brundtland Commission's report (WCED 1987), although the latter is clearly vital. It is also a particularly challenging requirement in situations of such widespread poverty, inequality and powerlessness as in African cities. Moreover, cities are not isolated entities but integral components of wider social, economic and political systems. These linkages must not be forgotten in the search for sustainability. In the words of Mitlin and Satterthwaite (1996:35),

> A concentration on "sustainable cities" focuses too much on achieving ecological sustainability within increasingly isolated "eco-regions" or "bio-regions." Seeking "sustainable cities" implies that each city has to meet the resource needs of the population and enterprises located there from its immediate surrounds. But the goals of sustainable development are the meeting of human needs within all cities (and rural areas) with a level of resource use and waste generation within each region and within the nation and the planet that is compatible with ecological sustainability. It is unrealistic to demand that major cities should be supported by the resources produced in their immediate surrounds but entirely appropriate to require that consumers and producers in high-consumption, high waste cities reduce their level of resource use and waste and reduce or halt the damaging ecological impacts of their demands for fresh water and other resources on their surrounds.

In recent years, issues of sustainability have gained international prominence and political legitimacy. Although the presence of world leaders at special UN-sponsored summits and their signatures on the declarations and conventions which result may ultimately have more symbolic than substantive value, this nevertheless represents a major advance from the situation just a few years ago where such concerns could be dismissed as the preoccupations of a lunatic environmentalist fringe. For example, Chapter 7 of Agenda 21, which was adopted at the United Nations Conference on Environment and Development in Rio de Janeiro in 1992, addresses ways to promote the sustainable development of human settlements. Similarly, the "Global Plan of Action" agreed at Habitat II, the Second Cities Summit, in Istanbul in mid-1996, contains two key national commitments. These deal with "adequate shelter for all" and "sustainable human settlements in an urbanizing world." Meanwhile, in 1995 UNEP and UNCHS established a joint Sustainable Cities Programme of technical co-operation and capacity building at the level of individual participating cities in different countries of the South. In addition, there is a growing academic and professional literature on the subject, including at least two books entitled simply *Sustainable Cities* (Stren et al. 1992; Haughton and Hunter 1994), one on *Sustainability, the Environment and Urbanization* (Pugh 1996) and one with sustainability in the subtitle (Cadman and Payne 1990); research initiatives or programmes are also currently being supported by two Research Councils in the UK.

RESTRUCTURING URBAN SPACE

Given the theme of this section of the book, I will concentrate now on promoting sustainability and equitability in the physical urban environment, i.e., urban space or morphology. Clearly, however, such concerns require appropriate local institutional contexts and appropriate financing mechanisms capable of providing both private and public funds into shelter and settlements development (UNCHS 1990a; Simon 1996b). Following from my discussion above about postmodernism, institutions and planning processes must become more flexible, participatory, transparent, responsive and better able to accommodate the diversity of competing views articulated by different community groups and interests. For example, South Africa's still unfinished transition to democratic rule at the level of local authorities has been providing some fascinating and very relevant examples in this context (Simon 1996b, 1996c). In what follows, I draw on ideas developed more specifically for southern Africa (Simon 1996b), duly modified to address conditions elsewhere on the continent.

In view of the inherent inequities and inefficiencies of current urban designs and layouts, it is necessary to consider potential changes to these areas as well as in the design of new urban extensions. Inevitably, though, there are numerous common issues, many of which will require amendment and adaptation of the existing planning system and design/building standards.

The continued reliance on expatriate consultants and Northern-trained planners unwilling or unable to adapt to very different planning contexts, has been well documented (Wekwete 1988; Simon 1992).

Densification and Residential Integration
By encouraging or requiring the subdivision of large plots and greater vertical development (i.e., the construction of double-storey homes, duplex or town house schemes, and blocks of flats), more people can be suitably accommodated and supplied with infrastructure within existing developed suburbs or townships, and at lower unit cost. There is certainly scope for this in many middle and high income areas across the continent. Some middle income areas in major South African cities have been experiencing considerable market-led densification of these types since at least the late 1970s (Dewar 1995; Simon 1992). Measures to encourage densification and the development of vacant plots of urban land held for speculative purposes could include modifying zoning density limits, and introducing differential property rates which discriminate proportionately more heavily against undeveloped plots or those with low bulk-density ratios. However, such intervention cannot alone address the scale and magnitude of the problems facing African cities, particularly as regards the needs of the urban poor and those previously suffering discrimination in access to urban spaces and opportunities. A more comprehensive approach is required.

One crucial issue to be addressed is whether market-led property redistribution and residential integration can or will change the complexion of urban areas substantially. The evidence from cities of colonial origin ranging from Dakar to Nairobi and Windhoek suggests very clearly that the class character and associated characteristics of existing residential areas have generally been maintained. This applies especially in the more exclusive middle and upper income suburbs, where only people with adequate financial means or status are able to gain a foothold (Cumming 1990; Simon 1991, 1992; Yahya 1990). Occasionally, in the context of a shortage of appropriate housing for a particular income group, refurbishment and upgrading of poorer quality areas may occur. This is sometimes known as "downraiding" in the literature, especially where people buy into supposedly low-income housing schemes. This has been well documented in Nairobi, for example (Simon 1992). A rather different case is Johannesburg's inner city Mayfair suburb, where substantial numbers of relatively well-off Asians from segregated townships on the outskirts of the city bought properties in the late 1980s and early 1990s, as apartheid laws were relaxed or defied. In many cases this enabled them to return to an area close to their businesses and from which they has suffered apartheid evictions (Parnell and Pirie 1991:

140). Class is thus becoming the basis of residential organization rather than imputed "race," but the legacy of apartheid and colonial segregation policies will ensure that a substantial overlap between the two remains for a considerable period.

Cities or city segments of indigenous origin where customary land and housing allocation processes have survived to some extent, are now also experiencing greater filtering by income, as well as densification through multiple occupancy as pressure on available shelter increases. Under such conditions, transactions are becoming commercialized and housing quality is often declining. This is well illustrated in villages enveloped by Lagos (Aina 1989), as well as by conditions within the old walled cities of Ibadan and Kano, for example.

Reclaiming the InnerCity

Generally, the most substantial residential opportunities for poor people within the former colonial or white cities have occurred where and to the extent that downmarket accommodation becomes available. Such properties are found especially in and around central business districts, in older cottages and blocks of flats. There is evidence of this in parts of Nairobi and Harare (Cumming 1990; Yahya 1990). The recent transformation of the formerly white Joubert Park-Hillbrow-Berea area of Johannesburg into 90-95% black occupancy is undoubtedly the most dramatic example in South Africa, on account of its size and the rapidity of the process (Crankshaw and White 1995). Since the late 1960s, whites had been suburbanizing at an increasing rate, precipitating a survival crisis for many flatland rentlords and for shops and offices in and around the CBD. Just as the clientele of these businesses became increasingly black, so landlords, managing agents and sectional title companies accepted black tenants in order to secure rents. Indeed, when the Group Areas Act was still in force (i.e. until mid-1991) higher rents could be charged on account of the illegality and attendant risks; at the same time, the need to provide formal leases could be avoided. Banks and other financial institutions "redlined" the area, refusing to provide mortgage bond funds out of a mixture of racial prejudice and fear that property prices would fall substantially.

In order to help meet such rentals, and to assist relatives or friends lacking housing or facing the long, expensive commute from the townships, tenants began taking in subtenants. Multiple occupancy became common, services and infrastructure were overloaded and landlords reduced or ceased to undertake maintenance. Tenants sometimes responded by withholding rent payments. Evictions were sought and occasionally carried out. Since most lacked formal leases, they were technically illegal residents. In some areas, conditions deteriorated rapidly, and crime increased. The term "slum" is used regularly by municipal officials and politicians, although the City Council took little action.

People occupying several apartment blocks in the Joubert Park neighborhood that had been effectively abandoned by their owners were faced with evictions in what became a celebrated case of resistance organized by community-based organizations. A resolution to the conflict gradually emerged with the tenants organizing on a co-operative basis in what became known as the Seven Buildings Project. Residents are organized into groups with responsibility for cleaning, maintenance and security. In March 1996, some six years after the conflict began, ownership of the apartment blocks was transferred from the existing owners, via the Gauteng Provincial Housing Board, to a specially formed company owned by the Project. The almost 2,000 tenants of the 446 apartments in the seven blocks have become sectional title shareholders, paying rent to the company, on the board of which one representative from each of the buildings with serve as a director. With a R5.9 million subsidy from the National Housing Forum, affordable, income-related rents can be charged (*Mail and Guardian* 1/12/95; *Star* 7/3/ 96; *Sunday Times* 13/10/96). If successful, this innovative scheme could serve as a model not only for the rest of what is colloquially dubbed Johannesburg's "lost city"[2] but inner city areas of other conurbations as well. It provides a mechanism for managed transition, giving poor black people a stake in accessible parts of the existing urban structure, and avoiding the downward spiral of living conditions and quality which would otherwise result.

In indigenous city centers, the issue is not so much reclaiming them as revitalizing and upgrading those which have suffered neglect and decline. Of course, a few have become attractive tourist foci. The old urban cores of North Africa are, in Kharoufi's (1994:95) words, "characterized by opposition between Arab-Muslim cultural values and Western values and symbols, and by the penetration of the systems and models of international tertiary industries into old city structures." I will return to the implications of such conflicts below.

Reversing Modernist Zonal Planning: Encouraging Multifunctional Landuse

Another important way forward is to encourage multifunctional landuse and different urban designs, something which was (and in some cases still is) characteristic of indigenous cities. Current zoning and development control practice in most formal urban areas of colonial origin or others which have come within the ambit of urban planning controls (e.g., through extension of

municipal boundaries) still has an acutely modernist thrust. It is very restrictive, favoring single functions in given zones, except within very clearly
defined limits for the number and variety of convenience and other shops
permitted in residential areas. Although certain office functions are now
sometimes permitted within homes or entire houses e.g., medical, architectural, accountancy and other professional practices, industries are almost
entirely banished from residential areas. Greater flexibility should be exercised in permitting non-disturbance causing industries, e.g. cottage industries, small-scale upholsterers, picture framers, repairers. Redevelopment,
development on vacant land and in new areas should also make explicit
design provision for a fuller mix of activities overall rather than on an exceptional permission basis. These principles have been adopted in the
South African government's draft urban development strategy as part of
their efforts to overcome the gross inefficiency of apartheid urbanism (Republic of South Africa 1995).

While not advocating a romantic return to preindustrial, indigenous or
colonial urbanism, it is worth noting that earlier forms of multifunctional
landuse, e.g. the "home above the shop or workshop" have largely been
eliminated through rigid application of modernist town planning. Apart
from providing a boost to municipal revenue from increased rates and taxes,
change in this respect would diversify the geography of employment, reduce
commuter traffic pressure (and the associated energy, pollution and time
costs[1]) and also provide greater convenience for local residents. As their
unit costs, installation and operating costs decline, new information and
communications technologies can also play a role in reducing the need for
travel and face-to-face contact. Overall urban efficiency would thus be
enhanced.

More appropriate and sustainable urban designs and standards can more
readily be incorporated into new township developments or new settlements.
These should aim to reduce the need for travel, especially by means of private motorized transport, utilize appropriate energy sources and technologies (including new information technologies), improve the living environment and be designed to accommodate often diverse existing social structures and senses of identity. This would mean innovation in terms of street
layouts and the creation of diversity. By contrast, conventional town planning has generally sought to erase such diversity in favor of an assumed
modern norm, namely geometric street grids and crescents. At least one
recent author has advocated drawing lessons from the design principles of
precolonial African towns and cities, especially in West Africa, albeit in a
somewhat romantic conception (Amankwah-Ayeh 1995). Rather, the most
likely prospects lie in developing hybrids able to draw on appropriate tradi-

tions and principles of urban design—be they Islamic, Akan, Sotho, Nguni or whatever—but adapt them to current urban and social realities (Simon 1992). Abu-Lughod (1987), has made a particularly eloquent case in respect of Islamic cities in North Africa and the Middle East. One crucial issue here is to address problems still arising from the co-existence, overlap and/or conflict between surviving indigenous and Western landuse and land allocation processes (Attahi 1994: 213; Simon 1992).

Official toleration of indigenous dwelling forms and materials in formal low-income urban settlements, hitherto forbidden in terms of existing town planning regulations in Anglophone countries and beyond, would probably have major benefits for residents in terms of cost, construction materials and social appropriateness, although care would be necessary to avoid excessive environmental pressures where the timber and clay, for example, are collected (Simon 1985, 1992). For example, in 1992 a few rondavels (traditional round huts), built from a mixture of commercial and local materials, appeared on an ultralow income housing scheme on the outskirts of Windhoek. Over time these structures could be upgraded to extend their useful lives or replaced if necessary. Indigenous materials may also find a useful role as a complement to conventional "Western" ones in higher income, commercial and public buildings as part of new hybrid styles. I should emphasize immediately that I am not advocating some kind of postmodern "free-for-all" in which planning controls are effectively abandoned. There will undoubtedly always be a need for planning mechanisms and procedures capable of mediation among conflicting needs and aspirations and with sufficient teeth to enable due enforcement. It is the nature, flexibility and legitimacy of such planning which is in question.

Addressing Class Segregation: Promoting Social Integration
Socially more diverse cities can also be encouraged through efforts to break the tradition of residential zoning in terms of plot size and associated dwelling density, which is a surrogate form of institutionalized class segregation operating through the property market. Instead, more diverse mixes of residential types and densities within individual residential areas can and should be encouraged. This will undoubtedly generate substantial opposition from high income groups, fearful of the unknown and probably disguised in rhetoric of social difference and thus conflict, rising crime and falling property prices. Ethnic minorities, such as the Asians in East Africa and Levantines in West Africa are well known to concentrate in a small number of high income areas of capital and commercial cities. However, the African inheritors of former colonial elite spaces have generally also perpetuated the social practices associated with their predecessors.

Encouraging change to such supposedly "natural" patterns of social reproduction will constitute no mean challenge, requiring considerable political will by local authorities. The way forward would seem to be through the
sensitive construction of a wider mix of housing styles, sizes and densities in
individual areas. Direct contact from such proximity could help people to
transcend inherited social prejudices and cleavages between "them" and "us,"
in other words, the fear of "alien" racial, cultural and poorer "others" (cf.,
Dewar 1995:417). Again, no single or uniform blueprint can or should be
imposed; local circumstances must be taken into account in determining an
acceptable and appropriate mix of densities, "income groups" and urban
designs within each area. In any event, the scope for implementing change
within many established suburbs is limited by the availability of open space,
large plots suitable for subdivision and dwellings in poor condition which
might be demolished, and possible problems resulting from the interfacing
of different land allocation systems and principles.

One notable exception to the foregoing is in allocation or divestiture
policies (in the case of privatization) pursued by state or parastatal bodies
with respect to their existing housing stock, where social policies can readily
be implemented and could have a significant influence on emerging social
complexions of particular areas within a city. This is relevant to many
African cities, but Mozambique provides an appropriate example. The
government's State Property Administration, APIE (*Administraçao do
Parque Imobiliário do Estado*), inherited the formal housing and blocks of
flats abandoned by the emigré settlers in the mid-1970s and other investment property in the "cement cities" nationalized thereafter. Although allocation criteria based on need were established, over time the bureaucratic
process became increasingly corrupt and subject to informal bypassing, while
maintenance was negligible. Today these units are in an appalling state,
especially with respect to infrastructure and services, and a major structural
survey has just been undertaken to assess refurbishment needs (*Noticias* 23/
6/95). Privatization has been commenced, with current tenants supposed to
have first option, although some properties (or substantial compensation)
are being claimed by *retornados* (returning emigrés). To date the state has
issued several assurances that such repossessions will not be granted. Nevertheless, access to and control over such properties, and the resource they
represent in a situation of chronic housing shortage, have become highly
contested in ways contingent upon the nature of economic liberalization in
this impoverished peripheral ex-socialist state and the effective recolonization
by foreign capital (Simon 1992; Sidaway and Power 1995; *Noticias* 7/11/
95). Privatization is now beginning to move rapidly. By the end of September 1995, requests for purchase had been lodged in respect of 16,000 of the

total national APIE stock of 56,500 dwelling units. 11,500 of these had been authorized, over 61% of them (i.e., 9,847) in Maputo city. Another 1,823 were in the rest of Maputo province and 1,526 in Sofala province, including Beira, the country's second city. No other province registered more than 600 (*Noticias* 5/10/95). Details of the purchasers and their relative social positions are unavailable, so it is currently impossible to ascertain the extent to which desired beneficiaries are actually able to do so.

Upgrading Low-Income Areas

Finally, we should not omit the well-known imperative of upgrading townships, shanty settlements and similar areas occupied principally by low-income households. Numerous such programmes have been undertaken across the continent since the since the first World Bank-assisted site and service scheme in Dakar in 1972. One of the principal lessons learnt in the process is that, as in rural sustainable development schemes, community participation and joint control are important ingredients of successful programmes. In other words, these need to be empowering processes, not merely housing or infrastructure delivery mechanisms (Friedmann 1992; Wisner 1988). Some of the issues raised in the preceding paragraphs apply here too, not least the question of planning for diverse income groups in areas from which higher income households have moved out as their financial resources have grown or more conveniently located alternatives have been identified. Addressing the needs of low-income areas (townships, informal settlements and low-income inner city neighborhoods) is regarded as the single most important priority in South Africa's new draft urban development strategy (Republic of South Africa 1995:24).

Conflicting land allocation systems have often had problematic consequences for planning and adequate housing provision, particularly by and for the urban poor (Peil 1976; Simon 1992), who increasingly have to seek their own land along the urban fringe. In Attahi's (1994:213) words, with reference to Francophone West Africa,

> ...traditional land owners have succeeded in maintaining some of their authority by creating subdivisions in the peripheral areas. Indeed, the scarcity and expense of lots produced by the official system, as well as the time taken to complete transfers, force the majority of citizens seeking land to fall back on the peripheral subdivisions produced by traditional land-owners. The coexistence of two judicial land authorities is a source of conflict, and interferes with the supply of urban land and the development of cities.

The objective of upgrading should be to achieve improvements in the overall quality of life, not merely in shelter quality through in-situ upgrading or some other form of aided self-help (cf., Hardoy et al. 1992; Wekwete 1992; Main and Williams 1994). Infrastructure, employment opportunities, recreational spaces and environmental improvements should all be included in such programmes. Especially in arid and semi-arid areas, which occur from the Maghreb to South Africa, access to adequate potable water supplies for a growing urban population and more water-intensive activities will represent a formidable constraint.

As vividly documented in the recent BBC TV documentary, *Cairo: Mother of Megacities*, the urgency of the challenge in that city of 11-12 million is underlain by the rate at which vital, fertile agricultural land in the Nile valley is disappearing under informal and illegal housing by poor migrants and long term residents and by rogue speculative developers respectively. State efforts to divert and rehouse such people in satellite cities in the adjacent desert have met with a generally poor response: new towns such as 10th of Ramadan and Sadat City remain largely uninhabited (see also Kharoufi 1994:60).

CONCLUSIONS

I have argued that current urban processes and planning/management practices needs to change substantially as Africa's towns and cities are highly inequitable and increasingly also environmentally and socially unsustainable. Although planning is inherently concerned with long range futures, the methods and objectives of inherited modernist town planning and urban management are increasingly inappropriate to the pressing tasks of post-structural adjustment (and in South and southern Africa also post-apartheid) urban reconstruction. Concerns with homogenization and standardization especially within individual urban segments, often militate against substantive change to the underlying character defined in terms of unifunctional zoning, plot size, housing density, building lines and the like. These have generally served as surrogates for racial exclusivity, but the process of market-led postcolonial or post-apartheid residential integration is producing increasingly class-based social and spatial cleavages, which nevertheless mirror their predecessors to a remarkable extent. On the other hand, formal processes and mechanisms are increasingly being bypassed by those who feel ignored or oppressed by the state; official incapacity and irrelevance have also been exacerbated by expenditure cuts. None of these developments will change the fundamental realities of unsustainable urbanism and urban social reproduction.

By contrast, the promotion of greater equity and sustainability, as well as accommodation (in both the physical and metaphorical senses) of the multiple, increasingly diverse, and even antagonistic social groups with distinct identities and agendas, will require very different visions and processes. These will need to be more participatory, decentralized, flexible, and empowering, capable of providing local access and accountability within a framework offering strategic metropolitan-wide integration. Such notions do borrow from concepts of agropolitan development, urban villages and suchlike but, importantly, also from certain indigenous traditions as well as from contemporary debates in social theory about sustainability, postmodernism, postcolonialism and development. This approach would not dispense entirely with planning, for some planning authority, procedures and enforcement mechanisms will always be necessary in order to address the inevitable conflicts.

Equally important, however, is to offer practical guidelines for operationalizing the concepts and goals outlined. The United Nations Center for Human Settlements (1991) offers four criteria for judging the sustainability of development in any human settlement:
1. The quality of life it offers to its inhabitants;
2. The scale of non-renewable resource use (including the extent to which secondary resources are drawn from settlement by-products for re-use);
3. The scale and nature of renewable resource use and the implications for sustaining production levels of renewable resources; and
4. The scale and nature of non-reusable wastes generated by production and consumption activities and the means by which these are disposed of, including the extent to which wastes impact upon human health, natural systems and amenity (UNCHS 1991:4).

None of these relates specifically to urban morphology, but addressing them will often have substantial spatial implications. Some require concerted institutional intervention, others can appropriately be addressed through local community action and participation. Resource mobilization and the transmission of international experience as a basis for local adaptation or adoption are very important support activities which can involve both official and NGO structures and channels at local and supra-local levels in complementary ways. The Dakar Declaration, "Environmental Strategies for African Cities," adopted in June 1995 and formally incorporated into the preparatory process for Habitat II at the African Ministerial Meeting in Johannesburg in October 1995, embodies these principles (UNCHS 1995).

I have explored how urban spaces and places can be modified or conceived in accordance with current perspectives on sustainability and equitability. The measures discussed have the common objective of promoting various forms of diversity and better functional, spatial, social and technological integration, so as to reduce energy consumption (UNCHS 1990b), pollution generation, travel time loss, both within and between parts of the urban mosaic. Interestingly and importantly, many of these have been echoed, at least in outline terms, in the draft urban development strategy of the South African Government of National Unity, published for debate at the end of 1995 (Republic of South Africa 1995).

There will undoubtedly be numerous obstacles and concerted political resistance to such proposals from those who stand to lose effective power or control over resources, or who feel participatory processes to be excessively time-consuming and inconclusive. At one level, the current privatization initiatives embracing urban land and various forms of property in many African countries create new opportunities for individual or corporate independence. Ultimately, however, they are likely to reduce the space for achieving the agendas outlined here in favor of increasingly market-led outcomes. These agendas are not prescriptive but indicative of more people-centered and flexible structures and procedures which are likely to facilitate the achievement of desired goals. Ultimately, it will necessarily remain the prerogative of those living in, and responsible for, individual cities and towns to negotiate their own futures. On the other hand, if the traditions of mobilization among civic associations in South Africa and equivalent community based organizations and NGOs elsewhere are not harnessed within such a facilitatory framework, and if expectations and basic needs are not at least partially met, the results will be renewed alienation, division and resistance. Equally, to abandon all planning mechanisms and controls in the name of postmodern fashion, a lack of resources and trained personnel or whatever, would be to entrench existing or emerging inequalities which will increase rather than decrease, and prove no more sustainable than existing urban centers are.

NOTES

1. Ironically, this status derived in no small measure from the sanctions-driven diversification of the UDI period.
2. This term not only refers to the "loss" of the area from the rest of Johannesburg through urban decline but represents an ironic contrast with the overexuberant kitch of The Lost City, Sun International Hotels' ruritanian resort in the former Bophutatswana bantustan.

3. In Bangkok Metropolitan Area, for example, it has recently been estimated that the monetary cost alone of vehicle fuel wasted through idling in the chronic traffic congestion in one of the world's fastest developing metropolises, amounts to at least US$500 million and possibly as much as $2.92 billion annually (Setchell 1995:9-10).

REFERENCES

Abu-Lughod, J. L. "The Islamic City—Historic Myth, Islamic Essence and Contemporary Relevance." *International Journal of Middle East Studies* 19(1987):155-176.

Aina, T. A. "Many Routes Enter the Market Place - Housing Submarkets for the Urban Poor in Metropolitan Lagos, Nigeria." *Environment and Urbanization* 1, 2(1989):38-49.

Amankwah-Ayeh, K. "Planning Environmentally Sustainable Cities in Africa." *Africa Insight* 25, 1(1995):37-47.

Attahi, K. "Urban Research in Francophone West Africa: Towards an Agenda for the 1990s." In *Urban Research in the Developing World: Africa*, ed. R. Stren. Toronto: Center for Urban and Community Studies, University of Toronto, 1994.

Cadman, D. and G. Payne, eds. 1990. *The Living City: Towards a Sustainable Future.* London: Routledge.

Comissao Nacional de Plano, Direccao Nacional da Estatistica, Unidade de População e Planificação. *Pobreza, Emprego e a Questao Demografica na Cidade de Maputo.* Maputo: CNP, 1993.

Crankshaw, O., and C. White. "Racial Desegregation and Inner City Decay in Johannesburg." *International Journal of Urban and Regional Research* 19, 4(1995):622-638.

Cumming, S. "Postcolonial Urban Residential Change in Zimbabwe: A Case Study." In *Cities and Development in the Third World*, eds. R. B. Potter and A. T. Salau. London: Mansell, 1990.

Dewar, D. "The Urban Question in South Africa: The Need for a Planning Paradigm Shift." *Third World Planning Review* 17, 4(1995):407-419.

Friedmann, J. *Empowerment: The Politics of Basic Needs.* Oxford: Blackwell, 1992.

Hardoy, J., and D. Satterthwaite. *Squatter Citizen.* London: Earthscan, 1989.

Hardoy, J., D. Mitlin, and D. Satterthwaite. *Environmental Problems in Third World Cities.* London: Earthscan, 1992.

Haughton, G., and C. Hunter. *Sustainable Cities.* London: Jessica Kingsley, 1994.

Holm, M. "The Impact of Structural Adjustment on Intermediate Towns and Urban Migrants: An Example from Tanzania." In *Structurally Adjusted Africa: Poverty, Debt and Basic Needs*, eds. D. Simon, W. van Spengen, C. Dixon, and A. Närman. London: Pluto, 1995.

Kharoufi, M. "Reflections on a Research Field: Urban Studies in Egypt, Morocco and the Sudan." *Urban Research in the Developing World: Africa*, ed. R. Stren. Toronto: Center for Urban and Community Studies, University of Toronto, 1994.

Mail and Guardian. 1 December, 1995. Johannesburg.

Main, H., and S. W. Williams, eds. *Environment and Housing in Third World Cities.* Chichester: Wiley, 1994.

Mitlin, D., and D. Satterthwaite. "Sustainable Development and Cities." In *Sustainability, the Environment and Urbanization*, ed. C. Pugh. London: Earthscan, 1996.

Murphy, D. *The Ukimwi Road; from Kenya to Zimbabwe.* London: Flamingo, 1994.

Noticias 23 June, 5 October, 7 November, 1995. Maputo.

O'Connor, A. *The African City.* London: Hutchinson, 1983.

Parnell, S. M. and G. H. Pirie. "Johannesburg." In *Homes Apart: South Africa's Segregated Cities*, ed. A. Lemon. London: Paul Chapman, and Bloomington: Indiana University Press, 1991.

Peil, M. "African Squatter Settlements: A Comparative Study." *Urban Studies* 13, 2(1976):155-166.

Potts, D. "Shall We Go Home? Increasing Urban Poverty in African Cities and Migration Processes." *Geographical Journal* 161, 3(1995):245-264.

Pugh, C., ed. *Sustainability, the Environment and Urbanization.* London: Earthscan, 1996.

Rakodi, C. *Harare; Inheriting a Settler-Colonial City: Change or Continuity?* Chichester: Wiley, 1995.

Republic of South Africa. "Urban Development Strategy of the Government of National Unity; A Discussion Document." *Government Gazette* (Pretoria) 3 November 1995.

Robertson, R. *Globalization: Social Theory and Global Change.* London/Newbury Park: Sage, 1992.

Setchell, C. A. "The Growing Environmental Crisis in the World's Mega-Cities: The Case of Bangkok." *Third World Planning Review* 17, 1(1995):1-18.

Sidaway, J. D., and M. Power. "Sociospatial Transformations in the 'Postsocialist' Periphery: The Case of Maputo, Mozambique." *Environment and Planning A* 27(1995):1463-1491.

Simon, D. "Independence and Social Transformation: Urban Planning Problems and Priorities for Namibia." *Third World Planning Review* 7, 2(1985):99-118.

Simon, D. "Windhoek: Desegregation and Change in the Capital of South Africa's Erstwhile Colony." In *Homes Apart: South Africa's Segregated Cities*, ed. A. Lemon. London: Paul Chapman, and Bloomington: Indiana University Press, 1991.

Simon, D. *Cities, Capital and Development: African Cities in the World Economy.* London: Belhaven (now Chichester: Wiley), 1992.

Simon, D. "Urbanization, Globalization and Economic Crisis in Africa." In *The Challenge of Urbanization in Africa*, ed. C. Rakodi. Tokyo: United Nations

University Press, 1996a [in press]. Draft version published as Research Paper 10, Center for Developing Areas Research, Dept. of Geography, Royal Holloway, University of London, November 1994.

Simon, D. "Equitable and Sustainable Urban Futures in Post-Apartheid Southern Africa." Paper presented at the IAI/ISER Seminar on 'Understanding Changing Patterns of Settlement and Resettlement in Southern Africa,' Rhodes University, Grahamstown, 22-26 January, 1996b; revised version in De Wet, C. and R. Fox, eds. *Settlement and Resettlement in Southern Africa.* Edinburgh: Edinburgh University Press for the International Africa Institute, 1997 [Forthcoming].

Simon, D. "Restructuring the Local State in Post-Apartheid Cities: Namibian Experience and Lessons for South Africa." *African Affairs* 95, 378(1996c):51-84.

Star, The. 7 March, 1996. Johannesburg.

Stren, R.E. and R. R. White, eds. *African Cities in Crisis: Managing Rapid Urban Growth.* Boulder, Colo.: Westview, 1989.

Stren, R.E., R. R. White, and J. B. Whitney, eds. *Sustainable Cities: Urbanization and the Environment in International Perspective.* Boulder, Colo.: Westview, 1992.

Sunday Times, The. Metro Edition, 13 October, 1996. Johannesburg.

Tevera, D. "The Medicine That Might Kill the Patient: Structural Adjustment and Urban Poverty in Zimbabwe." In *Structurally Adjusted Africa: Poverty, Debt and Basic Needs,* eds. D. Simon, W. van Spengen, C. Dixon and A. Närman. London: Pluto, 1995.

United Nations Center for Human Settlements. *Financing Human Settlements Development and Management in Developing Countries: A Comparative Overview of Case Studies.* HS/174/98E. Nairobi: UNCHS, 1990a.

United Nations Center for Human Settlements. *Use of New and Renewable Energy Sources with Emphasis on Shelter Requirements.* HS/183/89E. Nairobi: UNCHS, 1990b.

United Nations Center for Human Settlements. *People, Settlements, Environment and Development: Improving the Living Environment for a Sustainable Future.* Nairobi: UNCHS, 1991.

United Nations Center for Human Settlements. *Sustainable City News* (Nairobi) 1, 1(September 1995).

United Nations Development Programme. *Human Development Report.* New York: Oxford University Press, 1995.

Watson, S., and K. Gibson, eds. *Postmodern Cities and Spaces.* Oxford: Blackwell, 1995.

Wekwete, K. "Development of Urban Planning in Zimbabwe: An Overview." *Cities* 5, 1(1988):57-71.

Wekwete, K. "Africa." In *Sustainable Cities,* eds. R. E. Stren, R. R. White, and J. B. Whitney. Boulder: Westview, 1992.

Wisner, B. *Power and Need in Africa: Basic Human Needs and Development Policies.* London: Earthscan, 1988.

World Commission on Environment and Development. *Our Common Future.* New York: Oxford University Press, 1987.

Yahya, S. S. "Residential Urban Land Markets in Kenya." In *Housing Africa's Urban Poor*, eds. P. Amis and P. Lloyd. Manchester: University of Manchester Press, 1990.

3

THE SPATIAL ECONOMY OF STRUCTURAL ADJUSTMENT IN AFRICAN CITIES

PAUL TIYAMBE ZELEZA

INTRODUCTION
THE LITERATURE ON STRUCTURAL ADJUSTMENT IN AFRICA
is vast and still growing rapidly. Much of this literature examines the inception, implementation, and impact of structural adjustment programs on African economic, social, and political conditions and prospects. Often specific subregions, countries, or sectors are targeted for analysis, and normative generalizations are drawn for the whole continent on the efficacy or inefficacy, success or failure of economic and political liberalization. Needless to say, the debates are vigorous, sometimes vitriolic, reflecting the divergent paradigmatic premises, theoretical tendencies, ideological inclinations, and political preferences of the various writers. The aim of this chapter is not to revisit the debates, rather it is to recast the analysis by explicitly drawing out the spatial dimensions of structural adjustment. A careful glance at the conceptions and imputed consequences of structural adjustment reveal the ubiquity of spatial metaphors, such as urban-bias, globalization, and re-colonization.

Such metaphors aside, focusing on spatiality offers theoretical keys to opening new dimensions of understanding in so far as the social is spatially constituted as much as the spatial is socially constituted.[1] In other words, the concepts of the spatial division of labor and spatial structure are as critical as those of the social division of labor and social structure (Massey 1994). Structural adjustment as a project of capitalist reorganization seeks to restructure African social and spatial processes and relations, to map new geographies of production, in which, to quote Harvey (1993a:6), new networks of places arise, "around which new territorial divisions of labour and concentrations of people and labor power, new resource extraction activities and markets form." It is well known that the history of capitalist accumulation on a global scale has always been marked by complex and contradictory processes of uneven development. This entails uneven development of space, differentiation and hierarchization of places, spatial practices that are constructed and enacted through material, symbolic, and representational activities, and whose consequences for the organization of production and the orchestration of power are profound.

The representation and red-lining of much of Africa in the western mass and academic media, for example, as a degraded and derelict global slum, plays the discursive function of asserting the power of western spaces and social systems, thereby rationalizing the free-market interventions of structural adjustment authored and authorized by the international financial institutions and aimed at remaking and reinscribing African spaces and social systems into the restructured global capitalist economy. Spaces are of course not simply arenas of production, but also of politics, crucibles through which social identities and movements are stirred and shaped, formed and transformed, out of articulated moments and networks of social relations, experiences and understandings. As with all hegemonic projects, the ambitions of global capital to restructure the African material, symbolic, and imaginary landscapes, through structural adjustment, have been challenged, contested and constrained by the resistance of communities and movements ignited and invigorated by those very processes of social and spatial reorganization.

This chapter, then, seeks to unravel the spatialities of structural adjustment at various levels of analysis. Given the complexity of the subject and the length of this chapter it is obviously not possible to present a comprehensive study of the spatial dimensions of structural adjustment. What is offered amounts largely to a research agenda encompassing four elements. First, the centrality of spatial metaphors and maps in the conceptualization of structural adjustment programs is examined. Three are singled out: the theses of urban-bias, globalization, and re-colonization. Second, the development of new spatial divisions and devaluations of labour, in which the impact of structural adjustment on urban labor markets will be analyzed and assessed. Third, it will be argued that the coping mechanisms developed by the most affected communities exhibit strong spatial dynamics, including the ruralization of urban spaces and the intensification of urban-rural linkages, as well as the emergence of new patterns of national, intra-regional, and international migration. These migrations entail complex flows and movements of cultures within, into, and from Africa which African and Africanist social science research has yet to address seriously. Finally, the chapter briefly examines the spatialized and highly differentiated politics of structural adjustment by communities and groups repositioned and relocated by these programs.

TRADING PLACES

The economic crisis that spawned structural adjustment programs in Africa had both global and local dimensions. It is pointless to attribute the crisis solely either to external or internal factors, as many writers on the subject are inclined to, as if in the historical geography of capitalism the two have ever operated in splendid isolation from each other. Internal and external factors, conjunctural and spatial dynamics reinforced each other in producing and reproducing the differentiated conditions, consequences, and trajectories of the crisis among and within regions, nations, social classes and groups. During prolonged periods of crisis in the capitalist world economy, as was the case from the early 1970s, there are intense social and spatial struggles, within and between countries, over the reorganization of the disintegrating growth model and who is to bear the costs of constructing a new one. Classes and places with massive concentrations of economic and political power are often able to load and export the costs of devaluation of the old regime of accumulation and development of the new to the weaker classes and places in the global circuits of capitalist production and distribution. That, in a nutshell, is the spatial history of the African crisis of the 1970s and 1980s.[2]

Structural adjustment, imposed with exceptional ruthlessness in the underdeveloped regions, including Africa, in essence entailed a reversal of roles and responsibilities: the weight of reform was removed from the shoulders of the economically strong, who had generated the crisis in the first place, to those of the economically weak. This was facilitated by the predilection of the neo-classical paradigm to attribute the global capitalist crisis to contingent, not structural, factors, in which the "oil shocks" of 1973-74 featured prominently. "The commodity power of the Third World oil producers," Toye (1994:19) argues, "appeared to have succeeded in shifting the balance of advantage towards themselves and away from the industrial countries, within a more generally turbulent economic environment. This perception helped to undermine the post-war consensus that the adjustment burden should rest with the industrial world."

As the imperative for reform was being exported by the industrial world to the economically weak both at home and abroad, the industrialized countries adopted deflationary policies which compressed the growth of developing countries' exports and plunged them deeper into a yawning abyss of indebtedness, a descent that was exacerbated by the rise of interest rates to historically unprecedented levels. Shipping structural adjustment to the vulnerable peoples and places of the Third World, including Africa, reflected and reinforced, the death of the Keynesian orthodoxy with its structuralist faith in the hand of the state and planning and its dualist conceptions of development, which conceded difference and specificity to the economies of the underdeveloped countries. The applied rhetoric of development economics gave way to the theoretical rigor of "standard" economics, to the exhilarating creed of economic universalism; that all economies, developed and developing, were subject to the same economic principles and prescriptions. The rise of "monoeconomics," anchored on market fundamentalism, further "helped to undermine the notion that the industrial countries had a special responsibility to carry the burdens of global adjustment" (Toye 1994: 23).

Accompanying the globalization of neo-classical economic theory and policy, however, was the particularization and pathologization of African states, societies, and spaces. African economies and polities, the neo-colonial highpriests charged, were afflicted by the cancer of "urban bias" (Lipton 1977; Bates 1981, 1989; Bhagwati 1982; Lofchie 1989; Cornia et al. 1992; Sahn 1994, 1996). The state and development were held hostage by the unproductive rent-seeking urban coalition of corrupt elites and shiftless workers, who thrived on the exploitation of the rural peasantry and generated the economic perversions and political rigidities of "urban bias." Structural adjustment was, therefore, designed, so they claimed, to tame the malevolent postcolonial leviathan, to "clear" the factor markets, to level the economic playing field between the rural and urban communities by disciplining the latter and weaning them from the deforming comforts of urban bias, the unearned privileges of rent collection. The uncompromising and combative metaphor of "urban bias," that structural adjustment sought its erasure, to trade the places of winners and losers, sought to articulate the moral and material rationalities of economic equity and expansion. Opponents of structural adjustment could then be dismissed and accused of both economic immorality and irrationality, of compromising their countries' economic future at the altar of personal and factional greed and shortsightedness.

Globalization was another powerful spatial metaphor frequently articulated in the discourse on structural adjustment. To the proponents of these programs, it was waved as a fearsome whip to focus the attention of those who opposed the miracle of the market. The literature screamed deliriously that globalization made liberalization necessary and inevitable, that a global village had emerged; that the accelerated flows of capital, commodities, and cultures, of ideas, images, and ideologies were dissolving spatial barriers and the provincial fictions of national economies and sovereignties. Only those who restructured and rationalized their economies, made them more open, more efficient, more competitive; those who maximized their comparative advantage would benefit from this brave new world of "time-space compression," of instantaneous global communication, fierce international competition and capital's immense ability to roam the world at will. Those who did not would be left behind to wallow in the depressed and depraved fourth and other nether worlds. Marginalized African countries, many of them already barely hanging on to the Third World, had little choice but to adopt structural adjustment if they wanted to recover and get on the train bolting towards globalization.

For many of the critics of structural adjustment, recolonization was their favorite spatial metaphor. The painful sight of the international financial institutions, especially the World Bank and IMF, dictating structural adjustment programs, imposing an ever escalating array of conditionalities, sitting in the central banks and treasury departments, and managing whole economies, evoked bitter memories of colonial territorial invasion, in which African peoples and societies lost control of their economies and polities, of their landscapes and culturalscapes, their histories and futures. The secrecy with which these programs were designed and the authoritarianism with which they were implemented reinforced the sense of siege and imperial onslaught, of seizure and erasure of African autonomy and the achievements of independence. The gloomy rhetoric of African marginality, the unrelieved mood of Afropessimism, recalled the imperialist jingoism of the late nineteenth century in which Europe proclaimed for itself the right to appropriate and reshape African lands and societies, to catapult them from barbarism into history, in the name of "civilization"; now it was in the name of "liberalization."

The critiques of each of these metaphors are too well-known to detain us much here. The 'urban-bias' thesis has been accused of misconceiving and oversimplifying the processes and production of state power, and the complex intersections of state-civil society relations, and of rural and urban activities and communities in contemporary Africa. The discourse of "urban bias" not only seeks to internalize the economic crisis as Africa's own creation, spatially and structurally isolated from the rest of the global economy, and pits urban and rural communities, sectors, and spaces against each other, it evokes and deploys the anti-urban and anti-elite biases of colonial anthropology and populist nationalist ideology. It is a discourse, moreover, that in denigrating urban spaces, classes, and activities, such as industrialization, reinscribes African societies as the rural backwoods for the global commons and reinserts them as primary producers for the post-Fordist global economy. (Gibbon et al. 1992; Cornia et al. 1992; Hoeven and Kraaij 1994; Geest 1994; Mkandawire and Olukoshi 1995; Gibbon and Olukoshi 1996; Eyoh 1996; Engberg-Pedersen et al. 1996).

The globalization thesis is often reproached for telescoping history and exaggerating current trends, universalizing the experiences and anxieties of elites; homogenizing globalization when in reality new forms of globality and locality are simultaneously being produced and reproduced; and serving as a discursive arsenal to discipline, disorient, and disempower labor and nationalists and to silence the "uprising discourses" of class, gender, and national liberation (Ahmad 1992; Massey 1994; Holm and Sorrenson 1995; Appadurai 1996; Aina 1997a)[3]. Finally, in my opinion, the recolonization thesis sometimes verges on the conspiratorial; revives the Fanonist fable of false decolonization; and coalesces and collapses different moments and conjunctures of Africa's incorporation into the world system, thereby ignoring the profound changes that African political, cultural, and spatial economies have undergone in the period since independence.

These three metaphors have strongly affected the conceptualization, representation, and implementation of structural adjustment programs. They have helped structure the highly differentiated meanings and materiality of structural adjustment for people and communities in different spaces, places, and locations. Out of the concessions to, compromises with, and contestations against, structural adjustment have emerged new spaces, spectacles and signs of politics, new struggles and social and spatial imaginaries for the past, the present, and the future.

PRODUCING PLACES

Structural adjustment seeks to restructure the organization of production through the deregulation of markets, devaluation of currencies, internal and external trade liberalization, public enterprise privatization and public expenditure reduction. These policies, it was believed, would eliminate the balance of payments and government deficits, state intervention, price distortions, and promote private initiative, domestic savings, foreign investment, and exports, the end result of which would be the restoration of sustainable growth and development. Contrary to the commonly held populist assumption that from the very beginning structural adjustment programs were cast in stone and applied with the uniformity of the ten command-ments, the adjustment agenda underwent several changes as the crisis proved more intractable than the short-term analytical and prescriptive frameworks of the World Bank and IMF allowed for and the patients reacted poorly or violently to the lethal medicine. The first generation of SAPs consisted of initial adjustment policies aimed at economic stabilization; the second com-prised comprehensive adjustment policy packages; and the third paid more attention to the social factors. Given the fact that different countries joined the adjustment train at different stations carrying different baggages of eco-nomic challenges, they were served different courses culled from the same menu. Enormous intellectual capital has been spent in the literature mea-suring the costs and benefits of structural adjustment economically, socially, and politically. The protagonists have included the international financial institutions themselves, who periodically produce glossy reports filled with colorful charts and dense statistics comparing countries' macroeconomic performance "before and after" adjustment and between those of the "ad-justing" versus the "non-adjusting" countries, and further distinguishing the "strong" from the "weak" adjusters (World Bank and UNDP 1989; World Bank 1989, 1994, 1995). The conclusions are as varied as the countries chosen, the indicators and variables included, and the ideological and policy preferences of the assessors. To the architects and supporters of adjustment, SAPs have restored growth, facilitated the redistribution of resources and incomes between the urban-based rentier classes and the productive peas-antry in the rural areas, and even engendered good governance and democ-ratization. For the critics democratization has been spawned by the struggles against structural adjustment, which has led to increased poverty and social dislocation, and reinforced the economic marginality and deindustrialization of many African countries.

The main concern of this section, indeed, the chapter, is to demonstrate the impact of structural adjustment, or rather of developments that occurred during the era of structural adjustment,[4] on the spatial structure and the spatial division of labour within African countries. The argument is that from the 1980s there were significant changes in the ways the places of production and the production of places were organized and experienced. Economic liberalization and the other structural transformations that were occurring in African countries and the world at large, led to shifts in the patterns and processes of accumulation, in the locus and dispersal of pro-duction and power. Among other things, the extensive spatial and social restructuring of capital reverberated through the economically active popu-lation in the changing occupational structure and spatiality of the workforce.

The changing map of employment and unemployment in many African cities was related to the deregulatory and deflationary policies and deindustrialization effects of structural adjustment. Freeing labor markets from the strangulation of state control and the suffocating affections of trade unions were regarded as an essential component of SAPs, and the adjusting countries embarked on labor law reform, which entailed the removal of protective and "restrictive" labor regulations, standards, and institutions.[5] These reforms were meant to whip workers and labor movements into submission and tame them for local and global capital that was increasingly mobile and intolerant of the rigidities of fixity, of spatial stasis and permanent location. The swelling reserve army of the unemployed and underemployed limited labor's options for self-defense.

As might be expected, the decline of modern sector wage employment was differentiated according to sector and the social inscriptions of gender and age. The public sector, traditionally the engine of employment growth in postcolonial Africa, contracted more sharply than the private sector and began shedding workers as eagerly as it had absorbed them earlier in the days when the dreams of independence were alive and well. Within both the private and public sector, the most affected was employment in manufacturing, which either stagnated or fell, as factories downsized, relocated, raised productivity, or collapsed (Riddell 1990; Khennas 1992; Stein 1995; de Valk 1996).

Since public sector and industrial employment were concentrated in the urban areas, their contraction meant that these areas were the hardest hit by rising unemployment. The rural areas were, of course, not immune from unemployment and underemployment. But rural employment does not seem to have fallen as precipitously as in the urban areas. In fact, studies by the ILO's Jobs and Skills Program for Africa ILO/JASPA) suggest that 'the employment prospects in the rural areas have improved recently and look better than those in the urban areas (ILO/JASPA 1989:ix). This is largely attributed to the rise of agricultural employment and the increasing importance of non-farm activities (Vandemoortele 1991:14-17). What needs investigating is the specific composition of these activities and the possible impact of industrial relocation. Studies on more industrialized regions, especially Western Europe and North America, indicate that the desertion of manufacturing jobs from the cities corresponded to the dispersal of manufacturing capital to small isolated towns, semi-ruralized suburbia, or to the sweatshops of the Third World (Lash and Urry 1994; Bagguley et.al. 1990; Harvey 1993b; Massey 1994).

In addition to its differentiated sectoral and spatial impact, the employment crisis also affected households, men and women, youths and adults quite differently. In a detailed study on Francophone countries, it was found that 'the incidence of unemployment is between two and three times higher in poor households than in the well off ones' (Lachaud 1994:60). This partly reflected the difficulties of women from the poor households to access wage employment. Women's concentration in clerical and manual manufacturing jobs, compounded their vulnerabilities, for these occupations were the most affected by the retrenchment of the 1980s and early 1990s. The exceptions were those countries, such as Mauritius, which were able to attract export processing industries, exceptions that simply prove the rule. Similarly battered by rising unemployment were youths despite, some say because of, their rising levels of education in a world of shrinking or sluggish labor markets. Needless to say, female youths were more affected than male youths.

Urban unemployment rose at unprecedented annual rates. By the mid-1980s it ranged between 15% and 32% in such countries as Somalia, Kenya, Senegal, Mauritius, Liberia, Tanzania, Seychelles, Zambia, Botswana, Ethiopia, and Reunion, in that order (ILO/JASPA 1989:16). For Africa, altogether, recorded unemployment shot up from 5.3% in 1980 to 13% in 1987. Underemployment is also said to have risen from 40 to 50% over the same period (ECA 1988b). In some of the most blighted cities it was being estimated that unemployment "could be as high as 30-40 per cent, with as many as 70 per cent of the total population living below the poverty line" (Diejomaoh 1987:16).

In the meantime, real wages plummeted as well. Between 1980 and 1985, for example, they fell by an average of 6% per annum for the 18 countries for which comparable data was available to the ILO (ILO/JASPA 1989:8). Vandemoortele (1991:86) puts the number of countries at 27. This means that by 1985 workers in these countries earned, on average, about a quarter less than they did in 1980. One result was wage compression between the highest and lowest paid workers and between non-agricultural and agricultural wages. The income gap between urban and rural areas narrowed. As early as 1984, an ILO/JASPA study of 17 countries indicated that the gap had been reduced to 4:1 (ILO/JASPA 1984:31-38), a trend that accelerated in subsequent years (Jamal and Weeks 1988; Weeks 1995; Jamal 1995). The expectations that improving rural terms of trade would reverse rural-urban migration and that falling wages would increase wage employment failed to materialize.

That wage erosion and compression was more a result of political skull-duggery than market forces can be shown by the fact that real wages dropped more sharply in the public than the private sector. Overall, while public sector wages declined by 5% between 1980 and 1987 for the sub-Saharan region, government expenditure rose by 23% (Vandemoortele 1991:89-90).

Also, formal sector wages fell more rapidly than total urban incomes and national per capita incomes. ILO data for 14 countries shows that between 1971 and 1984 growth in per capita incomes outstripped growth in real wages in all but two of the countries (ILO 1987:99).

As evidence and criticisms mounted of cities and workers blighted by rising unemployment, chagrined governments and chastened donors began desperately searching for sponges that would absorb the problems away. They found salvation in the informal sector. And scholars seeking an intellectual antidote to Afropessimism latched on to the informal sector as the reservoir from which would spring "an indigenous, technically innovative, developmental bourgeoisie" (Berman 1994:254), and a revitalized civil society that would foster democracy (Azarya and Chazan 1987; Rothchild and Chazan 1988; Chazan 1988; Portes et al. 1989; Bratton 1989, 1990). Indeed, the expatriate friends of the informal sector soon declared that the formal-informal dichotomy was decomposing in favor of informalization. Interestingly, the ILO and JASPA which had popularized the term, became increasingly cautious about the informal sector's potential to create jobs and sustain development. Also unpersuaded by the developmentalist and democratic credentials of the informal sector were many African social scientists, some of whom dabbled in the sector and knew that it could be as corrupt, exploitative, and pernicious as the sectors controlled by the much maligned state.

Cast in dualistic and normative terms, the debate obscured what was really happening. What was referred to as informalization was in effect temporal-spatial dispersal of work and income generation activities. To meet the challenges they faced, working people in the cities were changing their places and times of production and producing new configurations of place and time; they were diversifying their range of remunerative occupations and locations in order to reproduce themselves; they were, in short, seeking to restructure the temporal geography of work. The apparent disruption of established rhythms and places of remunerative work, represented materially and visually by the increasing intermingling of previously separated urban architectural and functional spaces and forms, created the sense of disorder that fueled the inflationary discourse of informalization and the dread among the local and visiting elites that the boundaries of social and spatial modernity were dissolving.

COPING PLACES

It is clear that despite the severe erosion of public sector and manufacturing jobs and the fall in real wages, urban populations, while they may not have thrived, survived and continued to expand, thanks to the complex array of adaptation and coping strategies they devised. These included urban farming, resuscitating or strengthening rural linkages and supporting rural farming activities, the remapping of urban cultural spaces, and migration. Urban farming entailed the ruralization of urban spaces and changed the morphology of cities, local ecosystems, and the aesthetics of low-income and middle class residential neighborhoods.[6]

Urban agriculture was of course not new, nor was it confined to the Third World.[7] But from the 1980s the scale of urban farming seems to have expanded substantially in many African cities. The phenomenon affected or afflicted cities of divergent histories, economies, and spatialities, ranging from crowded Cairo (Khouri-Dagher 1986), austere Addis Ababa (Egziabher 1994), noisy Nairobi, (Lado 1990; Freeman 1991; Memon and Lee-Smith 1993), drab Dar es Salaam (Mosha 1991; Mlozi et al. 1992; Mlozi 1994, 1995; Sawio 1994), listless Lusaka (Sanyal 1985; Rakodi 1988), handsome Harare (Drakakis-Smith 1992; Drakakis-Smith et al. 1995; Mbiba 1994), to the vibrant cities of Nigeria (Tricaud 1987; Gbadegesin 1991; Andrae 1992), and the segregated cities of apartheid South Africa (Rogerson 1993; May and Rogerson 1995). To be sure, urban agricultural activities varied enormously, both within and between countries, as well as throughout the urban hierarchy, depending on the prevailing state policies and economic conditions, class structure and divisions of labor, land availability and tenure, cropping regimes and climatic conditions, food supply and marketing systems.

Previously, urban farming had largely been confined to the urban poor, many of them recent rural migrants with a reservoir of farming knowledge.[8] As structural adjustment began to pauperize segments of the middle classes, the latter increasingly resorted to farming.[9] In many cities farming became a major economic activity, indeed, in some cases one of the largest employers. The sites used for farming encompassed backyards or the so-called home gardens, land on the periphery of cities, and patches of available public land, including the sides of roads. Depending on the size of the land and other supply, marketing, spatial, demographic, environmental and policy factors the urban farmers grew food and cash crops and reared livestock, usually poultry as well as goats, sheep, and cattle. Like all productive activities, urban farming spawned and was sustained by complex social and spatial divisions of labor among and within households and income groups. For the urban poor located on congested and rugged plots, their farming activities were small-scale and consisted largely of food crops for subsistence, while the middle class farming households with large housing lots and the resources and influence to access urban and peri-urban farming land could produce larger quantities and varieties of crops as well as livestock for both self-provisioning and marketing. The latter were also more likely than the former to access extra-household labor, so that the gender and age divisions of labor varied between them. Women bore the burden of urban farming in the poor neighborhoods.

The ruralization of urban spaces diffused the sharp rural-urban spatial and analytical dichotomies. As part of the rural-urban interface, wherever and whenever possible urban dwellers sought to revitalize their linkages to rural land and kin, either by investing in rural farming or subsidizing the farming of relatives or members of their households left behind. The complex traffic of food and tastes, capital and labor, information and ideas between the rural and urban spaces was a testament to the straddling strategies of African households, the spatially diversified resource allocation decisions adopted by families to meet the challenges of their reproduction in a harsh economic world. It is the multi-occupational and multi-spatial nature of most African households that enabled them to cope.

All this facilitated the continuous remapping of urban cultural spaces, as evident, for example in the spatial reorganization of leisure activities. Research on structural adjustment, indeed, in African studies in general, has largely ignored questions of culture, how communities create and recreate their daily lives beneath all the structural conditions and systemic processes often analyzed. Leisure is one such activity of daily life whose systematic study has the potential of deepening our understanding of the dynamics of African societies, of the complex constructions and contestations over meanings, symbols, spaces, and time. The differentiated provision of work and leisure, and the composition and location of the leisure activities themselves for different social groups, poignantly unveils the inscriptions of class, status, gender, and other social markers, and their complex articulations with the structures of access to resources and power.

Space allows for only the most perfunctory notes to be made here.[10] It is clear that in the midst of all the hardships of structural adjustment, and because of them, the times and spaces of urban leisure and popular culture have been transformed in complex and unpredictable ways, generating new patterns and processes of cultural creation, conception, consumption, and contestation; giving African cities new social rhythms and rituals, sounds, sights, and smells. With SAPs costs of access to leisure places and activities rose beyond the means of growing numbers of working class, and elements of middle class, people.

Writing on contemporary Lagos, Aina (1997b:16-17) observes that "people sought out entertainment, leisure and diversion that were more informal, less organized on a grand-scale and which demanded less rigid and expensive payments. Activities shifted from commercial central locations such as movie-houses to home- or community-based or smaller-scale enterprise outlets (such as the small video-shops, the corner record stores, palm wine and other bars)." As their locations and functions spread, entertainment and recreation became highly improvised. To quote Aina (1997b:20) again: "One therefore finds spectacles at bus stops, market places, in between traffic on major road networks in which the intention is to entertain, to sell, to cheat or even to steal from the unwary onlooker. Even the commuter buses known as 'Molue' became sites of this multifunctional entertainment and diversion." He also notes the massive growth of revivalist churches and sects, whose gatherings provide redemptive moments and spaces of spiritual and social communion and "extensive leisure and entertainment through their highly spectacular dancing, drumming and singing, the opportunities for trances, and the drama of exorcisms, faith-healing and testimonies... the larger ones are increasingly shifting their places of worship to cinema houses and theaters, stadia, hotel halls and night clubs. Through colonizing and appropriating the places and sites of 'debauchery' and 'sin', they take their struggles against evil and for the hearts and pockets of the urban poor to the spatial level" (Aina 1997b:20).

Similar processes of the destruction and recreation of urban social space and time by structural adjustment is evident in Nairobi, whose color, texture, and vibrancy has changed noticeably since the late 1980s. As in Lagos, leisure and popular culture in Nairobi has become increasingly dispersed from the glitter, and increasingly litter, of the city center and the bourgeoisified spaces of elite and tourist entertainment to the multipurpose improvised recreation centers located in working class and some middle class neighborhoods. In these rustic squares, mostly open air spaces assembled with wooden benches and thatched stalls and reverberating with music and dance, drinking and drama, story-telling and seduction, the working people of Nairobi while away their evenings and weekends. In and through them, the ebbs and flows of daily life are being altered, a spatial spectacle is unfolding: urban neighborhoods and communities are not only recreating old and creating novel forms of leisure in new spaces and consuming it in innovative ways, they are domesticating and appropriating urban space. In short, they are producing a new urban experience for themselves in the process of which they are transforming Nairobi into a postcolonial city, shedding it of its colonial settler origins. They are inventing cultural copping strategies against the intolerant exactions of capitalist globalization mediated through structural adjustment.

Migration constituted another major coping strategy. Patterns of migration became more complex than ever as people looked for greener pastures elsewhere, internally, regionally, and internationally. Recent studies show that internal migrations—rural-urban, rural-rural, urban-rural, urban-urban—intensified and took new forms in the 1980s. It cannot be overemphasized there are considerable differences between and within countries. Despite almost universal projections that African countries were doomed to irrationally rapid urbanization, evidence is growing that the rate of urban growth slowed down considerably in several African countries as the effects of economic recession and structural adjustment began to bite. Available data from some of the worst hit countries, such as Ghana, Tanzania, Uganda, and Zambia, shows that in the 1980s and 1990s most of their major cities hardly grew above the national population rate, a marked reversal from earlier trends, especially in the 1960s (Potts 1995). Clearly, the rates of rural-urban migration were declining as potential rural migrants were discouraged by dimming city lights. It also appears that some cities were actually losing people to smaller towns or the rural areas.

The reversal of net migration to cities has been reported from such countries as Nigeria (Collier 1988; Peil 1988; Mosley 1992); Uganda (Bigsten and Kayizzi-Magerwa 1992; Weeks 1992; Zambia (Ferguson 1990; Macmillan 1993); and Tanzania (von Troil 1992; Mbonile 1995). "Return" migration to the rural areas was used as a coping mechanism against the trials and tribulations of structural adjustment mostly by the urban poor, unemployed, and the retired. Its utility as an "exit option" has depended on the availability of land and other rural resources and social networks to which the returning migrant could effectively lay claims of entitlement. Given women's unequal access to rural land and relatively weak nexus of connections, it stands to reason that return migration has largely been a male option. This might explain the rising sex ratios in African cities and even the growing predominance of women in some of them that has been noted by several observers (Gugler 1989; Gugler and Ludwar-Ene 1995; Trager 1995; Jones-Dubey 1995). The differentiated patterns of male and female return migration also reflects the growth of female headed households in cities and helps to unveil the realities of autonomous female urban migration that is often wrapped in stereotypes of women as associational migrants (Adepoju 1995:94-7).

There can be little doubt that economic hardships and premature layoffs have altered the retirement plans of African workers, including those of some professionals, forcing many of them to return to their rural "homes" or to smaller towns where opportunities for business are higher than in the villages and the costs of living are lower than in the large cities. Unfortunately, not much research has been done on African retirement migration. One of the few studies on the subject by Peil (1995) on five small towns, two in Nigeria, two in Sierra Leone, and one in Zimbabwe, demonstrates the growing popularity of such towns as places of retirment. They offer the welfare services and entrepreneurial possibilities of cities and the supportive social networks of village communities. As with return migration, retirement migration is a gendered process. Peil found that elderly women, often widows, were more likely than elderly men, who have larger economic, political, and social resources at home, to settle in a town. While she does not focus on the possible impact of structural adjustment, it would not be too farfetched to suggest that children might find it easier and cheaper to support their elderly mothers than their elderly fathers who can assist in informal sector trading activities and in looking after the children.

These new streams of migration may not justify premature prognoses of counter-urbanization, but they indicate complex changes in urbanization processes in Africa during the era of structural adjustment as rural and urban populations altered their assessments of, and access to, the diminishing opportunities of cities. Structural adjustment also affected, indeed accelerated, two other forms of migration, international and involuntary migration, which affected cities as recipients and generators of the migrants. These forms of migration cannot be easily isolated from internal and voluntary migrations, for the boundaries between them in countries that are often small and share contiguous economies, cultures, and ethnic groups are often fluid and porous. Quite often international migrations are extensions of internal national migrations.

Three major types of international migration can be distinguished on the basis of the economic purpose and class position of the migrants: commercial, labor, and agrarian migrations. Each of these can further be subdivided in terms of occupation, periodicity, destination, and gender. Commercial migrations across national borders, by both males and females, and by target, regular, and professional traders has always been significant in many parts of Africa. The scale of inter- and intra-regional cross-border trade, most of it unregulated by the state authorities, appears to have increased in the 1980s and 1990s. That this was connected to the impact of structural adjustment can be seen in the increased flow of traders and the expansion of trading diasporas from poorer countries and regions to the wealthier countries of Southern Africa, especially South Africa. Similarly, despite growing immigration restrictions, commercial migrations from Africa to the leading cities of western Europe, the United States, and the tigers of East Asia, increased, and new trading diaspora communities were established, or older ones, especially from West Africa, extended their tentacles overseas.

The patterns of international labor migration within Africa appear to have been affected by structural adjustment in several ways. As economic and employment conditions degenerated, pressures for labor migration intensified, while tolerance for labor immigrants deteriorated. By the mid-1980s about five to six million workers were crossing their border in search of work, mostly to Nigeria, Côte d'Ivoire, Libya, and South Africa. But few were welcome. The 1980s will be remembered as the decade when millions of migrant workers were brazenly expelled from fellow African countries. For example, in 1983 and 1985 Nigeria expelled over a million migrant workers from the neighboring countries, and in 1984 Libya expelled about 60,000 migrant workers from other African countries, including 30,000 Tunisians (Zeleza 1997:364).

Unlike before, the migrants were not restricted to ordinary laborers, but increasingly included professionals. Also, women began to feature prominently among both internal and international labor migrants, thanks to the post-independence expansion of female education and the economic changes taking place, as reflected, for example, in the growth of the service sector. Overlaid on already shifting cultural values and occupational roles, rooted in changing gender relations and divisions of labor, including the growth of female-headed households, structural adjustment reinforced women's poverty and the instability of marriage, thus bolstering their struggles for economic autonomy and new income-generating opportunities (Vaa et al. 1989; Adepoju 1990; Findley and Williams 1990; Ingstad 1994; Wright 1995).

Labour migration outside the continent also accelerated, especially among professionals, pushed out by harsh economic conditions and austerity programs and the resulting declines in salaries and living conditions, sometimes compounded by the political insecurities of civil strife and war. Many, about 30,000 between 1984 and 1987 alone, sought and found refuge in western Europe and North America. Notwithstanding remittances from the emigrants to their families, and other invisible benefits to their communities and the expansion of African diaspora communities in the western countries, the brain drain exacted a heavy toll on African economies in terms of lost skills and investment opportunities, specifically through delayed or unimplemented projects and the importation of replacement high-cost expatriate labor (Balogun and Mutahaba 1990).

More difficult to discern is the impact of structural adjustment on agrarian migration, that is, the seasonal and permanent migrations of farmers and pastoralists. Historically, such patterns of migration were widespread in many regions. For example, farming migrations were common in nineteenth and early twentieth century West Africa, and migrant farmers played a major role in the cash crop revolutions witnessed in some parts of the region (Zeleza 1993). Even more prevalent and better known are the pastoral migrations. International agrarian migration within the continent declined as the newly independent states consolidated their assumed sovereignty over borders, populations grew, and arable land became more scarce. Nevertheless, structural adjustment programs had repercussions on rural farming and pastoral communities, sometimes forcing multitudes to migrate within and across national boundaries to protect the integrity of their lives and livelihoods.

Indeed, the bulk of the swelling army of involuntary migrants in Africa in the 1980s and 1990s have been peasant farmers and pastoralists. Africa's refugee crisis from the 1980s may have coincided with natural disasters, but it was spawned by political and economic turmoil, in which the role of structural adjustment looms large. An examination of the political ecology of the refugee crisis indicates that the combination of historic struggles for resources, among ethnic or regional groups, in an era of intensifying pressures for democratization and deepening poverty and underdevelopment, can, and has in several countries—from Burundi and Rwanda in Central Africa; Ethiopia, Sudan, and Somalia in the Horn; Liberia and Sierra Leone in West Africa; and Angola and Mozambique in southern Africa—unleashed civil conflict which generated a flood of refugees (Alderman and Sorenson 1994; Oucho 1995; Kalipeni and Oppong 1997). Of the fifteen million refugees worldwide at the beginning of the 1990s, five million were in Africa, most of them from the rural areas, the purported beneficiaries of SAPs. Not only were the physical places and social spaces where the refugees came from transformed, often leaving behind various forms of environmental and human degradation, so were those to which they migrated.

FIGHTING PLACES

Coping was not always enough or, for that matter, possible. Failure to cope by individuals and communities with the debilitating consequences of structural adjustment was reflected in rising forms of social pathology, including escalating rates of crime, child abandonment, marriage breakdowns, homelessness, violence, and incivility. But African urban dwellers also responded to the changes in the production, organization, and distribution of urban space associated with structural adjustment by fighting for new modalities of local and national governance and for new structures of economic management and opportunity.

It was from the cities that the struggles for democratization which began sweeping across Africa from the mid-1980s emanated. One major city after another, in all the regions of the continent, was rocked by civil disturbances, from riots and uprisings to strikes and public demonstrations. Urban civil society began flexing its overstressed muscles to challenge the authoritarian and corrupt municipal and national governments, demanding popular participation, transparency, and accountability; in short, the democratization, decentralization, and devolution of power. The intolerant and incompetent political authorities were suddenly confronted with an unfamiliar social order: the resurgence of a powerful network of civil institutions, organizations, and associations. They included the older ethnic, professional, and workers' associations, such as trade unions, and religious institutions centered on churches, mosques and shrines, and the newer social movements of women, environmentalists, tenants, consumers, and vendors coalesced around community based organizations (CBOs) and non-governmental-organizations (NGOs). Often intimately involved in the provision of welfare services and the maintenance of public infrastructure and order abdicated by the state, these organizations increasingly intervened in public policy processes seeking fundamental changes in the organization of political power and the economy.

There were, of course, noticeable national and regional differences in the ways in which the urban social movements and struggles manifested themselves. In the Muslim societies of North Africa, Islam provided an important institutional and ideological framework for civil associations. From the 1980s Islamic groups, or organizations influenced by them, began to challenge autocratic rule as the developmentalist capacities and ambitions of the state were curtailed by economic distress and structural adjustment, and to compete for the political souls of the population with the secular civil institutions and organizations, whose allure was tarnished by their class elitism and the failures of a misguided modernity (Kharoufi 1997). The struggles between the three forces—the state, Islamic movements, and secular social movements—for hegemony turned into a deadly confrontation in Algeria, where a civil war erupted following the cancellation of the national elections in 1992 which the Islamicists were poised to win.

In Southern Africa, urban politics has been driven by the need to deracialize the colonial spatial order and political economy and realize the popular democratic and developmental dreams of the national liberation struggle. South Africa, the largest and last settler state to fall, captures most poignantly the problems and possibilities of restructuring urban governance in the region. Perhaps more than anywhere else on the continent, in South Africa urban-based social movements spearheaded and dominated the liberation struggle, so that by the 1980s communities and workplaces in the country's towns and cities had been transformed from bastions of apartheid control into bulwarks of resistance. As the tide of civil unrest and ungovernability rose through strikes, demonstrations, and the prolonged mass actions of consumer and rent boycotts, reinforced by the country's growing international and regional isolation, the shell of apartheid began to crack. Since it appeared neither the state nor the liberation movement were capable of decisively defeating the other, attempts were made to find a negotiated settlement. The search for a new dispensation were conducted from the local, to the regional and national levels, in which complex and tortuous negotiating forums were held between all the protagonists and stakeholders; those representing the beleaguered state and its historic allies and the liberation movement and other oppositional social movements. Besides the transition to a new democratic, majority rule government in 1994, new structures of urban governance emerged out of the hundreds of local negotiating forums (Swilling 1997). Despite facing enormous fiscal, technical, and administrative challenges, compounded in some areas by the persistence of the 'culture of boycott' and the non-payment of rent and services, which threatened the implementation of their ambitious plans, the new urban local governments were more integrated, inclusive, participatory, and accountable than any South Africa had ever known; indeed, they were more democratic than elsewhere in the sub-region and, for that matter, much of the continent.

By the 1990s the political map of Africa had changed significantly. Democratic elections were becoming as common as coups were in the 1970s, and a new political culture and culture of politics had emerged that valorized the trinity of good governance: participation, transparency, and accountability; and sought to realize the triple dreams of the African struggle for independence: democracy, development, and self-determination. It was an intense, intriguing moment, characterized by transitional modes and modalities of urban and national governance. In many of Africa's cities there emerged what Halfani (1997a:33) calls "a multiplicity of governance regimes." Writing on Francophone Africa Attahi (1997:198) makes the same observation, noting that "through their initiatives the local community organizations have brought about a new political culture, recognizing the plurality of actors in urban management together with the necessity of laying the foundations of cooperation between them." Similar developments were evident in Anglophone West Africa (Onibokun 1997) and East Africa (Halfani 1997b).

The growth of new forms of shared management of the city, or the multiplicity of governance regimes, often despite the monopolistic will of the discredited state, reflected the renewal of the social infrastructure of civil society beneath the signs of decaying physical infrastructure. This demonstrates that, as with most historical processes or events, the effects of structural adjustment programs, or of the moment in recent African history dominated by SAPs, spawned contradictory changes. While some responded to reduced urban opportunities and deepening poverty by migrating to greener sectors and spaces at home and abroad, it propelled many more to devise complex coping strategies and to fight for new modes of governance.

This reflected, it could be argued, a fundamental shift in the public imagination of the city and the closure of previous exit options (Herbst 1990). Long regarded by the poor as a transit area, as a place that was not quite "home" even for the middle class elites, the beleagured structurally adjusted city increasingly came to be seen as "home," a place that was worth struggling for. And so they sought to reinvent it, to reshape its spaces, signs, and symbols, to make it work for them. The struggles for remaking the city went beyond the immediate and most visible effects of structural adjustment. They became struggles about many other pressing questions, such as the nature of state power and local governance, the relationship between workplaces and community life, and the creation and consumption of popular culture. Many of the questions raised about the spatial and social dynamics of African cities during the era of structural adjustment attempted in this essay, could also fruitfully inform analysis of the spatial and political ecology of African urbanization in general.

CONCLUSION

Since the economic slowdown of the 1980s and the imposition of structural adjustment programs, African cities have undergone visible spatial changes and less visible cultural transformations. The first thing to note is that contrary to predictions, population growth rates in African cities began to slow down from the 1980s. The growth that took place was also more the result of natural increase than rural-urban migration. Moreover, the medium cities grew faster than the largest cities, leading to a wider dispersal of the urban population. Many of these trends were not restricted to Africa, but applied to many cities in the South as well (Habitat 1996).

As a result of the contraction of formal public and private employment, the informalization of the economy not only increased, but so did the unregulated provision of urban housing and other social services. This contributed to the proliferation of community organizations and the emergence of new forms of urban associational life; the decentralization and democratization of city governance; and the deregulation of urban space from being restricted enclaves of colonial power and privilege into bustling spaces increasingly driven and domesticated by the often desperate dreams and demands of the impoverished masses.

The spatial morphology of many cities in the continent was also transformed, not only as noisy hawkers invaded the previously staid business districts, but also as settlements expanded on the peripheries of the cities, thus dissolving the stern rural-urban separation. The expansion of urban agriculture added to the blurring of the economic and cultural differences between city and country. The African city of the 1990s was quite different in terms of size, spatial organization, infrastructural services, and cultural dynamics from the post-independence city of the 1960s and 1970s. Life for many in the city turned nasty, brutish, and short, but the city also became a place called "home," worth struggling for and reinventing and reimagining. In short, with structural adjustment the struggle for the city entered a new era, characterized by immense problems and new possibilities.

This Chapter has tried to outline the spatial economy and political ecology of African cities in the 1980s and 1990s during the period of structural adjustment. It has tried to combine an analysis that focuses on the changes in the structural processes and the built urban environment, on which many social scientists tend to dwell, with an examination of the transformations that were taking place in the realms of culture and governance. This enables us to understand contemporary African urbanization for the complex phenomenon that it is, as one in which structural conditions, human agency, and historical process are intricately woven.

NOTES

1. Spatiality, many Geographers are happy to note, is now in vogue, competing with historicity, in the formulation of social theory. See the following collections by Bird et al. (1993), Keith and Pile (1993), Duncan and Ley (1993), and the books by Harvey (1989), Lefebvre (1991), Lash and Urry (1994), and Massey (1994).

2. For a detailed theoretical and empirical discussion of these issues and an extensive bibliography see Zeleza (1997: Chapter 13).

3. These readings suggest the difficulties of defining globalization. Much of what is said about it is not new; many of the processes have been going on for centuries since the emergence of the modern world system. Massey (1994) suggests, quite perceptively, that the unsettling discovery of the dislocations of globalization among social theorists and commentators in the North is elitist and sometimes racist in that it reflects their apprehension of loss of control as their local streets and neighborhoods are "invaded" by cultural imports and communities from the ex-colonial world. For peoples who were once enslaved and colonized the feelings and realities of being dislocated/placeless/invaded is nothing new.

4. This distinction points to the difficulties of establishing specific causal connections between structural adjustment policies and socio-economic trends and outcomes. It also eliminates the need for counterfactual arguments, and enables us to incorporate into the analysis "events" that occurred that had little to do, in their causation not consequences, with structural adjustment per se, such as the weather, which probably had a far greater impact on variations in economic performance among countries than differences in policy.

5.   This section draws heavily on Chapter 14 in Zeleza (1997), which has an extensive bibliography, thereby eschewing the need for lengthy references here.

6.   "Urban agriculture," some have charged, is a euphemism for urban decay and has been blamed for exacerbating urban environmental degradation, see Bibangambah (1992).

7.   Urban agriculture has grown in the developed countries of Western Europe, North America and Japan for a variety of economic, cultural, nutritional, and social reasons, see Latz (1991), Bills (1991), van der Bliek (1992). The same is true for Asian and Latin American cities (Gutman 1987; Wade 1987; Yeung 1988; Lee-Smith and Trujillo 1992).

8.   In a survey of workers in Kaduna and Kano who lost jobs in the textile industry, those who had previous farming experience resorted to city farming at a higher rate than those who did not, see Andrae (1992).

9.   A survey of academic staff at Ahmadu Bello University showed that part-time farming activities pre-dated the imposition of structural adjustment in Nigeria, but accelerated following its implementation, see Defu (1992).

10. For a fuller treatment of the subject see the papers delivered at the 24th Annual Symposium of the Center for African Studies, University of Illinois at Urbana-Champaign, April 1997, "The Creation and Consumption of Leisure in Urban Africa."

REFERENCES

Adepoju, A. "State of the Art Review on Migration in Africa." Conference on the Role of Migration in African Development: Issues and Policies for the 1990s, UAPS, Dakar, Senegal, 1990.

Adepoju, A. "Migration in Africa: An Overview." In *The Migration Experience in Africa*, eds. J. Baker and T. A. Aina. Uppsala: Nordiska Afrikainstitutet, 1995.

Ahmad, A. *In Theory: Classes, Nations, Literatures.* London and New York: Verso, 1992.

Aina, T. A. *Globalization and Social Policy in Africa. Issues and Research Directions.* Codesria Working Paper 6/96, 1997a.

Aina, T. A. "Working People's Popular Culture in Lagos." Paper presented at the 24th Annual Spring Symposium, The Creation and Consumption of Leisure in Urban Africa,' University of Illinois at Urbana-Champaign, 1997b.

Alderman, H. and J. Sorenson, eds. *African Refugees: Development Aid and Repatriation.* Boulder, Colo: Westview, 1994.

Andrae, G. "Urban Workers as Farmers: Agro-Links of Nigerian Textile Workers in the Crisis of the 1980s." In *The Rural-Urban Interface in Africa: Expansion and Adaptation*, eds. J. Baker and P. O. Pedersen. Uppsala: Scandinavian Institute of African Studies, 1992.

Appadurai, A. *Modernity at Large: Cultural Dimensions of Globalization.* Minneapolis: University of Minnesota Press, 1996.

Azarya, V. and N. Chazan. "Disengagement from the State in Africa: Reflections on the Experience in Ghana and Guinea." *Comparative Politics in Society and History* 20, 1(1987):106-131.

Bagguley, P., J. M. Lawson, D. Shapiro, J. Urry, S. Walby and A. Warde. *Restructuring: Place, Class, Gender.* London: Sage, 1990.

Balogun, J. and G. Mutahaba. "The Dilemma of the Brain Drain." In *The Employment Crisis in Africa*, ed. C. Grey-Johnson. Harare: Sapes Trust, 1990.

Bates, R. *Markets and States in Tropical Africa.* Berkeley: University of California Press, 1981.

Bates, R. *Beyond the Miracle of the Market: The Political Economy of Agrarian Development in Kenya.* Cambridge: Cambridge University Press, 1989.

Bhagwati, J. "Directly Unproductive Profit Seeking Activities." *Journal of Political Economy* 90 (1982):988-1002.

Berman, B. J. "African Capitalism and the Paradigm of Modernity: Culture, Technology and the State." In *African Capitalists in Development*, eds. B. Berman and C. Leys. Boulder: Lynne Rienner, 1994.

Bibangambah, J. R. "Macro-Level Constraints and the Growth of the Informal Sector in Uganda." In *The Rural-Urban Interface in Africa: Expansion and Adaptation*, eds. J. Baker and P. O. Pedersen. Uppsala: Scandinavian Institute of African Studies, 1992.

Bigsten, A. and Kayizzi-Magerwa, S. "Adaptation and Distress in the Urban Economy: A Study of Kampala Households." *World Development* 20, 10(1992):1423-41.

Bills, N. L. *Urban Agriculture in the United States.* New York: Cornell University, Department of Agricultural Economics, 1991.

Bird, J, B. Curtis, T. Putnam, G. Robertson, and L. Tickner, eds. *Mapping the Futures: Local Cultures, Global Change.* London and New York: Routledge, 1993.

Bratton, M. "Beyond the State: Civil Society and Associational Life in Africa." *World Politics* 49, 3 (1989):407-23.

Bratton, M. 1990. "Non-Governmental Organizations in Africa." *Development and Change* 21, 1 (1990):87-118.

Chazan, N. "Ghana: Problems of Governance and the Emergence of Civil Society. In *Democracy in Developing Countries*, Vol.2, Africa, eds. L. Diamond, J. Linz and S. Lipset. Boulder: Lynne Rienner, 1988.

Collier, P. "Oil shocks and food security in Nigeria." *International Labour Review* 127, 6 (1988):761-82.

Cornia, G. A., R. van der Hoeven and S. Lall. "The Supply Side: Changing Production Structures and Accelerating Growth." *Africa's Recovery in the 1990s: From Stagnation and Adjustment to Human Development*, eds. Cornia, G. A., R. van der Hoeven, and T. Mkandawire, eds. New York: St. Martin's Press, 1992.

Cornia, G. A., R. van der Hoeven, and T. Mkandawire, eds. *Africa's Recovery in the 1990s: From Stagnation and Adjustment to Human Development*. New York: St. Martin's Press, 1992.

Defu, J. O. "Part-Time Farming as an Urban Survival Strategy: A Nigerian Case Study." In *The Rural-Urban Interface in Africa: Expansion and Adaptation*, eds. J. Baker and P. O. Pedersen. Uppsala: Scandinavian Institute of African Studies, 1992.

De Valk, P. *African Industry in Decline*. New York: St. Martin's Press, 1996.

Diejomaoh, V. P. "Welcome Address." In *Youth Employment Promotion in Africa*. Addis Ababa: JASPA, 1987.

Drakakis-Smith, D. "Strategies for Meeting Basic Food Needs in Harare." In *The Rural-Urban Interface in Africa: Expansion and Adaptation*, eds. J. Baker and P. O. Pedersen. Uppsala: Scandinavian Institute of African Studies, 1992.

Drakakis-Smith, D., T. Bowyer-Bower, and D. Tavera. "Urban Poverty and Urban Agriculture: An Overview of Linkages in Harare." *Habitat International* 19, 2 (1995):183-193.

Duncan, J. and D. Ley, eds. *Place/Culture/Representation*. London and New York: Routledge, 1993.

ECA (Economic Commission for Africa). "Long-Term Development and Structural Change: Manpower Planning and Utilization." Khartoum Conference on the Human Dimension of Africa's Economic Recovery and Development, ECA/ICHD/88/32, 1988.

Engberg-Pedersen, P., P. Gibbon P. Raikes, and L. Udsholt, eds. *The Limits of Structural Adjustment in Africa*. Oxford: James Currey, 1996.

Eyoh, D. "From Economic Stagnation to Political Liberalization: Pitfalls of the New Political Sociology for Africa." *African Studies Review* 39, 3 (1996):43-80.

Egziabher, A. G. "Urban Farming Co-operatives, and the Urban Poor in Addis Ababa." In *Cities Feeding People: An Examination of Urban Agriculture in East Africa*, ed. International Development Research Center (IDRC). Ottawa, Canada: IDRC, 1994.

Ferguson, J. "Mobile Workers, Modernist Narratives: A Critique of the Historiography of Transition on the Zambian Copperbelt." *Journal of Southern African Studies* 16, 3 (1990):385-412.

Findley, S. E. and L. Williams. "Women who Go and Women who Stay: Reflections on Family Migration Processes in a Changing World." *Working Paper Series*. Geneva: International Labor Organization, 1990.

Freeman, D. B. *A City of Farmers: Informal Agriculture in Open Spaces of Nairobi, Kenya*. Montreal and Kingston: McGill-Queen's University Press, 1991.

Gbadegesin, A. "Farming in the Urban Environment of a Developing - A Case Study From Ibadan Metropolis in Nigeria." *The Environment* 11, 2 (1991):105-111.

Geest, W. van der, ed. *Negotiating Structural Adjustment in Africa*. London: James Currey, 1994.

Gibbon, P., Y. Bangura and A. Ofstad, eds. *Authoritarianism, Democracy and Adjustment: The Politics of Economic Reform in Africa.* Uppsala: Scandinavian Institute for African Studies, 1992.

Gibbon, P. and A. O. Olukoshi. *Structural Adjustment and Socio-Economic Change in Sub-Saharan Africa: Some Conceptual, Methodological and Research Issues.* Uppsala: Nordiska Afrikainstitutet, 1996.

Gugler, J. "Women stay on the Farm No More: Changing Patterns of Rural-Urban Migration in Sub-Saharan Africa." *Journal of Modern African Studies* 27, 2 (1989)347-52.

Gugler, J. and G. Ludwar-Ene. "Gender and Migration in Africa South of the Sahara." In *The Migration Experience in Africa*, eds. J. Baker and T. A. Aina. Uppsala: Nordiska Afrikainstitutet, 1995.

Gutman, P. "Urban Agriculture: The Potential and Limitations of an Urban Self-Reliance Strategy." *Food and Nutrition Bulletin* 9, 2 (1987):37-42.

Habitat. *An Urbanizing World: Global Report on Human Settlements 1996.* New York: Oxford University Press, 1996.

Halfani, M. "The Challenge of Urban Governance in Africa. Institutional Change and Knowledge Gaps."In *Governing Africa's Cities*, ed. M. Swilling. Johannesburg: Witwatersrand University Press, 1997a.

Halfani, M. "The Governance of Urban Development in East Africa. An Examination of the Institutional landscape and the poverty challenge." In *Governing Africa's Cities*, ed. M. Swilling. Johannesburg: Witwatersrand University Press, 1997b.

Harvey, D. *The Condition of Postmodernity.* Oxford: Basil Blackwell, 1989.

Harvey, D. "From Space to Place and back again: Reflections on the Condition of Modernity." In *Mapping the Futures: Local Cultures, Global Change*, eds. J. Bird, B. Curtis, T. Putman, G. Robertson, and L. Tickner. London and New York: Routledge, 1993a.

Harvey, D. "Class Relations, Social Justice and the Politics of Difference." In *Place and the Politics of Identity*, ed. M. Keith and S. Pile. London and New York: Routledge, 1993b.

Herbst, J. "Migration, The Politics of Protest, and State Consolidation in Africa." *African Affairs* 89, 355 (1990):183-203.

Hoeven, R. van der and F. van der Kraaji, eds. *Structural Adjustment and Beyond in Sub-Sahara Africa.* London: James Currey, 1994.

Holm, H. and G. Sorenson, eds. *Whose World Order? Uneven Globalization and the End of the Cold War.* Boulder, Col.: Westview, 1995.

Ingstad, B. "The Grandmother and Household Viability in Botswana." In *Gender, Work and Population in Sub-Saharan Africa*, eds. A. Adepoju and C. Oppong. London: ILO, James Currey, 1994.

ILO (International Labour Organization). *World Labour Report 3.* Geneva: ILO, 1987.

ILO/JASPA. *Rural-Urban Gap and Income Distribution: A Comparative Sub-Regional Study.*   Addis Ababa: JASPA, 1984.

ILO/JASPA. *African Employment Report 1988.* Addis Ababa: JASPA, 1989.

Jamal, V. *Structural Adjustment and Rural Labour Markets in Africa.* New York: St. Martin's Press, 1995.

Jamal, V. and J. Weeks. "The Vanishing Rural-Urban Gap in Sub-Saharan Africa." *International Labour Review* 127, 3 (1988):271-292.

Jones-Dubey, E. "Non-Metropolitan Migration in Botswana with an Emphasis on Gender." In *The Migration Experience in Africa*, eds. J. Baker and T. A. Aina. Uppsala: Nordiska Afrikainstitutet, 1995.

Kalipeni, E. and J. Oppong. "The Refugee Crisis and Implications For Health and Disease in Africa: A Political Ecology Approach." Paper presented at the World Centers Symposium, University of Illinois at Urbana-Champaign, April, 1997.

Keith, M. and S. Pile, eds. *Place and the Politics of Identity.* London and New York: Routledge, 1993.

Kharoufi, M. "Governance and Urban Society in North Africa." In *Governing Africa's Cities*, ed. M. Swilling. Johannesburg: Witwatersrand University Press, 1997.

Khennas, S., ed. *Industrialization Mineral Resources and Energy in Africa.* Dakar: Codesria, 1992.

Khouri-Dagher, N. *Food and Energy in Cairo: Provisioning the Poor.* Research Report No.18, The Food Energy Nexus Programme. Tokyo: The United Nations University, 1986.

Lachaud, J. *The Labour Market in Africa.* Geneva: ILO, 1994.

Lado, C. "Informal Urban Agriculture in Nairobi, Kenya: Problems or Resource in Development and Land Use Planning." *Land Use Policy* 3, 7 (1990):257-266.

Latz, G. "The Persistence of Agriculture in Urban Japan: An Analysis of the Tokyo Metropolitan Area." In *The Extended Metropolis: Settlement Transition in Asia*, eds, N. Ginsburg, B. Koppel and T. G. McGee. Honolulu: University of Hawaii Press, 1991.

Lash, S. and J. Urry. *Economies of Signs and Space.* London: Sage Publications, 1994.

Lee-Smith, D. and C. H. Trujillo. "The Struggle to Legitimize Subsistence: Women and Sustainable Development." *Environment and Urbanization* 4, 1 (1992):77-84.

Lefebvre, H. *The Production of Space.* Oxford: Basil Blackwell, 1991.

Lipton, M. *Why Poor People Stay Poor: Urban Bias in World Development.* London: Temple Smith, 1977.

Lofchie, M. *The Policy Factor: Agricultural Performance in Kenya and Tanzania.* Boulder, Colo: Lynne Rienner, 1989.

Macmillan, H. "The Historiography of Transition on the Zambian Copperbelt - Another View." *Journal of Southern African Studies* 19, 4 (1993):681-712.

Massey, D. *Space, Place, and Gender.* Minneapolis: University of Minnesota Press, 1994.

May, J. and C. M. Rogerson. "Poverty and Sustainable Cities in South Africa: The Role of Urban Cultivation." *Habitat International* 19, 2 (1995):165-181.

Mbiba, B. "Institutional Responses to Uncontrolled Urban Cultivation in Harare: Prohibitive or Accommodative?" *Environment and Urbanization* 16, 1 (1994):188-202.

Mbonile, M. Structural adjustment and rural development in Tanzania: The case of Makete District." In *Structurally Adjusted Africa: Poverty, Debt and Basic Needs*, eds. D. Simon, W. van Spengen, C. Dixon, and A. Närman. London: Pluto Press, 1995.

Memon, P. A. and D. Lee-Smith. "Urban Agriculture in Kenya." *Canadian Journal of African Studies* 27, 1 (1993):25-42.

Mlozi, M. R. S. "Inequitable Agricultural Extension Services in the Urban Context: The
Case of Tanzania." In *Education in Urban Areas: Cross-National Dimensions*, ed. N. P. Tromquist. Westport: Praeger, 1994.

Mlozi, M. R. S. "Child Labour in Urban Agriculture: The Case of Dar es Salaam, Tanzania." *Children's Environments* 12, 2 (1995):197-208.

Mlozi, M. R. S., I. J. Lupanga and Z. S. K. Mvena. "Urban Agriculture as a Survival Strategy in Tanzania." In *The Rural-Urban Interface in Africa: Expansion and Adaptation*, eds. J. Baker and P. O. Pedersen. Uppsala: Scandinavian Institute of African Studies, 1992.

Mkandawire, T. and A. O. Olukoshi. *Between Liberalization and Oppression: The Politics of Structural Adjustment in Africa*. Dakar: Codesria, 1995.

Mosha, A. "Urban Farming Practices in Tanzania." *Review of Rural and Urban Planning in Southern and Eastern Africa* 1(1991):83-92.

Mosley, P. "Nigeria's Economy and structural adjustment." *African Affairs* 91, 361 (1992):227-40.

Onibokun, P. "Governance and Urban Poverty in Anglophone West Africa." In *Governing Africa's Cities*, ed. M. Swilling. Johannesburg: Witwatersrand University Press, 1997.

Oucho, J. O. "International Migration and Sustainable Human Development in Eastern and Southern Africa." *International Migration* 33, 1 (1993):31-51.

Peil, M. "Going home: Migration careers of southern Nigerians." *International Migration Review* 22, 4 (1988):563-85.

Peil, M. "The Small Town as a Retirement Center." In *The Migration Experience in Africa*, eds. J. Baker and T. A. Aina. Uppsala: Nordiska Afrikainstitutet, 1995.

Portes, A., M. Castelles and L. Benton. *Informal Economy: Studies in Advanced and Less Developed Countries*. Baltimore: Johns Hopkins University Press, 1989.

Potts, D. "Shall we go home? Increasing Urban Poverty in African Cities and Migration Processes." *The Geographical Journal* 161, 3 (1995): 245-264.

Rakodi, C. "Urban Agriculture: Research Questions and Zambian Evidence." *Journal of Modern African Studies* 26, 3 (1988):495-515.

Riddell, R., ed. *Manufacturing Africa: Performance and Prospects of Seven Countries in Sub-Saharan Africa.* London: James Currey, 1990.

Rogerson, C. "Urban Agriculture in South Africa: Policy Issues From the International Experience." *Development Southern Africa* 10, 1 (1993):33-44.

Rothchild, D. And N. Chazan. *The Precarious Balance: State and Society in Africa.* Boulder, Colo: Lynne Rienner, 1988.

Sahn, D. E., ed. *Adjusting to Policy Failure in African Economies.* Ithaca and London: Cornell University Press, 1994.

Sahn, D. E., ed. *Economic Reform and the Poor in Africa.* Oxford: Clarendon Press, 1996.

Sanyal, B. "Urban Agriculture: Who Cultivates and Why? A Case Study of Lusaka, Zambia." *Food and Nutrition Bulletin* 3, 7 (1985):15-24.

Sawio, C. J. "Who are the Farmers in Dar es Salaam?" In *Cities Feeding People: An Examination of Urban Agriculture in East Africa,* ed. International Development Research Center (IDRC). Ottawa, Canada: IDRC, 1994.

Stein, H., ed. *Asian Industrialization and Africa: Studies in Policy Alternatives to Structural Adjustment.* New York: St. Martin's Press, 1995.

Swilling, M. "Building Democratic Local Urban Governance in Southern Africa." In *Governing Africa's Cities,* ed. M. Swilling. Johannesburg: Witwatersrand University Press, 1997.

Toye, J. "Structural Adjustment: Context, Assumptions, Origin and Diversity." In *Structural Adjustment and Beyond in Sub-Sahara Africa,* eds. R. van der Hoeven and F. van der Kraaji. London: James Currey, 1994.

Trager, L. "Women Migrants and Rural-Urban Linkages in South-Western Nigeria." In *The Migration Experience in Africa,* eds. J. Baker and T. A. Aina. Uppsala: Nordiska Afrikainstitutet, 1995.

Tricaud, P. M. *Urban Agriculture in Ibadan and Freetown.* Food and Energy Nexus Program, Tokyo: United Nations University, 1987.

Vaa, M., S. E. Findley, and A. Diallo. "The Gift Economy: A Study of Women Migrants' Survival Strategies in a Low-Income Bamako Neighborhood." *Labour, Capital and Society* 22, 2 (1989).

Vandemoortele, J. *Employment Issues in Sub-Saharan Africa.* Nairobi: African Economic Research Consortium, 1991.

van der Bliek, J. A. *Urban Agriculture: Possibilities for Ecological Agriculture in Urban Environment as a Strategy for Sustainable Cities.* Leusden: CTC Foundation, 1992.

von Troil, M. "Looking for a better life in town: The case of Tanzania." In *The Rural-Urban Interface in Africa: Expansion and Adaptation,* eds J. Baker and P. O. Pederson. Uppsala: Scandinavian Institute of African Studies, Seminar Proceedings 27 (1992):223-37.

Wade, I. 1987. "Community Food Production in Cities of the Developing Nations." *Food and Nutrition Bulletin* 9, 2 (1987):29-36.

World Bank. *Sub-Saharan Africa: From Crisis to Sustainable Growth.* Washington D.C.: World Bank, 1989.

World Bank. *Adjustment in Africa: Reforms, Results, and the Road Ahead.* New York: Oxford University Press, 1994.

World Bank. *A Continent in Transition: Sub-Saharan Africa in the Mid-1990s.* Washington, DC: World Bank, 1995.

World Bank and UNDP. *Africa's Adjustment and Growth in the 1980s.* Washington, DC: The World Bank and UNDP, 1989.

Wright, C. "Gender Awareness in Migration Theory: Synthesizing Actor and Structure in Southern Africa." *Development and Change* 26, 4 (1995):771-791.

Yeung, Y. M. "Agricultural Land Use in Asian Cities." *Land Use Policy* 5, 1 (1988):79-82.

Weeks, J. *Development strategy and the Economy of Sierra Leone.* Basingstoke: Macmillan, 1992.

Zeleza, P. T. *A Modern Economic History of Africa.* Vol. 1: *The Nineteenth Century.* Dakar: Codesria, 1993.

Zeleza, P. T. *Manufacturing African Studies and Crises.* Dakar: Codesria, 1997.

4

THE SPATIAL CONTEXT OF LILONGWE S GROWTH AND DEVELOPMENT

EZEKIEL KALIPENI

INTRODUCTION

LILONGWE, OFTEN DESCRIBED AS A SMALL, QUIET, AND DUSTY outpost during the colonial era (see Cole-King 1971), has experienced rapid growth since its establishment in the early 1970s as the new capital city of Malawi. With a population of about 19,000 in 1966, Lilongwe's population increased dramatically to approximately 500,000 people in 1997 (Malawi National Statistical Office 1994). Between 1975 and 1985 the city grew at an astounding growth rate of 15.8 % per annum (M'manga 1986). Recent estimates indicate that the city is currently growing at a growth rate of 9% per annum and this growth is expected to decline further to about 5% per annum in the near future. While most of this growth is due to the move of the capital from Zomba to Lilongwe, it must also be kept in mind that the area of Lilongwe was redrawn to include a larger expanse of 350 square kilometers incorporating villages that surrounded the old Lilongwe.

From a theoretical point of view, one would expect that the rapid growth Lilongwe has experienced would threaten its function and survival as an engine of sustainable development. However, in spite of the external shocks in these times of structural adjustment, Lilongwe's economy, particularly the informal sector, is vibrant and continues to grow. The city is even more lively today than it was a few years ago. Using a spatial framework, this paper briefly examines how Lilongwe has been able to cope with such rapid growth. The major problems facing the city of Lilongwe are highlighted. It is argued that the "apartheid oriented" spatial planning of Lilongwe and the initial stringent land use zoning ordinances have had profound direct and indirect effects as well as positive and negative consequences on the livelihoods of the majority of the residents.

THE CITY IN AFRICAN ECONOMIES

McNulty (1986) notes that African towns and cities are like "economic islands" in a sea of underdevelopment. There exists an intricate relationship between these "islands of development" and the rural hinterlands which they serve and are served by. Towns and cities in sub-Saharan Africa are the main market centers and boast a disproportionate share of wage employment and manufacturing. Better medical facilities, schools, colleges, shops, entertainment and leisure amenities are all concentrated in the modern African city. On the other hand, the rural countryside within the area of influence of these cities provide them with food and labor (Danaher 1984). Furthermore, foreign exchange earned from the growing of cash crops in the countryside is invariably invested by national governments into the expansion of these cities at the expense of the rural areas. The major impact of the modern city, according to a number of scholars, has been the triggering of rural-urban migration of young people from the countryside (Stren and White 1988; Riddell 1978; Hanna and Hanna 1981; Ross 1973; Brockerhoff & Eu 1993).

During the early years of independence, the colonial tradition of encouraging the growth of urban areas was fervently adopted by post-colonial governments of Africa (Mijere and Chilivumbo 1992). Others such as Lipton (1977) have strongly argued that there has been heavy bias towards urban development during the post-independence period in most developing countries. Old cities have been expanded and new ones created. For example, Lilongwe in Malawi, Abuja in Nigeria, Dodoma in Tanzania, Yamoussoukro in Cote d'Ivoire, are post-colonial creations (Mlia 1975). The cities of Kinshasa in Zaire, Nairobi in Kenya, Dakar in Senegal, Lagos in Nigeria, Dar-es-Salaam in Tanzania and many others have been growing at annual rates of well over 6 % per annum (Onibokun 1989; Mbuyi 1989; Lee-Smith 1989; Ngom 1989). A growth rate of 6 % per annum implies a population doubling time of less than 12 years.

Although the level of urbanization, estimated at 30 percent for most African countries, is low by world standards, contemporary literature notes that African cities have not been adequately prepared to handle the postcolonial rural-urban influx of people. As Riddell notes, the situation is of such proportions that phrases such as "cities that came too soon," "exploding cities in unexploding economies," and "over-urbanization" are commonly employed to describe what is happening (Riddell 1978). This vein of the literature further argues that the unpreparedness of African cities for the massive influx has resulted in a number of unwanted consequences such as traffic congestion and substandard housing. Shanty towns and squatter colonies have mushroomed alongside the modern skyscrapers. For the majority there is no running water, no sewer facilities, no electricity or any of the modern amenities associated with cities. It is further noted that burgeoning city population is putting a lot of pressure on the existing facilities such as housing, hospitals, schools and that unemployment is on the rise. According to this rather pessimistic school of thought, the end result has been rising crime rates, theft, prostitution and other such vices (Danaher 1984; MacGregor 1990). Cities have thus been dubbed as centers of discontent and political agitation, inevitably culminating in riots, civil strife, military take over of governments and general political instability instigated by the dissatisfied urban masses (Noble 1991; Somerville 1992).

Why then do migrants pour into the urban areas when the chances of their finding steady jobs and adequate housing for their families are so low? A number of scholars have answered this question in the push/pull tradition or the much talked about "bright lights" theory (see for example Ross 1973; Mabogunje 1976; Riddell 1978; Bale and Drakakis-Smith 1990). The "push" side suggests that life is so bad in the rural areas that individuals know there is no chance for improvement. Rural poverty, overpopulation, lack of alternative wage employment other than agriculture are some of the factors which have, so it is argued, tended to push the youthful from rural areas to the city (Mabogunje 1976). The "pull" side emphasizes reasons why the city attracts migrants. Cities act like magnets for the young, especially those who have attained some sort of education. There is a promise of economic gain in the form of money and the benefits of modernity such as good housing, a car, a stereo and a television set. Due to these factors, the post-independence era in most African countries is said to have seen a massive influx into the modern African city. In contradiction to the rural-urban school of thought, recent studies indicate the growth of a strong urban to rural counter stream (Jamal and Weeks 1988; Becker et al. 1994; Potts 1995). While most studies have concentrated on the rural-urban push/pull factors, little has been done to look at intra-urban dynamics of space, politics, culture and the economy. In the following sections I outline the historical evolution of Lilongwe, its position in Malawi's national urban hierarchy, and problems engendered by its apartheid fashion urban morphology.

THE HISTORICAL EVOLUTION OF LILONGWE

Central Malawi has a long history of human settlement. When the first Europeans such as David Livingstone in the mid 1860s and early Portuguese explorers in 1811 passed through present-day Lilongwe area they found thriving communities led by powerful Chewa chiefs such as Tambala, Malambo, Chimphango, and Thope (Cole-King 1971). Simple and complex rock paintings dating back to 200 BC have been discovered in the hills to the south of Lilongwe. These paintings are thought to have been the work of the Batwa, a group of hunters and gatherers who inhabited the Lilongwe plains during the "Later Stone Age" between 8,000 to 200 BC (Mathews et al. 1991). Other stone age artifacts have been unearthed on the site of the New Capital City itself. Pottery and metal finds in this region also seem to indicate the arrival of Bantu speakers who brought with them the knowledge and art of iron smelting and farming around 300 AD. These new immigrants slowly displaced the original Batwa inhabitants. By the end of the fifteenth century, the Chewa of Central Malawi, a Bantu group, had established a powerful kingdom known as the Maravi Empire from which present day Malawi derived its name. Although Lilongwe was not the headquarters of this Kingdom, most of the chiefs in this area were sub-chiefs of the Maravi Empire.

The origins of Lilongwe as a modern town go back to 1904 when Lilongwe was made an administrative center for Lilongwe district and shortly thereafter a provincial headquarters for the Central Region (Cole-King 1971; Mjojo 1989). The choice of Lilongwe as a new administrative center by early colonial officers was dictated by its centrality in the newly created Central Province then known as Central Angoniland. Cole-King estimates that by 1905 the population of this new settlement was no more than 130 people. In 1920 the settlement had grown considerably and boasted a few buildings which included a small post office, a police station, a prison building and the resident's office. The resident was the person responsible for the day to day administration of the settlement. His tasks were multipurpose serving as judge, tax collector, administrator, etc. In 1930 the status of Lilongwe was raised to that of a sanitary area since the presence of a Sanitary Board was synonymous with a town council. The chairman of this board was the resident and soon his title was changed to that of a district commissioner. This board was responsible for public health, planning and raising of revenue for the development of the *boma*, i.e. the district headquarters. (For a detailed description of the historical origins of Lilongwe see Cole-King 1971; Mjojo 1989; Bandawe 1989).

By the 1950s Lilongwe was a flourishing administrative outpost in Central Malawi. A number of factors played a crucial role in the historical growth of Lilongwe during the colonial era. One important factor was the emergence of Lilongwe as a communication center in Central Malawi. The African Trans-Continental Telegraph company's line reached Central Malawi in the early years of the establishment of Lilongwe. Roads connecting Lilongwe to other administrative centers in Central Malawi were also built which facilitated the task of administration and commerce. In the 1920s tobacco emerged as the main cash crop in the Lilongwe environs and the colonial government was quick to realize and promote the growing of to-bacco by small farmers as a means to generate revenue for the colonial government. Lilongwe became the central collection point of the tobacco industry in Central Malawi. Soon trading companies such as Imperial to-bacco Company, the African Lakes Corporation, the Blantyre Supply Com-pany (Kandodo), the Kabula Stores Ltd. opened branches in Lilongwe to take advantage of the wealth generated from tobacco growing by both large scale agricultural estates and smallholder farmers. The tobacco industry in turn fueled the building of roads linking Lilongwe to many of the tobacco producing areas in Central Malawi. The booming commerce in Lilongwe created an atmosphere in which hawking and commercial trading of other commodities such as foodstuffs, cattle, fish from Lake Malawi, etc became a daily routine of urban life.

As Lilongwe grew, the physical layout of the town mirrored the colonial context characterized by imperialism and racial segregation. As Simon (1992b) notes, in the colonial city or town all potential urban inhabitants were not catered for on an equal basis. "Local indegenes were frequently allowed to live only in certain areas of the city, commonly under inadequate, degrading and tightly regulated conditions." In most colonial settings, physical space was invariably used to promote the separation of social space. In 1924 colonial Lilongwe was thus divided into sectors, one part for the na-tives on the eastern bank of the Lilongwe River and the other for the resi-dences of the district commissioner and his fellow colonial officers and other Europeans on the western bank of the Lilongwe River (Pennant 1985; Mjojo 1989). Thus while the initial city was founded on the western bank of the river, all natives were ordered to move to the eastern bank in 1924. The Asians were allocated the southeastern portion of the city on the same side as the indigenous people. It should be noted that the area on the western bank of the river was on higher ground and hence was thought to have a smaller risk of malaria, cholera outbreaks, and other diseases, i.e. prime ground for European settlement.

African workers in the colonial government such as police constables, court clerks and messengers were housed in less permanent houses made of mud and thatched with grass on the eastern bank of the Lilongwe River.

Housing for the expanding urban area became very acute that in the 1950s the colonial government was forced to build more permanent smaller houses for African civil servants in the area called the Falls Estate on the eastern side of the Lilongwe River. In 1958 the colonial administration introduced the now famous "site and service scheme" in peri-urban areas. In the "site and service scheme" such as Kawale and Nchesi on the far eastern outskirts of the original town, plots were demarcated and distributed to interested indigenous people to build simple traditional houses and/or more permanent structures with bricks. Piped water would be provided in kiosks at various points in the scheme and deep latrines would be built. Thus right from the start Lilongwe was a differentiated city, with the European core on the western side of the river boundary marker and the African and Asian cores on the eastern side.

In spite of the social and physical distances between the races, Lilongwe continued to grow and boundaries were adjusted as the city expanded outwards (see Figure 4.1). Lilongwe's fortunes changed significantly in 1930 when the Lilongwe Sanitary Board was established, which meant Lilongwe would soon graduate to a township with a town council (Cole-King 1971; Mjojo 1989; Bandawe 1989). Although it was a nominated not an elected board, the board had powers similar to those of a town council with regard to public health and planning albeit with limited revenue collection powers (Cole-King 1971:45). Without any African representation, the board consisted of the District Commissioner, District Medical Officer, the Engineer, two Europeans and two Asian unofficial members. By 1947 Lilongwe had graduated into a fully fledged township with slightly extended boundaries as shown in Figure 4.1. The segregated layout of the old part of Lilongwe can be traced to the zoning activities of the sanitary board and later the town council. Indeed many of the problems facing Lilongwe today can be traced to the philosophy of segregation that was instituted during the colonial era. Note that it was not until the early 1960s that the first African representative sat on the Lilongwe.

Figure 4.1: The Change in Lilongwe s Boundaries, 1936-1968

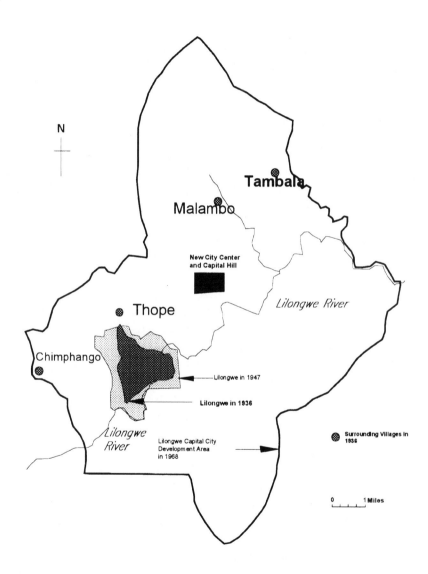

Source: Adapted from Coleman, G. (1973)

THE CHANGE IN LILONGWE S FORTUNES

Lilongwe's fortunes came to a pinnacle with the end of colonial rule and the ascendancy to power of Dr. Banda in 1964. Legend has it that while the late Dr. Banda was languishing in a colonial jail in Rhodesia (now Zimbabwe) he dreamt of building various projects in Malawi, one of them being the transfer of the capital city from Zomba to Lilongwe, a more centrally located position given the elongated shape of the country. The justification for the move of the capital city to Lilongwe was cleverly couched in economic rather than political expedient terms. In a speech given to parliament by Dr. Banda, then Prime Minister of newly independent Malawi, he voiced the need, firstly, to improve the efficiency of Government by concentrating Central Government administration in one city and, secondly, to stimulate development in the Central and Northern Regions by establishing a major focal growth point near the center of the country (Richards 1974; Mlia 1975; Matope 1984; Potts 1985). The argument was that the colonial arrangement of having Central Government administrative functions in two separate cities (i.e., Zomba and Blantyre) was wasteful and lopsided given that both Zomba and Blantyre were located in the Southern Region of Malawi. Further it was argued that the citing of a new capital in a more central location would encourage a broad national unity through widely shared development which could be enjoyed by all sections of the Malawian community. Finally, the creation of a new city in the central part of the country would act as an intervening opportunity and ease the population pressure on Blantyre, then a primate city and still the hub of industry and commerce in Malawi (Matope 1984). As Potts (1985) argues, it is evident that the idea of Lilongwe as a new capital city was pitched as a means of enhancing the regional spread of "development" which "fits with the general theories attached to the use of 'growth poles' as a means of alleviating regional disparities and simultaneously stimulating further development" (Potts 1985). Mlia (1975) and Potts (1985) further note that given the spatial imbalance in development that existed during the colonial era in favor of the Southern Region, the decision to move the capital city to Lilongwe was a logical and sound one.

Indeed even during the colonial era the re-siting of the capital away from Zomba had been a point of argument, but the alternative site had usually been considered to be Blantyre or Limbe, although a Finance Commission Report in 1922 recommended the establishment of a new capital at some unspecified central point north or Zomba (Richards 1974). Thus, the prison dream of Dr. Banda to move the capital to Lilongwe was a resurrection of an idea that had been debated in colonial circles for over 50 years prior to his dream. There is also a political subtext to this dream. It is a fact that Dr. Banda originally comes from Kasungu District northwest of Lilongwe and citing the capital city at Lilongwe may have been politically expedient as Dr. Banda's power base was among the Chewa of Central Malawi (Conell 1972). However, on balance, Lilongwe as a new site for Malawi's capital was more advantageous than both Blantyre and Zomba which suffer from constraints of space and rough topography with serious limitations to development and expansion while Lilongwe's terrain is generally flat or undulating without any major physical constraints to expansion. Additionally, Zomba is said to be on a cyclone path and in 1946 the town was severely affected by a cyclone which caused extensive damage to property due to landslides and flooding (Mlia 1975; Matope 1984:10; Potts 1985).

Once the decision to move the capital city to Lilongwe was made, a British Consulting firm, Brian Colquhoun and Partners, was contracted to conduct a feasibility study in 1965. These consultants submitted their report of recommendation in favor of Lilongwe during the same year and this was discussed with a visiting British Economic Commission. The British Government rejected the idea on the grounds that the project was too expensive and there were more pressing problems and priorities at the time than the move of the capital (Matope 1984, 1989). Dr. Banda turned to apartheid South Africa whose firm of IMEX began to prepare a report. A master plan for the new city was ready by August 1967 (see IMEX 1967; Gerke and Viljoen 1968). The following sections highlight the pattern of urbanization in Malawi, the implementation of the philosophy of spatially balancing development via the decentralization of urban centers, the contemporary spatial morphology and growth of Lilongwe and some of the attendant problems and coping mechanisms of the residents in these times of economic turbulence.

LILONGWE AND THE PATTERN OF URBANIZATION IN MALAWI

Socioeconomic development has historically been accompanied by an increase in urbanization. Malawi is no exception in this regard. Malawi's pace of urbanization has, however, hitherto been slow with urban population only increasing from 200,000 to 879,000 between 1966 and 1987 representing a change in the level of urbanization from 5 % to 11% (see Malawi National Statistical Office 1969, 1980a 1984, 1987a and 1991). The explanation of the low level of urbanization lies in the lower level of economic development. In the past this has meant that migration which would have been otherwise targeted to urban areas within the country has been directed to neighboring countries notably South Africa and Zimbabwe. Some estimates suggest that in the mid-sixties Malawi might have been exporting as much as a quarter of her male labor force (Coleman 1973; Gregory and

Mandala 1987). However, during the past 20 years, government policy and other factors both within and outside the country have significantly reduced the level of labor migration to neighboring countries (Kydd and Christiansen 1982). The curtailment of international labor migration would have resulted in the explosion of the two largest cities of Blantyre and Lilongwe. But such growth as occurred was, to a greater degree, moderated until 1994 when the Banda regime was still in power.

Between 1966 and 1977 Lilongwe, the newly designated national capital experienced the highest growth rate of 7 %. During the same period Blantyre, the country's primate city dominating in both commercial and industrial sectors, grew at 6.5% per annum. Other smaller urban centers generally grew at a slower pace with Mzuzu in the Northern Region growing at 6.0 % and Zomba at 1.9 % (Mlia and Kalipeni 1987; Mlia 1989; see Table 1 for rates).

The picture for the 1977-1987 period is different from that of the previous decade. The census results from the 1987 census indicate that during the 1977-1987 intercensal period, Mzuzu City, one of the smaller urban centers but currently the largest urban center in the Northern Region (with a total population of about 44,000), recorded the highest intercensal population growth rate of 10.6% per annum and a population increase of about 175% during this decade. This rapid growth for a previously small urban center in an area that has been dubbed as a the "Dead North" due to lack of any visible development in this region is due to three factors, namely, intrinsic natural increase because of high urban fertility rates, the redirection of rural-urban migration within the Northern Region to Mzuzu as Northerners within the Southern and Central region began to be increasingly persecuted by the Banda regime, and the designation of Mzuzu as a city which entailed a readjustment of boundaries and annexation of adjacent peri-urban villages. While the contribution of each of these factors is unknown research from elsewhere has indicated that rural to urban migration is the dominant force in urban growth accounting for about 40% to 50% of growth, natural increase 30% to 40% and annexation anywhere from 10 to 20% (Aryeetey-Attoh 1997).

In terms of annual growth rates during the 1977-87 decade, Mzuzu City was followed by the City of Lilongwe (9.0%), Municipality of Zomba (5.9%) and Blantyre City (4.2%). It is apparent from the data in Table 1 that the growth of the largest urban center, Blantyre, declined between the two census periods, 1966-1977 and 1977-1987 while that of the small urban centers rose during the same time periods. For example, Dedza which grew at 3.7% in the 1966-1977 decade registered a growth rate of 11.6% in the 1977-1987 decade and moved from a rank of 12 to the sixth largest urban center in the country. It may be argued that the rapid growth of Dedza is in part due to the influx of Mozambican refugees, and this pattern is also seen among such smaller urban centers as Mulanje, Salima, Liwonde, Mchinji and Monkey Bay, most of which were in close proximity to the major trouble spots that experienced the burden of refugees generated by the Mozambican civil war.

The rapid growth of smaller urban centers has reduced the primacy of Blantyre city. In a well integrated hierarchical system of urban centers the rank-size rule predicts that the population of the nth city is 1/n the size of the largest city's population. The fit between distributions of real cities and the idealized distributions predicted by the rule can more easily be compared if the axes on which the cities' size and rank are plotted are nonlinear or scaled in log form (this was done in another paper, see Kalipeni 1997). The results of this other study indicated that in 1966 Blantyre was a primate city with more than twice as many people as Lilongwe, the second-ranking city. At that time the urban-commercial-industrial complex of Blantyre alone is believed to have accounted for about 66% of the national monetary gross domestic product, 59% of the national total number of manufacturing jobs and 26.3% of all the paid jobs in the country (Mlia 1975; Blantyre Planning Team 1972). Despite the lopsided share of the national economic activities, this primate city only catered to 3.7% of the total population of the country. By 1977 the gap between the largest and the second largest urban centers in the country had been slightly narrowed. In 1987 the population of Lilongwe, the new capital city, was far above that predicted by the rank-size relationship (Kalipeni 1997).

In terms of distribution of urban population at district level the picture appears to have remained constant over the 20-year period, 1966-1987. However, when location quotients of the share of urban population were computed for each of the three census years (1966, 1977, 1987) a different picture emerged (see Kalipeni 1997). Location quotients measure the concentration of urban population. A location quotient of one or more than one indicates a relative concentration of urban population in that district compared with other districts. A location quotient of one signifies that the district has its fair share of urban population; if the quotient is less than one, the district does not have its fair share of urban population. Overall, the location quotients for the year 1966 were generally less than one for most of the districts in the country with the exception of Blantyre district. But interestingly, the location quotient for Blantyre district steadily declined between 1966 and 1987, while those for other districts in the Central and Northern Region dramatically increased. These simple descriptive statistics lend further credibility to the assertion that the share of urban population across the regions and districts of the country has been moving towards uniformity in proportion to the district's population base. This is certainly a testament of the re-distributive effects of Lilongwe as a new but formidable intervening opportunity for the previously only primate city of Blantyre.

SPATIAL STRATEGIES TO REDIRECT RURAL-URBAN MIGRATION

According to Riddell urban malaise, especially urban unemployment, must and can be overcome by the implementation of policies that either increase the number of jobs and/or reduce rural-urbanward migration. However, as additional opportunities for work will tend to "pull" more people into the towns, because of the reduction of unemployment there—given the present socioeconomic differentials—it would appear that migration is the variable most suitable to policy implementation (Riddell 1978). It can be strongly argued that it is easier to manage small to medium sized urban centers that are more or less evenly distributed throughout a country than it is to manage exploding cities. Indeed, as noted by Anyang' Nyong'o (1991), municipalities in Africa, as they grow larger both in population as well as size, become unmanageable as single entities in matters of government.

Riddell believes that the route to reduce the rural-urban invasion is through policies that address the rural-urban differentials head-on. He strongly advocates the diffusion of the development process to the rural countryside through the introduction of non-agricultural jobs, basic modern infrastructure and essential services (Riddell 1978). The following quote summarizes his views on this issue:

> Thus, the political leaders...have in their hands the tools by which some of the colonial legacies can be removed; specifically, they can alter a situation whereby in the past, and continuing today, their rural, agricultural economies are 'exploited' by those who live elsewhere—in the urban centres and in other countries. Should the governments so wish, the national income base could be shifted away from the rural areas, and a greater share of the revenue required to administer and develop the state could be derived from those who are relatively advantaged. (Riddell 1978 257).

The Banda regime took a similar path of development to that suggested by Riddell. The crux of the strategy was a concentration on development of available resources in predominantly rural districts and a creation and maintenance of what government documents dubbed as "efficient and livable urban environments and economies" (see Malawi Department of Economic

Planning and Development 1987). As pointed out earlier, at the time of independence in 1964, the leadership was aware of the regional imbalance in the country's development, which had increased land pressure, specifically in the Southern Region, and of the insufficient service infrastructure at district and subdistrict levels. In 1964, the bulk of public- and private-sector infrastructure was concentrated in the Southern Region, where British settlers had opened tobacco and tea farms to take advantage of the region's temperate climate. The Central and Northern regions were neglected by the British colonial government. The latter was usually referred to as the "dead north," a phrase that emphasized its economic underdevelopment.

Since 1964, there has been considerable effort to address this imbalance but in favor of Dr. Banda's own region with the Northern Region experiencing little development. The capital was moved northward from Zomba to Lilongwe, and a portion of the industrial and commercial activities at Blantyre, especially those focused on tobacco, was shifted to Liwonde and Lilongwe (Conell 1972; Mlia 1975; Kalipeni 1992). There has also been considerable investment in infrastructure in the Central Region and peripherally in the Northern Region, such as a paved road running between Salima and Karonga along the shore of Lake Malawi; the Blantyre-Lilongwe-Mchinji highway; the Lilongwe-Kasungu highway and the extension of the railhead from Salima via Lilongwe to Mchinji on the Malawi-Zambia border. Most of Dr. Banda's tobacco estates were concentrated in Kasungu, Mchinji and Lilongwe Districts. It can therefore be argued that the said infrastructure was developed to largely serve personal rather than national interests. Most of the people who were brought to work on the Kasungu and Mchinji commercial farms did not come on their own will attracted by the "carrot" but rather were those that had been evacuated from the environs of Lilongwe, the capital city designate, in the early 1970s. Those that came from the Southern Region had often been lured by scrupulous recruiters with promises of land to settle on only to find out that they were to serve as serfs on the tobacco estates (Msukwa 1984). Data indicate that paid employment in the agricultural sector rose from 42,600 in 1969 to 148,000 in 1978 (Malawi Department of Town and Country Planning 1987; Malawi National Statistical Office 1980b; Kydd and Christiansen 1982). This paid employment helped to absorb the returning labor migrants from South Africa and Zimbabwe in the late 1970s (Christiansen and Kydd 1982) and actually served as a safety valve to the likely rapid urban growth that would have been triggered by the large-scale return of migrants which in turn would have threatened the survival of the Banda regime.

Although moving from subsistence agriculture into non-agricultural occupations or paid employment is desirable, the issue at stake is whether such jobs pay well enough to fully provide for the basic needs of a family. The case of Mchinji district illustrates the importance of this issue. Mchinji district is one of the districts in the Central Region that has experienced an unprecedented growth of commercial agriculture. Paid employment during the 1977-1987 quadrupled, and yet during the same period, contrary to expectations, the district experienced an increase in its infant mortality rate, one of the major indicators of level of development (Kalipeni 1993). Laborers on commercialized agricultural estates were and continue to be paid the equivalent of US$15.00 a month or less (Msukwa 1984) which comes no where close to meeting the basic needs of the family such as food and clothing. The working conditions on these farms can hardly qualify as the "carrot". However, the increase in rural job opportunities appear to have helped in slowing down the flow of rural inhabitants to towns and cities within the country.

Urban growth was also contained directly through stringent zoning plans in the cities of Blantyre, Lilongwe and Mzuzu. The zoning ordinances were strictly enforced by the Department of Town and Country Planning which was under the direction of the Office of the President and Cabinet. Incentives such as tax breaks and government assistance were offered to lure industry to smaller urban centers in all the three regions. However, with a new post-Banda era of a democratically elected government the enforcement of zoning ordinances has been relaxed. As noted later in this paper, traveling through the cities of Blantyre and Lilongwe one cannot help but notice the proliferation of numerous stalls set up alongside major roads by small vendors in the informal economy. These stalls, made of cardboard materials and scavenged iron sheets would not have been tolerated during the Banda era on the grounds that they were an eye-sore.

THE INTERNAL SPATIAL STRUCTURE OF LILONGWE

The above sections have offered the macro-level picture of the role of Lilongwe in Malawi's urban hierarchy. The rest of this paper will examine the micro-level spatial context of this rapidly expanding city and the problems the city faces in these days of structural adjustment and a new political atmosphere. To begin with, urban spatial configurations have been studied by various disciplines such as sociology, economics, and geography, each one of them employing various methodologies. The result has been the creation of urban growth models such as the *concentric zone, sector* and *multiple nuclei* models that describe the internal spatial and social structure of the city. Most of these models were developed using the European or North American city. In describing the internal structure of Lilongwe the question is to what extent does Lilongwe conform to these models?

tively uniform land uses emerge away from the central business district (CBD) including a zone of transition into lower income residential areas followed by successively higher income neighborhoods at greater distances from the CBD (see Figure 4.2a; Hartshorn and Alexander 1988; Aryeetey-Attoh 1997).

The transitional zone in this model contains abandoned factories and warehouses and high density low income housing, slums, and tenement houses. The central argument of the concentric-zone model is based on the notion that "like plants and animals, people in cities develop a sense of territoriality and sort themselves out in relatively uniform neighborhoods based on ethnicity and socioeconomic status" (Hartshorn and Alexander 1988). The sector model of urban structure argues that the influence of transportation corridors creates axes of uniform development. The wedges of activity that develop may include industrial areas in low lying river valleys, middle class residential communities along major arterials, and upper income neighborhoods on high rolling, or wooded ground (see Figure 4.2b). On the other hand the multiple nuclei model recognizes that cities can develop around many centers and that different functions have varying locational and accessibility requirements. Hence multiple nuclei rather than a single CBD as hypothesized by the sector and concentric-zone models (see Figure 4.2c).

Figure 4.2: Models of Spatial Structure for Urban Areas

1. CBD
2. Wholesale, light manufacturing
3. Low-class residential
4. Middle-class residential
5. High-class residential
6. Heavy manufacturing
7. Outlying business district
8. Residential suburb
9. Industrial suburb
10. Commuter zone

a) Concentric-zone Model

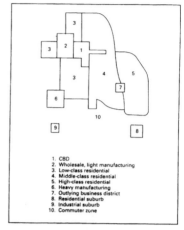

1. CBD
2. Wholesale, light manufacturing
3. Low-class residential
4. Middle-class residential
5. High-class residential
6. Heavy manufacturing
7. Outlying business district
8. Residential suburb
9. Industrial suburb
10. Commuter zone

c) Multiple Nuclei Model

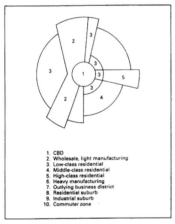

1. CBD
2. Wholesale, light manufacturing
3. Low-class residential
4. Middle-class residential
5. High-class residential
6. Heavy manufacturing
7. Outlying business district
8. Residential suburb
9. Industrial suburb
10. Commuter zone

b) Sector Model

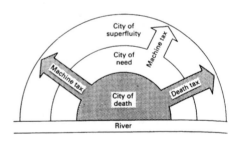

d) Bunge's Death City Model

While the above models give insights into the process of urban growth, each has strengths and weaknesses and explain only a portion of the complex internal structure of the city. Hybrid models have been developed to try to account for the complexity exhibited by city structure. Two such hybrid models seem to be relevant in trying to explain Lilongwe's urban morphology. The first is an adaptation of the concentric-zone model developed by Bunge (1957). Using Detroit as a case study, Bunge developed what he called the exploitative model of urban structure. This model divides the city into three functional areas based on the ownership of resources and ability to pay. As shown in Figure 4.2d, the "city of death" is the poorest inner-city area, which is exploited by the rest of the city through the exaction of a "machine tax," which results from wage payments below the workers' worth (Hartshorn and Alexander 1988). The poor residents in this area also pay a "death tax," which involves the payment of higher prices for food, housing, insurance, and other services in comparison to other parts of the city. This zone is surrounded by the "city of need," which is inhabited by blue-collar working class who are also exploited by business interests and the political machinery. Whereas the outer ring, the "city of superfluity" is the home to the upper classes who live a life of leisure and mass consumption subsidized by the exaction of payments from the other groups (Hartshorn and Alexander 1988; Bunge 1957).

A second hybrid model more pertinent to the internal structure of Lilongwe is the social area analysis model which superimposes social space with physical space. The model incorporates aspects of the concentric ring, sector, and multiple nuclei models which allows for the simultaneous operation of several patterns and processes as depicted in Figure 4.3 (see Shevky and Bell 1955). According to this approach uniform land use zones are demarcated based on three main characteristics, namely, family status, socioeconomic status, and ethnic status (as shown in Figure 4.3. These comprise the social space, which is then superimposed on the physical space. Research on cities in developed countries has demonstrated that family status variables (such as age, size of household, and marital status as well as other life-cycle characteristics exhibit) zonal or ring patterns, with older, smaller, renter households concentrated closer to the city center, and owner-occupied, newer, larger, family households farther from the city center, in suburban settings (Ley 1983; Hartshorn and Alexander 1988; Rubenstein 1989). On the other hand variations along socioeconomic status (such as income, occupation, education, etc.) have been found to follow the sector pattern while ethnicity exhibits a multiple nuclei pattern, as clearly shown in Figure 4.3.

Figure 4.3: Social Area Analysis Model City Structure

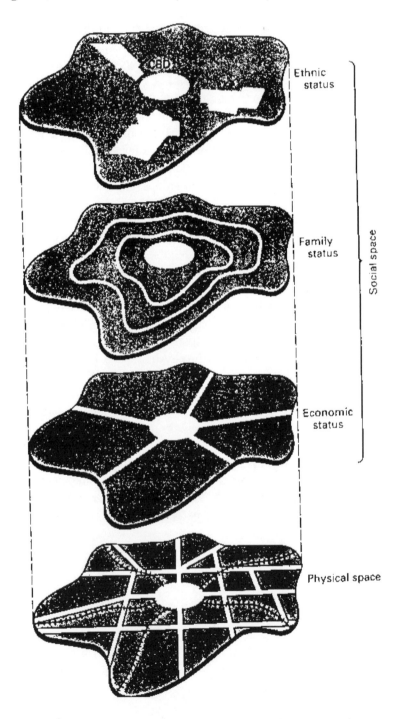

None of the three models by itself completely explains why different types of people live in distinctive parts of the city (Rubenstein 1989). These models have been criticized as being too simplistic and that since they are largely based on the North American city their relevance to modern urban patterns elsewhere in the world is also questionable. However, when these models are combined as in Figure 4.3, they can help in explaining spatial patterns within an urban area. In the case of Lilongwe, all three models seem to be applicable. Although ethnic family statuses have not been researched in Lilongwe, data on the spatial configuration of land use based on economic status is readily available dating back to the colonial era, as discussed earlier in this chapter. During the colonial era there was outright ethnic segregation based on race and socioeconomic status. Below is an examination of the land-use patterns in Lilongwe. The discussion is greatly informed by the theoretical models discussed above and how they were applied to marginalize the lower socioeconomic groups in the planning of Lilongwe both during the colonial and the post-colonial periods.

As of 1968 when the new Master Plan for Lilongwe was formalized, the existing land use pattern in Lilongwe followed closely the colonial imprint in which there were three clearly delineated sections. The western bank of the Lilongwe River was reserved for European development with its own commercial and recreation facilities. The eastern bank had an Indian commercial center to cater to the indigents. Figure 4.4a, shows the existing land use pattern as of 1968 with the river as the divide between the three racial groups. The Asian commercial center (CBD) was also the residential zone for the Asians with their living quarters on the second floor of their shops. The CBD is a linear sliver of land on both sides of the river.

In attempting to apply the three models of urban morphology discussed above to the Lilongwe of 1968 it is clear that the sector model fits the land-use pattern better than the other two models see (Figure 4.4b) with the European sector radiating from the linear CBD on the western bank of the river, which also happened to contain government and local authority offices and the golf course. The part of the CBD containing the Indian/Asian complex acted as a buffer zone, a zone in transition between the European complex and the African complex. On the eastern sector, the pattern is in a reverse fashion to that of the concentric zone model where the civil servants and other professionals had housing closer to the old city center while the poorer indigents lived further away from the city center in squatter like settlements of Kawale, Mchesi, and Biwi with few services provided. Kawale for example is the far removed, high-density residential zone in the northeastern portion of the map in Figure 4.4a separated by a large marshy open space occupied by a tributary of the Lilongwe River.

Figure 4.4: Pattern of Land Use in Lilongwe at the
Time of Independence

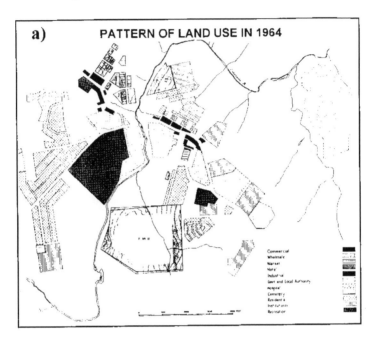

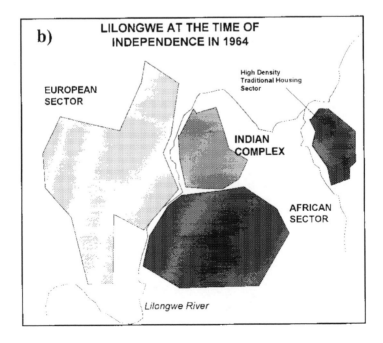

With the modification and acceptance of the new master plan crafted by a group of architects from the South African IMEX firm and the acceptance of South Africa to bankroll the new capital city venture, move of facilities from Zomba to Lilongwe began in earnest in the early 1970s. The urban design concept was simple with Lilongwe envisioned as a garden city with a linear form extending south to north on the main north-south highway that runs along the north-south axis of the country. The basic idea was to create a multi-purpose multi-center city with four main activity focal points, namely, the Old Town center in the southern part of the new city, the new City Center plus Capital Hill as the seat of Central Government offices, a new industrial area of heavy to medium industry located at Alimaunde/Kanengo, and the Lumbadzi Township to the extreme north to service the international airport (Gerke and Viljoen 1968; Richards 1974; Matope 1984; Yasini 1984). A total area of about 26,000 hectares (350 sq. km) of which 2,000 hectares comprised the original municipality of Lilongwe was designated as the New Capital City Planning Area and vested in the Capital City Development Corporation (CCDC). The new area in a linear fashion traversed 35km north-south straddling north-south main road and about 10 km in width from east-west. This is a vast expanse of real estate.

The expansive nature of the city made it easy for the south African team of planners to implement their South African planning experiences patterned along the "apartheid city". As Simon (1992a) argues the overall effect of apartheid city creation has not only been racial segregation but also increased separation between workplace and home for many working class house-holds. This spatial effect is clearly illustrated in the new master plan for Lilongwe. The multi-purpose multi-center vision evokes the tenets of the multiple nuclei model of urban development that has been central to the development of cities in South Africa at the height of the apartheid system. In the case of South Africa, "With both land and capital largely controlled by whites, the immediate burden was borne overwhelmingly by Black la-bor" (Simon 1992b) and in the case of Malawi the capital and other re-sources were largely to be controlled by the capitalist oriented CCDC. In these times of economic turbulence, this form of spatial planning ultimately created new problems and compounded the problems already in existence for the inhabitants of Lilongwe as will be amply demonstrated in the next section. In one extreme context, Lilongwe can be seen in the eyes of Bunge (1957) as having all three functional elements in his radical concentric-zone model in which one finds the zones of death on the periphery of the city exploited for its cheap labor and milked through other taxes such as higher transportation rates; the city of need are the civil servants who leave from paycheck to paycheck in the middle belt, and the superfluity zone of the rich close to the city centers. The expansive nature of Lilongwe made it easy to create this spatial configuration via the use of the multiple nuclei concept and social space segregation based on socioeconomic status. As Potts (1985) notes, Lilongwe's development has adhered strictly to the spatial allocation of land use planned by the Town and Country Planning Department based on the South African conceived master plan.

SPATIALITY AND PROBLEMS OF URBAN GROWTH

It has been argued that, given the relatively slow rate of urbanization Malawi, has avoided some of the worst problems associated with this phenomenon in many Third World countries. Supporters of the post-independence government of Dr. Banda have noted that the streets of Malawian cities were safe and clean in the Banda era (see, e.g., Waterford 1980). Although problems of urban employment, shanty towns, poor sanitary conditions, crime and other forms of social pathology were clearly visible, they seemed to be not as bad as in many other Third World countries (Mlia 1975). However, the situation has not remained static and, as the economic situation has changed and population increased, these problems have become exacerbated as illustrated by the case of Lilongwe. We argue in this paper that Lilongwe's master plan and the shocks from structural adjustment in the economy have exacerbated the problems that seem to be manifesting themselves at the present. Below we briefly highlight a few of the major problems facing the city of Lilongwe as it attempts to move into the twenty-first century.

Population Growth

The master plan was based on an estimated ultimate population of between 185,000 and 257,000 by the year 2000 (Gerke and Viljoen 1968). This estimate seems to have been completely off the target. Revised estimates based on the 1966-1977 and 1977-1987 intercensal growth rates indicate that Lilongwe will have a population of about half a million by the year 2000 (Malawi National Statistical Office 1994) double the population that was projected by the South African team in the master plan. During the intercensal period, 1977-1987, Lilongwe grew at a rate of about 9% in contrast to 10% per annum for Mzuzu, 5% for Zomba, and 4% for Blantyre (see Table 1). Potts (1985) argues that Lilongwe was probably growing at higher rates of between 10% and 12% per annum when one takes into consideration the fact that thousands of "rural" people have been resettled from within Lilongwe's city boundaries to nearby outside locations and some even as far as Mchinji. Needless to say, such a rapidly growing population (not envisaged in the original plans) has had to contend with scarce resources. The unequal nature of the distribution of such resources to the rest of the population is also a major problem. During the Banda era the philosophy was that of efficiency rather than equity (Potts 1985) compounding an already precarious position for many of the urban residents.

The age-sex structure of the total population of Lilongwe city is a less pronounced broad-based age-sex pyramid in comparison to the rest of the country. While at the national level about 45% of the population is below age 15, Lilongwe's proportion is 20%, an indication of lower than country-wide fertility rates (Yasini 1984; Malawi National Statistical Office 1994). Overall 50% of the population is below age 20 which implies the need for more schools and the generation of future jobs to care for this young population. Another significant phenomenon of the age-sex structure is the rapid decrease of population over 49 years of age. In 1967 5% of Lilongwe's population was over 49 years and this had declined to 4% by 1977 and to 3.8% by 1987. This is further evidence of the arguments advanced by Potts (1995) that economic decline in the 1980s, and the impact of IMF structural adjustment programs, combined to devastate the real incomes of a very large proportion of the urban population including many public sector workers that were previously considered to be part of the "labor aristocracy." The tough economic conditions in urban areas have tended to result in what Potts calls "reverse migration" from urban to rural areas particularly for those who have just retired. This partly explains the declining proportion of those aged 49 and over.

The rapid population growth Lilongwe experienced during the move of the capital had some serious consequences. It has become increasingly difficult to provide social services such as housing, schools and health services. Infrastructure such as roads, sewerage, water, power, and telephone lines have also become costly to provide. In most parts of the city potholes have replaced the once beautiful roads that were laid out in the early part of the cities development. Furthermore Lilongwe has relatively the highest cost of living when compared to the other towns of Mzuzu, Zomba and Blantyre probably due to the upsurge of population within such a very short period of time, which, in addition to the difficult economic conditions, has meant escalating inflation. The overall building standards set for most areas of the city are too high and unrealistic relative to incomes, source of funds, and level of economic development.

Housing

In most African countries housing is a major issue in urban areas (Schwerdtfeger 1982; Morrison and Gutkind 1982) and, as Aryeetey-Attoh (1997) notes, housing is a multi-dimension phenomenon since as a physical facility it provides shelter and consumes a fair amount of urban land; as an economic good, it generates equity; as a social good, it enhances one's social status and self-esteem; and as a bundle of services, it offers a range of neighborhood amenities that come with its purchase. During the initial phase of building the capital city, housing did not appear to be a serious problem (Matope 1984) since the Government, CCDC, statutory bodies such as the Malawi Housing Corporation and the private sector constructed and provided many houses of all types. However, by the early 1980s the general global recession and the imposition of structural adjustment programs made it increasingly difficult to build more housing units for the expanding urban population. Statistics reported by the Malawi Housing Corporation provided clear indications of a worsening situation in the area of housing during the early 1980s. The number of applicants on a waiting list to rent permanent houses increased from 7,000 to 32,000 between 1971 and 1982, while the gap between the demand and supply of serviced plots in traditional housing areas on the outskirts of Lilongwe grew from 500 to 11,000 during the same period (Malawi Housing Corporation 1984; Roe 1992).

Given the failure to meet the demand for both permanent housing and serviced plots, most low to medium income urbanites have little choice but to live in squatter colonies where, as in many other countries, conditions are sub-standard. The fall in real incomes or, worse still, the loss of jobs for the poor and middle class engendered by the imposition of structural adjustment programs which require retrenchment has meant more suffering for the poor and the marginally poor. It was estimated that in Lilongwe 17% of the population respectively were living in degraded squatter settlements in 1977 and this figure has since increased to over 47% (Du Mhango 1984). Recent estimates on the housing situation in the four major urban areas indicate that the economic crisis, coupled with an increasing urban population, has resulted in a dwindled supply of housing. Chakufa and Polela (1989) note that supply has by far failed to cope with the demand. Recently, the government has began to sell the housing units it built in the early 1970s to house its civil servants. Corruption and scrupulous speculators in these sales have also been quite common with those that have the means buying more than their fair share and renting such properties to expatriates and companies that can afford. It has been alleged that some greedy senior officials in government bought "ghost houses" and milked money from the government in the name of "home ownership scheme" (Mwale 1997). Even within the site and service scheme program for traditional housing overcrowding and corruption are common. The occupation of a plot by the legal plotholder's household alone is a rarity and 70% of plots are occupied by more than one household (Potts 1985). Furthermore, Potts notes that about half of the plots in Lilongwe are not resided on by the official plotholders who have managed to obtain them illegally and then rent them out, i.e., the problem of absentee landlords.

This process has inevitably contributed to the growth of squatter settlements on the outskirts of the city. The serious housing shortages have also led to overcrowding, poor sanitary conditions, and the escalation of rent, particularly of the houses provided by the private sector (Chakufa and Polela 1989). To accommodate the expanding urban population, it is estimated that Malawi as a whole needs to provide at least 4,500 additional housing units including site and service plots per year.

The Informal Sector as a Buffer to the Effects of Structural Adjustment

Besides, the government's and private sectors' inability to meet effective demand for housing, the growth of squatter settlements may be a result of unemployment, under-employment, and the relatively low salaries the majority of the urban inhabitants receive. Data on unemployment are not particularly reliable but the 1977 census suggests that in that year about 4.6% of the urban dwellers were unemployed. This is by all standards a low unemployment rate. However, some estimates suggest that around 1972 Blantyre might have had an unemployment rate of about 11% and under-employment was relatively high (Blantyre Planning Team 1972), and if this is correct there are no good reasons to believe that the situation now is different. The ability of the government to create jobs for the urban population and rural-urban migrants has declined with the recession that began in the early 1980s and the implementation of the World Bank imposed structural adjustment program during this recession and thereafter. Unemployment and inflation have been on the rise. Today, unemployment is recognized as one of the major problems facing the major urban centers in the country. The urban informal sector, defined as untaxable small scale enterprises such as petty trading, has tried to alleviate urban unemployment and the blow dealt to the majority of the people by structural adjustment. Informal activities are easy to enter, unregulated, predominantly family owned, small scale, labor intensive and rely on indigenous resources (ILO 1972; Aryeeteh-Attoh 1997; Nyakaana 1997).

While very little data is available on the informal sector in Lilongwe, the inability of scarce formal sector jobs to accommodate in-migrants and the general urban populace seems to have resulted in an increase in informal sector jobs. Throughout Africa informal sector jobs are estimated to have grown by 6.7% per annum between 1980 and 1989 and employed more than 60% of the workforce in Sub-Saharan African cities in 1990 (Aryeeteh-Attoh 1997; UNDP 1992). In a 1991 survey of the formal and informal sectors in Lilongwe, Chilowa (1991) found some interesting results. In a randomly taken sample in Lilongwe about 300 households (30% of the sample) indicated that they were involved in at least one small business or income generating activity. Selling goods or services was found to be the single most important survival mechanism and a significant proportion of households in all income categories reported that for at least a portion of the year they were obliged to become involved in some form of small business in order to make ends meet. In the Chilowa (1991) study, the average income earned per month by households with one small business was K70.00 in comparison to K100.00 for those involved in the "formal" sector (in 1991 K2.50 was the equivalent of US$1.00 but as of 1997 K17.00 was the equivalent of US$1.00 due to the spiraling effects of devaluation as mandated by structural adjustment). Although generally lower than earnings gained from the formal sector, the income generated from the small businesses captured within the confines of the Chilowa study was sometimes found to be relatively high, and for many households represented a viable source of income at the peak of the structural adjustment program (Chilowa 1991). This finding offers more evidence to the argument that contrary to the traditional views that suggest a gap between formal and informal sector wages and living standards, the distinction between the two sectors is becoming blurred as real incomes for those in the formal sectors decline (Jamal and Weeks 1988; Potts 1995).

Other coping mechanisms in times of economic turbulence have included borrowing from friends and relatives, and from small businesses or selling products on an irregular basis or engaging in urban agriculture. There also appears to be an increase in more negative aspects of the informal economy, such as smuggling, black marketing, and prostitution (Chilowa 1991; Mwale 1997). The business of smuggling goods to and from the surrounding countries of Mozambique, Zambia, and Tanzania is vibrant. *Katangale* or black marketeering ranges from petty thieving to a complex networking system which involves selling stolen goods (Chilowa 1991). Crime and violence by the unemployed youths in urban areas seems to be on the increase too. For some women it has become necessary to work as "bar girls" in order to buy food and other essentials. In the process these women, some as young as 14, turn to one form of prostitution or another in order to make ends meet (Kishindo n.d.). The rise in prostitution is more serious today in light of the high possibility of contracting and/or transmitting the AIDS/HIV virus. Data from Malawian urban centers indicate that Malawian cities are among the hardest hit by the AIDS epidemic. This is largely due to poverty compounded by the effects of structural adjustment which drives people to despair. Armed robbery, murders and rape are on the increase and the new government of

President Muluzi is finding it increasingly difficult to stem the tide of crime in the large and burgeoning cities of Blantyre, Zomba, Lilongwe and Mzuzu; Corruption at the highest level of government is also a source of great concern (Mhone 1995).

However, in spite of the darker side of the informal sector in today's Lilongwe, the contribution of informal and small-scale enterprises should not be underestimated. Informal activities have provided a major coping mechanism in a world of economic turbulence for the majority of the residents in Lilongwe. The side of the informal sector that consists of talented and creative individuals who make worthwhile contributions to the urban economy—artisans, basket weavers, tinsmiths, tailors, and vendors—seems to far outweigh the image of the informal sector as people who engage in social vices and criminal activity (Aryeeteh-Attoh 1997). More importantly it needs to be emphasized that the rapid growth of the informal sector, for good or for bad, has been a direct result of the structural adjustment programs.

Problems of Urban Morphology

One of the major serious flows in the planning of Lilongwe is that the new city is too dispersed and land use activities too scattered making it relatively costly to travel from one part of the city to the other in as far as time, money and effort are concerned and the maintenance of utility infrastructure and roads. While a great number of administrative functions have moved to Lilongwe successfully, very little of the designated area of 26,000 hectares has actually been built-up with many areas and empty spaces that need to be filled. Indeed the building of an expansive city may have been a deliberate move on the part of the South African planners to create a truly segregated city on the basis of income through strict application of the zoning ordinances. As noted earlier the city is linear measuring about 35 km by 10 km on average. The concept of creating four focal points, namely, the Old Town, City Center and Capital Hill, Alimaunde/Kanengo Industrial Area, and Lumbadzi Sattelite Town to serve the International Airport has resulted in considerable dispersal of development, with presently, extensive empty spaces in-beween (Matope 1984; Potts 1985). To prevent squatting in these empty spaces, fast growing gmelina trees were indiscriminately planted throughout the designated area on the justification that these plantations would provide fuelwood and poles for building.

As Matope (1984) notes, the idea was that each of the four centers would provide employment activities to the surrounding residents, but after 20 years of city implementation this has not occurred. The only viable employment centers remain the Old Town and the newly built City Center and Capital

Hill, all in the southern part of the city. The location of residential areas in the city of Lilongwe is such that the upper class live closer to the city center, the place of work. The poor have been deliberately pushed to the outskirts of the city around the two northerly focal points of Alimaunde/Kanengo and Lumbadzi. Yet the lower income classes do not possess the means to commute daily to the New City Center and the Old Town where most jobs in both the formal and the informal sectors are located. For example, residents of one site and service scheme (patterned along the South Africa township), simply christened "Area 25," have to cover a distance of 10 to 15 miles daily to travel to work in the Old Town (see Figure 4.5a&b). A substantial chunk of their meager monthly income (estimated at US$15.00) has to be spent on transportation. The few who can afford a bicycle commute to work by bike; the unfortunate majority have no alternative but to walk on foot, waking up at 3 a.m. every day to make the long trek to the new city center or the Old Town. Area 25 is not the only such place, but there are several other townships, or more appropriately, government sanctioned squatter colonies, strewn on the outskirts of the city; completely out of sight to prevent them from being an irritating eye-sole (see Potts 1985). With inflation and spiraling bus fares, the residents of these townships live in misery and destitution. In jarring contrast, the residents of "Area 10, 11 and 12" do not need to drive their automobiles to work since the offices are within a couple of hundreds yards away from their modern residences. It is this disparity that leads one to conclude that Lilongwe is a true replica of the spatial configuration of an apartheid city. In the South African context, the structure of the apartheid city, with its racially exclusive and unequal residential segments, educational, health and recreational facilities, was designed to minimize interracial contact, this being restricted essentially to the work-place (Simon 1992a). This urban structure, in which white control was paramount, and where the conditions of other races mirrored their socio-political positions —and relative class status within that—was explicitly implemented in the planning of the city of Lilongwe.

Figure 4.5: Lilongwe Urban Structure Plan

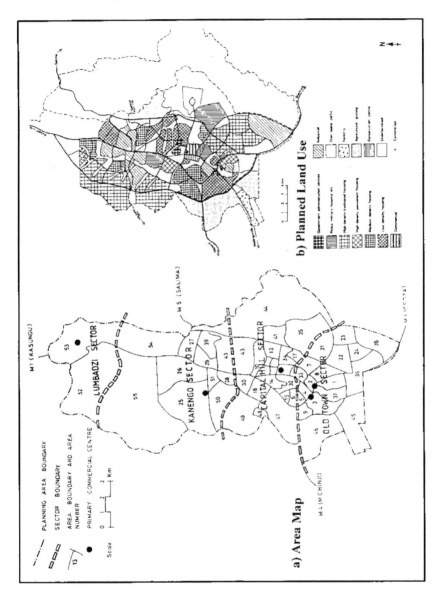

In short, transportation to and from work is a serious problem in the City of Lilongwe. The former public transport company, the United Transport (Malawi) Limited (UTM) (which has since been privatized under a new name: Stage Coach) failed to provide adequate public transport facilities to the expanding urban population. The economic crisis of the 1980s meant a severe shortage of foreign exchange allocated to the transport sector. The sector was unable to import new buses to meet demand and spare parts to repair the aging fleet. The limited capacity of UTM left open a great market for private public transport which currently meets a substantial proportion of the urban transport needs. It is estimated that private buses and mini-buses carry over 50% of the total passenger traffic every year (Malawi National Statistical Office 1987b). This sector too has been hit by the shortage of foreign exchange to import new buses or mini-buses and spare parts. It is not uncommon for both the private and public buses to overload. Buses that should normally carry up to 60 passengers, often carry over 100 passengers. Minibuses with a capacity of only 15 passengers normally carry double this capacity which brings into question safety concerns. Data indicate that the number of minibuses involved in accidents increased from a total of 224 in 1978 to 436 in 1987 (Malawi National Statistical Office 1987b). Some of the minibuses are not even road-worthy, but they continue to operate as the only available means to commute to work-place daily. The situation has changed slightly with new diplomatic and political alliances to the countries of the Gulf States given Muluzi, the new president of Malawi, is a Moslem. Used minibuses and salon cars are being supplied to the Malawian economy from the countries in the Gulf such as Dhubai and closer to home from South Africa.

CONCLUSION

From the above discussion two central spatial justifications for the development of Lilongwe as a new capital city emerge. First Lilongwe was developed to act as a countervailing national center to the dominance of Blantyre in the Malawian urban hierarchy. Lilongwe was seen as a means of spreading development northwards. Second, Lilongwe was "planned" to develop into a sustainable modern city that effectively caters to the needs of its residents. An assessment of these dual functions after almost 20 years of its inception indicates mixed results. While at the national level Lilongwe has grown remarkably into a formidable intervening opportunity to Blantyre's primate position, the spatial morphology of the city itself has created problems for most of the inhabitants, particularly the very poor.

At the national level, Lilongwe possesses most of the administrative functions and a small set of economic and social institutions. Examples of these include headquarters of government ministries, the police, the army, banks, the international airport, tobacco auction floors, Kamuzu College of Nursing (a constituent college of the University of Malawi), and the national grain silos. However, the parliament and the president's residence are still in Zomba and Blantyre respectively which calls into question Dr. Banda's criticism of the colonial arrangement in which functions of government were partly in Zomba and Blantyre. Locally Lilongwe seems to have failed to provide the growing population with adequate infrastructure. This is a direct result of the way the city was spatially planned with four nodes separated by large distances and empty spaces as buffer zones. The allocation of the poor to the most northerly sectors of the city that still remain undeveloped has exacerbated their precarious position. The propulsive effect of the international airport in Lilongwe has also fizzled out and the residents of Lumbadzi and northerly Areas such as Area 25, 55, and 53, have no recourse but to commute daily to the old town to engage in informal sector activities, a less than satisfactory survival alternative. Others are retiring back to the countryside as the economic situation becomes unbearable. While this study is an indictment of the spatially unsound planning of the city of Lilongwe, it also calls for a rethinking of Lilongwe's future. Policy makers need to revise the master plan in favor of a more realistic plan that could rationalize the currently planned land use pattern into a more compact city. A less ambitious and more spatially compact plan would make it easier for the provision of infrastructure and the growth of industries in close proximity to the place of residence for the majority.

REFERENCES

Anyang' Nyong'o, P. "Governing African Cities." In *Association of African Political Scientists (AAPS) Research Agenda, 1991-1993, No. 2*, ed. P. Anyang' Nyong'o. Nairobi: AAPS, 1991.

Aryeetey-Attoh, S. "Urban Geography of Sub-Saharan Africa." In *Geography of Sub-Saharan Africa*, ed. S. Aryeetey-Attoh. Upper Saddle, N.J.: Prentice Hall, 1997, pp.182-222.

Bale, J. and D. Drakakis-Smith. *Latin America*. London: Routledge, 1990.

Bandawe, C. R. "Aspects of Urban Society in Lilongwe: 1939-1950." *History Seminar 1988/89, Paper No. 8*. Department of History, Chancellor College, University of Malawi, Zomba, Malawi, 1989.

Becker, C., A. Hamer, and A. Morrison. *Beyond Urban Bias in Africa*. Portsmouth, NH: Heinemann, 1994.

Blantyre Planning Team. *Plan for Blantyre: Interim Report Number 1*. Blantyre: Department of Town and Country Planning, 1972.

Brockerhoff, M. and H. Eu. "Demographic and Socioeconomic Determinants of Rural to Urban Migration in Sub-Saharan Africa." *International Migration Review* 28, 3 (1993):557-577.

Bunge, W. "Detroit Humanly Viewed: The American Urban Present." In *Human Geography in a Shrinking World*, eds. R. Abler et al. North Scituate, Mass.: Duxbury Press, 1957.

Chakufa, C. A. and M. S. Polela. "Population Growth and Provision of Housing in Malawi." Paper presented at the National Seminar on Population and Development in Malawi, Chancellor College, Zomba, Malawi, June 5-9, 1993.

Chilowa, W. *Food Insecurity and Coping Strategies among the Low Income Urban Households in Malawi.* Bergen, Norway: Department of Social Science and Development, Chr. Michelsen Institute, 1991.

Cole-King, P. A. *Lilongwe: A Historical Study.* Zomba: Government Press, 1971.

Coleman, G. "International Labour Migration from Malawi." *Malawi Journal of Social Science* 2 (1973):31-46.

Conell, J. "Lilongwe: Another New Capital for Africa." *East African Geographical Review* 10 (1972):90-98.

Danaher, K. "Myths of African Hunger." Oakland, California: Institute for Food and Development Policy, an Occasional Paper, 1984.

Du Mhango, G. L. "Traditional Housing Areas (Site and Service Schemes) in Malawi." Paper presented at the Annual Conference of the Association of Local Government Authorities in Malawi, Salima, Malawi, 1984.

Gerke, W. J. C. and C. J. Viljoen. *Master Plan for Lilongwe: The Capital City of Malawi.* Johannesburg: Purnell, 1968.

Gregory, J. W. and E. Mandala. "Dimensions of Conflict: Emigrant Labor from Colonial Malawi and Zambia, 1900-1945." In *African Population and Capitalism: Historical Perspectives,* eds. Dennis D. Cordell and Joel W. Gregory. Boulder, Colo: Westview Press, 1987, pp. 221-240.

Hartshorn, T. A. and J. W. Alexander. *Economic Geography.* Englewood Cliffs, NJ.: Prentice Hall, 1988.

IMEX. *Capital City Project — Malawi.* Johannesburg: IMEX, 1967.

Jamal, V. and J. Weeks. "The Vanishing Rural-Urban Gap in Sub-Saharan Africa." *International Labor Review* 127, 3 (1988): 271-292.

Kalipeni, E. "Population Redistribution in Malawi Since 1964." *Geographical Review* 82, 1 (1992):13-28.

Kalipeni, E. "Determinants of Infant Mortality in Malawi: A Spatial Perspective." *Social Science and Medicine* 37, 2 (1993):183-198.

Kalipeni, E. "Contained Urban Growth in Post-Independence Malawi." *East African Geographical Review* 19, 2 (1997):49-66.

Kaunda, M. E. M. "The National Rural Centres Programme." Paper presented at the National Seminar on Population and Development in Malawi, Chancellor College, Zomba, Malawi, 5-9th June, 1989.

Kishindo, P. *Condom Use: Rapid Assessment Study, Draft Report.* Zomba: Chancellor College, University of Malawi, n.d.

Kydd, J. G. and R. E. Christiansen. "Structural Change in Malawi Since Independence: Consequences of a Development Strategy Based on Large-Scale Agriculture." *World Development* 10 (1982):355-375.

Lee-Smith, D. "Urban Management in Nairobi: A Case of the Matatu Mode of Public Transport." In *African Cities in Crisis: Managing Rapid Urban Growth,* eds. R. E. Stren and R.R. White, Boulder. Co.: Westview Press, 1989, pp. 276-304.

Ley, D. *A Social Geography of the City.* New York: Harper and Row, 1983.

Lipton, M. *Why Poor People Stay Poor: Urban Bias in world Development.* Cambridge: Harvard University Press, 1977.

Mabogunje, A. L. *Cities and African Development.* Ibadan: Oxford University Press, 1976.

Macgregor, J."The Crisis in African Agriculture." *Africa Insight* 20, 1(1990):3-16.

Malawi Department of Economic Planning and Development. *Statement of Development Policies 1987-1996.* Lilongwe: Office of the President and Cabinet, 1987.

Malawi Department of Research and Environmental Affairs. *Malawi National Environmental Action Plan Vols. 1 & 2.* Lilongwe: Malawi Department of Research and Environmental Affairs, 1994.

Malawi Government. *Lilongwe Outline Zoning Scheme.* Lilongwe: Office of the President and Cabinet, Town and Country Planning Department, Malawi Government, 1986.

Malawi National Statistical Office. *Malawi Population Census 1966: Final Report.* Zomba: Government Printer, 1969.

Malawi National Statistical Office. *Malawi Population Census 1977: Final Report.* Zomba: Government Printer, 1980a.

Malawi National Statistical Office. *Malawi Statistical Yearbook 1979.* Zomba: Government Printer, 1980b.

Malawi National Statistical Office. *Malawi Population Census 1977: Analytical Report, Vol. I and II.* Zomba: Government Printer, 1984.

Malawi National Statistical Office. *Malawi Population and Housing Census 1987: Preliminary Report.* Zomba: Government Printer, 1987a.

Malawi National Statistical Office. *Malawi Statistical Yearbook.* Zomba: Government Printer, 1987b.

Malawi National Statistical Office. *Malawi Population and Housing Census 1987: Summary of Results.* Zomba: Government Printer, 1991.

Malawi National Statistical Office. Malawi Population and Housing Census 1987: Analytical Report, Vol. II. Zomba: Malawi National Statistical Office, 1994.

Malawi Town and Country Planning Department. *National Physical Development Plan.* Lilongwe: Office of the President and Cabinet, 1987.

Mathews, A.; Myers, L. and Jubitz, N. *Lilongwe and the Central Region of Malawi: An Official Guide.* Blantyre: Central Africana Limited, 1991.

Matope, J. J. "Lilongwe: New Capital City of Malawi." Paper presented at the Workshop on New Capital Cities in the Developing Countries: A Critical Examination of Experiences, Abuja, Nigeria, 4-9 March, 1984.

Matope, J. J. "Spatial Aspects of Population and Development: Spatial Development Policy and Strategy." Paper presented at the National Seminar on Population and Development in Malawi, Chancellor College, Zomba, Malawi, 5-9th June, 1989.

Mbuyi, K. "Kinshasa: Problems of Land Management, Infrastructure, and Food Supply." In *African Cities in Crisis: Managing Rapid Urban Growth*, eds. R.E. Stren and R. R. White, 149-176. Boulder, Co.: Westview Press, 1989.

McNulty, M. "The Contemporary Map of Africa." In *Africa,* eds. P. M. Martin and P. O'meara. Bloomington: Indiana University Press, 1986, pp. 9-42.

Mijere, N.J. and Chilivumbo, A. "Rural-Urban Migration and Urbanization in Zambia During the Colonial and Post-Colonial Periods." In *Population Growth and Environmental Degradation in Southern Africa,* ed. E. Kalipeni. Boulder, Colorado: Lynne Rienner Publishers, 1992, pp. 147-178.

Mjojo, B. K. M. "Urban Development: The Case of Lilongwe: 1920-1964." *History Seminar 1988/89, Paper No. 12.* Department of History, Chancellor College, University of Malawi, Zomba, Malawi, 1989.

Mlia, J. R. N. "Malawi's New Capital City: A Regional Planning Perspective." *Pan African Journal VIII,* no. 4 (1975):388-401.

Mlia, J. R. N. "Spatial Dimension of Development in Malawi." Paper presented at the National Seminar on Population and Development in Malawi, Chancellor College, Zomba, Malawi, 5-9 June, 1989.

Mlia, J. R. N. and E. Kalipeni."Population Growth and National Development in Malawi." *Malaysian Journal of Tropical Geography* 15 (1987):39-48.

M'manga, W. R. "Population Estimates for the Four Major Urban Areas of Malawi, 1977-1986." Paper presented at the Seminar of the Analysis of the 1977 Malawi Population Census and Its Utilization in Development Planning held at Kwacha International Conference Center, 29th October-2nd November, 1984, Published 1986.

Morrison, M. K. C. and P. C. W. Gutkind. *Housing the Urban Poor in Africa.* Syracuse, N.Y.: Maxwell School of Citizenship and Public Affairs, Syracuse University, 1982.

Msukwa L. A. H. "Agriculture and Nutrition in Malawi." Paper presented at the Conference on Malawi: An Alternative Pattern of Development, Edinburgh University, 24-25 May, 1984.

Mwale, Costa. "Life and Living in Malawi Today." *NYASANET,* 11 January 1997.

Ngom, T. "Appropriate Standards of Infrastructure in Dakar." In *African Cities in Crisis: Managing Rapid Urban Growth*, eds. R.E. Stren and R.R. White. Boulder, Colo.: Westview Press, 1989, pp. 177-202.

Noble, K. B. "Zaire Ends 26 Years of Dictatorship." *The New York Times* (9/30/91):1.

Nyakaana, J. B. "The Informal Sector Employment and Its Contribution to Rural Development: The Case of Eldoret Municipality in Kenya." *The East African Geographical Review* 19, 2(1997):93-112.

Onibokuni, A.G. "Urban Growth and Urban Management in Nigeria." In *African Cities in Crisis: Managing Rapid Urban Growth*, eds. R.E. Stren and R.R. White. Boulder, Colo.: Westview Press, 1989, pp. 69-112.

Potts, Deborah. "Capital Relocation in Africa: The Case of Lilongwe in Malawi." *Geographical Journal* 151 (1985):182-196.

Potts, D. "Shall we Go Home? Increasing Urban Poverty in African Cities and Migration Processes." *The Geographical Journal* 161, 3(1995):245-252.

Richards, G. *From Vision to Reality: The Story of Malawi's New Capital.* Johannesburg, South Africa: Lorton Publications, 1974.

Riddell, J. Barry. "The Migration to the Cities of West Africa: Some Policy Considerations." *Journal of Modern African Studies* 16, 2 (1978):241-260.

Roe, Gillian. *Beyond the City Limits: Anatomy of an Unplanned Housing Settlement in Lilongwe, Malawi.* Zomba, Malawi: Center for Social Research, University of Malawi, 1992.

Ross, M. H. *The Political Integration of Urban Squatters.* Evanston: Northwestern University Press, 1973.

Rubenstein, J. M. *The Cultural Landscape: An Introduction to Human Geography.* New York: Macmillan Publishing Co, 1989.

Schwerdtfeger, F. W. *Traditional Housing in African Cities: A Comparative Study of Houses in Zaria, Ibadan, and Marrakech.* New York: John Wiley and Sons, 1982.

Shevky, E. and W. Bell. *Social Area Analysis: Theory, Illustrative Application, and Computational Procedures.* Stanford, CA.: Stanford University Press, 1955.

Simon, D. "Reform in South Africa and Modernization of the Apartheid City." In *Urban and Regional Change in Southern Africa,* ed. David Drakakis-Smith London: Routledge, 1992a, pp. 33-65.

Simon, D. *Cities, Capital and Development: African Cities in the World Economy.* London: Belhaven Press, 1992b.

Somerville, K. "One man Banda." *New Africa* (July 1992):11-13.

Stren, R.E. and R. R. White. *African Cities in Crisis: Managing Rapid Urban Growth.* Boulder, Colo.: Westview Press, 1989.

UNDP. *Human Development Index.* New York: Oxford University Press, 1992.

Waterford, S. "Kamuzu's Maverick Rule." *Africa Report* (September-October 1980):10-14.

Yasini, Patrick A. *Urban Project Implementation and Lilongwe—New Capital City Project Implementation.* M.A. Thesis, Department of Urban and Regional Planning, University of Nairobi, Nairobi, Kenya, 1984.

Table 1: Population and Growth Rates of Selected Urban Centers
in Malawi, (1966,1977and 1987)

Urban Area	Rank			Population			Growth Rate (%)	
(City/Town)	1987	1977	1966	1987	1977	1966	1966-1977	1966-1987
Blantyre	1	1	1	331,588	219,011	109,461	6.51	4.23
Lolongwe	2	2	2	233,978	98,718	45,380	7.32	9.01
Mzuzu	3	4	5	44,238	16,108	8,490	5.99	10.63
Zomba	4	3	3	42,878	24,234	19,666	1.92	5.87
Karonga	5	5	4	19,630	12,051	11,241	0.63	5.00
Dedza	6	11	12	16,735	5,578	3,762	3.65	11.61
Mangochi	7	7	8	15,329	7,764	4,770	4.53	7.04
Nkhotakota	8	6	6	12,149	10,316	6,425	4.40	1.65
Kasungu	9	8	9	10,848	6,488	4,266	3.89	5,27
Salima	10	14	11	10,606	4,712	3,900	1.73	8.45
Nsanje	11	9	7	10,042	6,400	6,019	0.56	4.61
Balaka	12	10	14	9,081	5,632	2,582	7035	4.89
Liwonde	13	18	-	8,685	3,738	-	-	8.80
Mzimba	14	12	10	7,735	5,396	4,156	2.40	3.67
Rumphi	15	16	16	7,147	4,003	2,429	4.65	5.97
Mulanje	16	25	21	7,112	3,001	2,221	2.77	9.01
Monkeybay	17	21	19	6,868	3,207	2,390	2.71	7.91
Nkatabay	18	15	18	6,492	4,048	2415	4.81	4.84
Luchenza	19	19	17	6145	3381	2416	3.10	6.16
Ntcheu	20	22	22	5808	3115	2105	3.63	6.24
Ngabu	21	13	-	5678	4848	-	-	1.59
Mponela	22	20	20	5609	3359	2304	3.49	5.26
Chitipa	23	23	24	5233	3110	1429	7.33	5.34
Mwanza	24	26	27	4710	2354	1000	8.09	7.18
Mchinji	25	28	26	4542	1957	1295	3.82	8.78
Chikwawa	26	24	13	4344	3036	2837	0.62	3.65
Thyolo	27	17	15	4251	3856	2480	4.09	0.98
Ntchisi	28	29	25	3060	1654	1368	1.74	6.35
Dowa	29	27	23	2704	1962	1857	0.50	3.26
Chiradzulu	30	31	28	1459	689	609	1.13	7.77
Machinga	31	30	29	913	697	402	5.13	2.74

*Ranked in descending order using 1987 population size   - Data not available
Source: Compiled by author from Malawi National Statistical Office (MNSO) (1969; 1980a; 1987a)
        and the Malawi Town and Country Planning Department (1987)
Note: Intercensal growth rates computed by author using expontial growth rates formula.

II
LANDSCAPES AS RITUAL AND THERAPEUTIC SPACES

5

THE CONSTRUCTION OF
THERAPEUTIC SPACES

WILBERT GESLER

INTRODUCTION

MEDICAL GEOGRAPHY, INFLUENCED BY SOCIAL THEORY, HAS Been shifting its focus over the last several years. One particular emphasis within this shift is toward a renewed concern with place (Kearns and Gesler, forthcoming). This paper extends that concern to Africa by employing a theoretical framework previously used in the investigation of "therapeutic landscapes" (Gesler 1992; Gesler 1993). Research for this paper consisted of reading and re-reading material on disease and health in Africa, written by scholars from different disciplines, in light of that framework. In the spirit of the Illinois conference, I am trying to tie together ideas about illness and healing through the concept of place.

The paper begins with a brief look at two traditional ways used by medical geographers to investigate disease and health: cultural ecology and health care delivery. Then, more recent work in a "reformed" medical geography - approaches based on context and meaning—are explored in some detail. These discussions will be supported with evidence from the literature on health in Africa. Then, one example—Kung healing rituals—will be explored in some depth, as it illustrates the main themes of the paper.

TRADITIONAL APPROACHES

Cultural ecology

This approach is based on human interactions with the environment. It is probably safe to say that all societies attribute healing power to the physical environment, whether it be from medical plants (Ayensu 1981), isolation and quiet, or scenic beauty. Many believe that relatively untainted rural environments are more conducive to health than cities which are spoiled by human habitation (Marx 1968). Certain natural elements have traditionally been associated with healing because of their material and symbolic properties. Primary among these is water, which accounts for the importance of sacred springs, the spa industry, and many healing rituals. Other environmental elements with perceived healing power include earth, trees, and stones.

Europeans since the early nineteenth century were interested in studying the environments of particular locations (in terms of soils, temperatures, rainfall, and so on) in order to determine which places were healthy or unhealthy (Curtin 1992). Continuing in this tradition, medical geographers and others trained in cultural ecology have had an important impact on the study of disease and health in Africa. Detailed and carefully researched studies include those on river blindness in Ghana (Hunter 1972), geophagy throughout the continent (Hunter 1973), schistosomiasis in Ethiopia (Kloos 1985), disease hazards in Ethiopia (Roundy 1978), sleeping sickness in different parts of Africa (Knight 1971), the interaction of migration and malaria (Prothero 1965), the diffusion of cholera (Stock 1976), and the impact of development on disease (Hughes and Hunter 1970). This research took place into account in the sense that particular sites were mapped out as the locations where disease agents, vectors, and human hosts with their accompanying characteristics and behaviors came together to create or mitigate disease. These studies were criticized, however, for being reductionist and for assuming the superiority and universal applicability of the biomedical model. What they lacked, for the most part, was a consideration of political, economic, social, and historical context and the meaning and experience of illness in places (Stock 1986; Kearns 1993).

Health Care Delivery

The bulk of the work by European, North American, and African medical geographers in health care delivery followed the spatial analytic approach. Most of this work dealt with biomedical personnel and facilities, although some attention was paid to indigenous healing systems. Some representative examples follow. In the area of the spatial distribution of health care resources, Jackman (1972) mapped out areas served by the flying doctor service in Zambia, Iyun (1983) looked at hospital service areas in Ibadan,

Lasker (1981) found that health care resources in Ivory Coast were placed in more productive areas, and Gershenberg and Haskell (1972) reported that six types of biomedical facilities had been located without careful planning in Uganda.

Turning to accessibility, we note studies by Thomas and Mascarenhas (1973) on distance to biomedical facilities in Tanzania, the advantage of being on or near feeder roads in Ghana (Ashitey et al. 1972), and Stock's (1981) demonstration that traditional health care resources in Northern Nigeria were more accessible than biomedical ones. During the 1980s, some medical geographers were beginning to think in terms of the political economic constraints on health care delivery. However, with some exceptions (e.g., Stock 1980; Okafor 1982), these kinds of studies lacked an emphasis on context and meaning. It is to these two considerations that we now turn.

CONTEXT

As social theory penetrated the social sciences of health from the 1970s onward, there was a concern for the wider context in which disease or illness occurs and how it is treated (Eyles and Woods 1983; Jones and Moon 1987). Of primary interest were the ways in which certain groups within society attempted to dominate others politically, economically, socially, and culturally, based on divisions such as race, ethnicity, class, or gender and how this hegemony affected health and disease. Within African medical geography, the seminal paper was Stock's (1986) review which strongly criticized previous work on health and development for largely ignoring political and economic themes. In Africa, control has mainly been exercised in both colonial and post-colonial times by the industrial nations operating within a global capitalist system. Although the effects on health of this control varied over time and space, some factors were common: simplification of the food crop regime, a weakening of support mechanisms based on kinship, and inequalities in payment of social costs to different groups of workers (Feierman and Janzen 1992); alienation of large tracts of fertile agricultural and grazing land, forced labor and labor migration, low wages paid to workers, and the creation of an African consumer class (Onoge 1975).

The work by Turshen, Wisner, and others, shows how contextual factors led to health problems in African places. For a rural district in Tanzania, Songea, Turshen (1977) demonstrated how, among other things, German and British colonial policies decimated cattle populations and opened up tsetse habitats, forced labor migrations to plantations and mines by requiring taxes to be paid in cash, restricted land use rights to peasants, and increased the birth rate in response to changes in the social relations of production. Land was left fallow for half the usual number of years, the women left behind on farms overcropped small plots, and soils became exhausted. This led to malnutrition and a higher toll of nutrition-related diseases. Turshen asserts (1977:9): "There are diseases of affluence and diseases of poverty, but there are few 'tropical' diseases; that is, there are few diseases in which a tropical climate is the leading or determining characteristic or ecological factor, whereas the incidence, course, and outcome of most common diseases are affected by poverty." Poverty, in turn, is brought about by ". . . increasing cultural, technological, and economic dependency on the international capitalist system . . ." (9).

Wisner (1980/81) has shown how colonial policies and the transition from a subsistence to a capitalist economy had serious consequences for the nutritional status of people living in Eastern Kenya. Land alienation forced agriculturalists onto marginal land and many were forced into wage labor. Farmers were marginalized politically, economically, and ecologically. Responses to drought conditions based on kinship reciprocity were drastically curtailed. Also in Kenya, Good (1987) looked at the impact on health of the introduction of a wage economy and European encroachment on African land. He shows how colonial governments and Christian missions disrupted indigenous medical systems and how capitalism produced a biomedical health care system which favored a small elite.

A major geographic manifestation of hegemonic control is segregation of populations, most often seen in urban places. Colonial authorities used ideas about disease and medicine to justify segregation. The idea was that Europeans and Africans should be separated in order to protect the former from diseases endemic among the latter (Curtin 1992). For example, in Leopoldville, the original European quarter was separated from the African quarter by a *cordon sanitaire* comprised of a zoo, botanical garden, and golf course. Malaria, and what little was known about its ecology around the turn of the twentieth century, was used as a thinly disguised excuse for racial segregation. Thus, in Freetown, disregarding Ross' advice to clean up breeding sites for mosquitoes, the government of Sierra Leone built "Hill Station" 750 feet above sea level and four miles from the central town in order to protect a colonial elite (Frenkel and Western 1988). Medical justifications for segregation varied from place to place over time (Feierman and Janzen 1992). In Dakar, for instance, racial segregation was established to prevent the spread of plague, but it continued after the plague had ended, at least for poor Africans; those Africans who could afford to were allowed to build houses alongside the French. In short, "The racial ideas of the conquerors shaped their understanding of medical problems. Their medical ideas shaped the landscape, and with it the pattern of urban disease" (Feierman and Janzen 1992:15).

Struggles for control have been investigated in health care delivery studies as well. One example is the history of the development of biomedical health care services in Nigeria (Ityavyar 1987). Here the British government and Christian medical missions established medical care that was focused on urban places and favored Europeans first and the Africans who worked for them next, to the exclusion of the majority of the population. This colonial hegemony was contested by both Nigerian physicians and native healers. Following independence, there was talk of expanding coverage and some progress was made in eliminating inequalities, but Nigerian doctors became a new controlling elite and regional, rural/urban, and class differences remained. For Zaire, Janzen (1978) has chronicled the attempts by different groups of healers—native Kongo *banganga* doctors, healing prophets, and those trained in biomedicine—to legitimize themselves and marginalize others.

MEANING
The humanistic perspective, which has, along with context, also played an important role in the investigation of health and disease, has brought to the fore what Good (1994) refers to as the meaning-centered model. People in all societies ask questions such as "What is this illness I am experiencing?" "What caused it?" "Why did this misfortune happen to me?" and "What can I do about it?" The answers, which might appear irrational to others, nevertheless have meaning for those who give them. Lay theories about illness causation, for example, take several overlapping forms, related to individual responsibility (e.g., diet, exercises), the physical environment (e.g., climate, pollutants), the social world (e.g., work stress, witchcraft), and the supernatural world (e.g., gods, spirits) (Helman 1994a). What is extremely important is that interpretations of illness raise questions about the meaning of much wider issues such as life and death, what causes misfortune in general, what is evil, what is dangerous, and what is polluting (Feierman and Janzen 1992). When one looks at illness in this way, the alleviation of physiological symptoms may become less important than the alleviation of suffering as a human condition which comes from understanding an illness (Davis-Roberts 1992).

Meaning is derived from the experience of illness in at least two ways, which are clearly interrelated: ritual and language. Ritual, which Helman (1994b:224) defines as "a form of repetitive behavior that does not have a direct overt technical effect" celebrates, maintains, and renews one's world and deals with its dangers. It acts to maintain relationships between people, between people and nature, and between people and the supernatural, employing ritual objects such as talismans, items of clothing, and words and songs. Turner (1969) finds that ritual symbols cluster around two poles—a social and moral pole and a physiological pole—and acts to join them together. Thus, for example, a woman's achievement of womanhood (social pole) is associated with menarche (physiological pole).

Particularly important to us here are *rituals of misfortune* which are performed at times of crisis, including the onset of ill health. These rituals are intended to heal both the individual and society. They function in three ways: (1) psychologically, to lessen anxiety and to produce catharsis; (2) socially, to expose and then heal conflicts and to recreate values; and (3) protectively, to guard people against physical and mental dangers (Beattie 1967; Helman 1994b). There is, of course a rich literature on the use of ritual in dealing with illness in Africa. Turner (1964), to take one example, has described how a diviner among the Ndembu of Zambia practices curative rituals.

Ritual often has transformative power. That is, it aids in changes in physiological or social status. Van Gennep (1960) has described three stages in rites of passage: separation, transition, and incorporation. Helman (1994b) applies this concept to healing rituals which are intended to transform the ill person into a healthy one. For example, the hospital in the biomedical system is intended to provide a setting for such a change. Davis-Roberts (1992) shows how illness narratives perform a transformative function among the Tabwa of Zaire. Ngubane (1977) explains how the Zulu of South Africa use the colors of medicines as an aid in the ill-to-healthy transformation. Black medicines (representing death, night-time, darkness, dirt, pollution, defecation, and danger) are given first; red medicines (representing a transition from black to white, growth, and association with blood) follow; finally white medicines (the good things of life, good health and good fortune, daylight, eating and social interactions) complete the order.

To discover the meaning attached to illness, it is important to pay attention to the language people use. Disease classifications reveal beliefs about etiology and causation: the Kamba of South-central Kenya use a taxonomy based on four systems: ultimate cause, mode of treatment, disease characteristics, and attributes of the afflicted (Good 1987). Naming a disease gives the namer power to say what creates suffering and thus shapes cultural ideas about misfortune (Feierman and Janzen 1992). Language is often part of ritual. Like ritual, it joins the experience of illness and experiences of other aspects of life. The Tabwa of Zaire use words drawn from nature to describe pathology; an example is to talk about hunger and gestation in terms of the actions of two *nsakes* or insects that occupy the human body (Davis-Roberts 1992).

Particular types of language can be used to explore meaning. Metaphors, such as those used in describing cancer or AIDS reveal not only cultural attitudes toward those diseases, but also what people fear about other aspects of life such as the breakdown of society or the fear of invasions (Helman 1994a). Metaphors "work" because they are multi-vocal; that is, they have reference to different arenas of experience. Good (1994) has worked with the concept of semantic networks or words used from different realms of experience which can be linked to produce a core set of symbolic associations. Semantic networks are "a way of conceiving how diverse and apparently conflicting claims about the nature of a specific illness complaint could be synthesized and culturally objectified, formulated as an "object" of personal and social awareness," (Good:171). Again, like ritual, these networks connect cultural events and physiological processes. The concept is used by Greenwood (1992) to show how a network based on the humoral paradigm connects natural science, cosmology, agriculture, nutrition, and medicine in Moroccan therapeutics. For example, foods are linked to environmental temperature, inner feelings, and illness by metaphor and metonymy through the ways in which they are classified.

In recent years, a great deal of attention has been paid to illness narratives which tell us how life's problems are created, controlled, and made meaningful; about cultural values; and about social relations (Kleinman 1988). In other words, when people are allowed to relate their experience of illness, they may reveal far more than the "facts" of the illness itself. They place the illness in the context of their life history and the values of the society in which they live (Brody 1987). "In Tabwaland, as elsewhere," Davis-Roberts (1992:376) says, "the medical system exists and is experienced not as the discursive, analytic prose of the specialist or the observer, but rather as the narrative or saga of specific illness occurrences, episodes that cut to varying depths across the normal flow of life". He relates the story of the illness of a three-year old Tabwa girl and shows how a diviner used the narrative to bring together the illness itself, both as physiological symptoms and important life event, the personal histories of the child's parents and grandparents, and "a category of etiological agent that contains implicit within itself a prognosis and a nonbodily therapy" (380).

PLACE

The description of places has traditionally been an important focus for geographic study. The quantitative revolution, which began in the 1950s, dominated geography in the 1960s, and is still a powerful force today, submerged place in its search for spatial regularities. Geographers tended to shut out the other social sciences. However, as Massey (1984) says, this could not last. Beginning in the 1970s, it was recognized that "There are no such things as spatial processes without social content" (Massey 1984:3). Geographers discovered that there was a reciprocal relationship between the social and the spatial: the spatial was socially constructed and the social was spatially constructed.

As geography reached out to other disciplines, the qualities of place were rediscovered (Gesler 1991). Much was made of the idea of sense of place, how specific places provide identity, security, and aesthetic meaning for people. Places acquire personality, a spirit; they are loved or hated. People create places, but places also create people (Kearns 1991). These ideas are easily applied to health situations. As part of his healing practice, the Ndembu diviner gathers the relatives of the patient before a sacred shrine and publicly exposes previously hidden social tensions; the GPs consultation room creates a certain atmosphere through its display of such symbols as the diploma, a cabinet full of instruments, and a set of family photographs (Helman 1994b).

The work of Victor Turner often has a spatial or place orientation. Space, along with ritual objects and gestures, he asserts, stands for something other than itself. Symbols used in rituals have interpretive, operational, and *positional* meaning (emphasis added) (Turner 1968:21). "Through the wide range of reference possessed by a single symbol, almost all the things that matter can be concentrated into a small area of space and time, there to be re-endowed with value" (p. 21). *Where* rites are performed is important. For example, a ritual to cure a woman of infertility takes place at the hole or burrow of certain animals. Furthermore, the performance of this ritual, which includes digging pits representing life and death and tunnels joining them, follows a carefully planned spatial structure, each part of which carries symbolic meaning.

Feierman and Janzen (1992:2) recognize the importance of place in African healing when they state that "What patients see, in Africa as in many other parts of the world, is a diverse, heterogeneous set of options for treatment--options that vary from place to place." This leads them to advocate a search for local coherences, to try and make sense out of the layers of medical conceptions and practices which become sedimented at particular locations. Thus one must consider the uniqueness of places. However, places share features common with other places and must also be seen in relation to other places. That is, we need to take both a centered and a decentered view of places; we need to examine the tension between particularizing and universalizing discourses (Entrekin 1991).

A study which very clearly brings out the importance of place is Janzen's recent work on what Turner termed the "rituals or cults of affliction." These cults are defined (Janzen 1992:1, quoting Turner 1968:15-16) as "the interpretation of misfortune in terms of domination by a specific non-human agent and the attempt to come to terms with the misfortune by having the afflicted individual, under the guidance of a 'doctor' of that mode, join the cult association venerating that specific agent." Some cults or communities are called "drums of affliction" because drumming and rhythmic song and dance are an important part of the ritual. Janzen (1992) looks both at a regional view of the cult and its changing economic, political, and social context over time. Of particular interest here is the fact that he examined eight aspects of the therapeutic dimension of cults of affliction in four urban settings: Kinshasa, Dar Es Salaam, the Mbabane-Manzini corridor, and Capetown, using a theoretical framework based on health, healing, and efficacy. Also of interest is Janzen's focus on the micro-geography of a healing space in each of his study sites.

Thus far, our discussion of place has tended to emphasize meaning as opposed to context. Place, however, can also be thought of as part of the setting for medical interactions (Helman 1994a) and it can be argued that places tie context and meaning together. The unifying power of place can be expressed in several ways. Structuration theory, advocated by Giddens (1976), Pred (1983) and others, develops the idea of an interplay between structure and agency within places. In Livingstone's words (1992:357), ". . . it is the interplay of subject and structure that gives both character and texture to places because they are at once the medium and outcome of social reciprocity." We could also think in terms of the interaction between public power and private choice (Feierman and Janzen 1992), society and the individual, hegemony and self-expression, cultural norms and individual biographies. Perhaps most useful is to think of places as negotiated realities (Ley 1981). In terms of illness and health, patients and healers come together in places, influenced by context and seeking meaning, to be diagnosed and treated through negotiation. Cultural values, social relationships, individual experience, rituals, and language all play a part in the negotiation.

HEALING AMONG THE KALAHARI KUNG

The Kung, who dwell in the Kalahari Desert area of southwestern Africa, practice a type of healing that, in Katz's words (1982:34), "seeks to establish health and growth on physical, psychological, social, and spiritual levels; it involves work on the individual, the group, and the surrounding environment and cosmos." On an average of four nights a month, a healing dance is begun around a camp fire. The dance activates *num* or spiritual energy and some of the dancers experience *kia*, an enhancement (not an alteration) of consciousness. Those in *kia* heal all those at the dance.

The context of Kung healing can be presented briefly. The Kung are a hunting-gathering people who live in a semi-arid environment. They survive in harsh climatic conditions through sharing collected food resources among allied bands. Although each subsistence space is bounded, territories are loosely defined and are not defended. Conflict is usually resolved either by groups breaking up or at a healing dance. The Kung are very egalitarian people with little disparity in wealth to divide them; there is a prohibition against "standing out" from others. This social, political, and economic organization is breaking down, however, under outside pressures. The Kung are being enveloped by an economy which is dominated by their black pastoralist neighbors, who in turn are succumbing to the penetration of a capitalist economy. The Kung enter this economy at the low end; some have become sedentary serfs and squatters at the margins of pastoral settlements. The old way of sharing is weakening, and the meaning of the healing dance is becoming altered. Kung healers are becoming more professionalized and are beginning to seek payment for their cures.

Among the Kung, sickness is thought to be an existential condition rather than a specific illness or symptom. Healing sickness both affirms the worth of an individual and creates meaning. The healing process expresses several meanings: it alleviates physical illness, enhances the healer's understanding, resolves conflicts, establishes proper relationships with the cosmos, and restores a balance between the individual, the culture, and the environment. Experiencing *kia* is similar to spiritual growth in other cultures; this growth is closely related to practical aspects of daily life. That is, ". . . healing is the application of spiritual knowledge to everyday life . . ." (Katz 1982:296).

The Kung dance obviously contains ritual elements: repetitive singing and dancing, "pulling out the sickness", and so on. The dancing is done to make the *num* boil and create a healing energy. Through language, boiling *num* is symbolically associated with other aspects of life, namely boiling water, meat cooked in boiling water, and ripened plant foods. All these items become powerful when boiled, cooked, or ripened. Language also plays a role during the dance when healers carry on extended dialogues with the gods and spirits.

Katz views healing as a process of transition toward meaning, balance, wholeness, and connectedness. Thus the healing dance can be seen as a transformative process. During the process, the healer locates and diagnoses sickness by "seeing properly"; then comes the act of "pulling out the sickness"; finally the healer "bargains" and "battles" (negotiates) with the gods and spirits over the sickness. To experience full *kia* is to die and be reborn. Healers take a journey which they fear "through a territory of consciousness which can never become known" (Katz 1982:118). The community as a whole also goes on a transformative journey, resolving conflicts and tensions and growing spiritually along the way.

What is the role of place in Kung healing? The healing dance is performed around a camp fire. A community of people, living for a time in camps around a water hole gather within what can be thought of as sacred space. As they sing and dance, they create a setting in which *num* can boil and *kia* can be experienced. The fire itself "creates a special space in which *num* can boil." (Katz 1982:121). At the dance, people are in the same space for many hours, often in close physical contact. Each Kung group seems to favor its own fire; one healer says it is easier to *kia* when he is dancing at his own camp. The camp thus become a community healer. In sum, "In kia, they are acknowledging, in yet one more time and one more place, the nature of their universe as a whole and their place in it" (210).

CONCLUSIONS

This paper has traced the history of changing approaches medical geographers have taken to the study of disease and health in Africa. Early work used the predominantly positivist approaches of cultural ecology and health care delivery. These studies made a substantial contribution, but they lagged behind new theoretical movements within the social sciences such as structuralism, humanism, and postmodernism. With some notable exceptions, Africanist medical geographers were slow to respond to new theoretical orientations. Meanwhile, pressures for a more theoretically informed medical geography of Africa arose from two sources: work by non geographers and work by medical geographers dealing with other areas such as Britain, Canada, the U.S., New Zealand, and some Latin American countries. What I have tried to show here is that a focus on the very geographic notion of place can blend these two pressures in a useful way. Geographers have thought a great deal about place as context and meaning; non geographers, represented by several studies cited here, seem to be quite well aware of the importance of place as well. My call is for a more conscious grounding of African studies of disease and health in notions of place by all social scientists.

I realized as I researched this paper that the examples found were heavily biased toward traditional healing practices performed to alleviate chronic illnesses. Perhaps this indicates that the literature review itself was at fault. If not, then there seems to be a need to widen the scope of health-in-place studies to encompass acute illnesses and the biomedical system. This does not mean going back to the almost exclusive focus on biomedical health care which predominated, in medical geography at least, several years ago. Rather, it is a recognition that people experience both acute and chronic conditions and that they are pragmatic and will seek care from a variety of sources. Context and meaning can be imputed to the experience of illness and the practice of healing of all kinds, and pluralism occurs in places. We need to ask about the experience of the hospital as place as well as the diviner's hut. Which features of each place are, or are not, conducive to health?

It is well to remember that it may be difficult to distinguish what is "modern" and what is "traditional" in African health care. For example, many Bariba women in Benin choose to have their babies in a hospital because if a baby is born in a breech position or in some other anomalous way in a village setting, the child would be declared a witch and killed. Still holding witchcraft beliefs, the women nonetheless rebel against them to preserve their own offspring (Sargent 1982). An example from Tanzania further shows how "traditional" women read the "modern." Roth (1996) found that in small towns nurses view a "pre-natal card" issued by the government as "symbolic capital" and turn away women having complicated deliveries and in desperate need of biomedical services if they can not produce the cards.

Studies of health in Africa should also cover far more than physical health. As Africans, along with many non Africans have long recognized, health and healing also have mental, spiritual, and moral components which are often difficult to separate out. In addition, as indigenous African healers know well, health and healing can not be separated from other aspects of daily life such as religion, commerce, and politics. That is why African healers so often successfully heal.

REFERENCES

Ashitey, G. A., et al. "Danfa Rural Health Centre: Its Patients and Services. 1970-1971." *Ghana Medical Journal* 11 (1992):266-273.

Ayensu, E. S. "A worldwide Role for the Healing Powers of Plants." *The Smithsonian* 12 (1981):86-97.

Beattie, John. "Divination in Bunyoro, Uganda." In *Magic, Witchcraft, and Curing*, ed. John Middleton. Garden City, NY: The Natural History Press, 1967:211-231.

Brody, H. *Stories of Sickness.* New Haven: Yale University Press, 1987.

Curtin, Philip D. "Medical Knowledge and Urban Planning in Colonial Tropical Africa." In *The Social Basis of Health and Healing in Africa*, eds. Steven Feierman and John M. Janzen, Berkeley: University of California Press, 1992:235-255.

Davis-Roberts, Christopher. "Kutambuwa Ugonjuwa: Concepts of Illness and Transformation among the Tabwa of Zaire." In *The Social basis of Health and Healing in Africa*, eds. Steven Feierman and John M. Janzen. Berkeley: University of California Press, 1992:376-392.

Entrekin, J. Nicholas. *The Betweenness of Place: Towards a Geography of Modernity*. London: Macmillan, 1991.

Eyles, John and K. J. Woods. *The Social Geography of Medicine and Health*. London: Croom Helm, 1983.

Feierman, Steven and Janzen, John M. "Preface and Introduction." In *The Social Basis of Health and Healing in Africa*, eds. Steven Feierman and John M. Janzen, xv-xvii & 1-23. Berkeley: University of California Press, 1992.

Frenkel, S. and J. Western. "Pretext or Prophylaxis? Racial Segregation and Malarial Mosquitoes in a British Tropical Colony: Sierra Leone." *Annals of the Association of American Geographers* 78, 2 (1988):211-228.

Gershenberg, I. and M. A. Haskell. "The Distribution of Medical Services in Uganda." *Social Science and Medicine* 6 (1972):353-372.

Gesler, Wilbert M. *The Cultural Geography of Health Care*. Pittsburgh: University of Pittsburgh Press, 1991.

Gesler, W. M. "Therapeutic Landscapes: Medical Geographic Research in Light of the New Cultural Geography." *Social Science and Medicine* 34, 7 (1992): 735-746.

Gesler, W. M. "Therapeutic Landscapes: Theory and a Case study of Epidauros, Greece." *Environment and Planning D: Society and Space* 11 (1993): 171-189.

Giddens, Anthony. *New Rules of Sociological Method*. New York: Basic Books, 1976.

Good, Byron J. *Medicine, Rationality, and Experience*. Cambridge: Cambridge University Press, 1994.

Good, Charles M. *Ethnomedical Systems in Africa*. New York: Guilford Press, 1987.

Greenwoood, Bernard. "Cold or Spirits? Ambiguity and Syncretism in Moroccan Therapeutics." In *The Social Basis of Health and Healing in Africa*, eds. Steven Feierman and John M. Janzen. Berkeley: University of California Press, 1992:285-314.

Helman, Cecil G. "Doctor-Patient Interactions." In *Culture, Health and Illness*. Third Edition. Oxford: Butterworth Heinemann, 1994a:101-145.

Helman, Cecil G. 1994b. "Ritual and the Management of Misfortune." In *Culture, Health and Illness*. Third Edition. Oxford: Butterworth Heinemann, 1994b:224-245.

Hughes, Charles C. and Hunter, John M. "Disease and 'Development' in Africa." *Social Science and Medicine* 3 (1970):443-493.

Hunter, John M. "River Blindness in Nangodi, Northern Ghana." In *Medical Geography*, ed. N. D. McGlashan. London: Methuen & Co, Ltd, 1972.

Hunter, John M. "Geophagy in Africa and the United States: A Culture-Nutrition Hypothesis." *Geographical Review* 63 (1973):170-195.

Ityatvar, D.A. "Background to the Development of Health Services in Nigeria." *Social Science and Medicine* 24 (1987):487-499.

Iyun, Folisade. "Hospital Service Areas in Ibadan City." *Social Science and Medicine* 17 (1983):601-616.

Jackman, M. E. "Flying Doctor Services in Zambia." In *Medical Geography: Techniques and Field Studies*, ed. N. D. McGlashan. London: Methuen & Co, Ltd, 1972:97-103.

Janzen, John M. "The Comparative Study of Medical Systems as Changing Social Systems." *Social Science and Medicine* 12 (1978):121-129.

Janzen, John M. *Ngoma: Discourses of Healing in Central and Southern Africa.* Berkeley: University of California Press, 1992.

Jones, Kelvin and Moon, Graham. *Health, Disease and Society: An Introduction to Medical Geography.* London: Routledge and Kegan Paul, 1987.

Katz, Richard. *Boiling Energy: Community Health among the Kalahari Kung.* Cambridge, MA: Harvard University Press, 1982.

Kearns, Robin A. "The Place of Health in the Health of Place: The Case of the Hokianga Special Medical Area." *Social Science and Medicine* 33 (1991):519-530.

Kearns, Robin A. "Place and Health: Toward a Reformed Medical Geography." *The Professional Geographer* 45, 2 (1993):139-147.

Kearns, Robin A. and Wilbert M. Gesler. *Putting Health into Place.* Syracuse: University of Syracuse Press, forthcoming.

Kleinman, Arthur. *The Illness Narratives: Suffering, Healing & The Human Condition.* New York: Basic Books, 1988.

Kloos, Helmut. "Water Resources Development and Schistosomiasis Ecology in the Awash Valley, Ethiopia." *Social Science and Medicine* 20 (1985):609-625.

Knight, Gregory C. "The Ecology of African Sleeping Sickness." *Annals of the Association of American Geographers* 61 (1971):23-44.

Lasker, Judith M. 1981. "Choosing Among Therapies: Illness Behavior in the Ivory Coast." *Social Science and Medicine* 15A:157-168.

Ley, David. "Behavioral Geography and the Philosophies of Meaning." In *Behavioral Problems in Geography Revisited*, eds. K. R. Cox and R. C. Golledge. New York: Methuen, 1981:209-230.

Livingstone, David N. *The Geographical Tradition.* Oxford: Blackwell, 1992.

Marx, L. "Pastoral Ideals and City Troubles." *The Fitness of Man's Environment.* Washington, D.C.: Smithsonian Institution Press, 1968:119-144.

Massey, Doreen. "Introduction: Geography Matters." *Geography Matters!* Cambridge: Cambridge University Press, 1984.

Ngubane, Harriet. "Colour Symbolism in Medicine." In *Body and Mind in Zulu Medicine: An Ethnography of Health and Disease in Nyuswa-Zulu Thought and Practice.* London: Academic Press, 1977:113-139.

Okafor, S. I. "The Case of Medical Facilities in Nigeria." *Social Science and Medicine* 16 (1982):1971-1977.

Onoge, Omafume F. "Capitalism and Public Health: A Neglected Theme in the Medical Anthropology of Africa." In *Topias and Utopias in Health*, eds.

Stanley R. Ingman and Anthony E. Thomas, 219-231. The Hague: Mouton Publishers, 1975.

Pred, Allan. "Structuration and Place: On the Becoming of Sense of Place and Structure of Feeling." *Journal for the Theory of Social Behavior* 13 (1983):45-68.

Prothero, R. M. *Migrants and Malaria.* London: Longmans, 1965.

Roth, Denise. *Bodily Risks, Spiritual Risks: Contrasting Discourses of Pregnancy in a Rural Tanzanian Community.* Ph.D. Dissertation, Department of Anthropology, University of Illinois at Urbana-Champaign, 1986.

Roundy, Robert W. "A Model for Combining Human Behavior and Disease Ecology to Assess Disease Hazards in a Country: Rural Ethiopia as a Model." *Social Science and Medicine* 12 (1978):121-130.

Sargent, Carolyn. *The Cultural Context of Therapeutic Choice: Obstetrical Care Decisions Among the Bariba of Benin.* Dordrecht: Reidel, 1982.

Stock, Robert. *Cholera in Africa.* London: International African Institute, 1976.

Stock, Robert F. *Health Care Behavior in a Rural Nigerian Setting, with Particular Reference to the Utilization of Western-type Health Care Facilities.* Unpublished Ph.D. Dissertation, Department of Geography, University of Liverpool, 1980.

Stock, Robert F. "Traditional Healers in Rural Hausaland." *Geojournal* 5 (1981):363-368.

Stock, Robert F. "'Disease and Development' or 'the Underdevelopment of Health': A Critical Review of Geographical Perspectives on African Health Problems." *Social Science and Medicine* 23 (1986):689-700.

Thomas, I. D. and A. C. Mascarenhas. *Health Facilities and Population in Tanzania. Part One, Hospitals in Tanzania and Population Within Given Distance of Their Sites.* BRALUP Research Paper, University of Dar es Salaam, 21 (1973):1-55.

Turner, Victor W. "An Ndembu Doctor in Practice." In *Magic, Faith and Healing,* ed. A. Kiev. New York: Free Press, 1964:260-263.

Turner, Victor W. "Introduction." In *The Drums of Affliction: A Study of Religious Processes Among the Ndembu of Zambia.* Oxford: Clarendon Press, 1968:1-24.

Turner, Victor W. "Planes of Classification in a Ritual of Life and Death." In *The Ritual Process.* Harmondsworth: Penguin, 1969:1-43.

Turshen, Meredith. "The Impact of Colonialism on Health and Health Services in Tanzania." *International Journal of Health Services* 7, 1 (1977):7-35.

Van Gennep, A. *The Rites of Passage.* London: Routledge and Kegan Paul, 1960.

Wisner, Ben. "Nutritional Consequences of the Articulation of Capitalist and Non-capitalist Modes of Production in Eastern Kenya." *Rural Africana* 8-9 (1980-81): 99-132.

6

Ethnomedicine, Sacred Spaces, and Ecosystem Preservation and Conservation in Africa

Charles Anyinam

INTRODUCTION

LINKS BETWEEN RELIGION AND CURRENT ENVIRONMENTAL crisis have received much attention in recent years. The debate going on in recent discourse concerns the various challenges to traditional Enlightenment values. Whether the challenges are dubbed "postmodernism," "deconstruction," or "multiculturalism," they have generated much interest in the literature (Rockfeller and Elder 1992; Bowman 1990; Carmody 1983; Hargrove 1986; Knudtson and Suzuki 1992). In 1990, for example, over one thousand scientific, religious, and political leaders gathered in Moscow to discuss the problem of environmental deterioration around the world. A footnote to the conference issued before the discussion began was a statement by a distinguished list of American scientists who asserted that efforts to safeguard and cherish the environment need to be infused with a vision of the sacred, because problems of such magnitude, and solutions demanding so broad a perspective, must be recognised from the onset as having a religious as well as a scientific dimension. (*New York Times* 1/20/1990:21)

The surprising feature of this message is the explicit acknowledgement of several scientists of the need to couple scientific knowledge with religious conviction in the current search for solutions to the increasing environmental crisis facing humankind. For years, science has been disdainful of religion especially when it appears to restrict the development and distribution of modern scientific principles and technology. This statement by a group of scientists shows that scientists have learnt, perhaps the hard way, that religion may in fact incorporate sophisticated environmental practices or keep the interplay between humans and nature in balance (Stevens 1994).

Anthropologists have long appreciated the interaction of religion and management of the environment, especially in agricultural systems. Some of these studies have shown how agricultural scientists plunged headlong into projects without regard for existing indigenous practices which, may at their base, be scientific, although the knowledge is dispersed through religion (Stevens 1994). Some have demonstrated the folly of ignoring local religious practices and shown the benefits that can be derived if scientists will swallow their prejudices and carefully examine the scientific reasons behind rituals concerned with nature.

Much of the discussion concerning ecology and religion has, however, tended to focus on links between ecology and Christianity and other major religions. Very few analyses have explicitly focused on the relationships between indigenous religious beliefs and practices and the current ecological problems facing developing countries. More so, very limited research has been undertaken to investigate relationships between the natural environment and the practice of ethnomedicine which is intricately intertwined with the practice of indigenous religion in Third World countries. The fact that indigenous medical practices are intimately related to biotic and abiotic environments, makes it imperative that a discussion of the links between religion and environmental degradation, as well as ecological conservation and preservation should include that of ethnomedicine. In the existing literature, explicit discussion of ecological dimensions of ethnomedical practices is almost non-existent even though, to a large extent, the practice of ethnomedicine is an important vehicle for understanding indigenous societies and their relationships with nature (Anyinam 1995). To ignore indigenous religious traditions in ecological discussions is ultimately self-defeating.

The links between ethnomedicine and ecology is exemplified by a long tradition of healing powers associated with the earth's natural systems, whether this entails medicinal plants and animal species, the ambient salubrious air, spring water, or the natural scenery. The pharmacopoeia of folk societies and professional medical systems like Chinese, Ayurvedic, Unani, and biomedicine contain thousands of medicines made from leaves, herbs, roots, bark, animal, mineral substances, and other materials found in nature. As well, practitioners of ethnomedicine employ methods based on the ecological, socio-cultural, and religious background of the people to provide health care.

The study of links between indigenous religious practices and of current ecological crisis requires, on the one hand, investigations into how environmental characteristics influence the practice of ethnomedicine, and, on the other hand, how traditional medicine affects the quality and sustainability of natural systems (Anyinam 1995). Both ecology and culture evolve and change and each produces alterations in the other. Recent decades have seen significant changes occurring within several aspects of ethnomedicine as a result of environmental degradation and tremendous changes in modern social and economic systems. As well, over the years, the practice of ethnomedicine has had both positive and negative impacts on local natural ecosystems. An exploratory discussion of these two-way relationships in developing countries was recently highlighted by Anyinam (Anyinam 1995).

The discussion here is limited in scope as it explores one aspect of these relationships in the context of African ethnomedicine. The paper focuses on the role that ethnomedical practices, particularly the creation of sacred spaces, play in the conservation and preservation of African ecosystems. The discussion is very exploratory and relies on materials scattered in the exisitng literature on African ethnomedicine because of the lack of any systematic research and hence lack of data on the issue. It is argued that loss of respect for nature in the contemporary world is a contributory factor for the estrangement of modern societies from nature and their consequent abuse of it.

The chapter begins with a review of the concepts of 'ethnomedicine' and 'sacred space'. This is followed by a discussion of the links that exist between ethnomedical practices and local ecosystems. How African belief and value systems, as well as the utilization of sacred spaces contribute to the conservation and preservation of the ecology of certain geographic areas will be illustrated. The paper concludes by emphasizing the urgent need to take into consideration both the scientific and religious dimensions of the issue of environmental degradation, conservation, and preservation.

DEFINING ETHNOMEDICINE AND SACRED SPACE

It is pertinent to define the terms "ethnomedicine" and "sacred space" as they are employed in the discussion. There is not much concensus in the definition of ethnomedicine. One view expressed by Charles Hughes defines ethnomedicine as those beliefs and practices relating to disease which are the products of indigenous cultural development and are not explicitly derived from the conceptual framework of modern medicine (Hughes 1968). For Fabrega, ethno-medicine is the study of medical institutions and of the way human groups handle disease and illness in the light of their cultural perspective (Fabrega 1979). Charles Good provides a wider meaning of an ethnomedical system. His definition integrates "in variable configurations, all of a people's strategies, beliefs, conscious behaviours and relations with the habitat that pertain to disease, its management, and health status (Good 1980). Thus, according to Good, an ethnomedical system "is the entire approach of a community to its health problems, organised spatially and changing over time" (Good 1980). In this sense, an ethnomedical system, he continues, incorporates all health care strategies acceptable by the community, including biomedicine.

In this paper, following Foster and Anderson, ethnomedicine is employed here to denote the totality of health knowledge, values, beliefs, skills, and practices of indigenous people, including all the clinical and non-clinical activities that relate to their health needs (Foster and Anderson 1978). The term is used here in a more restricted sense than Good's definition. Ethnomedical practitioners are, therefore, the indigenous healers recognized by their communities as qualified or competent to provide health care services, employing plant medicine, animal parts, and mineral substances as well as methods based on the ecological, cultural, social, and religious background of the people (Good 1980). They employ the prevailing knowledge, attitudes, and beliefs of their communities regarding physical, mental, and social well-being and the causes of disease and disability (ibid).

One of the prominent geographical dimensions of ethnomedical practices is the notion of "sacred space". The concept of sacred is one of the topics discussed in Malinowski's well-known essay, *Magic, Science and Religion* (Malinowski 1948). The classical view of the nature of the sacred is, however, associated with the name of Emile Durkheim and his influence has continued to dominate much of the anthropological writing on the sacred. Jackson and Henrie offer a useful definition of sacred space. They define it as

> that portion of the earth's surface which is recognized by individuals or groups as worthy of devotion, loyalty, or esteem. Space is sharply discriminated from the non-sacred or profane world around it. Sacred space does not exist naturally, but is assigned sanctity as man defines, limits and characterises it through his culture, experience, and goals. (Jackson and Henrie 1983)

As Yi Fu Tuan has elaborated, the true meaning of "sacred" goes beyond sterotype images of temples and shrines, because 'at the level of experience, sacred phenomena are those that stand out from the commonplace' (Yi Fu Tuan 1978). He puts emphasis on qualities such as separateness, otherworldlines, orderliness, and wholeness in defining what is sacred. Isaac also emphasizes the significance of awe and wonder in the experience of the holy and points out that 'on almost all levels of culture there are segregated, dedicated, fenced, hallowed spaces. The holy or hallowed, means separated and dedicated' (Isaac 1964). The concept of "sacred space" embodies all these features.

There is abundant evidence from many cultures that the notion of sacred space is deep-rooted and long-lived. Ancient cultures had their own definition of sacred space that controlled where people went, what they did, and how they did it (Park 1994). Many religions designated certain places as holy or "sacred". This designation puts responsibilities on religious authorities to protect them. Various studies have discussed reasons for defining some places as sacred and what implications such designation have for the use and character of such places. Eliade's work in 1959 has been very influential. In his book, *The Sacred and the Profane*, Eliade explored how ordinary (profane) space is converted into a holy or sacred one. He suggests that such a conversion reflects the spiritual characteristics associated with both the physical features and the deeper, abstract implications delimiting a particular site as sacred (Eliade 1959).

Many religions, particularly historic ones, have designated different dimensions of the natural world as sacred and have worshipped all or part of it. Many have done so through the belief that nature is the dwelling place of the gods. Examples can be found in many cultures and throughout history. The Romans and Britons believed that various natural features of the landscape had divine association, either as homes of gods or as gods in themselves (Blagg 1986). Nature spirits continue to play a central role, for example, in the Chinese and Korean Buddhist practice of geomancy, which is used to select spiritually appropriate sites for houses, villages, temples, and graves (Yoon 1976).

Particular environments are venerated in some religions. Hindus designate the River Ganges as holy (Gopal 1988). Pre-Christain religions often regarded caves as holy places. Holy status is bestowed upon particular stones in some religions, an example being the famous Black Stone at Mecca which Muslims believe was sent down from heaven by Allah (Jordan and Rowntree 1990).

Mountain peaks and other high places have been also regarded as holy sites (often as home of gods) since ancient times. Good examples include Mount Olympus in Greece, believed to be the dwelling place of Zeus and other gods, and Mount Fuji, which is sacred in Japanese Shintoism. Forests were often seen as the haunts woodland gods. Ethnic or local religions of the ancient Germans, Slavs, Celts, and Greeks venerated trees and forests. Yew trees, for instance, were worshiped as sacred trees in pre-Christian Britain (Wallace 1992). As well, heavenly bodies —the sun, moon and stars — were widely worshipped throughout the pre-Christian world and impressive ceremonial structures survive in some places today.

It must be noted that not all sacred sites have equal status or perceived holiness, even among believers. Jackson and Henrie suggest a typology for categorising sacred space at three broad levels based on their study of Mormon culture in the USA. They are: "mystico-religious sites" (shrines, cathedrals, sacred groves, mountains, or trees); homelands (representing the roots of each individual, family or people—sacred only to believers); and the lowest level of sacred space is the "historical sacred sites that have been assigned as a result of an event occurring there (Jackson and Henrie 1983). The concept of sacred space as a "mystico-religious site" is the type employed in this paper.

The religious expression of sacred space, however, varies greatly through space and time. The areal extent of "sacred spaces" varies from infinite to a finite point. As well, the cared view or esteem associated with them varies according to their roles. The relative permanence of a sacred space is also a function of the event associated with its recognition as a unique place and the permanence of the ideas which gave rise to the perception of its sanctity. Thus, while certain sacred spaces have lost their sacredness due to loss of belief in the efficacy of the 'spirit world', often the combined effects of modernization, Christianization, and formal education, others remain to function in various cultures as "places" or "spaces" of reverence and worship.

Designation of particular places as sacred can be a mixed blessing because while special status normally gives such places priority for preservation and protection, it also encourages large numbers of visitors who can damage the very thing they want to see and experience. There is evidence of sacred spaces which have been carefully managed and have made significant contributions to the preservation of local landscapes. For example, most of the islands in Japan's Setonaikai (Inland Sea) have been extensively developed in the post-war period, but some have been preserved as sacred islands (Kondo 1991). The preservation of Ikishima Island as sacred island is encouraged by local legends that foretell insanity for anyone who cuts a tree on the island. Such legends also guarantee local fishermen's catches so long as the area remains sacred.

Temple forests in India provide another example of sacred places that also benefit wildlife and landscape. Worship of trees and plants has been the religious practice in India since about 600 CE, although it has ned. Hindu theology requires people to worhip deities in order the Vanadevi deity is believed to be responsible for forests), and the very act of planting specific plants and trees is considered to be an act of worship in itself. Chandrakanth and colleagues describe a variety of different temple forest types in India (Chandrakanth et al. 1990). There are, however, examples of some sacred places suffering from degradation because of intese utilization. For example, Buddhist sites in India are visited by many Indians and growing numbers from South-east Asia and face mounting pressure from government-guided tourism development (Orland and Bellafiore 1990).

With this brief background, the discussion now focuses on ethnomedical practices and ecology in the African context. The links that exist between ethnomedical practices, sacred spaces, and local ecological systems are first identified.

LINKS BETWEEN ETHNOMEDICINE, SACRED SPACES, AND ECOSYSTEMS IN AFRICA

There are close links between ethnomedicine and ecology. Plant and animal species are used for medicinal purposes. As well, they are of cultural and religious importance, especially for rituals and festivals. Humankind, from time immemorial, has depended on plants in treating all forms of ailments. Probably the region that makes the widest use of herbal preparations is Africa where people reputedly depend on plants, via ethnomedicine, for as much as 95% of their drug needs in some places (Iwu 1993). Like many other Third world countries, spiritual or magico-religious healers, herbalists, technical specialists (e.g., bone-setters), and traditional birth attendants in Africa employ diverse forms of herbs, roots, leaves, bark, mammals and birds in the preparation of medicine (Odu 1987). Wild animals and their by-products (hooves, skins, bones, feathers and tusks), for example, form important ingredients in the preparation of curative, protective, and preventive medicine. More importantly for some, they are used to perform rituals and invoking and appeasing gods and witches (Ajayi 1978). Belts, necklaces and bangles made of wild animal by-products (e.g., skins of leopards, lions, gorillas, and monkeys) embedded with herbs are commonly utilized in some societies for preventive and protective measures against witches and for immunity from bad luck, diseases, and enemies. Wildlife species and their parts are also utilized for aphrodisiacs and potency purposes. In addition, a variety of wild animals form an integral part of cultural and religious festivals and ceremonies, some of which seek to promote the good health of local people and their communities (Adeola 1992). During the performance of some rituals and festivals, for example, certain specific wild animals may be sacrificed. In some communities, parts of animals (e.g., feathers of parrots) are used as special "tools" for making masks for masquerades. Tusks and skins of elephant, lion, and leopard are used for the installation of traditional rulers and are worn during cultural festivals in some parts of Africa.

Apart from ethnomedicine's reliance on flora and fauna of local ecosystems, since ancient times, Africans have believed in a wide variety of deities which reside in all sorts of natural phenomena. These natural features have religious significance to local people and practitioners of ethnomedicine. The magico-spiritual and religious aspects of ethnomedicine have particularly had much impact on space in areas where people assign religious values to natural phenomena. In many societies where the practice of ethnomedicine is predominant, the local people assign sanctity to certain portions of their natural landscape and regard them as worthy of devotion, loyalty, dignity, and worship.

Some natural objects and their surroundings are personified in gods, deities, and spirits and such ecological features are believed to emanate power. There are spirits of forests and trees. All trees are thought to have souls of their own and some are regarded as the dwelling places of other powerful spirits which take temporary abode there. Many villages have a sacred tree. For example, the iroko tree is held to be sacred in most places. Among the Yoruba, the iroko tree is believed to be inhabited by very powerful spirit. People fear having the tree near their dwelling place or to use it for furniture. The tree cannot be felled unless special rites are perfomed. Important meetings are believed to be held by witches at the foot or top of the iroko tree. Other trees believed to be the abodes of certain spirits include the silk-cotton tree and African satinwood. Baobab trees are regarded as sacred and are often believed to be the abode of spirits or the "meeting place of witches." There are, as well numerous animal spirits and sacred snakes. Many forest animals are considered sacred by different ethnic groups. There exists taboos with regard to the killing such animals as leopard, python, duiker, crocodile, and elephant in some socieites. Certain types of animals symbolise the vitality of their ancestors.

There are spirits of rivers, streams, and lakes. Wells, springs, rivers, lakes, and the sea are believed to have spirits dwelling in them and in some places great cults are made of these naiads. The greatest nature god of the Ashantis in Ghana is the Tano River whose fame spreads far and wide. It has many priests and temples. Some lakes like Lake Bosomtwi in central Ghana and Lake Bamblime in the Camerouns are considered sacred. The sea is the home of very powerful gods. The Yoruba sea god, *Olokun* is represented by one of the famous Ife bronzes. The Mende of Sierra Leone believe in nature spirits which are associated with rivers and forests. The Yoruba believe that there are spirits dwelling in rivers, lagoons, and the sea. *Yemoja*, for example, is believed to be the goddess of waters generally and from her body, according to the people's belief, all rivers, lagoons, and the sea flow out. Today, she is associated with the Ogun River and is given elaborate worship in those areas through which it flows, particularly, in Abeokuta (Awolalu 1979). *Oya* is the goddess of the River Niger. *Olukun or Malokun*—the lord of the sea or divinity that is in the sea—is given prominent worhip in Ugbo and Iigbo-Egunrin in Okitipupa Division, in Itebu-Manuwa, and in some parts of Lagos State and Ile-Ife (Awolalu 1979). *Olisa* is the spirit of the lagoon and is worshiped in Lagos and other towns and villages close to the lagoon. Gods of the storm are divinities in full right in many parts of West Africa. There is also the Yoruba God, *Shango*, god of lightining and thunder (Parrinder 1962).

Spirits may also have their abode in mountains and other physical land-scapes. Hills and outstanding rocks are likely haunts of powerful spiritual forces and many villages which nestle under these hills take the hill spirit as their principal deity. The town of Abeokuta in Nigeria is built "under the rock. The sacred cave of the hill spirit (called *Olumo*) survives. At Ibadan, the tutelary divinity of the city is a hill goddess (called *Oke-Ibadan*) in whose honour an annual festival is held. Throughout the Southern Lake Tanganyika region, there are a number of recognised territorial spirit shrines which are located at various natural phenomena, including caves, mountains, large rocks and trees and waterfalls, some of which are believed to be inhabited by pythons.

In number of places, the earth is revered but has no regular cults. The Ashantis believe that the earth is animated by a female whose sacred day is Thursday and so the spirit is called "Thursday earth"' (*Asase Yaa*). Yet the earth has no priest and is not consulted by divination in time of sickness as are other gods. But among the Yorubas and Ewes, the earth has a powerful cult. The earth is venerated in Yorubaland because it is believed to be inhab-ited by a spirit.

In various parts of Africa, features of the landscape are selected as natural shrines. Shrine cults in Zambia, Ghana, Uganda, Kenya, and many other African countries tend to have a strong ecological emphasis and hills, imposing trees, caves, streams, falls and rapids become associated with in-visible entities and become objects of veneration (van Binsbergen 1978). The personification of such objects in the physical environment and the in-tuitive rapport which both practitioners of ethnomedicine as well as lay people establish with their natural landscape are the way in which the ecology be-comes clothed with some divine qualities still displayed in many communi-ties in Africa and other developing countries. In some cases, these natural shrines are accentuated by the erection of man-made shrines. There usually exists more than one type of shrine in any one area, each type with its own features. Richard's description of Memba shrine religion in Zambia distinguishes six types of shrines: (i) individual's house; (ii) the village shrine; (iii) villages of deceased chiefs; (iv) natural phenomena; (v) chiefs' groves; and (vi) relic shrines containing the chiefly paraphernalia (Richard 1939)

A large number of active shrines continues to receive the attention of local people in African countries (Werner 1978). Sacred-healers, in particular, live as close as possible to these features which they regard as "sacred spaces" and where they communicate with their gods and obtain greater access to supernatural powers for the purpose of medical practices. This kind of devotion and loyalty to natural objects is termed by Wright as "geopiety" (Wright 1966).

Besides localized active shrines, there are a few complex territorial shrines which receive more than just local attention, because in addition to being used by the local people, they are in some way involved in ritual activities concerning the region's kingships. Territorial cults are one of the most prominent religious institutions in Central African societies. They occupy a central position in the moral and religious system; they are an important ecological factor and they represent a source and system of authority which is a direct parallel to secular authority. Watson has written about some Mambwe territorial shrines of this sort (Watson 1959:64-66). Robert has described others in Ufipa (Robert 1949). The Bemba chief Mwamba has such a shrine at Chishimba Falls as does the Tabwa chief Nsama at Chansa Ngulu in Zambia (Robert 1949:11-32).

PRESERVATION AND CONSERVATION OF NATURE: THE ROLE OF ETHNOMEDICINE AND SACRED SPACE

The ecological crisis the whole world is witnessing is indebted generally to certain conceptions of the natural world. These have been categorized as: (a) the *anthropocentrism* of the Greek and the biblical tradition that assumes humans superiority over nature; (b) the *mechanism* of the scientifc revolution of the 17th and 18th centuries that affirms the complete passivity of nature; and (c) the *utilitarianism* of the technological revolution of the last two centuries (Rutledge 1993).

Greek philosophers accepted that human beings were essentially, by virtue of their possession of reason, superior to all other forms of life. This was affirmed by Herodotus, Xenophon, Plato, Socrates, Aristotle and by the later Stoics (Glacken 1967:41-58). Contemporaneous with the earlier phase of Greek philosophy, the prophets, priests, and poets of ancient Israel were fashinoning their literary account of God's dealings with humanity and the first episode in that story records God's creation of the "heaven and earth". It is the 26th verse that we find the crucial words by God:

> Let us make humankind in our image, according to our like-
> ness; and let them have dominion over the fish of the sea, and
> over the birds of the air, and over the cattle and over all the
> wild animals of the earth, and over every creeping thing that
> creeps upon the earth (Gen 1:26).

In his now-famous speech before the American Academy for the Advancement of Science in 1967, Lynn White pinpointed this verse as the origin, the
first cause of the ecological crisis (White 1967). In a subsequent verse man
and woman are told to "multiply and fill the earth and subdue it and have
dominion over .... every living thing that moves upon the earth" (Gen 1:28).
These passages, according to White, indicated that God placed humans on
earth to dominate it. White's observation led to reactions from several scholars, some in support of his stand; others refuting his claim (Kay 1980).

Even though there are countervailing messages in the scripture, no later
message from God retracts this command and it takes little imagination to
see how Western culture might have used these verses to justify a boundless
exploitation and conquest of nature. The combination of the Greek and Christian conceptions of anthropocentricity produces habits of mind whose effects are still with us—that other living things exist to meet our needs; that
subjugation and domination are not only permitted but mandated (Rutledge
1993). The contemporary environmental movements, especially discussions
of environmental ethics, have sharply criticized this "human-centeredness."
Undoubtedly, both Greek and Hebraic forms of anthropocentirsm are logically flawed.

As well, the "mechanical" conception of nature has shaped our way of
dealing with the natural world. The mechanical view began with Galileo and
Descartes and was further developed in the writings of Hobbes, Gassendi
and Mersenne (Burtt 1954). The mechanism of the scientific revolution of
the seventeenth century describes nature in terms of passive materiality. Thus,
the core of the conception rested on a single, fundamental assumption: "matter
is passive."

The "mechanical" conception is reinforced by the utilitarian attitude of
western societies. Central to the "utilitarian" attitude is the assumption that
nature exists for the purpose of serving human needs. The utilitarianism of
the industrial revolution of the nineteenth and twentienth centuries applies
these earlier notions to the use and control of the natural world for human
benefit. Contemporary developments have put in the hands of human beings instrumental means to put their ideas of superiority into practice. Ba-
con held immense influence in propagating the idea of a systematic investigation of nature as a boon to social development. When coupled with the
mechanical model of nature, the utilitarian drive to harness nature provided

a powerful ideology to support the activity of progressive western governments in extending their control over nature as well as the social environments (Rutledge 1993).

While modern societies are characterised by the anthropocentric, mecha-
nistic, and the utilitarian attitudes to nature, the various traditions within
indigenous societies have intricate relationships with nature which reflect a
keen sense of the interdependence of human culture and nature and involve
a holistic ethic of respect for nature. Unlike the beliefs of the Judeo-Chris-
tian humanistic tradition which generated the view of the universe that sharply
separated God and the world and humanity and nature, encouraging, thus,
attitudes of conquest and exploitation in relation to nature, the religious
aspects of ethnomedicine generally encourage indigenous people to relate to
natural phenomena with reverence and dignity. This conception of reality is
a form of world view in which most indigenous people structure their world
and experiences.

From the ecological point of view, sacred spaces are jealously protected
from any forms of human pollution and environmental degradation and thus,
contribute to the preservation of nature. In some areas of Africa, the landscape is never completely humanized—certain places remain which have
never been subjected to man's ecological transformations or which, once
used, have been abandoned again. These places are of great significance:
they tend to represent the hidden forces on which humankind draws for its
survival. Mountains, hills, imposing trees, caves, streams, falls, and rapids
that are associated with invisible entities and thus have become objects of
veneration are usually natural objects which are outside the cycle of ecological transformations and do not serve any direct utilitarian purpose for
the people concerned.

In typical rural settings, the bonds existing between people, the bio-physi-
cal environment, and spiritual world exercise some restrictions on where to
engage in such activities as farming, hunting, and fishing. Charles Good
notes that in Ukambani in Kenya, cultivation, grazing and fuelwood collection in the hillls have left little of the natural vegetation undisturbed, except
the familiar fig trees whose large dark-green canopies often mark the location of sacred grooves. In the Kilungu Hills, fruit species like mango and
wild fig (the latter is a common marker of the remaining sacred groves) are
prominent among the few remaining trees in the Kilungu Hills (Good 1987).

Local spiritual healers may become a powerful force in the control and
management of resources. In Africa, cult organizations in some areas have
made tremendous contribution to the preservation of nature. In their studies
of indigenous people, Schoffeleers and van Binsbergen have argued that
shrine activities and ecological processes are mirror images of each other

(Schoffeleers 1978; van Binsbergen 1978). As Schoffeleers reports of the Malawians, the indigenous people maintain "a ritually directed ecosystem." Cult organizations regulated significant practical activities of the people. Large areas of wilderness were, for example, ritually protected from burning. Cults issued and enforced directives with regard to a community's use of its environment (Schoffeleers 1978).

Cult mediums could, at times, compel people to plant particular crops and restrict fishing and grazing so as to protect fragile resources. In the 1930s, it is reported that the Mbona cult pressured part of the population of the Lower Shire Valley to emigrate in order to relieve conditions of overcrowding (ibid). In many African societies, cults which function for the whole community—what Schoffeleers calls "territorial cults"—are known to perform rituals which they believe could counteract droughts, floods, blights, pests and epidemic diseases (Schoffeleers 1978).

There is also an existence of a plethora of spirit beings or 'divinities' with special moral and practical functions satisfying human natural needs. In some indigenous societies, prohibitions on the use of certain species of wildlife exist to protect animal species. Squirrels, for example, are considered sacred to the Afana people (Messenger 1971). The religious aspects and belief systems related to ethnomedicine tends also to instill some fear in local people about certain natural landscapes or spaces. In Uganda, for example, among some lowland communities, certain mountains are feared because they are believed to harbour supernatural spirits and diseases brought about by the spirits of the mountains. In such areas, mountain resources are consequently often left unexploited (Messenger 1971). In the Kwahu district of the eastern region of Ghana, an inselberg in the local landscape whose surroundings were thickly forested was very much revered by the local inhabitants who regarded it as the 'home' of one of the most powerful gods in the district. This peak and its surrounding forest remained unexploited for decades until relatively recently (Anyinam 1987). There are several other examples in the African environment where fears of certain physical features have tended to influence the use of such natural resources as rivers, shorelines, and forests.

Among the Shona of Zimbabwe, there is still great respect for the spirit mediums. An Association of Zimbabwe Traditional Healers has been established and one of the founders is a spirit medium. This organization operates from Masvingo, some 300 kilometers south of Harare and is centred on the protection of sacred areas such as the Matopo Hills, home of the High God cult and the "*rambakutemwa*"—sacred forests where spirits reside. More than 700,00 seedlings of indigenous trees, including baobab, mahogany, as well fruit trees such as oranges, mangoes, pawpaws and avocados have been planted by this organization (Tandon 1994).

Another example is the role played by voodoo priests in environmental management practices in Benin, West Africa. Here, in shallow freshwater lakes fed by the annual delta floods, voodoo healers adminsiter the commands of a deity. After the floods recede in the dry season, the lakes are no longer replenished by rain. At that time, priests forbid fishermen to use weighted nets in the lakes which have thick, soft, muddy bottoms. The priests say the nets disturb the deity who will kill the fish. In scientific terms, the weights stir up the mud, which releases iron oxide, which is usually not toxic to fish when the lakes are receiving plenty of oxygen-rich rainwater but is deadly in stagnant water.

Benin boasts of the most productive lagoon fisheries in the world. Lake Nokoue, the largest lagoon in the Oueme River delta produces more fish per acre than other West African lagoons (Stevens 1994). In recent years, the lagoon has been invaded by "Eichhornia crassipes," a water hyacinth that threatens to suffocate the fishery. Listed as one of the world's ten worst weeds, one plant can multiply to cover 350 acres in one year (Stevens 1994). To control these weeds, another type of hyacinth which is infested with beetle no larger that a head of pin is being used. They weaken the hyacinths by eating the surface layers of leaves, on which they lay their eggs. The beetle larvae hatch and kill the plants by devouring the centres of the leaves and stems.

The new hyacinths were often ripped out of the infested water by the local fishermen to protect their fishing areas. But, to be effective, the insect-laden plants must grow without disturbance for several months until the beetles multiply and spread to other plants. The experts called upon the voodoo priests for help. The priests proclaimed the area where the infested water hyacinths have been released as off-limits, the home of deities who cannot be disturbed upon penalty of serious harm. Fearing the wrath of vengeful deities, the local people left the water hyacinths alone. The project now shows signs of success. The beetles have spread many miles from where they were originally placed (Stevens 1994). This is an example of how science and religion can work together for the sustainability of the ecology. In some sense, as Reichel-Dolmatoff rightly puts it, indigenous priests play the role of an "ecological broker" (Reichel 1976).

Gottlieb reports of a case where logging was prevented among the Beng society in West Africa in spite of efforts by loggers to cut down some iroko trees in the forest. In Beng universe, iroko trees are not sacred but they are said to be the home to forest spirits or *bonzo* who have chosen to dwell in them. The cutting down of such trees are preceded by some ceremony which includes offering chicken as a sacrifice to the gods and spirits. A team of loggers learnt some bitter lessons when it decided to log the iroko trees. Such an attempt led to the death of some loggers (Gottlieb, personal communication). As Gottlieb observed, "while it is undeniable that parastatal amd multinational corporations usually prove decisive in their victories over local disempowered populations, and over the natural environment they set out to conquer, it is exhilarating to see, for a change, that invisible spirits get the better of those usually ovewhelming forces" (Gottlieb, personal communication). She also observed that it gives us hope that the earth itself, -which is worshipped under so many guises by local populations around the world, may yet find ways to assert itself in the face of populations who are only temporary visitors to the planet (Gottlieb 1992).

That the practice of ethnomedicine can safeguard natural phenomena is undeniable, though the resultant conservation and preservation advantages may be limited in their geographic scale. It is also worth noting that with increased population pressure and economic hardships, the protective tendencies of ethnomedical practices and indigenous culture in general are being weakened.

LOSS OF SACRED SPACES AND ESTRANGEMENT FROM NATURE

In several parts of Africa, the physical world has been progressively "despiritualized". Many shrines have fallen into disuse. There are some which have been forgotten altogether. Many sacred lands have been desecrated and their spiritual value destroyed. Desecration of spiritual spots, sacred spaces, and groves has tended to reduce the dignity of such "landscapes" and to encourage their abuse.

Forest enclaves which traditionally served effectively as "sacred spaces" used by religious healers and consequently were prevented from extensive utilization and exploitation, have been cultivated, wiping away the dignity, devotion, and fear usually attached to such symbolic landscapes. The desecration of such landscapes tends to dispell their sacral aura, resulting in a new relationship that usually leads to severe abuse especially by a large percentage of the new generation of population which has little or no knowledge of such hierophanes in their localities. In such cases, the fear of local gods has been "extracted" from the natural environment.

Thus, in the Shire Highlands of Malawi, where several important townships developed and large tracts of land were alienated, the territorial cults collapsed. Much the same can be said of the Chewa area in Malawi and Zambia where by the 1930s almost the entire Chisumphi organization had broken up. What survived in Malawi were the Mbona cult, some isolated shrines of the Chisumphi cult, and a number of chiefdom cults. Cult healers have been at a greater risk of extinction.

The real challenges of these territorial cults have been the combined forces of world religions, modern technology, capitalism, and the bureaucratic state. The result of that confrontation has been the collapse of some cults and the decline of many others. During the colonial period, the concept of territorial cults came to be challenged and the breakdown of an ideational and organizational complex which had sustained African societies for many centuries was initiated. More directly, the challenges came from the Christian churches which questioned the religious basis of the cults and from the colonial adminstration which became intermittently involved in sharp conflicts with the religious leadership.

A more radical threat came from other factors, one of which was the application of a rationalist interpretation of ecology in the form of modern forms of land conservation and animal husbandry. This affected the moral and communal basis of the cults. As well, the bureaucratization of the chieftainships considerably weakened the political support of the cults. The alienation of land also drastically changed the structure of social organization and settlement.

The decline of sacred spaces and their religous symbolic importance is attributed to several factors. European missionary activities led to the rejection of traditional beliefs, rituals, and other non-Christian observations which form an integral part of ethnomedicine and designation of sacred spaces. This seriously undermined the prestige accorded ethnomedicine and the influence wielded by its practitioners. Over time, Christian teachings and Western civilization created new attitudes, value systems, and expectations among potential adherents of ethnomedical principles, and African traditional religion in general. This has led to significant shifts in traditional beliefs of both the literate and illiterate in Africa.

The denigradation of folk cultures and the disappearance of indigenous medical practitioners not only pose a problem for the future practice of ethnomedicine, but also the protection of biotic communities which serve as sources of indigenous medicine. Loss of indigenous cultures as well as indigenous knowledge has had much impact on the role of sacred spaces. Suzuki is right in his observation that once the indigenous people have disappeared, their body of priceless thought, medicinal knowledge, and value systems painstakingly acquired and built over thousands of years, will disappear forever (Knudston and Suzuki 1992).

CONCLUSION

It is undeniable that culture influences the way people perceive and use the resources of their environment. The practice of ethnomedicine as an integral part of the culture of indigenous people in many parts of Africa has a close interface with local ecosystems. The continued adherence of indigenous people to traditional cultural principles and values of ethnomedical systems contributes to the preservation and conservation of several biotic communities.

While ethnomedicine, expecially its religious elements, generally do shape the value systems, attitudes, and behaviour of indigenous people towards a positive relationship with nature, modern developments appear to be steadfastly eroding the "core of respect" that is bestowed on nature. Indigenous cultures are increasingly being fragmented and threatened by development pressures. Folk knowledge, painstakingly acquired over thousands of years is also steadily disappearing. Threats to, and desecration of, sacred sites and spaces are destroying their spiritual value. The sacral aura of these 'places' are dissipating, resulting in a new relationship with nature that threatens the future sustainability of ecosystems upon which the practice of ethnomedicine is dependent.

In some cases, ethnomedical practices do contribute to the process of environmental degradation and disruption (Anyinam 1995), but the preservation of the world's indigenous cultures and practices may contribute to the preservation and conservation of the remaining undisturbed forests and other biotic communities. It is very encouraging that, in the last few years, the issue of religion and ecology has become a "respected" academic topic worthy of investigation. The news media, the publishing world, and academics have begun to promote indigenous knowledge and culture and their relevance for the sustainability of the earth's ecosystems.

Increasingly, the roles that indigenous cultures and their ethnomedical practices, in particular, could play in the preservation of nature are being investigated. The recent conference on the need for the conservation of medicinal plants by World Health Organization, the International Union for the Conservation of Nature, and World Wildlife Fund is a step in the right direction. This international consultation on the conservation of medicinal plants brought together leading experts in different fields to exchange views on the problems, determine priorities, and make recommendations for action (Akerele et al. 1991).

It is remarkable that environmentalists have tended to admire the values of native North Americans, Australian Aborigines and rainforest dwellers. The discussion in this chapter is a contribution to that effort and the purpose here is to hightlight links that exist between ecology and a particular cultural practice. The ideas and thoughts of indigenous African societies are worth studying because they have, over the years, contributed to the preservation and conservation of nature. As African societies have developed from small scale hunter-gatherers through agriculture to manufacturing their value systems have also changed and their impact on local ecosystems has generally been negative.

Hopefully more detailed empirical studies will be undertaken to shed more light on the broader question of the relationship between culture and ecology in Africa. Our estrangement from nature is caused in part by the anthropocentric attitudes which still seem to guide human-nature relationships. The Humanities disciplines have a crucial role to play in bringing the cultural tradition to bear on the ecological issue. Without doubt, there is much to learn from the sacramental views of nature which is found among indigenous people.

REFERENCES

Adeola, M. O. "Importance of Wild Animals and their Parts in the Culture, Religious Festivals and Traditional Medicine in Nigeria." *Environmental Conservation* 19(1992):125-134.

Ajayi, S. S. *The Utilization of Tropical Forest Wildlife: State of Knowledge and Research Priorities.* Jarkata, Indonesia: 8th World Forestry Congress, 1978.

Akerele, O., et al. eds. *The Conservation of Medicinal Plants:. Proceedings of an International Consultation 21-27 March 1988 held at Chiang Mai, Thailand.* Cambridge: Cambridge University Press, 1991.

Anyinam, C. A. *Persistence with Change: A Rural-Urban Study of Ethno-Medical Practices in Contemporary Ghana.* Unpublished Ph.D. Dissertation, the Graduate School, Queen's University, Kingston, Ontario, 1987.

Anyinam, C. A. "Ecology and Ethnomedicine: Exploring Links Between Current Environmental Crisis and the Practice of Indigenous Medicine." *Social Science and Medicine.* 40, 3(1995):321-329.

Blagg, T. "Roman Religious Sites in the British Landscape." *Landscape History* 8(1986):15-26.

Bonati, A. "Industry and the Conservation of Medicinal Plants." In *The Conservation of Medicinal Plants*, eds. Akerele O.et al. Proceedings of an International Consultation 21-27 March 1988 held at Chiang Mai, Thailand. Cambridge: Cambridge University Press, 1991, pp. 141-145.

Bowman, D. C. *Beyond the Modern Mind: The Spiritual and Ethnical Challenge of the Environmental Crisis.* New York: The Pilgrim Press, 1990.

Burtt, E. A. *The Metaphysical Foundations of Modern Physical Science.* Garden City, N.Y.: Doubleday and Co, 1954.

Carmody, J. *Ecology and Religion: Toward a New Christian Theology of Nature.* New York: Paulist Press, 1983.

Chandrakanth, M. G. "Temple Forests—Their Role in Forestry Development in India." In *Headwater Control*, eds. J. Krecek et al. Prague: WASWC/IUFRO/CSVTS, 1989.

Chandrakanth, M. G. et al. "Temple Forests in India's Forest Development." *Agroforestry Systems* 11(1990):199-211.

Cohn, J. P. "Culture and Conservation." *BioScience* 38 (July-August, 1988):450-453.

Eliade, M. *The Sacred and the Profane: The Nature of Religion.* New York: Harcourt, Brace and World, 1959.

Fabrega, H. and P. K. Manning. "Illness Episodes, Illness Severity, and Treatment Options in a Pluralistc Setting." *Social Science and Medicine* 13B(1968):277-284.

Foster, G. M. and B. G. Anderson. *Medical Anthropology.* New York: John Wiley and Sons Ltd., 1978.

Gesler, W. M. "Therapeutic Landscapes: Medical Issues in Light of the New Cultural Geography." *Social Science and Medicine* 34(1992):735-746.

Glacken, C. *Traces of the Rhodian Shore. Nature and Culture in Western Thought from Ancient Times to the End of the Eighteenth Century.* Berkely, Calif.: University of California Press, 1967.

Good, C. "Ethno-medical Systems in Africa and the LDCs: Key Issues in Medical Geography." In *Conceptual and Methodolgical Issues in Medical Geography*, ed. Melinda S. Meade. Studies in Geography No. 5, Chapel Hill, NC: Unversity of North Carolina at Chapel Hill, 1980, pp.93-116

Good, C. *Ethnomedical Systems in Africa: Patterns of Traditional Medicine in Rural and Urban Kenya.* New York: The Guilford Press New York, 1987.

Gopal, B. "Holy Mother Ganges." *Geographical Magazine* (May, 1988):38-43.

Gottlieb, A. *Under the Kapok Tree: Identiy and Difference in Beng Thought.* Bloomington: Indiana University Press, 1992.

Hargrove, E. C. ed. *Religion and Environmental Crisis.* Athens, Ga: The University of Georgia Press, 1986.

Hughes, C. "Ethnomedicine." In *International Encyclopedia of the Sciences.* New York: New York Free Press/MacMillan, 1968.

Iwu, M. M. *Handbook of African Medicinal Plants.* London: CRC Press, 1993.

Jordan, T. G., and L. Rowntree. *The Human Mosaic: A Thematic Introduction to Cultural Geography.* New York: Harper and Row, 1990.

Kay, J. "Human Dominion Over Nature in the Hebrew Bible." *Annals of the Association of American Geographers* 79, 2(1980):214-232.

Knudtson, P. and D. Suzuki. *Wisdom of the Elders.* London: Stoddart Publishing Co., Ltd., 1992.

Kondo, M. "The Formation of Sacred Places as a Factor of the Environmental Preservation: The Case of Setonaikai (Inland Sea) in Japan." *Marine Pollution Bulletin* 23(1990): 649-52.

Messenger, J. G. "Ididio Drama." *Africa* 12(1971):208-222.

Mkali, H. "Traditional Medicine Under the Spotlight." *Africa Health* 10 (Dec.1987/Jan. 1988):36-37.

New York Times, January 16, 1990, p.21; Jan 20, 1990, p. 12.

Odu, M. "The Art of Traditional Healing in Nigeria." *National Concord* (July 17, 1987):5.

Orland, B. and V. J. Bellafiore. "Development Directions for a Sacred Site in India." *Landscape and Urban Planning* 19(1990):181-96.

Parrinder, G. *African Traditional Religion.* London: Sheldon Press, 1962.

Reichel-Dolmatoff, G. "Cosmology as Ecological Analysis: A View from the Rain Forest." *Man* 11 (Sept. 1976):307-328.

Richard, A. I. *Land, Labour, and Diet in Northern Rhodesia.* London: Oxfrod University Press, 1939.

Robert, J. M. *Croyances et Coutumes Magic-Religieuses des Wafipa Paiens.* Tabora: Tanganyika Mission Press, 1949.

Rockfeller, S. C. and J. C. Elder, eds. *Spirit and Nature: Why the Environment is a Religious Issue?* Boston: Beacon Press, 1992.

Rutledge, D. W. *Humans and the Earth: Toward a Personal Ecology.* New York: Peter Lang, 1993.

Schofeleers, J. M. "Introduction." In *Guardians of the Land: Essays on Central African Territorial Cults,* ed. J. M. Schofeleers. Gwelo: Mambo Press, 1978.

Stevens, Jane E. "Science and Religion at Work." *Bioscience* 44, 2(1994):60-64.

Tandon, Y. *The Ecologist* 24, 1(1994):4.

Tuan, Y. F. "Sacred Space: Exploration of an Idea." In *Dimensions of Human Geography,* ed. K. W. Butzer. University of Chicago, Department of Geography, Research Paper 186. Chicago: University of Chicago, 1978, pp. 84-99.

van Binsbergen, W. H. J. "Explorations into the History and Sociology of Territorial Cults in Zambia." In *Guardians of the Land: Essays on Central African Territorial Cults,* ed. J. M. Schoffeleers. Gwelo: Mambo Press, 1978, pp. 47-88.

Vos, A. de. "Game as Food: A Report on its Significance in Africa and Latin America." *Unasylva* (FAO Rome) 29(1978):2-12.

Wallace, D. "Dreaming of Yew." *Geographical Magazine* (February, 1992): 40-43.

Watson, W. *Tribal Cohesion in a Monetary Economy.* Manchester: Manchester University Press for Rhodes-Livingstone Institute, 1959, pp. 64-66.

Werner, D. "Miao Spirit Shrines in the Religious History of the Southern Lake Tanganyika Region: The Case of Kapembwa." In *Guardians of the Land: Essays on Central African Territorial Cults,* ed. J. M. Schofeleers. Gwelo: Mambo Press, 1978.

White, Lynn Jr. "The Historical Roots of our Ecological Crisis" *Science* (March 1967):10.

Wolalu, J. O. *Yoruba Beliefs and Sacrificial Rites.* London: Longman Group Limited, 1979.

Wright, J. K. *Human Nature in Geography.* New York: Harper and Row, 1966.

Yoon, H-K. *Geomantic Relationships Between Culture and Nature in Korea.* Dissertation Abstracts International A, 1976: 77-4661.

7

"Stray Women" and "Girls on the Move":

Gender, Space, and Disease in Colonial and Post-Colonial Zimbabwe

Lynette Jackson

INTRODUCTION

During several visits to Zimbabwe between 1983 and 1992, I was struck by a curious yet common association between mobile African women, criminality, and the spread of sexually transmitted disease. Each time I visited Zimbabwe, I witnessed political campaigns, conducted in the name of public order, apparently targeting single African women. The media referred to these campaigns as "clean-up," "crackdown" and/or "blitz" operations. They were ostensibly aimed at cleaning up the city streets of prostitutes, squatters, hawkers, beggars, and petty thieves and generally preceded an international conference or other important events for which foreign media were expected.[1] But, while these petty criminals were said to be the targets, these campaigns netted a wide variety of women, some of them members of the "informal sector" of the economy (independent beer brewers, women engaged in forms of sexual commerce, and hawkers) along with others who were not.[2] It began to appear as if Zimbabwean women had fallen under a new form of colonialism, one in which being single was a crime. Indeed, one scholar has argued that, during such moments, the Marriage Certificate became a Zimbabwean woman's *de facto* "town pass" when travelling "alone" (that is, without a male escort) after sunset.[3]

During the early 1990s, within the framework of the escalating HIV/AIDS crisis, the aforementioned process of criminalization was joined with pathologization. In other words, not only had young, unattached and mobile women come to signify a kind of social disorder; they began to signify a physical one as well. Single African women came to represent the single most important vector of HIV transmission. Indeed, "single mothers at growth points," or sometimes simply "young mothers," became the media shorthand for HIV/AIDS transmission.[4]

The association of single African women with both badness and disease appeared in some of the earliest AIDS education material. In the case of one educational poster put out by the Ministry of Education that hung in the University of Zimbabwe's Medical School library, two African women are pictured wearing thigh high boots and miniskirts and smoking cigarettes. The two "bad" women stood at the entrance to a long, dark tunnel. A man stood a short distance away, as if pondering what to do next. The following words appeared: "Choose your partners wisely." The clear and intended beneficiaries of this message were men; while the diseased escorts into the tunnel of death were women.[5]

Such messages pervaded the media of this period. A cartoon in the February 12, 1996 edition of *The Herald* newspaper contained this image. A stereotypical "loose woman" is shown chasing a stereotypical "fat cat"—an overweight, well dressed business or professional man. The woman's lips are puckered, her arms are outstretched, and the caption reads: "It [is] indeed possible for AIDS to be transmitted by saliva."[6] The agency of the man in this image is nowhere signified. Even in situations where a rural wife was infected, the role of the husband in linking up the so-called "single mother" and the rural housewife is rarely if ever enunciated.[7]

I encountered the above images, concepts and representations from 1990 to late 1992. What follows is an exploration into their historical antecedents. I will attempt to shed light upon questions of causations like: what led to the development and entrenchment of the stigmatizing association of mobile and independent African women with infectious disease and pathology? How did disease metaphors function in the gendered policing of colonial social boundaries? In other words, I explore the process by which power over mobile African women was medicalized and attempt a historical contextualization of recent dispensations of images and stereotypes relating to gender and disease. Particular emphasis will be placed on the development of a specific approach to medicalizing power, the venereal disease "inspections" which became compulsory for African women seeking economic opportunities, and admission to enter and reside within certain colonial spaces.

A few points need to be made by way of qualification. For one thing, evidence exists to suggest the probability that associations of African women with venereal disease transmission may have preceded the colonial era; or may be the product of African cultural concepts. We know that African men in 1940s Southern Rhodesia referred to sexually transmitted diseases as "woman's diseases," and that this was and remains a convention in other African societies as well.[8] But, while African patriarchal attitudes certainly played a role in ensuring the effectiveness of disease metaphor in discourses about uncontrolled African women, the most profound influence appears to have been colonial anti-venereal disease campaigns and related discourses. It was within this context where African women's mobility was explicitly linked to criminality and pathology.

To relate this issue directly to the theme of this volume, the question of space, I argue that to truly understand the ways in which African women were integrated into colonial discourse, it is necessary to explore the nature of colonial space, social, ideological and physical space; and ways in which African women were inscribed therein. As in contemporary Zimbabwe, women who moved between spaces, into spaces where they were not supposed to be, e.g., urban, after dark, single and independent, were suspected of disease and disorder. Thus the mediating factor in ascriptions of pathology was and remains, space. Finally, the implications of what was by the 1940s, a policy of policing black women's genitalia, will be explored as will the troubling continuities between past and present day realities concerning the framing of African women.

THE "STRAY WOMAN" IN
MEDICO-PATRIARCHAL DISCOURSE

A striking characteristic of the public health files for colonial Zimbabwe (Southern Rhodesia) is the frequency with which one encounters references to African women as disease hosts or agents. In a series of public health reports and correspondences of the late 1920s, the issue of venereal disease among Africans was the topic of note. During this period of escalating concern over the issue, a meeting was called at the behest of the Rhodesian Land-Owners' Association and held at the Bulawayo City Hall. Dr. Andrew M. Fleming, the Minister of Public Health for the colony, presided. As the colony's public health czar since 1896, the beginning of Southern Rhodesia's existence, Fleming's assessment that the crux of the problem lay in the bodies of mobile African women carried considerable weight.[9]

A few months later, a conference was held to determine how to develop efficient methods of surveillance and control, Fleming elaborated on his earlier assessment and stressed the particular role that "stray women" played in "spreading disease all over the country."[10] In other words, he presumed that the bodies of these African women were diseased and that, through their bodies, the disease was spread around. In a similar vein, other authorities identified the problem as women and "girls on the move" and the noxious and hard to keep track of "travelling prostitute(s) who changed their names" as they moved. The unregulated African female, the "stray woman" became synonymous with disease and disorder.

A NOTE ON STRAY WOMEN

By applying the word "stray" to these women, Dr. Fleming was suggesting that they had deviated from some "right place" on the social, spatial, and ideological maps of colony. The word implies disorder. In fact, the adjective is more commonly applied to domestic animals than to people, and confers no social agency. But, to the colonial mind, to those colonial authorities who spoke and wrote on the issue, there was no dissonance. African women had long been associated with brute beasts in the Western imagination. Since the eighteenth century, the natural sciences had been premised upon some variation of the "chain of being" concept in which European men were the apex and African women were just links above the simian beasts at the bottom.[12] So, when agents of colonial public health and public order spoke of these women, they did not describe them as *leaving* one place to *go* to another; but described them as straying beyond prescribed boundaries. "Stray women" was thus a negative metaphor for the transgressive relationship that African women had to colonial space. What is more, it is a metaphor which helps us understand why relations to space factored so centrally in designations of pathology among African women.

BEHOLDING THE OTHER'S OTHER

In the book *Difference and Pathology*, Sander Gilman explored the ways in which "the Other" is seen as both sexualized being and in association with the image of illness. However, Gilman never actually explains the social function of "the Other." His is a psychoanalytical approach which explores the process of projection. The individual projects that which it cannot control onto a bad Other. And, for some reason, otherness interacts with a deep structure of stereotypes and takes the form of disease and sexual pathology (Gilman 1985:23). While the role of "deep structures" is no doubt central to the ways in which people tend to represent difference, we are no wiser on the issues of social action, social structure or social relations of power and subordination or, as Vaughan (1991) states, we are no wiser as to the difference that differences made. In her own work, Vaughan (1991:12) has explored the intersections between discourses of disease and pathology with those of race and to a much lesser extent, gender. But while her work is very good at elaborating the ways in which social power relations informed knowledge of the Other and colored the ways in which the Other could know him or herself, she pays little attention to the reinforcing role that patriarchy played in the process. This, however, is key to my analysis of the shared preoccupations, the collaborations of European and African patriarchies, around key issues regarding African women. These two patriarchies, while unequal in terms of the colonial dispensations of power, were in rough agreement about where African women belonged and when they strayed from that place.

In the early years of colonial rule, when the missionaries and colonial authorities were still speaking about the emancipation of African women, problem women were those who stood in the way of change. Prior to the inauguration of Southern Rhodesia's own version of Indirect Rule, these authorities linked the undermining of indigenous institutions with the emancipation of African women and fashioned themselves saviors of an oppressed black womanhood.[13] Legislation was passed providing women and girls with channels through which to appeal against traditional authorities (Jeater 1990:120). These policies and the so-called emancipation project, have been interpretted by some as part and parcel of the process by which both missionaries and colonial authorities sought to permanently wound if not destroy any coherence in the African social order.[14]

Much work has been produced of late discussing the shifting of power over African women away from traditional patriarchy and towards the colonial state. This literature has registered the disapproval of traditional authorities to the dimunution of their control over women's sexual and reproductive powers. Diane Jeater has described the shift as one from "answerability to the ancestors to answerability to the state," a shift which had negative consequences for the authority of "big men" (Jeater 1990:124). Recent work has been more nuanced in its assessment of the impact of colonization on the lives of individual Africans. For instance, it has been noted that numerous African women, along with hardship, gained certain new opportunities to evade dependence upon and therefore control by senior men. Some, for instance, took their male guardians to colonial courts rather than accept arranged marriages to persons whom they disliked (see Schmidt 1992:chap. 3). "Big men" in turn, thought that women and girls were getting out of control and sought the colonizers' assistance in preventing missionaries from taking in runaway women and girls. They also requested state assistance in preventing women and girls from obtaining passage on rick-shas and trains.

The initial response of the the colonial state to these pleas was indifference and even scorn. In fact, the colonial state initially joined the missionaries in encouraging African girls to escape from African patriarchal controls. For instance, in his 1903 report to the London Missionary Society, Reverend Cullen Reed wrote the following:

> The heathen are realizing that a girl who learns the love of Christ will not submit to polygamy, and as nearly all the girls of the Makalanga are promised in infancy, this naturally produces strife...the result is that they do their best to prevent their girls coming to us, and even beg us to drive them away if they come. (Reed 1903)

This example not only illustrates the missionary view of Christian virtue and devotion, but reflects what the missionary felt of African patriarchal institutions. In essence, African women and girls were actively encouraged to abandon one form of patriarchal control for another.

It was quite common to read editorials and official documents and correspondence during the first decades of colonial rule in which African manhood was labeled as lazy, and African womanhood as downtrodden, something akin to connubial slaves. In a 1902 editorial of the *Rhodesian Herald*, the ideological importance of these stereotypes is made clear. According to the editorial, "the African had to learn that men and not women were designed to go out to work."[15] Such sentiments supported the image of Europeans as civilizers who would teach African manhood to become "real men" by selling their labor on the market. MacClintock (1990:110) has noted that the discourse on male idleness seemed to surface whenever the need arose to legitimize land plunder and generally perpetuate the colonial capitalist system.

During the first three decades of colonial rule, the dominant version of the "bad" African woman was not the one who escaped parental control which would come later; but rather the one who stood in the way of "progress," who represented tradition. She was invariably an older woman, like the grandmothers who prevented young girls from attending mission schools; the wives and mothers who objected to the migration of their husbands and sons; or the adherents of indigenous religious faiths.[16] But, over a rather short period of time, the dominant image of the problem African woman changed from the fiendish retarding agents of the old order, to the "stray women" of the colonial towns and industrial compounds. The colonial state and those capitalists and settlers whose livelihoods were dependent upon the steady flow of single male migrant laborers to towns, farms and mines, gradually realized the value of traditional gender relations.

The colonial state with interests rarely distinct or separate from those of colonial capitalists, conducted a commission of inquiry in 1910/1911 to figure out how best to proceed on the project of colonization.[17] The officials decided to try a modified form of "Indirect Rule" whereby control over African female productive and reproductive powers was again left in the hands of African men. They sought to reinvent indigenous gender relations and to reconstitute patriarchy within the subjugated Shona and Ndebele societies. The African man was re-imagined. Neither did he need to be viewed as inherently lazy and unmanly, nor did African women need to be viewed as oppressed and pitiable in their traditional states.[18]

Notions that black women and girls were inherently inferior and degraded, while an attitude of considerable age, seems to have gained currency with this transformation. By the 1920s, when the concern for the problem of the venereal native took center stage, African women were indeed at a low position on the colony's social totem pole. And, as has been suggested above, the fixity of their low status position became a requirement. The colonial authorities sought to invest as little as possible in apparatuses of social control and to mitigate the resistance of African village authorities, by reinforcing African patriarchy when possible. Thus the development of the Other's other status for African women. Put differently, African women were twice displaced from power.

Opinions like those expressed by the Native Commissioner of Hartley district to the Superintendent of Natives in 1924 were common. The Native Commissioner described a kind of generic African woman in the following manner: "her brain is not sufficiently balanced to allow her to think and act for herself." The Native Commissioner of Sinoia held a similar view. In the same year, he stated that, not only were African women inferior to both European men and European women, they were also "unfit to be granted any measure of freedom for the present as their instincts are almost purely *animal.*"[19]

As always, there were contradictions and inconsistences. There were contradictions inherent in the objectives of colonial capitalism. While the active dismantling of indigenous authority and institutions seen to hamper the flow of male labor migrants to the mines, farms and towns had been beneficial, the need for an inexpensive means of social control required that African male authorities in the rural areas maintain control over the sexuality and mobility of African women and girls. At the same time, the demands for social control on the mine compounds and in the urban areas were facilitated by a reasonable flow of single African women into those areas providing for the "daily reproduction" of the African male labor migrant population.[20] Hence, single women were allowed to live on the labor compounds (see van Onselen 1977:48) and were neither marginal or superfluous from the point of view of colonial capital, nor were they unequivocally undesirable. In other words, the state and capital were hesitant to eradicate the migrating women. Economic movement was another matter and, during the 1920s and 1930s, women were placed in a very precarious position as they were progressively relegated to illegal spaces and placed in a very precarious position as they were progressively marginalized from legality and respectability.

DANGERS OF MOBILITY

The period under analysis overlapped with the expansion of the independent urban migration of African women and girls.[21] To understand these developments, a picture of the broader economic and social environment is helpful. During the 1930s, the economic and social status of the majority of Africans was on the decline. African reserves were devastated as the colonial authorities averted the consequences of the Great Depression onto the African peasant and worker.[22] African access to land, to skilled and higher paying jobs were restricted through a series of legislative acts.[23]

As a result of these developments, more and more African women and girls migrated to the towns of Southern Rhodesia. Between 1929 and 1936, for example, the African female population of the Bulawayo Municipal Location grew from an estimated 750 women (and 4,500 men), to 1,237 women (and 6,816 men).[24] Betweem 1929 and 1944, the percentage of women in the Location's adult African population increased from sixteen percent of the total population to near thirty percent of the total population.[25]

But, while it is probable that African men who were single labor migrants in the colonial towns and on the mine compounds were pleased by this increase of female migration, much displeasure was expressed by the African male guardians and husbands of these women. In efforts to rectify the situation, some of the more nationalist and uplift minded African men occasionally submitted petitions to the colonial authorities. One such group was the Loyal Matabele Patriotic Society, a group established in Bulawayo in 1915 and consisting largely of the last Ndebele king, Lobengula's, descendants and a young and educated cadre of Nguni men. Interestingly, the second most pressing issue identified by this group, that is, after the restoration of the Ndebele monarchy, was the problem of single African women in the towns and labor compounds (see Ranger 1970:39).

The protests of African men concerning the "emancipation" of African women were common and appear in many of the Chief Native Commissioner's annual reports. In 1932, for instance, Chief Native Commissioner Charles Bullock reported that the "new freedom of women" was "repeatedly brought up at meetings of the district native boards."[26] In the same annual report, Bullock highlighted an all male delegation of Mfengu elders who, like the Ndebele nationalist, feared that women's emancipation would lead to a rise in immorality.[27]

By the 1930s, there was broad-based agreement on the need to restrict the mobility of African women. Official and unofficial policies and procedures were adopted towards this end. What is interesting about these efforts is what they reveal about the areas of contestation and cooperation between the different patriarchies; and the fact that African women voiced issues and concerns through their feet. Responses to these "voices" varied. In the case of the Bulawayo Municipal Native Location, the policy followed by its superintendent, Mr. Collier, was to "return all (female) minors" whom he suspected of traveling without parental consent, back to their rural homes.[28] Collier admitted, however, the women and girls would simply return and that there was little he could do about this.

In 1936, a more formal effort was made to deal with the "influx of young women who evaded parental control," the Native Registration Act. This Act was part effort to appease African patriarchy, and part effort to appease the rapidly expanding European population which was increasingly in competition with all levels of African petty-entrepreneurial activities. The Act was a serious blow to all Africans operating in the "informal" economic sector as keepers of rooming houses, beer brewers, wood collectors and food hawkers, and made African participation in all of these activities more difficult if not illegal. All in all, African women in urban spaces found themselves progressively on the wrong side of the law.

The growing anxiety and the inter-group collaborations over the control of mobile women and girls, coincided with other developments. As in much of the world during the period under analysis, both colonial and metropolitan worlds, social problems moved from the realm of morality, of good and evil, into the realm of science.[29] Recent works in United States and British social history have shown that, from the late 1920s on, perceived social disorders like single motherhood and female sexual assertiveness, were pathologized and appropriated by the medical sciences.[30] In Southern Rhodesia like in the United States, science truly seems to have become an encompassing idiom for the "policing [of] black women's bodies."

Anxieties over order and control focused on the problem of uncontrolled African womanhood framed more and more as a problem of public health. One could say that the degree to which African women were perceived as dangerous bore a direct relationship to the degree to which they were perceived as mobile. To paraphrase Sander Gilman, difference and otherness are frequently expressed in terms of disease and sexual pathology. What is more, the disease and the diseased other become one in the mind of the Western observer. This is precisely what the public health records for Southern Rhodesia reveal in their references to, and representations of, African women. They were represented and increasingly treated as contagious pathogen for whom regulation and monitoring was sought.

THE MEDICALIZATION OF URBAN AFRICAN WOMEN
A fear of infectious diseases, particularly venereal diseases like syphilis, produced a sustained murmur and occasional hysteria in Southern Rhodesia's settler population. From the early twentieth century, the *Reports on the Public Health* provided annual accounts of the extent of venereally infected Africans. This was the case even though the Medical Director consistently stated that "they [venereal diseases] have not the hold that has been popularly supposed."[31]

But there was enough of a problem for the authorities to enquire into the feasibility of opening a local hospital to deal with Africans with syphilis. This project was shelved, however, due to a lack of funds.[32] The colony's District Surgeons continued to report on the prevalence of venereal disease and on its alarming spread at centers of mining activity where a large number of African men lived without their wives or families. In 1913, one District Surgeon warned that "a grave danger undoubtedly exists with natives suffering from this disease being brought into contact with Europeans." And the Medical Director made the point that he would reiterate in 1928 and at many times between, that unmarried African women residing in the vicinity of the mining compounds were a growing menace and should be combated.[33]

By 1917, the general concern over the "venereal native" reached a fever pitch and led to long and drawn-out debate on the merits and demerits of compulsory detention and examination of all Africans seeking employment and likely to come into contact with Europeans, in other words, a kind of spirochaete screening process.[34] In 1918, an amended Native Registration Act was passed which contained a clause providing for the compulsory vaccination and medical examination of natives applying for certificates of registration. Like so much of Southern Rhodesia's legislation, however, this Act failed to provide for its own funding. The issue still had not been resolved by 1920 when the Town Clerk of Bulawayo requested clarification on the issue of funding.[35] In addition to the funding dilemma, the 1918 legislation was considered flawed by many officials and concerned citizens precisely because it neglected to address the problem of mobile African women who were increasingly viewed as the main source of venereal infection. African men also appear to have attributed the venereal scourge to these women. According to a 1921 petition signed by a group of Christian men working at the Falcon mine, "loose women" were at the root of all of the problems facing the urban black community and not caused by European domination. According to the petition:

> For some time we have considered that there is something wrong with a people to give rise to the great amount of quarreling, fighting and burning of houses, and also the vast amount of venereal disease. All those happenings are interfering with the morals and welfare of the man in employment and the only cause of the trouble is the number of loose women, who are permitted to roam about without hindrance.... Men have evil communication with them, the result is that the men are stricken with foul disease.[36]

To give strength to their argument or, to gain the sympathy of whites, they warned that "many of these loose women are decaying the white people when taken on as nurses to white babies."

In the above examples one sees that African women in town were seen as synonymous with disease from both African male and European settler points of view. What follows is a discussion of how the process of criminalization, in conjunction with the growing association of mobility of African females with the spread of disease, led to more aggressive policies for dealing with so-called venereal African females.

CHIBEURA OR THE AFRICAN WOMEN'S "TOWN PASS"

Rather than stave off the flow of African female migration to the towns, the clear desire of the numerous delegations and petitions from African men, the colonial authorities decided rather to regulate the bodies of these mobile women. In 1922, a motion was put forward in the Legislative Council at the request of the Chamber of Mines. The proposal called for the imposition of compulsory medical examinations on mines and urban locations for "all native men and women found to be infected." But, while both men and women were being targeted, the discourse was overwhelmingly centered on the idea that African women were the agents of infection. During the debates in the Legislative Council, the Medical Officer at the Globe and Phoenix Mine stated that "immoral native women plying their trade in the big compounds" spread their diseases from compound to compound because there were no compulsory medical examinations. Evidence was presented to the effect that where examinations were conducted, such as on the large mines like the Falcon and Shamva mines, the incidence of the disease decreased.

On the Falcon Mine, the term "medically inspected" was used, and women were required to carry medical certificates with them or risk arrest and compulsory examination. Similar "inspections" were conducted at Shamva Mine on males upon engagement, and females when they were "seeking permission to live on the compounds." The women were "examined by a committee of native women."[37] Southern African economic and social historian, van Onselen (1977:51) has interpreted African participation in conducting these exams as a sign of African agency and indicative of the perceived "failure of the state or industry to take decisive action." Whether or not this was the case, it is likely that some women would find participation in these regularized exams preferable to more rough and erratic raids and expulsions at the hands of state authorities. In an attempt at regularization, a new Public Health Act was passed in 1925. Part three, section 47 of the Act made it an offence for any employee with a venereal disease to knowingly continue in employment:

> in or about a factory, shop, hotel, house or other place in any capacity entailing the care of children or the handling of food or utensils intended for consumption or use by any other person.

This section also penalized employers who knowingly allowed persons with venereal diseases to remain in employment. Section 52(3) of the Act authorized the compulsory medical examination of inhabitants in areas where venereal disease was believed to be prevalent, stating that "any person who refuses to comply with such order or with any lawful instructions shall be guilty of an offence."[38] And finally, the last section of the Act, section 54, attempted to stave off criticism by stating that the colonial authorities would see to it that female practitioners would examine female patients when possible.

But chronic resistance among the various settler institutions against taking any responsibility for the implementations of the amended Act surfaced again. The Chamber of Mines found fault with this legislation which they felt was too burdensome upon employers, felt that pass officers should bear more of the responsibility. But, since African women were not issued passes, they had to be addressed separately. The Chamber of Mines resolved that "no native female servant be allowed to accept a post as general servant, housemaid, nurse or children's attendant except she be in possession of a clean bill of health signed periodically by a suitable medical attendant."[39]

This takes us back to the 1928 Conference at which Dr. Fleming and others discussed the issue of how best to institute a system of systematic medical surveillance which would effectively tackle the venereal disease problem.[40] The issue was again couched, however, because of the fear that an aggressive policy of compulsory examinations would potentially net "respectable people" and be politically inopportune.

Thus, more years passed and in the early 1930s, Mr. Collier, Superintendent of the Bulawayo Native Location, complained that there was no means of controlling the African women and girls who constantly drifted onto the Location. He estimated that in 1931 alone, 135 "girls" arrived in the location. He and his African police force sent the women away, but they simply returned and there was little that the Superintendent could do about it as women were not covered under the pass regulations. Thus, Collier and other Location and compound superintendents instituted informal policies such as sporadic raids whereby "unmarried native women" were rounded up and examined by "a coloured nurse." Each month, some fifteen to twenty women were sent to the hospital for treatment, and if one is to believe Collier, the "women [did] not object to this."[41]

Of course, there is absolutely no reason to believe Collier. Whether or not "native women" objected to these exams is certainly not something that Collier was in a position to judge. In fact, contradictory evidence abounds. Indeed, there was a history of resistance from organizations like the Rhodesia Bantu Voters Association's Women's League. One of the League's most outspoken members, Martha Ngano, even defied the colonial authorities to have their women compulsorily examined and let her know how they felt.[42] The colonizers did not take Mrs. Ngano up on her offer, but they did maintain a general reluctance to subject so-called "respectable native women" to the exams. The non-respectable African women, however, the "stray women," the illegal and marginal within colonial urban spaces, had few advocates.

During the 1930s and 1940s, the situation of non-wage laboring African town dwellers grew in precariousness as they, along with their rural, non-wage laboring compatriots, felt the burden of legislation passed during the Depression years, legislation which sought to buffer the economic strength of the European settler population and, as Robin Palmer has put it,"divide the country into non-competing castes." (Palmer 1977).

Following World War II, however, the settler government once again decided to reconsider its Native Policy due to the growing African and European urban populations, the rise in secondary manufacture and the consequent desires of the colonial state and colonial capital to stabilize the African wage labor force. Tighter controls were placed on the urban African population in general and, what is more, African women became more formally incorporated into the colony's influx control discourse. When Bulawayo was declared a proclaimed area under the Native Urban Areas Act in 1949, all African women "not in employment or seeking work," except those who were wives, were required to submit to a venereal disease exam. Thus, unlike the Public Health Act of 1925 which only applied to African women employees and work-seekers, this legislation netted the "informal sector" women as well.[43] All but married African women were required to obtain passes to verify that they were, among other things, not suffering from a venereal or other contractible disease, and that the pass officer did not suspect them of attempting to evade parental authority.

By the late and post World War II period, the colonial authorities were in a state of high anxiety about what they labeled the "urban African problem." In 1943, The Howman Report described how appalling the living condition of the urban Africans were, and warned of the disastrous effects that such disregard for their comfort was having upon their industrial performance. By way of solution, the Commission suggested a more family friendly Native policy, noting that African wives played a major productive role in the stabilization and health of the industrial workforce.[44] Another report sponsored by the Southern Rhodesian Government was conducted in 1946 by a member of the Native Welfare Association, Percy Ibbotson. Ibbotson's report concurred with Howman's concerning the need to accommodate African marriage and family life in the urban areas (see Ibbotson 1946). But while the grass may have looked greener for married and thus "respectable" African women, pathologization and medical policing of the unmarried through compulsory venereal disease examinations continued unabated.

THE WILLCOX REPORT

In 1949, the colonial authorities appointed a respected South African venereologist, R.R. Willcox, to conduct a formal survey on venereal disease among Southern Rhodesia's African population (see Willcox 1949). Willcox's report is an interesting document as it very clearly illustrates how, in his mind and in the minds of many of his peers within the fields of colonial medicine and public health, the African patient really did become the disease. He referred to prostitutes who plied their trade near the Zambian border as "the venereal filter," and to prostitutes in general as a "reservoir of infection." He complained vociferously about the "girls on the move [who] frequent the road camps and infect the transport drivers while in transit" (Willcox 1949:46).

Willcox's solutions were draconian. Not satisfied with the policy of compulsory exams on the compounds and urban Locations and for those seeking employment already in place, Willcox sought an even more all-encompassing solution. For instance, he believed that raids on the various urban sites should be better coordinated ventures to assure the maximum benefit, e.g., to net as many of the targeted human pathogens as possible. In addition, Willcox suggested that the authorities take advantage of the increasingly numerous opportunities to bring African women under the "official eye," through vagrancy and trespassing ordinances, to compulsorily examine them.

BACK TO THE PRESENT

While Mr. Collier of the Bulawayo Location stated that African women did not mind these examinations, one has reason to believe that they did. The problem is, it is extremely difficult to recover the voices of these women as they were so infrequently recorded. Thus we often only "hear" from African women through their feet, as they moved from place to place. However, it is probable that their day to day attitudes were those of resignation. According to Mary Ncube who was a sadza maker at the Mashumba Beer Garden in Mzilikazi African township when I visited in 1991, and who had lived at Makokoba (the old Bulawayo Location) in the 1950s, poor and working class women called these screening procedures, "Town Pass" examinations. And, according to Mrs. Ncube, whether or not they objected to the exams was quite besides the point. The general philosophy was: When in the white man's town, one does what the white man says.[45]

Mrs. Takawire who lived in Shabani Asbestos Mine compounds in the late 1940s, described the procedure to me. According to Mrs. Takawere, both married and single women were examined upon entry. They were led into public showers and instructed to remove their undergarments, lie on the concrete floor and open their legs by a Colored "nursing" staff. The women called this procedure *Chibeuru* which means to forcefully and rudely open something. While many found it humiliating, they had very little alternative if they wanted to maintain access to the economic and other opportunities found in the towns and compounds. Mrs. Takawire found it particularly insulting that, during the periodic raids conducted by the compound's African police, the men would walk through the compounds yelling: " *Chibeura, Chibeura, madzimai* (all mothers) *Chibeuru.*"[46]

The last piece of information that Mrs. Takawire shared with me and my interpreter was the following encounter. Mrs. Takawire went back to Shabani, now Zvishavane township, a few years after independence was won in 1980. She went back to visit family members who had remained there after she, her husband and children had moved to Harare. By chance, she ran into a woman who she had not seen in many years, a woman who had been one of the Coloured "nurses." The woman told Mrs. Takawire that she was no longer a "nurse." Apparently, the compulsory examinations were discontinued at Shabani sometime before independence. The woman described how she and the other "nurses" were each given a pair of gum boots and a mop and sent to clean the municipal toilets. The discomfiting laughter which followed this story spoke volumes to what African women thought of these examinations and generally about how they experienced their ranking within colonial spatial, social and ideological order. Before sharing this story and the other disclosure to me and my research assistant, Elizabeth Ncube, Mrs. Takawire sent the children and husbands out of the room and changed the food of the women left behind to a coarser grain, a kind of sandy green and curdled milk. The creation of this almost ritualized atmosphere is also indicative of the subjective meaning of these exams. While the women's humiliation was public, their memories, the space in which they will remember Chibeura, is private.

CONCLUSIONS

In the introduction of this paper I spoke of the contemporary ranking of African women within the post-colonial order as reflected in the intersecting discourses of public health and public order. The continuities apparent betweem the intersecting colonial and post-colonial discourses on gender, space and disease, point to the necessity of examining the ways in which power was exercised over the bodies of black women and how they experienced this power; of exploring how colonial attitudes vis-a-vis African women often reinforced or were reinforced by African patriarchal attitudes and through such an analysis, gain insight into why these stereotypes remain today.

I argue that colonial anti-venereal disease campaigns were expressions of both colonial/race and patriarchal/gender power. Furthermore, I explore the role of space in the making of objects of colonial public health discourse. In other words, while all African women may have been viewed as abnormal from the standpoint of the colonizer self, it generally took other factors associated with space and mobility for them to become public health menaces. Like pathogenic agents in general, they are only menacing when they spread. Thus I have found Dr. Fleming's term, "stray women" a useful metaphor for the African female in colonial public health discourse.

Of course, another side of this equation, one that the colonial authorities would not act upon and dared not speak about, was the fact that the major population of concern was the European population and, while African women were not a major employee group, they were certainly objects of European male desire and thus, in keeping with the notion that women transmit STDs, European males were perhaps unduly concerned with the danger potential of African women in the urban areas and most invested in inspecting them genitally.

While the compulsory exams have been discontinued in post-colonial Zimbabwe, the association of single, mobile African women with disease has not. The colonial face has receded, while the patriarchal face has come to the fore. The late twentieth century versions of the the Loyal Matabele Patriotic Society and the African Chrisians at the Falcon mine are now in power. And, while single African women are no longer represented as the venereal filters sapping away at colonial capitalist efficiency, they are represented as angels of death in the age of HIV/AIDS.

NOTES

1. See, for example, *The Herald:* "Police Image Discredited," 12/4/83; "Innocent Blitz Victims Freed," 11/28/83; "Prostitution and arrests," 1/28/83; "84 Women Held in Gwanda as Blitz Continues," 11/21/83; "Police Launch Massive Clean-Up before CHOGM" and "Women Criticize Police Operation," 6/14/91; "Don't Keep Street Safe Only for CHOGM," 6/15/91.
2. For a review of these campaigns see Susie Jacobs and Tracy Howard (1987:42).
3. I am indebted to Teresa Barnes, who drew this analogy in a paper entitled "Differential Class Experiences amongst African Women in Colonial Harare," Conference on Women & Gender in Southern Africa, University of Natal, Durban, January 30 through February 2, 1991.
4. See, for example, Never Gadaga, "AIDS: What Others Say," *Sunday Mail,* 9/15/1991. Note, the "others" that Gadaga referred to are the single mothers that he interviewed for the article.
5. As of October 1991, this poster could still be seen in the library at the University of Zimbabwe Medical School.
6. Cartoon by Stephan Mazere in *The Herald,* 2/18/92. Examples of articles and editorials which scapegoat women as the spreader HIV incude a series of articles written by Never Gadaga: "AIDS: What Others Say," *The Sunday Mail,* 9/15/91; "Anatomy of AIDS in Mashonaland," *The Sunday Mail,* 9/8/91.
7. According to an article by Mary Bassett and Marvelous Maloy 1991, African mothers were seen by the international epidemiologists as "contaminated vessels bearing diseased babies."
8. It is unclear how long this appellation has been in use. Whether this concept is a product of European public health policies or whether it was an indigenous African construct is not known. According to Michael Gelfand, a very prolific white doctor in Southern Rhodesia, African men described STDs in this way at least by the early 1940s. See Gelfand 1943. Lewis Wall discusses

how groups like the Hausa of northern Nigeria refer to venereal diseases in a similar fashion. See Wall 1988:186.

9. See National Archives of Zimbabwe (NAZ) S1173/220. Minutes from the Conference on Venereal Diseases, Bulawayo, October 6, 1928.

10. See NAZ S1173/220. Colonial Secretary, May 6, 1929. Re: Anti-Venereal Clinics.

11. These comments were made later in Willcox 1949. I discuss the Wilcox report in more detail below.

12. I am thinking here of the ways in which "the Hottentot Venus" and other Khoisan woman were represented by Western science in the first half of the nineteenth century. See, for example, the representation of Saartjie Baartman by Georges Cuvier in his autopsy of her. Cuvier likens Baartman to an orangutan. See Georges Cuvier 1817.

13. See Peaden's (1970:624-625) discussion of this and similar colonial campaigns among the Shona.

14. See Fanon 1967:35-67. Note that I do not adhere to Fanon's argument concerning the symbolism of the veil.

15. See *The Rhodesia Herald*, March 1, 1902.

16. See Bhebe's (1979:123) discussion of the ferocity with which a Father Prestage of the Jesuit mission station at Empandeni and other missionaries, battled against the female practitioners of cults like the Shumba cult of the Kalanga. The missionaries described the women as "hags," beat them with *sjambocks* (whips) and threatened them with expulsion from the mission station.

17. See NAZ SRG/410, Native Affairs Committee, 1910-1911.

18. Needless to say, it was a very self-interested about-face, necessary for paving the way for a de-emphasizing of the "emancipatory" role that the new colonial order had previously attributed to its interactions with and about African women and girls.

19. See NAZ S138/150, Native Commissioner of Hartley to Superintendent of Natives, Fort Victoria, March 26, 1924; Native Commissioner, Sinoia to Superintendent of Natives, Salisbury, February 23, 1924.

20. This concept of "daily reproduction" is developed in Luise White 1983.

21. There is a growing body of literature on the independent urban migration of African women and girl, and the patriarchal anxieties which this unleashed. The strongest published works on the phenomenon in Southern Rhodesia from the 1920s through the 1940s are: Barnes 1992; Schmidt 1990; and Jeater 1993: chap 9.

22. For a good discussion of the European war on African agricultural competition see Palmer 1977:195-230. For a good discussion of the impact of these changes on African women specifically, see Schmidt 1992:chap 3.

23. For a detailed discussion of these acts and their impact, see Phimister 1988.

24. See NAZ S235/394, "Commission of Inquiry on the Control and Welfare of the Native Population of Bulawayo," 1930, p.3; and Ibbotson 1946:74.

25. This increase was due, in part, to the post-World War II increase in the European population which led to an increase demand of African labor in

secondary industries and households and the growing willingness to employ African women.

26. See S.R., Report of the Chief Native Commissioner, 1932, p. 1.
27. See S.R., Report of the Chief Native Commissioner, 1932, p. 2.
28. See NAZ S235/594, Native Domestic Labor Committee Evidence, 1932.
29. A good discussion of this transformation is found in Humphries 1988. Also see Kunzel 1993 for an examination of a similar transformation in the United States.
30. The following authors have discussed the pathologization of female sexual assertiveness and indiscretion: Kunzel 1993; Humphries 1988; Ussher 1991:chaps 4 & 5; Showalter 1985:chap. 8.
31. See S. R., Report of the Medical Director and Principal Medical Officer of the British South Africa Police, 1901, pp. 4,5.
32. S.R., Report on the Public Health, 1912.
33. S.R., Report on the Public Health, 1914.
34. NAZ H2/9/2, Town Clerk's Office, Salisbury to the Administrator, May 11, 1917.
35. NAZ H 2/9/2, Town Clerk's Office, Bulawayo to Medical Director, Salisbury, September 7, 1920.
36. NAZ A 3/12/7-10, "Appeal from the Leaders of the Christian Mission at work at Falcon Mine and the Township of Umvuma" to Medical Director, April 21, 1921.
37. S.R., Legislative Council Debates, May 30, 1923.
38. These sections of the Act remained unaltered until 1991 when they were rewritten so as to be less punitive and more educative. Timothy Stamps, the Minister of Health in 1991, stated that "We do not achieve anything by punishing people suffering rom VD, because some of them contract the disease innocently, and do not deserve to be punished for it." "Ministry sets up body to rewrite Public Health Act," *The Herald,* Friday, August 18, 1991.
39. See NAZ S241/531, "Anti-Venereal Disease Clinics in Urban Areas," 1929.
40. See NAZ S241/531, Dr. Andrew M. Fleming to Colonial Secretary, May 6, 1929.
41. See NAZ S235/594, Native Domestic Labor Committee, 1932.
42. See NAZ S138/37, Superintendent of Central Investigation Department, Bulawayo, to Native Commission, Bulawayo. May 17, 1925.
43. See NAZ S51/5. Extracts from the Mayor's Minutes, Salisbury, 1944-1952.
44. S.R., "Report of the Select Committee to Investigate Urban Conditions in Southern Rhodesia (Howman Report)" (Salisbury: Government Printer, 1943).
45. Interview with Mrs. N. Ncube, Mashumba Beer Garden, July 23, 1991.
46. Interview with "Mrs. Takwarire," Harare, Zimbabwe. July 16, 1991.

REFRENCES

Barnes, Teresa. "Differential Class Experiences amongst African Women in Colonial Harare." Paper presented at the Conference on Women & Gender in
Southern Africa, University of Natal, Durban, January 30 through February
2, 1991.

Barnes, Theresa. 1992. "The Fight for Control of African's Women's Mobility in
Colonial Zimbabwe, 1900-1939." *Signs* 17, 3 (1992):586-608.

Basset, Mary, and M. Maloy. "Women and AIDS in Zimbabwe, the Making of an
Epidemic." *International Journal of Health Services* 21, 1 (1991).

Bhebe, Ngwabi. *Christianity and Traditional Religion in Western Zimbabwe.*
London: Longman, 1979.

Cuvier, Georges. "Summary of Observations Made on the Corpse of a Woman
Known in Paris and London by the Name of the Hottentot Venus." *Memoires
du Museum d'histoire Naturelle* III (1817).

Fanon, Frantz. *A Dying Colonialism.* New York: Grove Press, 1967.

Gadaga, Never. "Anatomy of AIDS in Mashonaland." *Sunday Mail* September 8,
1991.

Gadaga, Never. "AIDS: What Others Say." *Sunday Mail* September 15, 1991.

Gelfand, Michael. *The Sick African.* Cape Town: Juta and Co., 1943

Gilman, Sander. *Difference and Pathology: Stereotypes of Sexuality, Race and
Madness.* Ithaca: Cornell University Press, 1985.

Herald, The. "Police Image Discredited." December 4, 1983.

Herald, The. "Innocent Blitz Victims Freed." November 28, 1983.

Herald, The. "Prostitution and Arrests." January 1, 1983.

Herald, The. "84 Women Held in Gwanda as Blitz Continues." November 21,
1983.

Herald, The. "Police Launch Massive Clean-Up Before CHOGM." June 14, 1991.

Herald, The. "Women Criticize Police Operation." June 14, 1991.

Herald, The. "Don't Keep Street Safe Only for CHOGM." June 15, 1991.

Herald, The. "Ministry sets up body to rewrite Public Health Act." August 18,
1991

Humphries, Steven. *The Secret World of Sex.* London: Sidgewick & Jackson,
1988.

Ibbotson, Percy. "Report on a Survey of Urban African Conditions in Southern
Rhodesia." *Africa* 6, 2 (1946).

Jacobs, Susie, and Tracy Howard. "Women in Zimbabwe: Stated Policy and State
Action." In *Women, State and Ideology: Studies from Asia and Africa*, ed.
Haleh Afshar. London: MacMillan Press, 1987.

Jeater, Diane. "Marriage, Perversion and Power: The Construction of Moral Discourse in Soutern Rhodesia, 1890-1930." D. Phil. thesis, Oxford University,
1990.

Jeater, Diane. *Marriage, Perversion and Power: the Construction of Moral Discourse in Southern Rhodesia, 1894-1930.* Oxford: Carendon Press, 1993.

Kunzel, Regina. *Fallen Women, Problem Girls: Unmarried Mothers and the Professionalization of Social Work, 1890-1945*, 1993.

MacClintock, Anne. "Maidens, Maps and Mines: King Solomon's Mines and the Reinvention of Patriarchy in Colonial South Africa." In *Women and Gender in Southern Africa to 1945*, ed. Cheryl Walker. Cape Town: David Philip, 1990.

Palmer, Robin. *Land and Racial Domination in Rhodesia*. Berkeley: University of California Press, 1977.

Peaden, W. *Missionary Attitudes to Shona Culture, 1890-1923*. Salisbury: Mambo Books, 1970.

Phimister, Ian. *An Economic and Social History of Zimbabwe: Capital Accumulation and Class Struggle, 1890-1948*. New York: Longman, 1988.

Ranger, T. O. *The African Voice in Southern Rhodesian, 1898-1930*. Evanston: Northwestern University Press, 1970.

Reed, Cullen. *Report of the London Missionary Society*. Harare: Special Collections Library, University of Zimbabwe, 1903.

Rhodesia Herald. March 1, 1902.

Schmidt, Elizabeth. "Negotiated Spaces and Contested Terrain: Men, Women and the Law in Colonial Zimbabwe, 1890-1939." *Journal of Southern African Studies* 16, 4 (1990):622-648.

Schmidt, Elizabeth. *Peasants, Traders and Wives*. Portsmouth, NH: Heinemann, 1992.

Showalter, Elaine. *The Female Malady: Women, Madness and English Culture, 1830-1980*. London: Penguin Books, 1985.

Ussher, Jane M. *Women and Madness: Misogyny or Mental Illness*. Amherst: University of Massachusetts Press, 1991.

van Onselen, Charles. *Chibaro*. London: Pluto Press, 1977.

Vaughan, Megan. *Curing Their Ills: Colonial Power and African Illness*. Stanford: University of California Press, 1991.

Wall, Lewis. *Hausa Medicine: Illness and Well-being in a West African Culture*. Durham, NC: Duke University Press, 1988.

Willcox, R. R. *Report on Venereal Diseases, Survey of the African in Southern Rhodesia*. Salisbury: Government Printer, 1949.

White, Luise. "The Colonial State and an African Petty Bourgeoisie." In *Struggle for the City*, ed. Frederick Cooper. London: Sage, 1983.

III
NARRATING AND
IMAGINING SPACES

ART AS TIME-LINES:

SACRAL REPRESENTATION IN

FAMILY SPACES

NKIRU NZEGWU*

INTRODUCTION

THIS PAPER BRINGS TOGETHER STRANDS OF PHILOSOPHY AND modes of African representation to explore the intersecting categories of time, space and reality in the creative expressions of African artists. Taking family spaces as points of departure, I focus on the complex idea of time-lines that family memorials and artists' representation of sacral objects reveal about how we inhabit spaces, inscribe values to such spaces, and carry the articulated systems within us. Drawing attention to the philosophical ideas behind these memorials and artistic forms, I trace the temporal lines these objects chart in expanding our spatio-temporal notion of reality, and in linking our experiential present to the past, future, and the afterlife. The idea of objects as "time-lines" speaks to the imaginative ways forms of representation code information and knowledge, and allude to the existence of different spheres of life. To better describe our situatedness in the realms of the physical, the mental, and the pneumatic, I use the terms "body-space," "ideational space," and "spirit-space" to capture the different conditions and qualities of the three environments, and to simultaneously complicate and enrich our understanding of *uwa* (universe). "Body-space" refers to the physical environment of our everyday pattern of action and social interaction; "ideational space" refers to the non-tangible mental realm of thoughts, ideas and concepts; while "spirit-space" refers to *mmuo* or the pneumatic realm of the spirit where ancestor figures, supernatural beings and entities are held to dwell.

The distinguishing feature of these three spaces is that they are mutually permeable and interpenetrable, hence none is "behind" or "under" or "above" the other. Additionally, the three spaces may, but need not, occupy the same spatial location, since they are not necessarily coextensive. For example, an ideational system in which thought processes occur may occupy the same spatial location as physical bodies and pneumatic entities but would still retain its specific temporality. It is important to state that the relationship between the three spheres is not epiphenomenal since they possess the power to impact and affect each other. According to Onitsha metaphysical scheme that informs the standpoint of this paper, though *oge mmuo* (spirit-time) is different from *oge madu* (human-time that encompasses body-space), the two spaces are interconnected through the ideational-space, and sometimes impact on each other. Thus, on this picture, *uwa* or the universe is a multiplicity of intersecting spatial spheres with different conditions of temporality, constantly shifting and changing, and without a permanently fixed or static location.

By contrast, in the everyday reality of the typical Western frame of reference, time and space are conceptualized as three dimensional, physical reality. Within this reality, there are private and public spaces: geographical and architectural spaces are represented as being in the public domain, the psychological, symbolical and spiritual spaces are relegated to the private domain, but the idea of a spiritual realm is poorly articulated and developed. Contrapositively, in the Onitsha intellectual scheme, notions of the spiritual are fully developed and are a constitutive part of the everyday explanatory model. As a result, notions of publicity and privacy are radically altered with new theoretical meaning. All objects in their respective spaces are publicly accessible subjects, in principle. This means that objects in ideational-space and spirit-space are accessible in much the same way objects in body-space are accessible. Nothing can remain inherently private or hidden. Hence it is logically possible for two people to apprehend and think the same idea in ideational-space; they can also apprehend the same entity in spirit-space, provided they have learned the processes of thinking and perceiving under these spatio-temporal conditions.

Disciplinarily, because reality is empirically conceptualized in analytic philosophical tradition as a unitary whole with fixed essences,[1] it is possible to miss the way people shift "in and out" of space and time as they think their thoughts, and live their lives. This occurs because of the illusion of permanence and uniformity that underpins the notion of reality in European philosophy, compels scholars to view reality in one definite way, and to reject the idea that there are variable conditions of time and states of being. In fact seduced by the analytic relation of permanence and uniformity inherent in the idea of three dimensional reality, most people ignore the way in which this view of reality is fundamentally a fictive construction, an abstraction that yields a specific explanation about the world. However, if we drastically slowed down the hermeneutic reel-of-life, it is possible to examine our everyday process of life, and observe our oscillations between the discontinuous conditions of the body-space, ideational-space, and spirit-space.

Minimally, three questions arise in any serious discussion of time and space. Specifically, how do we know that time exists and that it extends beyond our actual perception of them? What is the nature of the connection between the three delineated spaces: the physical realm (body space), the mental realm (ideational space), and *mmuo*, the pneumatic realm (spirit space)? What do these three states tell us about ourselves?

In this essay I argue that certain representational forms that arise in family spaces function as temporal pathways to an expanded notion of reality. Part one is divided into two sections. In its first section, I slow down the hermeneutic reel-of-life and draw attention to the shifting time frames and spatial zones in which we live and the web of family relationships that initiate the creation of memorials and representation of sacred forms; and in the second section, I examine the skeptical implication of this methodology and its negative impact on identity. In part two, I examine an aspect of the views of the Beninoise philosopher, Paulin Hountondji, on knowledge production in Africa and argue that a recovery of Africa's indigenous knowledge must recognize the challenge it poses for the conventionalized view of reality that prevails in philosophy. And in the third part, I deal with the significance of sacral representation as time-lines, and the role they play in family-identity and family-cohesiveness within an expanded notion of space and reality. The last part focuses on the impact of these forms of representation on contemporary artists.

PASSING THROUGH SPATIO-TEMPORAL FRAMES

In the evening of Wednesday February 2, 1994 I arrived at Murtala Muhammed Airport Lagos to begin a major research project on Yoruba arts and aesthetics. Moving along the immigration line and circumspectly checking my environment to anticipate unusual activities, I shifted to another mode of consciousness; in which I was physically on the line but ideationally absent.

While in Nigeria, I planned to conclude my five-year research on Nigeria's internationally renowned artist, Odinigwe Ben Enwonwu, whom I had learned was seriously ill and may not have very long to live. Before anything happened to him, it was imperative that I probe the underlying rationale and significance of his *Agbogo mmuo* and *Ogolo* series, and as far as possible elucidate the deeper mysteries associated with these "spirit" forms. As a non-initiated woman in *mmuo* mysteries,[2] I was not supposed to know the secrets of *mmuo* (spirits). Thus the challenge I faced was how to get him to discuss the matter knowing that he knew that to speak about such matters with a non-initiate would violate his oath of secrecy.

Discussions with Enwonwu would center on what his rationale were for taking *mmuo* as a basis of creative expression. Such insight would be important if I am to write convincingly about what the *Agbogo mmuo* and *Ogolo* meant to him. For over forty years, he had diligently sketched and painted these spirit forms with such regularity that some of his ardent critics had claimed that he must have lost his imaginative vision. From my research perspective, however, it was unimportant that he may be in a creative rut. What was important was for him to elaborate on the values, ideas or messages to which he sometimes alluded when confronted with his near obsessive preoccupation with the forms of *Agbogo mmuo* and *Ogolo*.

I recalled intriguing comments that his brother's funeral had given him a whole new perspective from which to understand *Agbogo mmuo*. A close study of his work from 1987, when his brother Ike Francis Enwonwu died, and 1993, when he grew too ill to paint, reveal a profusion of fully developed character studies of *Ogolo* and *Agbogo mmuo*. Caught in various dynamic poses his forms pulsated with life and motion. *Ogolo Metamorphosis* (1990) depicts an *ogolo* in a powerful spectacular leap, heroically separating into two distinct parts amidst the clouds, in a reproductive rite of continuity. A transcendent twin *ogolo* was emerging from the frontal body of the *ogolo* with its back to the viewer. Clearly, Enwonwu's consuming interest in these forms suggest that something quite enigmatic and compelling was at stake.

Randomly, in an associative process, I wandered off to the works of Sokari Douglas Camp. I recalled the central enigma in her 1988 exhibition at the National Museum of African Art in Washington D.C. Her large welded metal construction *Church Ede (Decorated Bed for Christian Wake)* (1984), was a memorial tribute to her father, simultaneously representing an artistic exploration of Kalabari funeral rites and the ritual of transcendence and transfiguration. I'd always wondered why her creative energy and inspirational insight coalesced on the funeral bed, resulting in an intricately constructed large steel four-poster bed. No doubt, this grand steel bed referenced Kalabari ceremonial brass beds on which the death-stilled body of a transcending spirit is usually laid in state. Made out of artfully placed metal strips, evocative of the strips on *duein fubara* (Kalabari ancestral screens), the steel bed held the suggested outline of Sokari's absent father. On either side of the bed, two female figures devotionally sketched the pathway of the receding spirit as they solicitously fanned the stiffened body, whisking away all obtrusive flies.

Sokari had touchingly personalized her memorial tribute by incorporating a motorized part that simulates the swirling motion of handkerchiefs and fly whisks which daughters typically use to fan the deceased, and by so doing affirm their filial relationship to the deceased. It was unclear whether Douglas Camp was consciously using the materials of body-space to give physicality to her lament in ideational-space for a father who now exists in spirit-space. It seemed to me that in so far as Sokari, the daughter, was concerned with sketching out her father's ancestralized state, she was intuitively responding to the maxim "Life never dies, it simply transforms."

Madam this way..Passport.

Running the gauntlet officials at the arrival lounge at the airport of immigration and custom, some of whom were extorting "dash" (gift), it was clear that my entire research was going to be a tough job to pull off. First of all, the multiple locations which the research on Yoruba art and aesthetics called for me to visit were far removed from the Ikoyi residence of Enwonwu. As if this logistical problem were not enough, I wondered whether my uncle who had died in late December had been buried. If not, I knew I was in trouble, since I would have to radically alter my plans. My worst fears were confirmed when my brother sardonically greeted me at the airport with the following words: "Perfect timing! Akunne is going to be buried in two days time. We really should leave for Onitsha tomorrow."

Akunne Uwechia was my father's eldest full brother, by virtue of which position he was the "big father" (*nnukwu nna*). As the first child of my father, it was incumbent on me as the *ada* (first daughter) to organize my deceased father's unit so that it could play its rightful role in the unfolding ritual drama within the wider lineage. Thus, right from the airport, I had less than twenty-four hours to perform two major mental switches, which involved temporally and spatially relocating myself into the conceptual space of Onitsha. It was from there that I had to begin preparing for the task at hand. The first switch took me out of the existential framework of life in upstate New York to the social scheme of Lagos. After being filled in on the woeful social and political events of Nigeria, the second switch had to be thrown to relocate me from the Lagos world-scheme to the ritual-cum-ceremonial framework of Onitsha funeral obsequies.

Crossing time frames, entailed re-membering histories, shifting spatial locations, re-situating myself in appropriate temporal spaces, listening to stories and narratives. In the process of crossing time frames, I recalled and called forth different facets of well-worn selves that had been ignored and forgotten, yet were etched into the many crevasses of memory that glued together my identity. The complex process of relocation and change forced to attention the way in which we carry our histories. The rite of conversing and trading *our* stories triggers metamorphic changes that more firmly situates an individual within the social matrix of the everyday "body-space" of his or her culture. The mental changes I was undergoing helped me to inhabit the space more securely by displacing my Americanized professional veneer for my Onitsha cultural identity. Switching the psychological "skins" of my numerous identity transmutations enabled me to "step out" of the commodified efficiency time mode of the American cultural scheme in which a paid job was more important than family obligation. In "stepping out" of that condition of temporality, I "stepped into" a culturally validated temporal space in which family-connectedness and family obligations constituted the central basis of time-allocation, time-management, and personal identity.

Most assuredly, this process of "stepping in" and "stepping out" invokes the manner in which at the transfiguring moment of death, we permanently step out of the conditions of the everyday three dimensional reality, and into the pneumatic *mmuo* conditions of spirit-space and time.

SKEPTICAL THRUST OF SPATIAL SHIFTS

Although exceedingly mechanical, the preceding description of a self as extended in time and space, allows us to see the different means and modes by which humans traverse reality, in the process shifting from one temporal state to the next. But herein lies a paradox. If selves are extended in time, and each new state carries with it a different set of value expectations, would this not imply that there is no fixed identity and no underlying essence at the center of our identity. As the eighteenth century British philosopher, David Hume once puzzled over, if experience is a series of fleeting impressions that are spatio-temporally extended, where is the "self" that gives unity and coherence to these experiences? Succinctly put, how is personal identity constructed under a theory of experience that reduces knowledge to impressions in a stream of consciousness? How is the idea of a self, the owner to which these stream of impressions belong, to be understood?

The theoretical problem attendant to conceptually slowing down the hermeneutic reel-of-life is that we run the risk of discovering that there are no overarching essential features or traits to which personal identity hangs.

Experience becomes a constant stream of fleeting impressions or perceptual stimuli that subverts our idea of self. This skeptical problem, a slightly different variation of Zeno's paradox of change, exploits the seemingly discontinuous character of changing frames of experiences to launch a skeptical assault on personal identity. Consider that if life consists of an infinite series of changing frames of experiences, there is no one enduring event that is spatially extended in time or remains the same to assign unity to these experiences. Thus, on what basis can the existence of an enduring entity be postulated to give unity and coherence to our experiences?

Although it seems that it does, but switching from time-frame to time-frame, and questioning the corresponding conditions associated with each frame in the reel of life does not subvert the unitary character of the self or personal identity. We remain the same person with enduring characteristics, values, experiences, motivating narratives even as we examine what occurred in changing our experiences, values, and narratives. Within the framework of the intersecting conditions of time and space that is spatio-temporally extended, we selectively add to, organize, and reorganize our experiences by reference to what we privilege as meaningful. Our personal identity (constitutive of the stock of imaginative narratives, values and experiences through time) remains basically the same even as we continue to evolve and develop through life. Our ability to remain the same person comes from the fact that the enduring narratives of our lives are equally extended in time and space, and are held together by the glue of memory. Thus, we (meaning, the characteristics, enduring values, imaginative narratives that guide us) undergo each new experience by injecting newly acquired stories into the experiential frame where they are mixed with older experiences to produce new coagulates.

What the skeptical thrust of this extension of self in space plays up is the transformational impact of change that problematizes and contests the existence of real essences. In *Impossible Dreams* (1995), Susan Babbitt offers an epistemological argument that convincingly undermines the legitimacy of the anti-foundational thesis that sequential change implies that there is no fixed essences. Her argument rests on the contention that a commitment to the idea of real essences does not automatically imply "a commitment to the idea of fixed, eternal essences that separate one group from another with sharp discontinuity" (Babbitt 1996:145-146). The fact that something is temporarily extended and endures over time does not mean that what is extended is fixed and unchanging. A self or an identity extends over time, with new experiences informing the constitutive character of self identity. But this does not imply that identity is dissolved. As she puts it: "Indeed if knowledge claims are contingent upon the emergence or bringing about of the right sorts of theoretical and practical transitions, there is no reason to expect that the identification of real essences should result in precise sets of categories with clear boundaries and fixed content" (146). The thrust of Babbitt's argument is that "an opposition to a particular conception of justification, [in]...which standards and concepts are justifiable a priori and...precludes the proper appreciation of difference" (152), does not provide adequate grounds for denying that there are real essences or an enduring identity.

An understanding of the hermeneutical sequences of spatio-temporal extensions and shifts in frames of identity is useful for seeing that interspatial shifts need not necessarily be conceived of as involving geographical displacement. The spatio-temporal relations of specific spaces enter into the structure of what is apprehended in those environments. The fact that spatial and temporal shifts can occur without physically displacing a body from a specific location, as occurs under meditation and divining states, forcefully highlights the many possible ways in which trans-spatial communication and contact occurs between physical, mental and pneumatic states. From the standpoint of physical body-space reality, erstwhile impenetrable barriers and chasms between the physical world or body-space, the mental world or ideational-space, and the pneumatic world or spirit-space assume a different quality when conceptualized on a framework that recognizes the complex, extensively permeable nature of the universe.

In consciously recognizing the occurrence of interspatial shifts and becoming more adept in inter-spatial interaction, we find that the conditions of *mmuo* or pneumatic space which previously had seemed incomprehensible and impenetrable become intelligible and passable as explanatory paradigms emerge to offer grounds of openings. In Onitsha cultural logic, for example, an endless cycle of coming and going in the nexus of family is witnessed between the body-space and spirit-space and are socially highlighted. This permeability gives spirit-space a definite kind of concreteness and familiarity by treating it as a natural extension of the physical realm. The cycle of birth and death of which the death of Akunne Uwechia is one aspect of the cycle, is seen as a normal passage between body-space and spirit-space, in which the incarnate spirits of his grandchildren emerged, and in which he had once resided prior to his incarnation. Following his death as an initiated elder, he is seen to have passed into the state of *ndi ichie* or ancestor. Most significant, in this transformation into an *ndi ichie* is the idea of a passage through the outermost boundary of our three-dimensional constitution of body-space into *ani mmuo* or spirit-space, that may best be described as the fourth dimensional state of reality.

LISTENING CLOSELY, INTERROGATING
THE REALITY OF SCIENCE

The problem Africans have consistently faced in the study of our cultural reality and episteme is that the theoretical investigations of the latter have routinely been driven by the positivistic imperatives of European and European American structures of knowledge. In invidious imperializing moves, African pneumatic concepts and methodological moves that do not conform to the positivistic standards of validation and verification are summarily dismissed as erroneous and primitive. This imperious attitude, fostered by the intuitive belief of European and European American scholars that African culture is primitive, has become the dominant theoretical standpoint for most Africanists' investigations of Africa's material culture. As a result, the central logic of various African cultures are irrationalized before the "superior" rationality and value system of Europe and the United States. Not only has this posture of arrogance shaped knowledge production about Africa, it has enthroned a mode of epistemic interpretation that stymies understanding.

Generally, discussions about Africa's socio-cultural life proceeds by prefacing or highlighting the continent's economic and scientific backwardness, in the process, building up a conflicted wall of pressure which African scholars have to confront to prove that they know. Directly responding to this pressure in the Second Bashorun M.K.O. Abiola Distinguished Lecture at the African Studies Association, Hountondji deplores the scientific and technological failures in Africa, explaining that these shortcomings are a consequence of the subordinate way in which Africa's traditional knowledge has been integrated into the world-system of knowledge. In his view, this current state of scientific and technological underdevelopment parallels the early twentieth century integration of Africa's subsistence economies into the world capitalist market. As he sees it, the problem is not "from any original backwardness", as it is from the mode and character of integration (Hountondji 1995:2). At the end of his multipronged explanation Hountondji revisits what he takes to be the root of the problem and asks in evident exasperation: "Why is positive knowledge in Africa so often mingled with mythical beliefs and practices? Why does the 'traditional' healer always begin this [sic] cures by an invocation to gods, spirits and the ancestors and by all sorts of less intelligible incantations? Why not develop this knowledge for its own sake and rid the horizon of all these gods and goddesses"? (8).

Hountondji's frustration is certainly not new. It has been echoed by numerous Africans some of whom have indicted the backwardness of their people and the primitive state of their traditions as responsible for the European subjugation of the continent. It is to this well-known sentiment of cultural despair that Hountondji responds in answering his questions in ways that directly address and seek to correct past misinterpretations of Africa's traditional knowledge. He rejects Levy-Bruhl's patronizing thesis that this integration of gods, spirits, and ancestors with positive knowledge reflects a primitive mind unable to distinguish between the natural and the supernatural. By contrast, his explanation for the integration of positive knowledge with gods, spirits and ancestors accords with the views of scholars, like Eric Havelock in orature, who hypothesized that reference to "gods and goddesses" is a shorthand way by which people in oral structures of knowledge understand and theorize about abstract concepts (1991:24). Essentially in agreement with this position, Hountondji's argues that "the personification of basic categories" and "the mythical projection of configurations of the divination material into deities" are reducible to mnemotechnic devices (8). Although he does not go as far as Haverlock who claims that abstract reasoning exists only in a literate alphebetic context (1990:24),[3] Hountondji's position on "gods, spirits, and ancestors" coheres with Haverlock's views that personification of basic categories are features of information storage in contexts of memorization and recall.

Epistemologically, Hountondji's position also overlaps with that of Robin Horton, the English anthropologist, who views spirits in African traditional thought as attempted theoretical explanations (Horton 1982). On this framework of explanation, science is the marker of knowledge that maps out the true nature of reality. It is for this reason that Hountondji finds the traditional healer's references to "gods, spirits, and the ancestors" as unnecessary mythologizations that do not add anything positive to what we know. It seems that having found a perfectly "scientific" rationalization for the occurrence of these mythical entities in African thought, Hountondji is not prepared to entertain any further complication of this "scientific" (read, physicalist) picture with the presence of any unwarranted unverifiable entities. Thus, in trying to understand why the "traditional" healer always begins his cures "by an invocation to gods, spirits and the ancestors and by all sorts of *less intelligible incantations*" [emphasis mine], Hountondji failed to ask the following pertinent questions: What evidence is there that the "gods, spirits and the ancestors" are simply mnemonic devices, or tentative theoretical explanations of physical events in body-space reality? Why does he believe that the diviner's explanations are specifically limited to the body-space manifestation of a malady of an individual who exists in three different locations? What makes it so easy to privilege the physical imperatives of science and its body-space reality, and to devalue the pneumatic imperatives of spirit-space reality? Why does Hountondji believe that the pronouncements of traditional healers are not directed both to the physical and the pneumatic sides of life?

Evident in Hountondji's writing, and the other mentioned scholars, is a tacit hierarchical ranking of cultures and a conscious privileging of science. Though progressively positioned, Hountondji's assessment of the state of science in Africa reflects a settled view of it that is substantially informed by the imperatives of three dimensional space. Like all world-views, the logic and metaphysics of this three dimensional construction of space treats it as implicitly logical, fixed, predictable, and subject to comprehensible physical laws, that eliminates anything which is counterintuitive. Efficacious and predictive in some cases, this Newtonian conception of space and time loses its predictive power in some equally important cases. Its intuitive abstraction of space and time is primarily an abstraction, not an accurate description of reality, even though this hardly appears to be the case when its construction of reality is evaluated within its legitimizing principles.[4] But regardless of the plausibility of this physicalist view of science, and our commitment to its idea of absolute space, time and motion, this three dimensional reality must be subject to radical interrogation because of the inherent limitations of its explanatory myths, narratives and solutions. A critique of its physicalist imperatives require putting its ontological ethos under critical scrutiny, and seeing that the view of reality it offers is a theoretical abstraction that effectively transforms time and space into immutable categories with a propulsive force of their own.

In *Dangerous Currents: The State of Economics*, Lester C. Thurow gives an elaborate description of how economics "still rests on a behavioral assumption—rational utility maximization—that has long since been rejected by sociologists and psychologist who specialize in studying human behavior" (1983:216). The point of his example is that people not only construct models of interpretation that are based on erroneous abstraction, but that they end up living that reality too. The relevance of this insight to this argument is that our understanding of science in most cases still rest on the ordinate points mapped out by Isaac Newton that have been proven to entail an erroneous construction of reality. Even today, there is inadequate recognition, in most traditional philosophical circles, that the universe is not exhaustively defined or understood by the physicalist laws of three dimensional reality. Furthermore, there is inadequate appreciation that to speak of the universe as constitutive of events rather than points in absolute space is to speak of a relational network in which events are woven in an interconnected format. Under this different ontological condition, a different way of knowing prevails, since the old physicalist logic and metaphysics underpinning our definition of identity and logical relationships are radically transformed. In a language that sounds suspiciously similar to those used by some traditional healers, we learn that every event has "some bearing on everything else", and "everything is everywhere at all times"; for "every location involves an aspect of itself in every other location."[5] In the traditional healer's language and relational structure of explanation, it makes sense to use the familial concept of ancestors to speak of the ways in which the living are embodiments of ancestors at the same time that they are also aspects of future descendants. Thus, what may appear as the "irrational" postulations of traditional African healers become more intelligible when they are treated as epistemic claims, and the appropriate relational structure of interpretation is used to decode their articulations.

It is worthwhile to point out that Hountondji's evident neglect to seriously treat the "sorts of less intelligible incantations" of traditional healers comes from prejudging Africa's traditional cultures and their knowledge claims as primitive. Yet, most strongly reflected in this stance, is Hountondji's philosophical training and European biases. The fact that he neglected to question the idea that the basic structure of reality is exhaustively physical, reveals his theoretical commitment to a mode and manner of thinking that irrationalizes whatever deviates from it. Because of his acceptance of the immutability of this structure of reality, Hountondji fails to consider that the personification of basic categories may not entirely be reducible to mnemotechnic devices, but are coded capsules of knowledge that draw attention to the wider more expansive view of reality that conflicts with the arbitrarily narrow limits of the European conceptualization of space and time. Indeed, if for the moment, attributions of backwardness are set aside, it would become clearer that the language of "gods, spirits, and ancestors" is actually forcing a theoretical rethinking of the currently accepted limits and constitution of the world. Thus if Hountondji's injunction to African scholars to critically assess, test, update, and reappropriate Africa's ancestral heritage and creativity is to have revolutionary potential, then we must adopt a relevant framework of interpretation to understand the significance of the pneumatic concepts and ideas that are currently being dismissed as pre-theoretical and primitive. Also, we must work towards an epistemic break with the prevailing positivistic metaphysics and paradigm of science, so that a critical re-evaluation of the structure of reality can begin.

The critical issue at the heart of my argument is not that scientific knowledge *per se* is unimportant and irrelevant, but that the deployment of a specific conception of science and reality ignores the implicit nature of its own abstraction. In calling for a serious treatment of African ideas and concepts, it is important to call attention to this fallacy of misplaced criterion in which inappropriate yardstick is employed. This routinely occurs when scholars ignore the specificities of reality of their preferred model of explanation, and deploy that model in a differently constituted context. This sleight-of-hand trivializes important ideas of Africa's endogenous system which fails to conform to the physicalist criteria of evaluation. It is true that sometimes the underlying assumptions of technology and natural science many differ or conflict with pneumatic ideas, but this should not become the basis of rejection. After all, the reality defined by Newtonian physics, while useful, is also highly problematic, and it is not the *only* possible way of conceptualizing reality.

What is valuable about Hountondji's intervention is that it urges us to radically interrogate Africa's conceptual schemes as well as the celebrated paradigms of science and its initiating conditions. Conceptualizing the spatio-temporal conditions of reality as body-space and spirit-space enables us to see the many different interpretive possibilities and options available in understanding the spatial and temporal conditions of life in all their different manifestations. Since other models exist for interpreting reality, Hountondji must consider that nothing invalidates the healer's conceptualization of treatment as a healing of both the physical body and the pneumatic self. As the analysis in the following section makes clear, category personification may, in fact, be alluding to a view of reality that is better characterized by the relativity and quantum view of reality.

CONVERGENCE OF SPACE-TIME
CONTINUUM IN FAMILY SPACES

The climatic event of my uncle's funeral was the appearance of the venerable *mmuo ogonogo* (the tall spirit of the threshold/crossroad) to conduct the concluding part of the burial rites. This event is significant since it collapses the time-space continuum in ways that transforms our conception of death, and makes it a natural extension of life. Additionally, the appearance of the concretized manifest spirit is significant since it is a messenger, an inter-spatial traveler and custodian of the market site, where the world of humans (body-space) converge with the world of spirits (spirit-space). Known as *mmuo afia* (spirit of the market/crossroad), *mmuo ogonogo* prepares the deceased elder and initiate to encounter its fate by "seeing" in spirit-space. Prior to this rite, the feeble spirit of the departed is in a liminal state of indeterminacy, preparatory to its being born in spirit. Unable to comprehend what is happening, it remains umbilically tied to its discarded physical body until its formal birth into spirit-space is fully completed. Only with the process of *iwanye okpa n'anya*, a process of clarifying the vision with a drop of blood (from a chicken) into the eye, is the wraith of the deceased fully born into the reality of spirit-space and its visual impairment removed.[6] This clarifying process is the reverse process encountered in earthly birth, in which a baby begins to see only after wiping the blood from its eyes. Still feeble, the newly born spirit-elder locates the path that leads to its first resting stage in *obodo mmuo* (spirit land), where it awaits for the second funeral rites to open the doorway into the ancestors' realm.

As Basden reported in 1921, the resurrection ritual of the deceased in spirit was re-enacted as part of the second funeral obsequies. After the burial of *igbudu*, a "catafalque made out of white bamboo mat that is placed on four vertical sticks with white strips of cloth across it" (Bosah 1988:130):

> the *maw-afia* appear escorting the "spirit" of the dead man from his house beneath the floor of which his body lies buried. On his return to this world, the spirit walks slowly with tottering uncertain steps and muttering words with a feeble voice - his speech being disguised similarly to that of the *maw-afia*. The poor "spirit" is as yet weak from its enforced imprisonment in the grave, it need time and food to recover its lost strength. Meanwhile the escorting *maw-afia* are busily engaged in dusting down the "spirit" to remove earth stains of the grave. Amidst profound expressions of joy on the part of the assembled relatives and friends the "spirit" meanders round...His strength is soon exhausted and he returns to the house and disappears. (Basden 1921:124).

When the spirit appears again:

> He can walk faster, and speak loudly and clearly. He goes in and out amongst his kinsfolk comforting and exhorting his wives and children. After this tour he returns to his house and assumes his former position on the "ukpo" (seat of honour), his attendants all the time vigorously fanning him. His daughters bring presents of gin and cowries, and to manifest his gratitude for the gifts a day is appointed by the men present, acting on behalf of the "spirit," on which he will make a special visit to the women-folk of that particular village. The "spirit" then retires to his own place once more.
>
> On the appointed day he tours the whole town speaking words of comfort and counsel, and in return receives abundant presents, and thus having fulfilled every duty of a good, kind-hearted and contended "spirit" he disappears finally. (Basden 1921:125).

This rite of resurrection (*ipu mmuo ofuu,* coming out in new spirit) is still being performed as the culmination point of an elder's second funeral obsequies. The only change is that it has become a one day event, occurring on the third day of a four-day funeral ceremony. Today, as in the early twenties, the family expresses its delight at the resurrected *mmuo ofuu* (or new spirit). Needless, to say, there is no visible resemblance between the deceased and the resurrected apparition, nor is there any attempt to create one. People are keenly aware that the existential conditions of being a spirit and existing in spirit-space are radically different from the physical conditions and logic of the body-space that it is misguided to so attempt to create or simulate a resemblance. Following this logic, actors within the Onitsha metaphysical scheme never strive for physical resemblance for an embodied spirit since they are truly viewed as an "other" transcategory being.

Although Basden, like most colonial officers-cum-anthropologists of the period, claimed intimate knowledge of the people he wrote about, his description showed superficial understanding of the logic and metaphysics of the cultural practices. If anything, Basden's distanced white gaze saw as "curious and interesting" the "habits, customs and beliefs of a little known African people" whom he clinically examined. Perhaps, more important in our reading of Basden's account of the Igbos, is our recognition of the sorts of intellectual absurdities that follow when colonial officers like Basden attempt to understand the death and life-after-death rituals he encountered on the standards and conditions of the body-space. An instance of this absurdity occurred after he was informed that "Ezira" was the resting-point of ancestral spirits on their way to the spirit-realm. To "test" the credibility of the narrative, Basden rushed off to a neighboring geographical village of Ezira and imperiously claimed to have proved that no such spiritual place exists. No doubt, his need to establish the low-level nature of the people's intelligence and philosophical thoughts, explains his willingness to apply a highly inappropriate criterion of verification to determining the validity of this symbolic location.[7]

Cognitive aberrations of this sort are eliminated if attributions of primitivity are not made prior to analysis, and if the specific cultural practices are correctly explained by an interpretive framework that understands the operative ontological imperatives of the culture, and the people's construal of reality. Any interpretation must recognize that central to the enactment of this resurrection rite is an awareness and recognition of the complexity of life and conditions of temporality in the spheres.

Although a psychological explanation of these resurrection rites may construe them as manifestations of people's subliminal desire for assurance that their beloved ones are in good spiritual state. But this preferred line of interpretation, does not entirely explain the non-autobiographical aspect of the rites. The resurrection rite makes important philosophical statements about the regenerative character of life as well as an even deeper statement about death, as an intermissive transfer station in the cycle of life. What is being asserted is that death is not the cessation of life, but merely its transformation as we know it. As the resurrection ritual indicates, family cohesion is promoted and lineage memory is reinforced, through knowing that life continues after death in a new state after going through a transition process of birth into spirit-space. Aware of the psychological impact of death in this transition rite, it is incumbent on the living to help facilitate the passage of the newly dead into their new life just as the birth or passage of a new born child or incarnating spirit into life as we know it, is facilitated by other-worlders who are grieving the lose of their own. Thus, the epistemological importance of the rites performed by *mmuo ogonogo* or the tall spirit is that it reaffirms the cycle of life, and underscores people's awareness of the distinct difference in the metaphysics and logic of existential conditions of the two spaces.

Against this conceptual background, it is crucial to see *mmuo ogonogo* more as a theoretical confirmation of the multiplicity of spatio-temporal states of reality, and in which the possibility of inter-spatial and inter-temporal travel exists. As an embodied sojourner of the spirit-realm, *mmuo ogonogo* articulates the principle of *mmuo* or pneumatic space, in the process, affirming the role of embodiment as a prerequisite for existence in physical space. Given the intangibility of pneumatic-space, physical embodiment is crucial for being in body-space, while the reverse is true for humans seeking to journey into spirit-space. The body has to be shed either in death, sleep, or meditation so that the spirit can be released to function in the nontangible, conditions of spirit-space. The conditions of intangibility associated with pneumatic space means that there are no fixed geographical points, stations (as Basden assumed), or locations-in-the-clouds called heaven. *Mmuo* or pneumatic space is both everywhere and nowhere.

Theoretically sophisticated, the Onitsha ontological framework ensures that its ideas and concepts are logically consistent. This consistency is evident in their recognition and insistence that the physical conditions of life in body-space is a prerequisite for interaction in body-space. Thus, when spirits are invoked they have to appear embodied so as to intermingle with the inhabitants of physical space. This need to visually and conceptually satisfy the logic and conditions of body-space reveals a strong awareness of the laws of physics of the two realms of life. Because the creation of *mmuo ogonogo* involve a convergence of physical laws and pneumatic principles, the invocation of *mmuo* (or spirit manifestation) is never viewed as masking, nor can the word be plausibly used to represent the practice. The word "mask" and the concept of masking suggests that faking, playfulness, and intentional concealment are the objectives of the institution. Yet, nothing can be further from the truth, as has consistently been pointed out by Igbo scholars.[8] In assuming a privileged position of knowing, and assuming that what is known is an instance of faking, the word "mask" delegitimizes the profound ideas at the heart of the practice, and misrepresents the event as noncognitive and devoid of theoretical significance.

The art of spirit manifestation or invocation consciously works on the principle of embodiment, not concealment. Embodiment works on the premise that invoked spirits have to be given the necessary receptacles for appearance in body-space, preparatory to interacting with people in this sphere. In spirit manifestation, the physical receptacles are human mediums whose consciousness are temporarily used as media for communication, while *awolo* (or skin) represents the personality of invoked spirit and cloaks the identity of the medium so as not to distract people's attention. Because the central process involved in achieving this trans-substantiation is out of the scope of this paper, the topic will not be examined here.

What is important in all this, is that on the one hand, *mmuo ogonogo* (the tall spirit) is a concrete representation of people's theoretical beliefs, that dramatically reenacts both the miracle of resurrection and the central principles of life in expanded space and time. On the other hand, the traveling spirit is a visible temporal capsule that links the afterlife with the past and through the present. It points out, and constantly reminds us of a radically different conception of reality in which time and space are illusive, and are not the restraining barriers they seem to be. Lastly, as if to underscore this point, *mmuo ogonogo* concretely affirms the principle of family cohesiveness by validating the belief in ancestors, and in life after death.

SPATIAL RECONFIGURATIONS: ART AS TIME-LINES

Creative forms, of which the tall spirit is one, function as philosophical tools for traversing the conditions of temporality we know as past, present and future. The references to spirit-space and the conception of art as sacred object are grasped only if one listens attentively to artists' discourses on creativity, and their rationale for choosing their themes. In the case of Enwonwu, creativity and art are seen as an "invocation of ancestral spirits through giving concrete form or body to them before they can enter into the human world" (1968:421). In his view, art enables the artist to treat the present as a point of transition to and from the past into the future, and to and from the future into the past. Since the present moment or "the here-and-now" is not actually extended in three dimensional space, art becomes the vehicle for extending it, reminding us that the present finds extension in future states.

Construing artistic production as a creative ritual of spirit embodiment allows Enwonwu to participate in the mysteries of his culture while relishing the sacredness of his professional role as a creator. Following the death of his brother Ike, Enwonwu entered a different metonymic phase in his work in which art became the key for understanding the mysteries of *mmuo* (spirit), his past and his place in it. He focused on spirit forms that he said took him back to the time with his father when he saw carved spirit images in the shrine.[9] Through successive paintings and sketches of *Ogolo*, (runner-spirits) that are closely related to *Agbogo mmuo* (maiden-spirits) and *Ayolugbe* (singing-spirits), he reconciled his concept of art with deep mysteries, intuitively attending to the sacred rite of creation involved in the transformation of these forms into receptacles of life. *Ogolo* are lithe, skittish figures with long conical-shaped head and multicolored, appliquéd "skin." Stealthy runners, with a reputation for savagery in whipping, they are beautiful to behold, but dangerous to encounter. The following are some of the paintings of *Ogolo* in Enwonwu's post-1987 series that capture the rhythm and force of this *mmuo* (spirit) in various forms and movement: *Ogolo Adonis* (1989), *Ogolo Metamorphosis* (1991), *Ogolo* (1989), *Ogolo in Motion* (1989), *Nne Mmuo* (1987) and *Ogolo Emerging* (1989).

While contemplating the spirit-identity of these forms, and the color, tonal values, and vibrancy of *Ogolo*, Enwonwu's visual objective was to represent the inherent beauty of *Ogolo*, which in his view, has universal appeal.[10] The linear shapes of the canvases Enwonwu chose to capture the spirits wonderfully accentuate their vertical elongated forms and amplifies their beauty. The yellow and red colors of the fabric "skin" are intersected by the black lines of *uli* "body" markings. Created immediately after the funeral ceremony of his elder brother, the painting *Nne mmuo*, becomes an exhortatory reminder of the immutability of life. The appearance of this spirit and others at the funeral remind people that earthly life is not the only expression and form of life. Their presence reinforces the message that celebrating the departed's exit from earthly life constitutes a grand welcoming of a new spirit into spiritual life and space. The interconnectedness of earthly life (in body-space) and pneumatic life (in spirit space) breeches the artificial worldly separation of the two realms. Through dance, the *Ogolo* rechoreographs this grand drama of life and death, and validates the oneness of life by drawing from the interpretive dance movements of earthly life.

Nne mmuo is captured in the validatory throes of an intricate *iru ani* (couching low) dance motion, displaying humanoid skills that reenacts the metaphysical maxim about parallel states of existence: *as it is above, so it is below; as it is in humans, so is it in spirits.* The visual language of interpretation captures the dramatic intensity, color, and emotional style of the spirits. With dignity, respect and sensitivity, Enwonwu captures the movement of the spirit's hands, the intense concentration on its face, and the suggested ripple of muscles in the thighs. Becoming one with the *Ogolo* means cathartically moving with the spirit to the point where one memorably grieves through dance, and heals by realizing the transformatory potentials of death and that there is life after death.

Enwonwu's strong attachment to this sacral forms reveals that he also utilized them at a personal level to negotiate, come to terms with, and pass through the portals of death.[11] With the resurfacing of his prostrate cancer in 1993, Enwonwu faced the prospects of his own mortality. Sometime in October, four months before his death in February 1994, he had a premonitory experience that for him marked the turning point of his illness and his serious encounter with the afterlife. "Woken" by a presence that drew him to the window facing his hospital bed, he found himself at the edge of a cliff that abruptly plunged into a dizzying chasm. On the other side of this awesome vista was his mother and immediate elder brother, Francis. The mother beckoned, but he faltered as he tried to approach. Explaining that there was something he had to do since he was too afraid to cross, the next morning he asked for the painting he was working on before his illness. Still in hospital, he steely worked to finish the painting, weakly dabbing on paint onto canvas until he could no longer continue. The spiritly *Ogolo* that emerged was unusually frisky and elegant suggesting that it was an evocative form of his own inner spirit, being freed from the encasing prison of his feeble disease-ridden body. The colorful, cheery dancing form validating the resilience of life, and was the medium he utilized to draw together his last resources and energy to cross the chasm of death, into afterlife.[12]

In this example, Enwonwu presents a model of using the creative process to facilitate transition from one spatial condition to another. A different model occurs with the creative process of Sokari Douglas Camp, who uses it to chart a different time-line to an ancestral past. Born in Buguma, Nigeria, in 1958, Douglas Camp now lives and works in London. A sculptor of international standing, Sokari brings a sophisticated understanding of metal to her creative vision. In an important sense, she sees her work as both an expression and a continuation of Kalabari–Izhon creative principle. Within the aesthetic universe in which she creates, Sokari is aware of the intrusion of spirit forces into people's lives, and into the creative process. Spirit possession amplifies the power of art; the corporeality of embodied Sekiapu spirits inspire her art, and by virtue of spirit-channeling, the objects and forms created are power objects.

Being a Kalabari expatriate in England has mediated Douglas Camp's creative lens in profoundly deep ways. In a series of brilliant large-scale sculptures of Kalabari festival scenes, she imbues her steel constructions with rhythmic vitality that dissolves the solidity of steel, robbing it of its rigidity. Her Sekiapu-inspired dancing spirits appear mobile even in their immobility and as they are rooted to their spots. *Bird Masquerade with long tail* (1995) provocatively "swishes" its behind as well as the two brooms in its hands, while firmly balancing an reddish-orange egret on its head. The spirit-figure formed by the ultramarine blue steel lattice wrapper suggestively "flutters" as the dancing spirit "moves." Caught in a swashbuckling swagger with arms slightly crooked in a dance gesture is *Dandy Masquerade* (1995). This self-assured, dandy male spirit is decked out in a coppery waistcoat of *pelete* cloth (native cut) with four mirrors hanging low at the level of its behind from the dull grey sash encircling its waist.

The ferocious powerful *Big Masquerade with the boat and household on its head* (1995) wields two cutlasses with the bright red blood of a recent sacrifice splattered on its titanium white apron. It bears an architectonic Kalabari wooden boat on its head on which the artist has a carved family inscription. Equally fiercesome, the energy of the powerful *Otobo (Hippo) Masquerade* (1995) dominates its space. Its look is also remarkable: a dull-grey rectangular-shaped large steel head is vitalized by dominant blue-and-white piercing eyes, prominent steel fangs for teeth, small humanoid wooden skulls indelicately dispersed around the base of the head, and green palm fronds jutting askew all around the base of the head. Intricately crafted, the sculptures collectively underscore the evocative quality of some of the performances of the Sekiapu Society, and Douglas Camp's interpretive vision of the vitality of the dancing spirits.

Sokari comes to her steel representation of the Sekiapu dancing spirits whilst participating in the Buguma Centennial celebrations in 1987. Prior to that, her metal constructions had been restricted to *Church Ede* (1984), a decorated steel bed she constructed to rechoreograph her father's Christian wake, and to memorialize his absence. She began a tradition of personalizing her work by motorizing sections of it to fuse together three major qualities of the three dimensional space: visual, locomotion, and auditory. Her next steel project was the grand festival boat or *Alali Aru*, evocative of the elaborate festival boats used in Buguma during the Centennial regatta. Standing on the stern of the boat is the motorized lead Sekiapu dancing spirit, whose windswept wild appearance, and occasional stomping of its feet adds an unusual auditory zest to the sculptural piece.

Douglas Camp's interest in spirits was first kindled by dance and the transgressive character of choreographic dance patterns performed by priestesses. She studied the mannerism and gestures of a specific Kalabari priestess, Amonia Horsfall, who performs a trance inducing dance in which she traverses and collapses gender categories. Possessed, Horsfall role-plays and dances men's steps then switches in mid-dance into the choreographed patterns of women's dance. Working with Horsfall, Douglas Camp found herself being gradually pulled into the spirit sphere by the good relationship she claimed she developed with Horsfall's main spirit guide (1988:16). Consequently, "I made spirit objects that...I imagined because of the way she danced...I felt it was all right to make these things" (Douglas Camp 1988:16).

The Sekiapu-inspired sculptures commemorating the spirit-dancers contextualizes Kalabari-Izhon aesthetics, the philosophical concerns of Sokari, and her fascination with inspired dance, spirit possession, and movement. Fascinated by the intricate interplay of possession, creativity and dance, and the idea that possession is a medium for creativity, Sokari focuses on the movement and gestures of the dance performances of the Sekiapu or Ekine Society, capturing the modes and moods that she takes to be the essence of the society's spiritual drama. Unlike Enwonwu who utilized the *Agbogo mmuo* to deepen his knowledge of mysteries, Sokari's sculpturally nuanced spirits are deployed to recover history and assert her identity in the context of her life in London. Separated from the material aspects of Buguma culture, yet desirous to validate it, her metal sculptures become ways of asserting her difference and idenitity. By this means, she inscribes her values in the British environment as she engages in a nuanced, multi-layered exploration of self-identity in a migratory context of transitoriness. In this journey of self-assertion, Douglas Camp simultaneously proceeds in a journey of self-recovery. Unwittingly, she apprehends the female roots of the Sekiapu society, and in transforming herself into Ekine Erebo or Ekine woman, intuitively recovered the history of Ekineba, the female deity that is the founder and patroness of Ekine society.

Although today the Sekiapu dance drama of the Ekine Society is represented as an all-male institution, this was not historically the case. The origin of the Ekine Society, as recounted by Horton in "The Kalabari Ekine Society: A Borderland of Religion and Art," lies with Ekineba, a beautiful woman who was abducted by the Water People or water spirits (1963:94) Carried into spirit-space at the bottom of the creeks by these Water-People, Ekineba was shown a vast array of different plays by each water spirit, and according to Horton was, indeed, the first Kalabari person ever to have seen spirit embodiments dancing on the mud-flats by Water People (1995). After this epiphanous revelation Ekineba was returned to the "land of humans" (body-space) at the command of the mother of the water spirits. Coming to, she narrated her experiences and taught Kalabari people all the plays she had seen, which soon became very popular. The plays were regularly performed in accordance to a stipulated set of rules in which Ekineba had to initiate each performance by beating the signal tune. Chaffing under this rule which they found unduly restrictive, a group of young men refused to obey the rule which the Water People had stipulated must be performed before any of the play was performed. On three separate occasions they failed to let her beat the signal. Losing patience with this violation of their pact, the Water People abducted Ekineba for failing to enforce the code. Perhaps in remorse, the men made Ekineba the patron Spirit of Sekiapu, named the society after her, but promptly barred women from it.

CONCLUSION

The primacy of Ekineba in the Ekine Society speaks to the clairvoyant powers of an Ekine woman both in spirit possession and in creativity. Sokari's sculptural representation of the Sekiapu dancing-spirits (or masquerades as she calls them) excavates a historical time-line that links the past to the present, pronounces on the possibility of human interaction with the inhabitants of the spirit-space. Because African art came to art history via anthropology, and because anthropology is the handmaid of imperialism, no indication is ever given in the writings of anthropologists of the deep philosophical ideas underpinning the conceptualization of artifacts in Africa's material culture. Rarely is any hint given of the sophisticated ontological framework, ritual of resurrection, or the potentialities of human's capacity to transcend the three dimensional conditions of space and time. Since the objective of imperialism is to legitimize the dominance of Europe by racializing and primitivizing all non-Europeans, the discipline of African art history was consequently founded on a patronizing treatment of its culture and practices that stymies understanding.

It is worthwhile to recognize that estrangement from Africa's material culture led to an aberrant intellectual situation in which Africa's philosophy of life and mode of visual representation are presented to the world by European and European American collectors, anthropologists, historians and museum officials, most of whom lack an adequate grasp of any African language to participate in any meaningful intellectual discourse. A direct impact of their "scholarly" claims is the validation and grounding of knowledge on ignorance, the effect of which is the construal of sculpture as the dominant category of analysis in the concept of spirit manifestation. Most collectors, many scholars and museum officials treat the wooden face of the spirits as the most significant aspect of the manifested spirits, even when they assert that, in its cultural location, the created form is much more than its sculpted face or headdress.[14]

*   I would like to acknowledge the Senior Getty Grant that supported my research travel to Nigeria, and which yielded the experiences that are the subject of discussion in section one.

NOTES

1. This tradition has its roots in Plato's ontological concept of *eidos* (type). Even though John Locke's nominalism is an epistemological reaction to the idea of fixed real essences, his theory is ontologically caught within the metaphysics and logic of fixed reality.

2. It is important to correct the widespread assumption that women do not know the secrets of *mmuo* institution. Suffice it to say that, in Onitsha, post menopausal women are initiated into the *mmanwu* society if they so choose. Thereafter, they are known as *nne mmanwu* (mother of spirits) and are accorded the same respects that are due to any member of the institution. A different situation exists with the female members of *Ogbe otu* ward in Onitsha. By virtue of tracing their ancestral roots to Igala, the home of *mmuo ogonogo* (the tall spirit), *Ogbe otu* women do not require to undergo any process of initiation. In fact, initiation comes by birth, and at funerals, they freely escort the tall spirit of their ward.

3. Haverlock insists that because the rhythmic and narrativized syntax of information storage in memory discourages abstract formulation of principles and concepts individuals in contexts of orality "could reflect, but always as a human being, never as a philosopher, an intellectual, a theorist" (1991:24).

4. An example of our "scientific" myth is the belief that ulcers are caused by the high acidity content of the stomach, rather than by the pylori bacteria. Armed with the weight of medical tradition, but more concerned with maintaining the huge lucrative market offered by the production of acid-neutralizing solutions, the pharmaceutical industries and the medical establishment waged a ferocious battle against this medical breakthrough. Of course, on the model of science privileged by the establishment, the new ideas appeared unscientific and wrong-headed.

5. I was struck by the strangeness of the language prescribed by an Einsteinian view of science while reading a short biography of Alfred North Whitehead (Etienne Gilson et al. 1966:507-519). The selected quotation appears in (511).

6. According to S.I. Bosah this smearing of blood on the eyelids of the deceased distinguishes him or her as an initiate of *Mmuo* institution (Bosah 1988:129).

7. This is very much like the Soviets "proof" that God did not exist after their first successful mission to space and failed to discover the Christian Grandfather God.

8. See the works of Nnabenyi Ugonna, Onuora Ossie Enekwe, and Meki Nzewi. Of all the writers only Nzewi addressed the mystical implications of *mmuo* or *mmanwu* while Ugonna focused more on the dramatic character of the form.

9. The importance of this period to Enwonwu career is argued in another paper, "Immortal Sculptor and Painter: The Art of Odinigwe Ben Chukwukadibia

Enwonwu" in Contemporary Textures: Multidimensionality in Nigerian Art (Binghamton: International Society for the Study of Africa, forthcoming 1998).
10. Interview May 22, 1989.
11. He was diagnosed with prostate cancer in 1986, which went into remission after intensive chemotherapy treatment.
12. He died at home early Saturday morning, February 6, 1994.
13. Horton 1963:94.
14. Numerous exhibition catalogues on African art testify to this Western initiated prominence of sculpture in the masking tradition. Segy 1958; Fagg 1964, 1978, 1981; Bascom 1974, 1967; Cole 1978; Leiris and Delange 1968; Willett 1971; Leuzinger 1972; Fry 1974; Laude 1971; Ottenberg 1975.

REFERENCES

Bascom, William. *African Art in Cultural Perspective.* New York: Norton, 1973.
Bascom, William. *African Arts: An Exhibition at the Robert H. Lowie Museum of Anthropology.* Berkeley: University of California Printing Department, 1967.
Basden, G. T. *Among the Igbos of Nigeria.* London: Frank Cass & Co. Ltd., 1921
Babbitt, Susan. *Impossible Dreams.* Boulder, CO.: Westview Press, 1996.
Bosah, S. I. *Groundwork of the History and Culture of Onitsha.* Apapa, Nigeria: Times Press Ltd., 1988
Carruthers, Mary. *The Book of Memory: A Study of Memory in Medieval Culture.* New York: Cambridge University Press, 1990.
Cole, Herbert. *Male and Female: The Couple in African Sculpture.* Los Angeles: Los Angeles County Museum of Art, 1983.
Enekwe, Onuora Ossie. *Igbo Masks: The Oneness of Ritual and Theatre.* Lagos: A Nigerian Magazine Publication, 1987.
Fagg, William Buller. *African Majesty: From Grassland and Forest: The Barbara and Murray Frum Collection.* Toronto: Art Gallery of Ontario, 1981.
Fagg, William Buller. *Divine Kinship in Africa.* London: Published for the Trustees of the British Museum Publications, 1978.
Fagg, William and Margaret Plass. *African Sculpture.* London: Studio Vista, 1964.
Fry, Jacqueline. *The Art and Peoples of Black Africa.* New York: Dutton, 1974.
Gilson, Etienne; Thomas Langan and Armand A. Maurer. *Recent Philosophy: Hegel to the Present.* New York: Random House, 1966.
Haverlock, Eric. "The Oral-Literate Equation: A Formula for the Modern Mind." *Literacy and Orality,* eds. David Olson and Nancy Torrance. New York: Cambridge University Press, 1991, pp.11-27.
Horton, Robin. "Sokari Douglas Camp: Ekine Woman in London?" In *Play and Display: Steel Masquerades from Top to Toe.* London: Museum of Mankind, 1995.
Horton, Robin. "Tradition and Modernity Revisited." In Martin Hollis and Steven Lukes eds. *Rationality and Relativism.* Oxford: Basil Blackwell, 1992, pp.201-260.
Horton, Robin. "The Kalabari *Ekine* Society: A Borderland of Religion and Art." *Africa* 33, 2 (1963):94-113.

Hountondji, Paulin J. "Producing Knowledge in Africa Today: The Second Bashorun M. K. O. Abiola Distinguished Lecture." *African Studies Review* 38, 3 (1995):1-10.

Hubbard, Sue. "The Sculpture of Sokari Douglas Camp." In *Play and Display: Steel Masquerades from Top to Toe.* London: Museum of Mankind, 1995.

Laude, Jean. *The Arts of Black Africa.* Berkeley: University of California Press, 1971.

Leiris, Michel and Jacqueline Delange. *African Arts.* New York: Golden Press, 1968.

Leuzinger, Elsy. *The Art of Black Africa.* Greenwich, Conn.: New York Graphic Society, 1972.

Nzewi, Meki. "The Concept of Spirit Manifestation: Categories and Roles." In *The Masquerade in Nigerian History and Culture,* ed. Nzewunwa, Nwanna. Proceedings of a Workshop Sponsored by the School of Humanities, Port Harcourt: University of Port Harcourt, 1982.

Ottenberg, Simon. *Masked Rituals of Afikpo.* Seattle: University of Washington Press, 1975.

Segy, Ladislas. *African Sculpture Speaks.* New York: Dover Publications, 1958.

Thurow, Lester C. *Dangerous Currents: The State of Economics.* New York: Random House, 1983.

Ugonna, Nnabenyi. *Mmonwu: A Dramatic Tradition of the Igbos.* Lagos: Lagos University Press, 1984.

9

SELF AND PLACE IN AFRICAN AND AFRICAN-AMERICAN AUTOBIOGRAPHICAL PROSE:

EQUIANO AND ACHEBE, SOYINKA AND GATES

F. ODUN BALOGUN

INTRODUCTION

A CASE COULD BE MADE FOR ANALYZING CHINUA ACHEBE'S *Things Fall Apart* as an autobiographical fiction; however, the primary reason for including the novel in a study of autobiographies is that close observation reveals numerous parallels between it and *The Interesting Narrative of the Life of Oluadah Equiano, or Gustavus Vassa, the African.*[1] Both Equiano and Achebe come from the same Igbo ethnic culture and geographical location of Nigeria, but more important, both adopted similar stylistic strategies to portray the Igbo culture as a representative African culture and in response to the challenges of slavery (in the case of Equiano) and colonialism (in the case of Achebe). What specifically these strategies are, will soon become evident because their analysis constitutes a major focus of this chapter. Indeed, the thematic and stylistic parallels between both works are such that one could easily assume that Achebe had consciously modeled his novel after the manner of Equiano's autobiography: in many respects *Things Fall Apart* is the fictional elaboration of the first two chapters of Equiano's *Interesting Narrative*. Such an assumption, however, would be wrong because Achebe did not become acquainted with Equiano's narrative until about 1964, five years after he had published *Things Fall Apart*.[2]

The similarities between Wole Soyinka's memoir, *Ake: The Years of Childhood*, and Henry Louis Gates, Jr.'s *Colored People: A Memoir* are equally striking. Indeed, the biographical details selected for portrayal and the style in which they are portrayed are so close that it seems the former memoir has directly influenced the latter. Both are written in the mode of the bildungsroman, except that Soyinka's remains consistent throughout with the perspective of the growing child, since his story ends with the character still in childhood. Specifically, the story terminates as the young Wole is about to leave home for a boarding secondary school at the early age of nine-and-a-half years because of a precocious academic maturity. Gates, on the other hand, frequently editorializes his childhood narrative from an adult perspective, because he does not wish to limit the interpretation of things portrayed to the naive child's point of view, since, after all, the history captured in his narrative transcends his years of childhood. Young Henry's story stops at the point when he leaves home to enroll in a university. Aside from this and some other stylistic differences, the two works closely echo each other, beginning with the emphasis on the place of birth and growing up—Ake for Soyinka, Piedmont for Gates, both of which are located on picturesque hilly terrains. The evocative description of these hilly towns, the close attention paid to both the paternal and maternal sides of the families, the similar roles played by the mother, the father, and maternal uncles, the character of childhood education under paternal guidance and at school, the precocious excelling in academic learning, the childhood infatuation with grown-up women and the manner of recording this infatuation, the precocious interest in the contradictions of adult life, the love of physical nature, the early awakening of social and political consciousness and involvement in political actions—these and many others are details that have been given similar treatment in both works.

Soyinka and Gates, like Equiano and Achebe, wrote their respective memoirs as an intellectual response to a contemporary socio-political reality. The social implication of Soyinka's emphasis on dynamic individuality and informed political leadership which characterizes *Ake* (as almost everyone of Soyinka's works, especially the plays), is to be considered in light of the prevailing socio-political atmosphere in Nigeria. Corrupt leadership and political dictatorship by an unenlightened military, resulting in political disorder, social chaos and economic poverty, prevailed in Nigeria of the late

1970s and early 80s when *Ake* was written. Similarly, *Colored People* appeared in 1994, a time in America when the gains of the civil rights movement were actively being rolled back, when the Black family began to come under incessant attack for supposedly lacking in family values, when economic hardship—artificially created by the downsizing of business—was blamed not on the greedy multinationals, but on the Black poor who were supposedly sucking the economy dry through welfarism; when, in short, resurgent racism was so rampant in the society that the jury system became the standard mirror for reflecting the collapse of the social contract. It is against this background that Gates intended his audience to read his memoir and its implicit message about the need for informed and dynamic leadership which would socially engineer the return of sanity to race relations.

THE SUBTLETY OF NARRATIVE STRATEGIES
Anyone can be easily fooled into believing that these four works were written solely to provide unalloyed aesthetic pleasure for the reader, and this perception is the stronger for the deft manner narrative competence has been deployed in each case to maximally enhance the pleasure of reading. Equiano knew his time quite well; so, he adopted the prevailing—and, for that reason, captivating—genre of the adventure story. He wasted no time but proceeded immediately to whet the appetite of his eighteenth-century audience, who were in love with the primitive, by plunging them straight into the exotica of a sociological description of his homeland in the supposed dark continent—a ticket that was sure to be a winner since it had the advantage of being the first by a native and, therefore, fascinating for its authenticity and seeming confirmation of white cultural bias. At the appropriate time and before audience attention wanes, Equiano varies the modes of his ostensible tale of adventure by constantly alternating the narration from the details of merchant ship voyages to those of man-of-war military expeditions, each of which guarantees excitement because of inherent danger.

Equiano does not disappoint his audience in providing this pleasure, frequently and grippingly describing the dangers that regularly attend his travels at sea during shipwrecks, pirate attacks, military engagements, and accidents. Thus, as occasion demands, Equiano alternates his identity between that of a native providing exotic sociological details about the "primitive" people populating "the heart of darkness,"; that of a seasoned sailor on merchant voyages; that of a courageous aide-de-camp on military campaigns; and that of the member of an audacious crew on a scientific expedition to locate a sailing route from the Atlantic Ocean through the Arctic to India and the Pacific Ocean. When Equiano tells his audience, as he constantly does, that the sea is already in his blood and that he is restless except when sailing at sea, he is credible because he has so pandered to the taste of his eighteenth-century audience that his story appears to have no other purpose than to satisfy the audience's thirst for adventure. This impression is all the greater because the details of his personal experiences as a slave and the harsher experiences of his fellow African slaves, bitter and excruciating as they are and as he portrays them, are always expressed in a language of diplomacy calculated to show that he recognizes his place as an obedient subordinate to his superiors, that there is nothing he would not accomodate to maintain this decorous subordination to the superior culture of his white masters, that his only quarrel is with those trying to defame this superior culture by perpetuating the nefarious slave trade, and, finally, that this is all the more regrettable since trade in agricultural and industrial goods would be far more profitable than the objectionable trade in humans, particularly since the latter offends the tenets of Christianity.

Thus, with his manners perfect and his protests decorous, as befits a British Christian gentleman, all of which he has become by the time of writing his narrative, and with his tale maximally and exotically exciting, no one could claim that Equiano is gainsaying when he qualifies his narrative as "interesting" because the way he tells it makes it genuinely so. Nor could anybody effectively object to his strongest condemnation of the barbarity of the slave trade since it is understood that this nefarious trade is merely a removable blemish in the otherwise superior culture of the white race. Moreover, as interesting as his story might be, Equiano has not been so pretentious as to dream of imposing himself on his superiors if it were not for the hope that it could afford some satisfaction to his "numerous friends, at whose request it has been written, or in the smallest degree promotes the interest of humanity" (32). This quotation reveals the vintage Equiano style at its most subtle if it is observed that the actual reason that has motivated the writing of his narrative (to "promote the interest of humanity") is supremely understated. Equiano, the diplomat and strategist, knows how to stoop to conquer, and the success with which he garners the support of the high and mighty in the British society for his abolitionist cause shows how effective his strategy is. It is my contention that Equiano had decided that there was no sacrifice he could not make as long as it advanced the interest of his fellow Africans, and hence it should be seen as part of his strategy of stooping to conquer that he chose to flatter the British ego by referring to their culture as superior, chose to settle in Britain, become an Anglican, and marry a white lady. This seems to be the only way to understand the great thematic paradox or contradiction in Equiano's narrative. On one hand, there is the subtle— and, for that reason, devastating—exposure of white racism and the hypocrisy of a Christian culture that permitted slavery. On the other hand, there is

an equally subtle depiction that systematically reveals that the so-called hea-
thenish and savage people of Africa were, in fact, more civilized in the true
humane understanding of that word than their pretentious deprecators.
Equiano achieved this diplomatic coup with a subtle compositional structure and characterization, both of which transform the narration from its
delightful subterfuge of a tale of adventure to his true story—a tragic account of the life of "Oluadah Equiano, the African." This main story is ably
narrated in a manner that makes it possible to equate the self with the self's
place—Africa. The details of how Equiano does this in his narrative, acknowledged by Carretta Vincent (1995) as also highly intellectually learned,
will be seen below (xxiii-xxvii).[4]

In *Things Fall Apart*, Achebe stages a similar literary coup that turns the
table on the white ego which fed on the illusion of a racial and cultural
superiority, again using subtle compositional structure and characterization
whose details shall similarly be revealed below. Meanwhile, at the surface
level, Achebe's story is as diplomatically subtle and deceitful as Equiano's,
and it is just as arrestingly entertaining. Again, like Equiano, Achebe dangles
the exotic carrot of a sociological description of a "primitive culture" as he
narrates the captivating story of Okonkwo. Again, Achebe knows the taste
of his twentieth-century white audience, who have substituted the romantic
love of adventure (inherited from their eighteenth-century forebears) for the
love of realistic fiction complexly rendered in psychological details that are
the more captivating when the protagonist is a tragic super-hero. So, Achebe
intricately delights his audience with the analytical story of the complex
psychological elements responsible for Okonkwo's rise into a heroic star-
dom only for the same elements to engineer his tragic demise. The twentieth-
century reader vicariously experiences Okonkwo's taste of the tragic abyss,
psychologically and realistically rendered, and is as delighted and satisfied
as his/her eighteenth-century predecessors who enjoyed Equiano's romanti-
cally exotic adventures. The pleasure was all the more guaranteed because
Achebe has graduated from the same Igbo school of cultural diplomacy as
Equiano, and is as adept in the subterfuge language of entertainment. As
critics have unanimously attested, to read Achebe is to experience a linguistic delight, the result of Achebe's subtle aesthetic sensibility, the secret of
which consists in a certain manner of expressing the African thought while
using the English sentence structure and in the end producing an unobtru-
sive, smooth communication, redolent with the poetic cadence of African
proverbial idiom. This dexterous combination of linguistic narrative idioms
to achieve an entertaining surface story is what has made *Things Fall Apart*
one of the best-selling novels in the world today. Meanwhile, beneath the
surface entertaining story Achebe has also carefully plotted another story

—his main story, one in which Okonkwo is depicted as a representative tragic product of a representative African culture that has created him as much as he has created it. How Achebe fashions this story of the self that can be equated with the self's place will be examined below.

Soyinka adopts in *Ake* the child's naive point of view which enables adults to perceive with fresh insight the reality of their lives, especially those contradictions that occasion the child some worry and concern. At the same time, the naivete of the child becomes an endless source of discretely enjoyed humor and entertainment for the adults. Explaining, for instance, why he anticipates no problems with marrying Mrs. Odufuwa, "the most beautiful woman in the world," young Wole reasons in the following manner: "I bore her husband no grudge, after all, he was my godfather, so he should prove no obstacle to my marrying this goddess once I had grown to manhood" (101). After overhearing some conversation concerning the manner local tax collectors abuse their office, Wole sedately resolves that when he "grew up, no khakied official was going to extract one penny in tax from my hard-earned salary" (184). Also when conflicting signals, playfully given by adults, led to a fight between him and his brother Dipo, Wole summarily concludes that "there was neither justice nor logic in the world of grown-ups" (104). With an uncanny insight, Wole perceives in his naive way the similarity between traditional African religion and the Christian religion, and he expresses the similarity by equating traditional African masquerades with the images of venerated Christian personalities painted in Church stained-glass windows (32-33). Those familiar with the religious and philosophical debates between the missionary Mr. Brown and the old man Akunna in *Things Fall Apart* would recall that the issue Wole has so simply (naively) resolved is the weighty theological point of contention at the root of Western denigration of African religious practices (179-81). It is obvious, of course, that the child's naive point of view is not as innocent as is pretended, since it is remotely controlled by the worldly and experienced adult Soyinka, who, no doubt, thinks like Akunna on this theological issue.

What Soyinka does in *Ake*, then, is to capitalize on the directness and innocence of the child's perception of reality to convey his insight into the truth of the socio-political and economic reality of Ake, the place, as apprehended through the self of his child protagonist. This is why, as the memoir progresses, the story grows imperceptibly from the narration of the experiences of the child Wole to a tale of Ake, the representative African city (comparable with Essaka of the *Interesting Narrative*, the Umuofia of *Things Fall Apart*, and the Piedmont of *Colored People*) and as experienced by the reliable child narrator. Thus, Ake and Wole are intricately intertwined just as Equiano is inseparable from Essaka, Okonkwo from Umuofia, and Skip

Gates from Piedmont. While the details of this narrative strategy will be discussed below, it is pertinent at this point to observe that much of the aesthetic pleasure of reading Ake derives from Soyinka's attempt to convey the poetry and mystery in young Wole's imaginative apprehension of his natural environment and social reality. Being the accomplished poet he is, Wole the adult is able to find the appropriate language to capture the fascinating world of his childhood. Typical in this regard is the very first page of the memoir with its poetic language of personification and ironic allusions to contending deities, contending cultures and contending tongues. Poetically captured is the mysterious and sacred geographic landscape of the imposing Itoko heights that merges with the sky, recalling Mount Olympos and the Greek gods and goddesses. The "pagan" Chief with his stable is the guardian of the "profane" crest of the sacred Itoko heights that magisterially commands a panoramic view of the settlement located below its steep descent, and from where every Sunday God descends, taking "gigantic stride over those babbling markets—which dared to sell on Sundays—into St. Peter's Church, afterwards visiting the parsonage for tea with the Canon"; the same God who "reserved his most exotic presence for the evening service which, in his honor, was always held in the English tongue. The organ took on a dark, smoky sonority at evening service, and there was no doubt that the organ was adapting its normal sounds to accompany God's own sepulchral responses, with its timbre of the egungun, to those prayers that were offered to him" (1). While delighting in the share poetic beauty of this imaginatively heightened passage, the informed reader is also aware of its hidden polemics because the whole question of colonial cultural imposition and the defiant resistance of traditional culture and the manner in which this cultural contest should be mediated—the central theme of the memoir—is indirectly raised and also resolved here in the very first page for the perceptive reader.

The delight of *Colored People* reminds one at once of both *Ake* and *Things Fall Apart*. Gates's use of the naive child narrator and his variation on the application of the mode that both links it to, and differentiates it from, Soyinka's employment of the device in *Ake* has been earlier remarked. The point to insist on is Gates's preference for telling his story from the "point of view of the boy I was" (xvi), rather than telling the story as if he were still a child as does Soyinka. While this perspective justifies the learned character of the child's story, it denies it the disarming, innocent humor emanating from the irony of naivete. For instance, the captivating humor in the manner Wole presents his childhood infatuation for a married woman, Mrs. Odufuwa, is not matched by Skip's comparable declaration of love for the middle-aged Matilda mainly because the freshness of humor is robbed out of the irony of naivete by the analyzing learnedness that went along with it—what I referred to earlier as Skip's editorializing style: "... Matilda, always wore luscious red lipstick. She was not a pretty woman, perhaps, but with her light-beige powdered cheeks, her dark-brown, almost black hair and dark-brown eyes, and that red lipstick, when she stood before the golden and dark-brown breads, cookies, and pastries, or wrapped the blood-red links of her daddy's bologna in white waxed butcher's paper with that deliberate way she had, she was, I was convinced, one of the loveliest creatures on God's green earth" (37). The realistic description of Matilda's features denies Skip's rendition of his infatuation with Matilda the mystery and romantic power that attend Wole's love declaration. By not exposing Mrs. Odufuwa, his beloved, to the scrutinizing lenses of realistic description, Wole enhances the alluring power of the beloved who thus becomes reified, as befits a goddess, to the realm of the mysterious, the unknowable. But, of course, what is lost in comparison with the innocent pleasure of a child's naivete, characterizing Soyinka's ironic style which permits on the authority of a child's romantic infatuation the elevation of a mortal to the status of a goddess, is regained in Gates's learned or conscious irony implicit in the waxed beauty of a powdered old maid in a bakery, as well as in the sexual suggestiveness of the "red-blood links of her daddy's bologna."

The greatest linguistic appeal of *Colored People*, however, is in its pervasive irony, humor and hyperboles, the intense, passionate moment of love evocatively recalled, and in its Achebean approach to the language of colored people. The ironic, extended religious anecdotes of chapter ten "Joining the Church" are perhaps the most entertaining for their straight-face tall tales, verbal ironies in reference to the conversion of Mr. Les and the beliefs of Miss Sarah, "Sister Holy Ghost," who "talked to the Lord directly—on the phone, in her living room, or wherever she felt like it" and with whom "the Lord consulted ... on a daily basis, giving her full reports on all the seraphim and the cherubim" (118). Humor is so pervasive that it would not desert Gates even in the most personally tragic of situations such as when he jokes about his "first glimpse of eternity" on his hospital bed and about the northward migration of his hip's metal ball (142, 146). Aside from the emotionality of the account of his mother's depression, perhaps the most gripping pages of *Colored People* are in chapter nine "Love Junkie" where the doomed love for Linda Hoffman is evocatively recalled with accuracy and a truthful, bare-all candor—an evocation that leaves no doubt about the fact that the love for Linda lingers there still today in Gates's adult heart. In spite of the proliferation of learned allusions, and the intrusion of the professoral diction such as the search for fine distinctions ("Sports on the mind, sports in the mind" 20), the highfalutins ("this voyeuristic thrill of the forbidden contact" 20), or the involved imagery ("My metaphor was an unthethered craft, battered by frigid waters, too far out for me to bring back to shore" 130)—in spite of these reminders of the Ivy League professor-author, the linguistic idiom that characterizes *Colored People*, in the main, is not that of the learned English professor of Harvard University, but that of the colored people. Because of the choice of narrated direct speech, the voice transmitted is invariably that of the speaker or the character, and only rarely that of the narrator, and even when it is the latter, Gates often affects the language of ordinary folks. In fact, in an interview with Diane Middlebrook, Gates says "I wrote this portrait in honor of my mother in my father's voice. My father is a wit" (190).

Black speech resounds throughout *Colored People* in a way similar to how the Igbo speech resounds in the English syntax of *Things Fall Apart.* We read, for instance, that "he was beat so bad" (25); that "Mama read her minutes, just to represent the race, just to let those white people know that we was around here too" (33); that "Now, Murray was some serious grease" (45); that Skip Gates is the outsider "who enjoyed being on the edge of the circle, watching ... trying to strip away illusions, getting at what was really coming down" (83); and that Nemo's "God was one jealous Dude" (159). Black speech as a rule cherishes its freedom and refuses to be constrained by any taboos, and certainly not one imposed by any hypocritical prudish-ness; so, there is no surprise reading a comparison such as this: "In the newly integrated school system, race was like an item of apparel that fitted us up tight, like one of Mama's girdles or the garters that supported her hose" (92); or this: "Like when some white man would show up at the Le-gion, cruising 'to get laid by a colored woman,' or some jug-headed loader would bring his white buddy to a dance and then beg some woman to 'give him some' " (8); nor this: "... like the way Bobby Lee Jones ... looked that day he beat his woman, his tacky red processed strands getting dangling down the middle of his forehead, his Johnson getting harder each time he slapped her face. They say he would have fucked her right then and there if he hadn't been so drunk that his arms got tired of swinging at her. ... Or the time some guy cut off the tip of Russell Jones's nose after he had grabbed him for feeling up Inez, Inez's thighs smoking from doing the dog, her hand-kerchief wet from her rubbing it between her legs, men fighting for the right to sniff that rag like it was the holy grail" (10-11). But as with Equiano, Achebe, and Soyinka, whatever the nature of the linguistic idiom or the pleasure it might give in Gates's memoir, it exists mostly as a medium of communicating the protagonist's perception of self and the self's place—Piedmont, the representative abode of representative colored people.

PLACE AS SELF SELF AS PLACE

Setting, that is, time and place and the intellectual and cultural atmosphere that substantiates them, has always been important in imaginative literature. With the best writers, setting provides not merely a decorative geographical and temporal background where characters act out their fates, but itself functions as a major character in the plot, actively influencing and being influenced by the human protagonists. The naturalists, more than other writers, fully recognized the importance of setting in fiction and, having taken a cue from Darwin's biological determinism, they proceeded to valorize a theory of environmental determinism that over-empowered the social factors residing in a place in time, as if humans were mere passive victims. The four writers under consideration show in the works that we have been examining that they recognize, like the naturalists, the enormous power of environment, but at the same time, they also recognize, unlike the naturalists but like the Marxists, that human beings possess the will to remold their environment. Indeed, in the portrayal of the dialectical complexity of the relationship of self and place, they tend to be the opposites of the naturalists by tilting the balance in favor of the human agent.

There are not too many works in which place assumes as much significance as in the works under examination. So important is place that it not only supplies the title to one of the memoirs, *Ake*, but also becomes the first item to claim narrative attention in all the four works without exception. More than that, the amount of pages devoted to space, understood as the combination of geographical location and physical land as well as the historical and intellectual atmosphere within which a people exist creating a culture, is disproportionately higher than that strictly devoted to the story of how the biographical or fictional self exists within the identified space. The story of the self in Equiano's *Narrative*, where space is the most varied among the four texts, is presented in three major phases, each of which approximates a space: the phase/place of liberty, the phase/place of tyranny, and the phase/place of partial restoration to liberty. The story of Equiano is the story of his movement within and from one phase/space to another and the role his will plays in each stage. Three major phases/spaces are similarly delineated in the life of Okonkwo in *Things Fall Apart*: the phase and space of liberty, the phase and space of exile, and the phase and space of return to partial liberty. The play of will during each transitional phase provides the central plot for Okonkwo's story. There are two major phases/spaces in each of the other two memoirs *Ake* and *Colored People*: the phase of innocence, and the phase of maturity or experience.

Self and Place in Equiano's *Narrative*

With regard to the representation of self and place in his narrative, Equiano adopted three strategies that were designed to effectively counter the three basic white racist arguments characteristically advanced in his time as justification for the enslavement and subhuman exploitation of Africans; namely, that Africa was a dark continent peopled by a primitive race who needed to be civilized; two, that Africans were heathens who needed to be converted to Christianity for the salvation of their souls; and three, that Africans constituted an intellectually inferior race when compared to the people of the white race who, therefore, were justified in enslaving, exploiting and treating Africans as subhuman. The first of the three major phases of his memoir is constituted by the first two chapters where Equiano provides a detailed geographical, social, and cultural description of his country, his family and his upbringing as a strategy for demolishing all the aforementioned three racist fallacies about Africans. The second phase which consists of the narration of his experiences as a slave focuses on Equiano as an individual whose ability to survive the harshness of slavery derived from a combination of three factors: first, the character traits implanted by his cultural upbringing in Africa, second, his great intellectual ability which enabled him to learn fast and excel under unfavorable conditions, and third, God's providential selection which had marked him out for success—a providential favor that was already manifest in his home in Africa before he was captured into slavery. The three factors were especially emphasized because again they effectively undermined the racist fallacies about Africa and Africans. The third phase culminates the memoir with an account of his life as a freed man, an account that once again effectively levels all the three racist arguments for justifying the enslavement, oppression and exploitation of Africans.

For good reasons, Equiano takes pain at the beginning of the first phase of his autobiography to point out the representativeness of Essaka, the village where he was born on the bank of the River Niger: "the history of what passes in one family or village may serve as a specimen of the whole nation" (32). Similarly, Equiano takes care to represent himself as a typical Essaka child despite the fact that he also regards himself "as a particular favorite of Heaven" and that his name Olaudah "signifies vicissitude, or fortunate also; one favoured" (31, 41). As examples of his providential selection for favors, Equiano cites the instances of good omens associated with the crowing of harmless serpents "as thick as the calf of a man's leg" which had crept at different times into the room where he and his mother slept. One other instance that he recalls was when a poisonous snake he had stepped on moved away without harming him (43). These incidents were interpreted by the village wise men, his mother, "and the rest of the people, as remarkable omens in my favour" (43). What Equiano wishes to impress on his reader with these details is that even though he was "a favorite of Heaven," he was by no means unique. If the latter had been the case, the wise men, let alone the ordinary people of the village, would have been unable to interpret the snake omens. Indeed, the impression the passage creates is that these were pretty common omens, of which Equiano happens to be one among other beneficiaries. Equiano was not treated differently from other children of the village because of these propitious omens: he lived the life of a typical village child, intermingling and playing with his mates. Equiano acknowledges his typicality as a child of his village by the choice of the qualifier he selects for his title: it is not just the narrative of Oluadah Equiano, but Oluadah Equiano, the African. Of course, the naming also ensures that he is not mistaken for a European.

Having established himself as a typical African child and his village as a representative African village, Equiano meticulously provides details of what life in a typical African village was like, and the details leave no one in doubt as to the fact that Africans were a well organized, well governed, well behaved, and humane people; in other words, a truly civilized people.

The identification of the geographical location of Essaka[3] on the bank of the River Niger is followed by a detailed description of every aspect of the life of the inhabitants. What emerges is that Essaka is an autonomous governing constituent of a district of the most powerful empire then on the coast of West Africa—the famous Benin Empire. The Essaka people, who are farmers, operate an impartial judicial system that shows no favor to anyone irrespective of the individual's social standing. The son of a chief, for instance, is as liable before the law as anybody else. Though the law is sometimes harsh, it is always enforced with humane considerations. For instance, a woman caught in adultery, a crime whose usual penalty is death, is spared life because she nurses a baby. Marriage is regarded as sacred, there is strong love for one's kins, and the ethics of communalism rules behaviors: a person building a house, for instance, uses free communal labor. The people are industrious and modest in their habits, and there are no excesses or debauchery, the people being "totally unacquainted with strong or spiritous liquours" (35). Equiano says of his people, "Our manners are simple, our luxuries are few." He also affirms that organized ceremonies and entertainments are a regular part of life: "We are almost a nation of dancers, musicians, and poets" (34). He shows that medical practice is organized and religion is sacred, with religious rituals closely resembling those performed by the Jewish people. Education of children is undertaken with care: "The manners and customs of my country," he informs the reader, "had been implanted in me with great care." Being a favorite of his mother, he was always with her "and she used to take particular pains to form my mind. I was trained up from my earliest years in the arts of agriculture and war: my daily exercise was shooting and throwing javelins; and my mother adorned me with emblems, after the manner of our greatest warriors. In this way I grew up till I was turned the age of eleven" (46).

Equiano never pretends that his people were perfect; he reveals their limitations, which include the unequal treatment of women by men, and the fact that slavery was practiced in Africa. He points out, however, the vast difference between African and European slaves, noting that among Africans slaves are treated as family members:

> "With us they do no more work than other members of the community, even their master. Their food, clothing, and lodging were nearly the same as theirs, except that they were not permitted to eat with those who were free born and there was scarcely any other difference between them ... Some of these slaves have even slaves under them, as their own property, and for their own use" (40).

By providing this meticulous description of his cultural origin, Equiano obviously wishes to prepare the mind of his readers to understand the source of the calibre of man he turns out to be in spite of the adversities of slavery during the second phase of his life. His strong faith in God's providence in the face of extreme hardships during slavery, for instance, has its root in the faith he had while still in his village where he believed that he was "a favorite of heaven." The statement about his military training in his village, an obvious allusion to the training of Greek warriors as made famous by Homer's epics, is meant to explain why later, as a slave, he was constitutionally prepared to withstand the rigors of slave labors and why he was such a capable hand as an *aide-de-camp* on British naval campaigns. The allusion, as well as the direct comparisons of his people's culture with those of the Jews and the Turks and other groups regarded as civilized by whites, was, of course, meant to underscore racist lies about Africans' supposed lack of civilization and also to pinpoint the immorality of the double standards employed by the white race in matters concerning Africa.

Chapters 3 through 7 detail his experiences as a slave, beginning with his transit through the horrors of the middle passage, the degradation of the auction block, his purchase by and service to his quaker master, the harrowing experiences leading often to near death experiences at the hands of white men like Dr. Perkins of Savannah, the shipwrecks, the diseases, and the injustice and cheating he suffered at the hands of those he trusted, as well as many other such misfortunes during numerous trips on commercial and naval ships on the seas between England and America or between America and the Caribbean islands. Equiano's narrative shows that he was able to survive the harrowing experiences of slavery because of the quality of his character, the foundation of which had been laid by his African upbringing. He was an industrious person, and as he attests "The West-India planters prefer the slaves of Benin or Eboe to those of any other part of Guinea, for their hardiness, intelligence, integrity, and zeal" (38). He was, in addition, a likeable individual because he was humble, ready to be of service, tactful and diplomatic in his relationship with people, quick to learn, patient, and all-forgiving even to those who clearly did not deserve his forgiveness. These qualities as well as his courage, optimism, unwavering faith in divine deliverance, and, above all, his determination, perseverance, thriftiness, and great commercial instincts as he pursued his freedom through purchase were what made it possible for him to finally leave the phase of slavery to the final and third phase of his return to freedom.

Characteristically, Equiano welcomed his freedom which he had purchased in terms that link him to Africa and his original state of natural freedom though he chooses for good reasons to go to England than to return to Africa: "and now, being as in my original free African state, I embarked on board the Nancy" (138). Chapters 8 to 12 record this final phase of Equiano's memoir which comprises of his journeys in Europe, his cross-Atlantic trading (paradoxically in slaves, among other things), his scientific expedition to the North Pole, his conversion to Christianity, the self-publication and self-marketing of his narrative, his marriage, and his far-reaching and successful efforts to disseminate information about the evil of slave trade and to lobby the queen, members of the House of Lords and House of Commons for the abolition of the trade. The qualities that enabled him to survive slavery and to purchase his freedom — humility, congeniality, intelligence, tact, diplomacy, hard work, courage, faith, entrepreneurial instincts, and thrift (qualities that he associated with his African upbringing) — (were the same as assured his success as a British subject. By the time he died in 1797, Equiano had amassed considerable inheritance for his two daughters, one of who did not long survive him (Carretta 1995:305).

Every phase of Equiano's narrative achieves his intended goal. The first phase establishes with a series of indisputable evidence that Africans were a civilized race. The evidence include his people's well structured governmental, economic, social, legal, and cultural systems and the fact that Africans were a God-fearing people who had a structured religious system quite similar to those of the Jews. This phase of Equiano's narrative leads readers to the inevitable logical conclusion that only an intelligent people could organize the kind of efficient, God-fearing and moral society as Equiano has described, and that it was a sign of God's approval of the Africans that He would favor one of them and appoint him (Equiano) as His instrument for their deliverance from the bondage of slavery. The obvious allusion here is to the prophets and to Christ whom God sent to deliver the Jews, His chosen people, from bondage. Phase two reinforces phase one by showing how Equiano, a representative African, survives the horrors of slavery with fortitude, dignity, faith in and support from God, a situation in which an intellectually less endowed person would have perished. The intellectual and material success of Equiano which phase three of the narrative depicts also further reinforces the conclusion already made manifest by the earlier two phases. The enormous success of Equiano in garnering the support of the peoples in the influential circles of England to use his popular narrative as an anti-slavery instrument shows the hand of God who had chosen Equiano from the very beginning in Africa as a "particular favourite of heaven." Obviously, a people by whom God so firmly stands cannot be seen as heathens. Clearly, a people who could produce a personality as Equiano could not be regarded as unintelligent or uncivilized. Equiano's learned and carefully structured narrative, let alone his great personality and material success in hostile environments, was itself an irrefutable confirmation of his people's superior intellect, their superior civilization, and their godliness. Anyone who perceptively read Equiano's narrative could not have escaped arriving at these conclusions; hence those who fully understood the import of Equiano's narrative were quick to deny that he really was an African (Carretta 1995:6-7, 261, 286, 347). This was why Equiano calls himself "a stranger" even after he has successfully integrated himself as a British subject (31). It is what also explains the reason Equiano consistently links the self (Olaudah Equiano, the African) with the self's place (Essaka/Eboe/Benin Empire—Africa) throughout his narrative. Equiano knew only too well that the greatest insult an individual African could receive was, and still is, to denigrate the individual's home by saying that he or she lacked home training. It was, therefore, one's obligation and honor to defend one's home/place as a way of defending one's dignity/self. Equiano succeeded admirably well in carrying out the dual task.

Self and Place in Achebe's *Things Fall Apart*

The task that confronted the Black intellectual during slavery was practically the same as later confronted their descendants during colonialism, except that in the seventeenth and eighteenth centuries, alleged African primitivism, heathenism, and intellectual inferiority served as the European pretext for the enslavement of Africans, whereas in the nineteenth century, the same allegations, though already discredited in works like those by Equiano,

Frederick Douglass, and other Black intellectuals of the eighteenth and nineteenth centuries, nonetheless became the pretext for a new form of enslavement—colonization. In dealing with this similar problem, Black intellectuals often employed approaches that were similar to those used by their own intellectual predecessors. This is why it is not surprising that the artistic strategies of Achebe's novel, *Things Fall Apart* resemble those deployed by Equiano in his *Interesting Narrative*. However, in using the tactic of defending one's honor by linking the self to the self's place of abode or origin, Achebe goes into greater psychological details than did Equiano.

Achebe's novel is divided into almost two equal halves, with the first half (chapters 1 through 13) devoted to the era preceding the European incursion into Africa, and the second half (chapters 14 through 25) dealing with the European encroachment and consolidation of colonialism. The first half of the novel also coincides with the first phase in the life of the novel's hero, Okonkwo. The second half of the novel neatly subdivides into two equal parts, with the first part consisting of six chapters (14 through 19) depicting the second phase in Okonkwo's life; the third phase is treated in the last six chapters (20 through 25). As in the case of Equiano, the narrative of the first phase of Okonkwo's life displays microscopic details of the cultural milieu in which the hero's character was formed and in a manner that comprehensively refutes European justifications for colonialism. Phase two, also as in Equiano's case, reveals that the ability of the hero to survive the adversities of exile has everything to do with the manner in which his culture of origin has positively conditioned his character; thus, twice refuting white racist justification for colonialism. Again as in Equiano's memoir, the third phase of Okonkwo's life in Achebe's novel is a climactic affirmation of the dignity of African culture in a manner that suggests its moral superiority to the aggrandizing, duplicitous and pretentious culture of the intruding colonizers.

What Essaka was to Equiano is what Umuofia is to Okonkwo—home, the cultural bedrock of character, and almost every aspect of Okonkwo's character is a reflection of Umuofia's social, political, philosophical, economic, legal, religious, military, and family values. Although Okonkwo is a forceful, assertive personality, he moderates his individualism in conformity to the communal republicanism that governs Umuofia. Hence, for instance, even though he would have always wished to have his way in public affairs, he goes to the village commune to argue his case, and he listens to and reasons with other people's views until a communal decision is taken from reasoned arguments. Okonkwo does not always like the communal meetings because he knows that his people have a great love for the speech delivered with aesthetic beauty and oratorical flourish, and in this department,

Okonkwo is a nonstarter, being a man, not of words, but of action. But the people of Umuofia are not a narrow sort of people; they have a democratic accommodativeness for the varieties of life. Hence they love Okonkwo, a poor orator, for what he has in plenty and which they need for their communal protection: his strength, courage, military prowess and leadership. Okonkwo is a battle-tested, highly-decorated, and greatly respected war general of Umuofia, one whose name generates widespread fear in the enemy's camp. Because of the advantages of such a dreaded military leader in instances of war, the people of Umuofia conscientiously promote an environment for the emergence of fighters like Okonkwo. To this end, they have promoted the contest of strength into a popular public entertainment. Indeed, Okonkwo's story begins with the description of a historic wrestling match that establishes his unparalleled strength and fame in the nine villages of Umuofia and beyond.

Though the Umuofians valued military prowess, they also appreciate people who cultivate the refined taste of the arts, like music; in any case, they love entertainment, and hence they accommodate the likes of Unoka, Okonkwo's father whose laziness is proverbial. A cardinal virtue in Umuofia is industry, and Okonkwo assiduously and successfully cultivates this virtue primarily because he does not want to be a failure like his father and because material success is a way to rise to the position of importance and reverence in the society. The ever-present and terrifying fear of becoming like his father, whom Okonkwo judged a material failure and a weakling for displaying a love for songs and music, is the psychological fuel that supplies energy to the fire of Okonkwo's ambition and iron resolve to successfully climb the ladder of social success and recognition. Although Okonkwo's success is phenomenal, the fear of falling back from the height of his many-titled rank to the social abyss of his father's nothingness remains with him forever, cornering him into a position in which he feels compelled to constantly prove his strength and courage. This psychological liability or tragic flaw becomes the regular source of his human errors and lack of sufficient demonstration of tenderness of feeling toward even those he dearly loves. To show love, he believes, is to show weakness.

Okonkwo's view on this matter, as on some other issues including his attitude to his father's material failure, contradicts the position of his society which celebrates memorable love like that between Ozoemena and Ogbuefi who even death could not separate. Umuofia is a society that democratically appreciates variety and dissent and whose philosophy can be summed up in the dictum: live-and-let-live. For a people who love the word beautifully spoken and who believe that "proverbs are the palm oil with which words are eaten" (7), it is no surprise that their philosophy of live-and-let-live has been neatly framed in a memorable proverb: "Let the kite perch and let the eagle perch too. If one says no to the other, let his wing break" (19). Because of their democratic disposition, the people of Umuofia prefer to dwell on an individual's strength rather than the weakness. Hence, in spite of the premium they place on material success and military prowess, epitomized by individuals like Okonkwo, the Umuofians have an accommodative space for materially unsuccessful peoples like Okonkwo's father, Unoka. The latter's failure and debts are treated with jovial levity while he is valued for his musical accomplishments and is respected as a traditional musician.

As the proverb that sums up Umuofia's democratic accomodativeness also shows, the Umuofians are a people with a very strict sense of justice. They have an efficient judicial system that settles everything from family quarrels between husband and wife like that between Nzowulu and Mgbafo (86-93), to land disputes and impending wars between villages. As we see twice in the experience of Okonkwo, the people of Umuofia practice an absolutely incorruptible system of justice. No one, irrespective of his or her social status, is above the law. Okonkwo, in spite of his many titles and the great respect he commands as a great warrior, a patriot, and an extremely wealthy man, twice receives judicial punishment, the first time for breaking the sacred Week of Peace by beating his wife, the second time for accidentally killing a kinsman. In the distant past, the sentence for the first offense used to be death, but it has been reduced to material fines by the time of Okonkwo, whose punishment for the second offense was more severe— seven years of exile. The nature of these punishments reveals that Umuofia is not a society that is rigidly frozen in the past but one that regularly modernizes. Also it reveals the great regard the people have for life which they want to protect against preventable accidents. The strictness of the law discourages the sort of carelessness that led to Okonkwo's accidental killing. The high regard that the people have for life is further made evident by the fact that they do not lightly go into war, except it has become inevitable and only when they are in the right. Umuofia, the narrator affirms, "never went to war unless its case was clear and just and was accepted as such by its Oracle" (12).

The Umuofians are a deeply religious people, and the essence of their religious practices, as the conversation between the missionary Mr. Brown and the old man Akunna shows, is little different from that of Christianity, consisting as they both do in beliefs in a supreme deity, God/Chukwu, a hierarchy of what Akunna calls "lesser gods," and the use of symbolic physical images to represent spiritual objects of worship or adoration (179-81). The observance of the rituals of certain social functions like marriage, naming and burial ceremonies, harvesting and the taking of titles are also performed with almost a religious zeal. The people practice medicinal and psychiatric treatment with efficiency, as is evident in Okonkwo's use of herbs to cure Ezinma who was suffering from fever, the same Ezinma whom Chielo, the priestess of Agbala, mounts on her back and in the middle of a particularly dark night takes from one village to another and back as a way of psychologically conditioning her against the fear of darkness and the fear of the unknown. The priestess knows what is not known by charlatans like the medicine man Okagbue who has fraudulently diagnosed Ezinma as an ogbanje, a spirit child who mercilessly plagues parents with repeated cycles of births and premature deaths.

The people of Umuofia also know how to enjoy their leisure: they love sports, festivals, feasting, and the conversation that goes with it. They are a people of ceremony and social decorum, meticulously observing the specified details of social rituals and taking great delight and pride in the perfection with which they execute such details. For instance, every breaking of the kola and the drinking of palm wine when welcoming friendly visitors, or during social ceremonies like marriage negotiations, or during religious observances like sacrifices to gods or goddesses, is a complete ritual on its own and is meticulously performed.

Thus, Okonkwo's phenomenal achievements in Umuofia are attributable both to his ability to correctly identify what his society values and to his ability to pursue single-mindedly what he has set his mind on until it is achieved. For his success in measuring up to the standards set by his society, the latter generously rewards him by placing him in a position of honor and leadership, in which capacity, he helps to set standards for the rest of the society, especially in areas where he is regarded as a great specialist: industriousness, strength of character, ability to make wealth, unalloyed patriotism, courage, and military prowess.

The qualities that elevated Okonkwo to the position of prominence during the first phase of his life in Umuofia do not desert him during the second phase when he is compelled to go into a seven-year exile to his motherland, Mbanta, following his carelessness, involving an accidental gun discharge that killed a kinsman, the son of Ezeudu during the performance of the latter's burial ceremony. In time, Okonkwo overcomes the adversities of exile and starts to prosper after a fashion, thanks to the cooperation he receives from his maternal relations, the support given by the friends he left behind in his fatherland, principally Obierika, and, above all, because of his industriousness, courage, and experience as a great farmer. However, a new phenomenon—the arrival of white missionaries and colonial administrators—which at first manifests itself as a manageable, if curious and annoying nuisance, begins to establish a presence in Igboland during this second phase of

Okonkwo's life. Before long his son Nwoye, soon to be renamed Isaac, abandons him and joins the white missionaries. Painful as this experience is for Okonkwo, he is able to live with it because he has long suspected Nwoye to be a reincarnation of his father, the weakling and materially unsuccessful Unoka, whose failure, coupled with the great premium Umuofia placed on material success, have supplied the psychological motivation that propelled Okonkwo to wealth, military distinction, and social success. So, though painful, it is not too difficult for Okonkwo to dismiss Nwoye as a predictable failure.

However, when at the end of seven years of exile, Okonkwo returns to his fatherland, laden with evidence of material prosperity and ready to start the third phase of his life, he discovers that the white missionaries and colonial administrators have fully entrenched themselves and are working hard to consolidate themselves as sole authority of government in Umuofia. Okonkwo, of course, cannot accept such an eventuality and he fully expects his country men to join him in driving away the pretentious strangers, but to his utter amazement his people act as if their subjugation to an alien rule is already a forgone conclusion. In view of what he has known about the white intruders, Okonkwo cannot contemplate willingly yielding authority to them. He can see no moral ground on which to justify the demands of arrogant foreigners who have shown gross insensibility to the rightful owners of the land, their religion, leaders, culture, and everything they hold sacred. Okonkwo, the soldier cannot conceive being ruled by foreigners who have displayed the worst form of military barbarity, ambushing a whole village of women, children, and men, all of whom were unarmed and unwarned, and mowing them all to the ground in retaliation for a white man who was killed more out of freight and ignorance than for any ulterior motive. Okonkwo sees no sense in submitting to governance by a people whose only claim to power rests on their arrogance, insensibility, and inhumanity, and who have introduced a perverted judicial system where their "District Commissioners judged cases in ignorance" (174), in addition to having succeeded in dissociating governance from the governed by introducing the first corrupt and alienated officials into the administration of the land (197). Okonkwo prefers the dignity of death to the indignity of being governed by his moral inferiors.

Viewed in this manner, Okonkwo's death in spite of its method is a death with dignity and a credit to the land which has produced a man with such a high sense of honor. In the end, Okonkwo is a historical landmark, bearing the language of African protest against colonialist racist arrogance, unprovoked aggression, and economic greed. Meanwhile, Umuofia which has retained its traditional resilience in the face of adversities, its flexibility and democratic accommodation of variety, its philosophy of "live-and-let-live,"

and its modernizing capacity, survives and lives on in its younger generations like Nwoye who would design new ways of dealing with the new reality.

Achebe depicts not only the details in Umuofia's culture that unequivocally refute the groundless and racist claims of African supposed primitivity, intellectual inferiority, and heathenism, but also the weaknesses of
Umuofia, notably, the treatment of twins who are regarded as taboos and are
thrown away into the so-called bad bush, the *osu* caste system which dehu-
manizes those regarded as unclean, the mutilation of the corpse of those
children identified as ogbanje, and human sacrifice, epitomized by the memorable killing of Ikemefuna. However, Achebe's artistic strategies show that
these weaknesses were not the cause of, but only a convenient pretext for,
colonization. The barbaric incident at Abame, the insensitive treatment of
the elders of Umuofia, and the corrupt nature of the administrative governance set up in Umuofia and neighboring populations like Mbanta and Umuru
show that Umuofia's weaknesses serve the colonizers merely as pretext for
gaining a foothold among a people for whom they already have a design that
is anything but humane, civilized, or Christian. Thus, it is obvious that in
Things Fall Apart Achebe intentionally depicts the relationship between a
fictional character's self and place as a narrative strategy for defending his
fatherland against colonialist racial pretense and imposition. In the process
of accomplishing this patriotic goal, Achebe cleverly turns the tables on the
colonialist claim to racial and cultural superiority. Every observant reader
of *Things Fall Apart* recognizes not only the baselessness of these claims,
but also the essentially uncivilized nature of any culture that produces people
who would use such lies as pretext for colonization and dehumanization of
fellow human beings.

Self and Place in Soyinka's *Ake*

At the height of the Ake women's revolt against unfair taxation when the
Alake's palace is besieged, an insolent colonial District Officer rudely shouts
at the women's leader, Mrs. Kuti, commanding her to "SHUT UP YOUR
WOMEN!" After deliberately allowing a weighty moment of silence to
register the gravity of the insult on everybody's mind, Mrs. Kuti angrily
remarks: "You may have been born, you were not bred. Could you speak to
your mother like that?" (*Ake* 211). Beyond corroborating the remarks I
have earlier made regarding the importance Nigerians attach to proper upbringing ("home training," in popular parlance), this revealing episode, as I
understand it, underscores Soyinka's motive for writing *Ake*. Home training, for the Nigerian, explains everything: it shows whether a child would be
well mannered or prosper in the world, but, more important, it reveals the

texture of a people's culture, because a child is the ambassador of the home and of its culture. In *Ake* Soyinka reveals the texture of his culture and the people that have bred him, the better for his observers to understand how he became who he is—a world-renowned intellectual, writer, and political activist. This, as we have seen, is the same motive behind Equiano's and Achebe's works, and, as we shall soon discover, behind Gates's memoir as well. Additionally, and equally important, Ake is Soyinka's comment on the culture debate as it relates to contemporary times and that also answers back to the sort of racism that produced slavery and colonialism.

Although the last words in *Ake* are remarks concerning Wole's confusion about the "irrational world of adults and their disciplines," these words are not to be taken as literally as on earlier occasions in the autobiography when he used a similar expression. This is because at this point Wole is already over ten years of age and is used to the strange logic of the adult world in which he already participates, not just vicariously by observing and listening to, but by himself directly engaging in, adult conversations with well-informed intellectual and political leaders like Mr. and Mrs. Daodu Ransome-Kuti. There is, however, genuine confusion on the part of young Wole the first time he makes the remark. This is when the same adults who in the first place had instigated a fight between him and his brother Dipo proceeded afterwards to blame him for the fight. Then he has sweepingly concluded that "there was neither justice nor logic in the world of grown-ups" (104). When Dipo's name is changed to Femi, he also expresses similar sentiments: "Once again I felt a helpless confusion—did these grown-ups ever know what they wanted?" (125). The difference between the genuine and the pretended confusion expressed in the same phrase is the difference between the first and second phases of Wole's childhood as recorded in *Ake.*

The first phase—the years of innocence—is characterized by a curiosity about, and fascination with, the natural environment which is imbued with intelligence and mysteries and which is constantly changing and expanding in horizon and character. At first, it is a limited small world of the parsonage compound which contains the Canon's residence, school buildings, play fields, the Orchard, the mission bookseller's compound, the headmaster's residence where the Soyinkas live, and Bishops Court where the famous Bishop Ajayi Crowther once lived but which now serves as an Anglican school girls dormitory. Nearby is St. Peter's Church which together with the parsonage, in Wole's highly creative imagination, constitute an embattled island of faith, surrounded by a hostile world, chief of which is the pagan Itoko heights that with its pagan priest, the Chief, and his stable, looks hostilely down on the parsonage. The parsonage is in addition bordered by formidable thick woods, the abode of spirits and ghommids and the shrine of the dreaded oro cult. The stories recounted in Wole's house concerning the fearful spiritual battles which the faith-emboldened parsonage and its legendary occupants like Rev J. J. Ransome-Kuti had fought with the equally awesome and determined mysterious forces of the pagan world bordering its compounds further mystify and sharpen Wole's imagination. Consequently, as he moves around the compound, young Wole begins to see pictures and statues like that of Bishop Crowther come alive. And God, of course, lives at the top of the Itoko heights in spite of the pagan presence of the Chief and his stable on its crest, and it is from there that God descends every Sunday to visit St. Peter's Church and the parsonage. Wole spends many long hours alone exploring the mystery of the compounds, the boulders, the orchards and their fruits and flowers which re-enact for Wole's benefit their biblical stories as he keeps their company. And there are the heavenly fruits like the guava and the pomegranate, for which, following the example of the battling parsonage and its pagan surrounding, Wole soon learns to stake a proprietary claim, and fights with his sister and other children of the house.

In time, the small world of the parsonage gradually expands to include spaces outside its walls, and before long young Wole soon comes to know the whole of Ake township and suburbs, and even his father's village, Isara, some forty miles away. Repeatedly Soyinka nostalgically comments on the changes that have overtaken the parsonage and, no doubt, part of the purpose of describing it is to preserve the checkered history of the cradle of his life in printed memory.

The contest of will and of faiths between the evangelizing Anglican missionaries, many of whom are Africans like Bishop Crowther and Rev. J. J. Ransome-Kuti, is exemplified by a story narrated to young Wole by his mother, Mrs. Eniola Soyinka, and which, no doubt, Soyinka recounts because of its telling ambiguity. This happened in an Ijebu village. Rev. Ransome-Kuti had ignored warnings not to evangelize on a given day because it was sacred to followers of traditional religion who were going to have an outing for their egungun masquerades. While Rev. Ransome-Kuti was performing service, the egungun procession arrived and one egungun demanded that the service be stopped, but the Rev. carried on. Before departing, the egungun tapped thrice with his wand on the church main door and almost immediately, the church building mysteriously collapsed. The other mystery was that none of the members of the congregation was hurt by the collapsed roof and walls, nor was Rev. Ransome-Kuti at all intimidated. In fact, he merely paused to calm the worshipers, and after offering a thanksgiving prayer, he carried on with his service as if nothing had happened.

This incident as well as others, some of which Wole personally witnessed (like the mysteries of the abiku child Bukola or the mysterious paralysis of an ogboni cult member supposedly caused by "the collective psychic force of the women" whom the victim publicly derided during the Ake women's uprising 212-3), or those that were authenticated by reliable witnesses (like his mother's accounts about his uncle Sanya, who was reputed to be an *oro* —a spirit man) influenced Wole in two ways. They conditioned him to have an open mind towards both the Christian faith and African traditional beliefs, and they demonstrated to him what faith and a strong will can achieve. The significance of the latter lesson would further be impressed on him by both his father and grandfather on separate and significant moments in his childhood. The grandfather, for instance, who assures him that "there is more to the world than the world of Christians, or books," advises him never to run away from a fight because determination and his will power will eventually make him the winner (143, 147-8). When his father thinks that he is about to die, he gives Wole a death-bed advice: "You are not to let anything defeat you.... You will find that only determination will bring one through, sheer determination. And a faith in God—don't ever neglect your prayers" (162). With these influences, Wole with ease conflates the Christian and traditional beliefs, speaking of St. Peters as "my special egungun" (33) and expressing admiration for the magician's "language of a dual force" (152). This is doubtlessly the root of the cultural and spiritual eclecticism that would later enrich Wole's works with a conflation of African and European myths and that would condition his choice of the Yoruba deity *Ogun* as the patron of his art as a writer.

Wole's childhood education also is characterized by this duality both in its content and agent. His father's house is "the intellectual watering-hole of Ake and its environ" (19) and Wole listens and is encouraged by his father to listen to the endless intellectual arguments and debates that go on there. Furthermore, his father actively promotes in him the development of an inquiring critical mind that accepts nothing on faith and that "lawyers" every presented opinion. The father constantly engages in disputations with his young son who soon becomes notorious for "lawyering people to death." Joseph the house boy is sure Wole will turn out to be a troublesome native, a prophesy that has come true as all Nigerian unpopular leaders and dictators know only too well. During the brief period Wole attends Abeokuta Grammar school, its principal, Daodu Ransome-Kuti who is his maternal uncle, also organizes the curriculum to emphasize the training of assertive, independent-minded, critical intellects. He is encouraged to read, and he reads fast and beyond his years. His education is consciously ordered by his parents to emphasize both Western knowledge and knowledge of his Yoruba culture. Traditional values are impressed on him and they feature prominently in the life of his parents. His father, a school headmaster who religiously cultivates a rose garden, who eats elegantly with fork and knife and with impeccable English table manners, and who performs calisthenics every morning, is also an Isara Chief who uses the traditional chewing stick for teeth hygiene, narrates folktales to his children, wears both European and traditional clothes, and takes his family home to Isara, his village, every Christmas to perform his duties as chief and to expose his children to the local traditions. His mother trades in assorted African and European retail goods and combines African and European menus in feeding the family. The medicines used to treat ailments in the house are also an assortment of African and European preparations. Because his education has also stressed intelligent and critical evaluation of phenomena, the principle of multiculturalism which he thus imbibes eschews mindless imitation of foreign cultures, a prevalent habit of some segments of contemporary Nigerian youth which he sternly rebukes (155-6).

The traditional communal ethics of sharing and the Christian tenet of hospitality are exemplified in the family often to the inconvenience of young Wole who hates the "maternal dormitory" that resulted from the general sleeping arrangement in his mother's room. The house which already has a multiethnic composition of kins, servants, and visitors, becomes a regular guest house for visitors from Isara, including the peasant women who bring their produce every market day to sell at Ake. The house is also an abode for strays, and one of them, nicknamed "Mayself," becomes notorious for his abuse of the family's hospitality at meal times. In spite of the inconvenience of the "maternal dormitory," young Wole learns the crucial lesson that life is meaningful when it is not lived selfishly but is governed by the precepts of communal ethics. This is doubtlessly the root of the communal principle that has subsequently and consistently guided his social activism in the Nigerian polity. In Wole's household, punishment is regularly used as an instrument for inculcating discipline; however, while the mother prefers the cane, the father chooses psychological weapons that test the mind and train the will. The manner in which the mother handles the case of Mr. "Mayself" and others who overstep their bounds teaches Wole the value of tact, diplomacy, firmness, and decisiveness in dealing with people.

The second phase of Wole's childhood education—the phase of experience, is associated with the events surrounding the Egba Women Movement which practicalizes for him in a summary sort of way all the lessons of the first phase of his education—the phase of innocence. At this time, Wole is about nine-and-half years old and is temporarily attending Abeokuta's Grammar School, pending his securing a government scholarship to attend the more prestigious Ibadan Government College. He witnesses the unraveling of all of the events that led to the formation of the women's movement and knows that it is the concern for the common plight of Egba peasant women who are being unfairly taxed that makes Mrs. Daodu Ransome-Kuti, Wole's mother, and a few other influential Ake middle-class women decide to do something about the situation. The women are angry because the unfair tax shows that the government has violated the traditional communal ethics, which require that governance be in the mutual interest of the governed and the governor, but they can do nothing about it until they are organized and until the people they are trying to help become well informed.

So they begin the formation of an association, start adult education for the peasant women, and commence to canvass grassroot support. To succeed, they have to be strong; consequently, they broaden the base of their women union by forming a nationwide Nigerian Women Union which they affiliate to nationalist political parties working for national independence. Mrs. Kuti even carries the women's case and presents it to the colonial government in Britain. Wole sees the daily details of the Egba Women activism, the labor, perseverance, debates of tactics and strategies, the cost for printing and distributing material to educate the public on the matter within and outside Ake, and, above all, he sees the intellectual leadership, courage, sheer determination and will power provided by Mrs. Kuti, backed by her formidable husband, Daodu Ransom-Kuti. At every stage, Wole is involved in the movement as errand boy, as peasant women teacher, and as secretary, and is there at the scene of action observing from a safe distance when the movement climaxes into the uprising that rocks Ake, shakes the powerful ogboni council, disorganizes the local colonial District Officer and the national colonial administration in Lagos, and nearly topples the Alake from his throne. He sees the ups and downs of the events leading to and during the revolt and the central role organization, knowledge, strategy, courage, will power, and leadership play to make the revolt a success. In short, the young Wole has seen details of a successful revolution and how it works, is impressed by it, and he chooses to make the documentation of these details the significant conclusion of his memoir.

The major lesson of *Ake* is that government is not sacrosanct and that it could and should be made answerable to the people it governs. In order to ensure that full implication of this lesson is not lost on the reader, Soyinka makes the reader realize that the target of the women's uprising was as much against local as external tyranny by pointing out that the Alake, who at the height of the rebellion was a prisoner of the women trying to depose him, was indeed also "the slave of the [colonial] District Officer—if not the present one, at least of the earlier, insolent one" (220). The women revolt then was actually against colonial domination whose philosophical root was white racism. This was why the women movement was affiliated to the independence-seeking nationalist political parties and why Mrs. Kuti went to England, seat of colonial government, to argue the women's case. It was also the source of the vehemence with which Mrs. Kuti repeatedly charged the allied forces with white racism for choosing on racist grounds to bomb Japan, and not Germany, during the second World War. As Wole prepares to leave for Ibadan Government College, to which he has won a scholarship, he is warned by his uncle, Mr. Daodu Ransome-Kuti, of the miseducation that awaits him at that colonial college which is run by white racist principals and teachers. It is of the greatest significance that Soyinka should end his childhood autobiography on this note.

What Soyinka shows in *Ake*, then, is first the progress of the fight that Okonkwo in *Things Fall Apart* began but could not win because his people were then not prepared. Thanks to the liberationist education provided by the Egba Women's revolt, the contemporary Okonkwos are now a match for their oppressors. Second, it is a portrayal of how he, Soyinka, reflects the best tradition of his land by virtue of how the land had bred him in childhood to become as an adult a world-renown intellectual, writer and political activist. Soyinka is thus in agreement with Equiano and Achebe in the understanding of how the self reflects the self's place.

Self and Place in Gates's *Colored People*

Gates begins his memoir with a nostalgic view of Piedmont, his place of birth which is in danger of disappearing: "You wouldn't know Piedmont anymore—my Piedmont, I mean—by its silhouetted ruins" (3). "My darkest fear," he writes, "is that Piedmont, West Virginia, will cease to exist, if some executives on Park Avenue decide that it is more profitable to build a completely new paper mill elsewhere than to overhaul one a century old" (xi). One of Gates's reasons for writing the memoir, then, is to preserve in printed memory the record of the Piedmont that he knew, his Piedmont, the Piedmont of colored people. But colored people were not the only people who lived in Piedmont; whites lived there also, and were in the majority. Moreover, this was pre-civil rights times and Piedmont, therefore, was a segregated town. Segregation was so pervasive that young Henry, lovingly nicknamed Skip by his maternal grandmother, "assumed that this dispensation could no more be contested than the laws of gravity, or traffic lights" (19).

Racist segregation was everywhere: whites lived in their own streets in their own beautiful houses; colored people congregated in their own poor streets in houses owned by whites because they had no rights to own property. Churches were segregated; whites had theirs, the colored had theirs, and if it happened a colored went to a white church, as Skip's father once

did, he would be asked "to sit in the back pew" (115). Hospitals did everything they could to avoid treating colored patients, as Skip discovered when
taken in excruciating pains to a hospital where a doctor played dumb, claiming Skip was faking his pains. The schools too played tricks, as Skip's
brother, Rocky, discovered when he was cheated of a prestigious scholastic
award he had won—the Golden Horseshoe award, which ranked as "the
Nobel Prize of eighth graders in West Virginia"—because he was colored
(98). Work was segregated, and at the paper mill where "almost all colored
people in Piedmont worked," they all "made the same money, because they
all worked at the same job, on the platform" as loaders (8). Services and
entertainment, of course, were likewise segregated; Skip recalls: "For most
of my childhood, we couldn't eat in restaurants or sleep in hotels, we couldn't
use certain bathrooms or try on clothes in stores" (17). Inter-racial dating
was a taboo: "Colored go with colored; white with white" (92); consequently,
Skip's and Linda Hoffman's spontaneous and mutual love for each other, a
love which Skip nostalgically and lyrically evokes, was doomed from the
beginning by racism. As for television, Skip says that because "we were
starved for images of ourselves... we searched TV to find them," but "except for sports, we rarely saw a colored person" (19, 20). The consolation,
however, was that television provided the only window they had into the
tightly segregated middle class world of the whites, "a world so elegantly
distant from ours, it was like a voyage to another galaxy, light-years away"
(21).

Obviously, it is not this segregated Piedmont for which Skip is nostalgic
or worried because it might disappear. From colored people, racist Piedmont elicited one of two emotions, typified by his mother's deep hatred, or
his uncle Nemo's deep fear. As for Skip, he was only too glad to grab at
opportunities that enabled his mental horizon to expand beyond the suffocating confines of Piedmont.[5] This was why he loved geography and map at
school, why he enjoyed his trips to the Peterkin Church camps, and was glad
when he eventually left the town for college. This was why, when the civil
rights movement which "came late to Piedmont, even though it came early
to our television set" (19) finally arrived, Skip embraced it whole-heartedly
as did members of his activist group, the "Fearsome Four." For them, the
movement "was an exciting and sincere effort to forge a new communal
identity among a people descended from splendid ancient cultures, abducted
and forced into servility, and now deprived of collective economic and political power" (186).[6]

The way of life that these abducted, economically exploited, and politically deprived people have carved out for themselves amidst hostile segregation, and the history and cultural traditions of this life are what constitute

the Piedmont— "my Piedmont"—of which Skip nostalgically speaks and whose possible disappearance, caused by a capitalist fiat in factory relocation, he expresses fear. This is the Piedmont of colored people, and it is how he, Skip, was bred in and experienced this Piedmont that he presents in *Colored People*. In his interview with Middlebrook, Gates explains: "We [colored and white Americans] didn't want to be forced to live with each other, but we were forced to live with each other, and we developed a culture out of that. We didn't want to be slaves, but we created a culture, even as slaves. And I think we tend to forget that there was a tremendously vibrant, wonderful, compelling culture that black people created before integration, and a lot of that has been lost" (196).

As stated earlier, Skip narrates his story in two broad phases. The first (the phase of innocence) portrays his birth and upbringing, while the second (the phase of maturity) depicts Skip as one of the prime movers in the creation of a new Piedmont. This is the phase of action involving the demolition of the walls of segregation in Piedmont.

Two Black intellectual traditions—one linked to Booker T. Washington, the other to W.E.B. DuBois—characterized Skip's family education, and they were associated with the two sides of his family: the Colemans (the maternal) and the Gateses (the paternal). The Colemans, made up of nine brothers and three surviving sisters, did not want the applecart of race relations to be upset; rather, they promoted advancement through industry, self-reliance, cooperation between kins, discipline, and religious faith. They were very ambitious, very enterprising, imaginatively resourceful in the use of their hands, and thrifty: "They'd drive fifty miles to save cents ... Carpentry, masonry, gardening, hunting, fishing. Just fixing things in general. If you can hammer it or oil it up, dem coons can do it," concedes Skip's father who, being the Gates that he is, does not particularly like his in-laws (64). The Colemans were closely knit, self-reliant, deeply involved in church-going, ascetic in their habits, rather clanish, and were chauvinistic in the treatment of women: "They didn't drink, they didn't smoke, and if they weren't especially religious, they were especially self-righteous" (61). They lived a double life in order to accomodate white segregationist laws: "They would mouth the white man's command in the day, to paraphrase Hurston, and enact their own legislation and jurisprudence in their sepia world at night" (64). With these characteristics, it was only a matter of time before they became prosperous: "Born barely working class—clawing and scraping your way out of starvation class, Daddy says—they carved out a dark-chocolate world, a world as nurturing as the loamy soil in Nemo's garden at the bottom of Rat Tail Road" (64). Their success brought respect from everybody, including whites who treated them with some preference: "The Colemans were the first among the colored to be allowed hunting licenses and their own rifles and shotguns" (159) and to own property. "They had a weighty sense of family and tradition," Skip says, and one tradition they religiously observed was the annual family reunion, which "was the social event of the season" and for which it was an honor to be invited. Their table manners were as impeccably aristocratic as that of Soyinka's father in Ake: "The Colemans were serious about their cooking and their eating. There was none of this eating on the run; meals lasted for hours, with lots of good conversation thrown in"(39). Thus, "being a Coleman was a very big deal in Piedmont" (53).

Naturally, the Colemans wanted Skip, who was a favorite of the head of the Colemans family—Miss Maggie, his maternal grandmother—and of his oldest uncle, Nemo, to follow their foot steps. However, Skip says "As years went by, I grew more critical, deciding that I was more like the Gateses than the Colemans" (61), and the distance between him and the Colemans widened even further during the civil rights era when Skip became an activist and became rebellious against family control, doing things like drinking and smoking that offended the Colemans' code of conduct. Worse still was the fact that Skip was breaking the principal rule of the Colemans' philosophy of racial accomodation by agitating for equal rights. For the Colemans, by whom "integration was experienced as a loss," Skip's radicalism was worrisome: "Because I flouted the rules, they thought I would come to a bad end, and they took pleasure in letting me know that. Deep down, I think they were freightened for me. And deeper down, I think I frightened them" (184, 185).

The influence of the Gates side of his family was in the tradition of DuBois—intellectual and radical. The Gateses descended from Jane Gates, "our missing link with Africa," writes Skip. Jane inherited landed property from the white man for whom she had all her children. Her descendants multiplied that property, establishing businesses, and they prospered. At the time Skip's paternal grandfather died, for instance, the children had much property to share, and "Everything [was] paid for, every deed unencumbered. Never use credit, Pop had told my daddy for as long as he could remember" (70). Skip's paternal grandmother was partial to her three daughters, whom she gave college education, while sending all her seven sons to work in factories. Because of the college education of his aunts, the Gateses by Skip's time were already a family of intellectuals that boast "Three generations at Howard, including the board of trustees, two generations at Harvard, including Harvard Law School. Three generations of dentists and three of doctors" (72). The intellectual atmosphere of the Gateses was visible in their abode and in their pastimes: "The rooms of their house had a

certain worn and aging depth and the sort of dust-covered calm that suggested tradition. They drank beer and Scotch, played cards, read detective
novels and traded them with each other, did crossword puzzles, and loved
puns" (67). And they love "analyzing things when they were over, breaking
things down one by one. Second-order consciousness. Metamouthing. Scrutinizing. Reading the signs. Explicating the implicit" (169).

Even though Skip's father did not possess a college education, he steered
his son in the direction of the intellectual life of the Gateses. He encouraged
in Skip the development of a critical, inquiring, and analytical frame of
mind, and to this end, he often played the role of the devil's advocate in
debates with Skip: "By the mid-sixties, we'd argue about King from sunup
to sundown. Sometimes he'd just mention King to get a rise from me, to
make a sagging evening more interesting, to see if I had learned anything
real yet, to see how long I could think up counter arguments before getting
so mad that my face would turn purple" (26). Later, he would play the same
intellectual game with Skip and Skip's radical friends—"The Fearsome
Four"—who had adopted him as surrogate father: "and the four of us would
sit for hours arguing with Daddy and Mama, eating dinner, watching television, and arguing some more. ... We'd fall asleep in my bedroom ... then get
up and argue with the Old Man some more. We'd argue with Daddy for
hours on end" (187). Skip's house was, in effect, the "intellectual watering
hole" of Piedmont, much like Wole's house in *Ake*.

Skip's father, however, was not a "race man" and did not fully embrace
Skip's radicalism unlike the other Gateses who were intellectual "freethinkers" towards whom Skip gravitated (85, 188). On the other hand, Skip's
mother was unlike her family, the Colemans, being a radical herself: "she
did not seem to fear white people" and "it was Mama ... who showed us how
to fight" (34, 98). She had three related methods for fighting—one psychological, one physical, and the other intellectual—and she fought because
"Mama did not play when it came to her boys, and she wasn't going to let
any white woman or man step on her babies' dreams" (92). She was involved in a protest march to demand education for colored children before
Skip was born. When Skip's brother, Rocky, was cheated in the Golden
Horseshoe competition, she "took the battle to them" in open protest (98).
She displayed psychological finesse in her battle with stores that would not
allow colored people to try on clothes, and she took her children along to
observe this refined mode of fighting. But her greatest weapon was intellectual, doing everything to ensure that her children excelled in formal education and showing her children the power of education. She was respected in
Piedmont by both white and colored on account of how she used her intellect
and limited education. Her eulogies at colored funerals was memorable for

their psychological insight and oratory. She was the first colored to be appointed secretary of the PTA and she produced admirable minutes: "It was poetry, pure poetry. She'd read each word beautifully, mellifluously, each syllable spoken roundly but without the hypercorrection of Negroes who make 'again' rhyme with 'rain'" (33).

Given this paternal and maternal encouragement, it was clear that Skip would prefer the Gateses' DuBoian radical intellectualism to the Colemans' Washingtonian accomodationism as a mode of dealing with racism. Skip's background and education also ensured that he would not confuse race with racism. Each side of his family has a generous dose of white blood; indeed, "until a generation ago, most of the Gateses qualified as octoroons—'light and bright and damn near white'" (73). Besides, in spite of prevalent racism, Skip's personal experiences showed him that the white skin must not be confused with racism. For instance, even though it was racism that prevented the natural love between him and Linda Hoffman from blossoming, his first fulfilling love affair was with another white girl, Maura Gibson. Also, the first individual who had provided him the best intellectual stimulation outside of family was a white liberal professor at Potomac State College, Duke Anthony Whitmore, who taught him the virtue of intellectual courage and boldness: "Sin boldly," Whitmore had insisted. Thus, Skip makes it abundantly clear in his preface, that while he identifies fully with colored people, he would not wish to be defined exclusively by that identification: "I rebel at the notion that I can't be part of other groups, that I can't construct identities through elective affinities, that race must be the most important thing about me" (xv).

Young Skip was very much attracted to religion and, like his father in his youth, he had wanted to go into the priesthood. Church-going appealed to him for a number of reasons. One was socio-cultural: "What the church did provide was a sense of community, moments of intimacy, of belonging to a culture" (116). Church gave him a sense of African-American history: "I'd sit next to her, trying to learn the words of the traditional gospel songs and the camp songs, listening to my past and future through Andrea's lovely voice" (148). A second reason was entertainment—he loved gospel music because it "could make you feel good, with people 'patting their foots' and nodding their heads and being in tune with the message." For this reason the revival meetings of the Holiness Church was his favorite: "that was a camp meeting," Skip ironically enthused, "It was part of the ritual: working hard on Saturday, partying Saturday night, picnic and camp meeting on Sunday —an ideal weekend" (116). His favorite was when Miss Toot sang "The Prodigal Son," half drunk, obliterating the distinction "between the sacred and the secular" (116). A third reason was spiritual and intellectual: Skip liked good sermons. But the fourth reason was perhaps the most important and it was psychological. Church promised a heaven of equality, justice, and happiness that segregation had denied on earth and it assuaged his fear of hell: "I supposed the shake-up of my spiritual creed was hastened by my realization that I was religious in part because I was scared, scared of Jesus coming back to earth and sending me to Hell, scared of being liquidated or vaporized in a nuclear holocaust, scared of what was happening to my mother —scared, in all likelihood, of life itself" (137). It was after this discovery that Skip abandoned the intention to dedicate his life to the priesthood and discovered a personal relation to God: "What I did feel was that God spoke His will to my heart if I asked what I should do in a given situation. I still ask, and, generally, I still hear. Sooner or later" (134). No doubt, the igno-rance or the intellectual fraud or religious hypocrisy of the Colemans churches and the "Sister Holy Ghost," on one hand, and the racism of white churches, on the other hand, also contributed to Skip's disenchantment with organized religion, and the cultivation of a preference for a truly protestant personal approach to religion. Indeed, what Skip discovered was his true self—the Gates who belonged to the intellectual tradition of freethinkers.

Skip also imbibed from his family and the Piedmont colored community the colored people's intense love of life, which consisted of an appreciation for humor and a disregard for social taboos that killed the joy out of life. "Daddy, loved telling stories about his family," Skip writes, "and I loved listening to them, mostly because they were so funny" (68). Colored people of Piedmont so loved life that it was fun to them to openly discuss how everybody was cheating on everybody else and accepting their bastard chil-dren without complaining. This love of life was also reflected in the atten-tion the colored of Piedmont paid to their style of clothing, hairdo, music, and dancing at the colored Legions. The cultural symbolism of this colored Piedmonts' love of life was the annual mill picnic, which drew Piedmont indigenes from whatever corners of the United States they might be located because they wanted to share in the special tradition, the love of life, that was Piedmont's. It is for this reason significant that Skip should nostalgi-cally and symbolically signal the disappearing of "his Piedmont" with the termination of the tradition of the mill picnic, the description of which also ends his childhood memoir.

Before this conclusion, however, Skip had presented the final element of his Piedmont education or upbringing—that which constitutes the second phase of his memoir: the Age of Maturity. If the first phase—the Age of Innocence—portrays Skip's education, how he was bred, the second phase is the phase of action and it depicts how Skip shows the tenor of his charac-ter and started giving back to the community which had given so much to him. The central element of this phase is the civil rights movement, which was for Skip what the Egba Women revolt in *Ake* was for Wole. Just as the watching of the Egba Women's movement taught Wole the process of how a people can assert their will and make government accountable to the community, so did the watching of the civil rights movement on television educate Skip on how to integrate segregated Piedmont. Given his age, Wole's participation in the Egba revolt was necessarily limited to that of errand boy, secretary, or teacher for the women; in his case, Skip and members of his "Fearsome Four" were the civil rights movement in Piedmont, having personally taken the risks of integrating many of the segregated facilities in Piedmont. Skip also personally integrated a section of Rehoboth Beach in far-out Delaware, and was, in fact, paradoxically the deciding factor in the mayoral election of the city of Keyser, West Virginia, by virtue of his radical courage in dating Maura Gibson and becoming "apparently the first interracial couple in Mineral County" (196). His book report on Dick Gregory's *Nigger*, his high school valedictory address, and his college application to Yale rang with the assertive radicalism of his integrationist crusade. For all this, he entered the security police's bad book as "that troublemaker Gates," a service of naming that Joseph, Wole's family houseboy, had performed for the colonial security police by prophetically calling Wole the "troublesome native." In time, even white Piedmont accepted the radically-emerged and academically-promising Skip Gates, whom they invited to help that Piedmont's rock of segregation (Westvaco paper mill) to integrate. This was one of the first confirmations of how right Skip's mother and the Gates were in bringing up their son to believe that intellectual radicalism — the tool promoted by W.E.B DuBois — was the right weapon to fight racism. Thus, even though Skip Gates refuses to be generalized ("I am not Everynegro ... this story is not the story of a race but a story of a village, a family, and its friends" xv-xvi), the way it has been told undeniably makes it the representative story of a representative African-American in a representative town. This is so because the family education of every African-American child even today has had to confront at some point a choice between the accommodationist philosophy of Booker T. Washington and the radical intellectual tradition of W. E. B. DuBois, and because every adult African-American has had to make this choice, even if the adult finally settles for neither the one nor the other, but rather a judicious selection of either, as circumstances dictate.

Thus, *Colored People* demonstrates that the autobiographical self is a reflection of the autobiographer's place, a reflection whose primary strategy is to undermine the racist definition of the biographer's place and, as such, the biographer's self. To this extent, therefore, Equiano's *Narrative*, Achebe's

Things Fall Apart, Soyinka's *Ake*, and Gates's *Colored People* can be said to be uniform in artistic purpose and strategy.

NOTES

1. The autobiographical details of *Things Fall Apart* should become somewhat clearer after the release of Ezenwa-Oheato's awaited *Chinua Achebe: A Biography* and much clearer still if Achebe chooses to publish an autobiography and addresses the matter in it. Meanwhile, one can only speculate on the basis of seeming similarities. The most obvious in this respect is the parallel between Achebe's birth place, Ogidi, described in the autobiographical notes at the end of the novel as "one of the first centers of Anglican missionary work in Eastern Nigeria," and Umuru, a geographical locale within the novel, described as situated "on the bank of the Great River, where the white men first came many years before and where they had built the center of their religion and trade and government" (174). It was "to the new training college for teachers in Umuru" that Mr. Brown (who was more rational and more diplomatic than his successor Reverend James Smith) had sent Okonkwo's rebellious son Nwoye, now renamed Isaac (182). As one of the first to receive missionary (Western) education in Nigeria, Nwoye belongs to the generation of Achebe's father, and my speculation is that Nwoye might in fact be more than just a fictional representation of a member of the generation of Achebe's father; perhaps he is the artistic depiction of his father. If this is true, then *Things Fall Apart* could be described, using the title of Allison Kimmich's and Vivian May's proposed 1996 MLA Convention panel, as an "Autobiography by Other Means, Writing the Self through Other Selves" (18). The "other selves" in this case would be Nwoye (the fictional representation of Achebe's father according to this speculation) and Okonkwo (the speculated grandfather of Achebe). Even if there were no iota of truth in this speculation, *Things Fall Apart*, as Achebe's creation, is his authoral statement on the cultural and political history of his people, expressed through the indirect medium of fiction. As the rest of this chapter reveals, *Things Fall Apart* is a devastating anti-colonialist critique that turns the table on the colonialist claims to racial and cultural superiority.

2. This information was provided by Chinua Achebe during a private telephone conversation on January 1, 1997, in response to my question regarding the first time he became acquainted with Equiano's narrative.

3. Chinua Achebe confirmed in the already cited telephone conversation that Equiano's village still exists today, but that "Essaka" was Equiano's Anglicized phonetic rendering of the true name Iseke. He further explained that the orthographical variation can be understood, given the fact that no standardized form of writing the Igbo language existed since writing had not been introduced to Igboland at the time that Equiano was kidnaped and transported as a slave to North America.

4. To have a full grasp of how highly knowledgeable Equiano really was in the literary and intellectual traditions of his time and how adept and subtle he was in utilizing this knowledge in his narrative, one must read Vincent Carretta's meticulous and rich explanatory and textual notes covering pages 237-305.

5. Most of the contributors to *The City in African American Literature* agree that, while exemptions exist, African American writers generally depict the city, or the urban milieu, as a more positive force than the village, or the rural setting, on Black protagonists. This is in contrast to mainstream American literature which more often presents a romanticized, idealized image of the rural setting, while the urban background is negatively depicted (Hakutani and Butler).

6. References in *Colored People* to Africa—sometimes direct, sometimes veiled—are positive and suggest Gates's identification with Africa, though this is to be received in the context of his desire not to be restricted by race in the matter of "constructing identities through selective affinity" (xv). See, for instance, pages 9, 42, 70-71, 79, 101-2, 109, 112, 143, 186, 208-9.

REFERENCES

Achebe, Chinua. *Things Fall Apart.* New York: Anchor, 1994. [First published in 1959.]

Carretta, Vincent. ed. *The Interesting Narrative and Other Writings by Olaudah Equiano.* New York: Penguin, 1995.

Equiano, Olaudah. "The Interesting Narrative of the Lfe of Olaudah Equiano, Or Gustavus Vassa, The African." (Written by Himself). In *The Interesting Narrative and Other Writings by Olaudah Equiano.* New York: Penguin, 1995. [First published in 1789].

Ezenwa-Ohaeto. *Chinua Achebe: A Biography.* London: James Currey Publishers (forthcoming).

Gates, Jr., Henry Louis. *Colored People: A Memoir.* New York: Alfred A. Knopf, 1994.

Hakutani, Yoshinobu, and Robert Butler. eds. *The City in African-American Literature.* Madison: Fairleigh Dickinson University Press, 1995.

Kimmich, Allison, and Vivian May."Autobiography by Other Means, Writing the Self through Other Selves." Proposed 1996 MLA Convention Panel. *MLA Newsletter* 28, 1 (Spring 1996):18.

Middlebrook, Diane Wood. "The Artful Voyeur." *Transition* 67 (1995):86-97.

Soyinka, Wole. *Ake: The Years of Childhood.* New York: Vintage, 1989. [First published in 1981.]

10

THE NIGER DELTA, NATIVITY, AND MY WRITING

TANURE OJAIDE

THE CREATIVE WRITER IS NEVER AN AIRPLANT, BUT SOME-
one who is grounded in some specific place. It is difficult to talk of many
writers without their identification with place. Every writer's roots are very
important in understanding his or her work. For example, though born in
Harlem to southern migrants in 1924, James Baldwin told an interviewer:

> I am, in all but in technical fact, a Southerner. My father was
> born in the South—my mother was born in the South, and if
> they had waited two more seconds I might have been born in
> the South. But that means I was raised by families whose roots
> were essentially southern rural.... (qtd. in Hall 22)

Similarly, Zora Neale Hurston, wherever she lived, considered Eatonville,
Florida her home. As Cheryl A. Wall (1985:27) puts it, wherever Hurston
journeyed, she "was able to draw on this heritage and find the strength to
remain herself." Claude McKay, of Jamaican origin but living in Harlem,
wrote *A Long Way from Home*. Many African-Americans see Africa as
their ancestral home. Even in the so-called mainstream American literature,
William Faulkner's strength as a novelist comes from his Southern nativity.

Nativity has much to do with creating literature, especially poetry. The
writer tends to exploit memory and return to childhood days to garner images to clarify his or her vision. This memory might be of the writer's

birthplace or of the place he or she lived in and associates with. I may have traveled extensively all over the world, I may have lived in different parts of my country Nigeria; I may be currently living and working in the United States, but my native home is the Niger Delta. Friends and readers of my writing say that I light up and become passionate when I write about the Niger Delta. Call that nostalgia, but I call it the immense power of the Niger Delta as my native place, the constant backdrop to my inspiration. In this essay I will use the Niger Delta in the context of my nativity to discuss the inexhaustible field of imagination that the writer draws from in the creative process.

Space is a major defining factor in African culture. Every African is expected to be connected or linked to some specific place. In other words, space defines the rootedness of people in Africa. That is why where one is born is important. It is a life-long badge one wears. Nativity in this essay means birthplace and/or the place where one grows up to imbibe its worldview. Generally, where one is born or lives the formative years of childhood defines the person's nativity.

Nativity is some specific place whose air, water, crops, folklore and other produce nourish the individual. One can say that space in this context is geography. However, as Jose Ortega y Gasset hypothesizes, "Each geographic space, insofar as it is a space for a possible history, is . . . a function of many variables" (qtd. in Mudimbe 1988:188). These "variables" include biology, economics, language. Biologically, humans submit to the "demands of an environment, coming to terms with the modifications it imposes" (Mudimbe 1988:190). Foucault sees humans as having needs and desires which they seek to satisfy economically. He also sees the human need for *meaning* resulting in arranging a *system* of signs (qtd. in Mudimbe 1988:190-191). V.Y. Mudimbe (1988) further sees "a spatial configuration" in imagining "a panoramic view of African *gnosis*" (191). Discussing space therefore involves a complexity of ontologies, cosmologies, and many other *systems* that it holds together or connects with.

In traditional Africa, land (a major component of space) is highly valued. Ngugi wa Thiongo (1964:22) in *Weep Not, Child* says of land among the Gikuyu people:

> Any man who had land was considered rich. If a man had plenty of money, many motor cars, but no land, he could never be counted as rich. A man who went with tattered clothes but had at least an acre of red earth was better off than the man with money.

So space-bound on the physical plane is the African worldview that when old people die, they are expected to be taken to their homeplaces for burial. It is as if the individual who was given his or her first nourishment in an area upon birth should return to the spiritual realm upon death through the same gateway in order to complete a life cycle.

My Urhobo people of the Niger Delta have the concept of *Urhoro*. It is the mythical place—ironically aspatial—through which people in the spiritual world make their pre-natal choices and are then born into this world. Every individual, according to this mythical concept, is fated to live in accordance with his or her choice at *Urhoro*. In other words, we are predestined in the Urhobo worldview. Sometimes, according to elders of the group, sacrifices can be offered to ward off negative forces. There is thus traffic between the spiritual and physical worlds of the Niger Delta. When somebody dies, the person passes through the gate of *Urhoro* into the spiritual world to be an ancestor, who will be reborn again and again. Among the Urhobo, people talk of *this* world and the *next* world.

The Urhobo concept of *Urhoro* not only ties space to the physical and the spiritual, but also to the temporal and the a-temporal in the unending cycle of reincarnation. Nativity is significant here as the known and familiar each seeks its own kind. The Urhobo myth of *eda*, what the Yoruba and Ibo call *abiku* and *ogbanje* respectively, can be anchored on this spiritual dimension of beliefs in my native Niger Delta home.

Urhoro appears directly and indirectly in my writing. A recent long poem is titled "Urhoro: Going in Cycles." In it I reflect not only on my personal condition and the impact of relatives (daughter and father) on me but also on the human condition and the ironies involved:

> I who side-slipped every ambush on the road
> am bound to a survival kit,
> thrown into a rioting mass of currents.
> Buoyed by precedents of crossing rivers
> in *Olokun*'s arms, without a boat,
> I can understand why the champion swimmer
> drowns in a knee-depth, while
> the novice doomed to disappear
> escapes the shark bite of bad mouths.

Later in the same poem,

> I surrender my garments and property,
> but will not give up the bird

that flies and flies, brightening
my eyes beyond the horizon. . .

That "bird" is my soul with its possibilities that emanate from the place, from *Urhoro,* the outer and spiritual space of my native Niger Delta.

Space is more meaningful when seen through time. The singularity of reality lies in the connection of a point in space with a moment in time. As Mudimbe (1988:195) puts it, "all cultural figures determine their own specificity in apparently regional ruptures and continuities, whereby the otherness of their being appears as dynamic event, and thus history. All temporal pasts expose an otherness of the same ontological quality as the otherness unveiled by anthropologists." Time transforms a place and accelerates its culture in the changes which occur. Culture is thus dynamic. A place can expand or become narrow but the theoretical space remains in memory even if re-occupied. It is for these dynamics that culture and society are redefined by the transformation of space through human contact in time. Values of a people change, social and cultural icons also change. The creative writer finds himself or herself in the vortex of this socio-cultural flux set about by the impact of time on place.

The writer attempts to bridge time and space. He or she can only reflect, for the most part, the time of his or her existence. I see myself, if not consciously but subconsciously, as chronicling the time in which I live from the positionality of the Niger Delta. To put it differently but in a Chinua Achebe (1958) image, I am watching the masquerade of life from my Delta foothold. This positioning no doubt has advantages and disadvantages, because seeing things through this local but specific perspective could bring an intense vision. At the same time, narrowness to a specific place is bound to obscure some distant angles. To put this more bluntly, because of my Niger Delta nativity I am subconsciously conditioned to respond to reality in a way unique to me and different from others who are strangers there. People who share the same birthplace, culture, and society are connected in their group values and interests.

The Niger Delta is the three-dimensional space that time continues to change. As Nadezhda Mandelstam (1970) asks of the Russia of the Stalinist period, can I escape the Niger Delta? My life on earth started from here. If the purpose of life is to build, there is so much in the area to build on. However, to avoid a constraining parochiality, the writer needs "friends and allies across barriers of both time and space" (Mandelstam, 1974:229), hence I open myself to other worlds. But significantly, the writer nourished by a specific place gives back something by assuming the responsibility of being an honest, sincere, and passionate witness of his place and time. If my writing in part reflects the zeitgist and volkgist of the Niger Delta, then I feel I have performed a duty. After all, the attributes of a place's culture are equivalent to the attributes of a period's culture.

A signifying icon of a place's culture is the prevailing pantheon. Of course, gods are indigenous to specific ethnic places. The Romans and Greeks had their gods with specific localities as their haunts. Homer and Ovid, among other classical writers, utilized the presence of gods with great effect. Closer home, Wole Soyinka demonstrates the power of one's people's gods in the creative writing process. *Idanre and Other Poems* and *Ogun Abibiman*, two poetry collections, have Ogun as the central "character" (see Soyinka 1965, 1976b). In fact, Ogun defines the poet's persona in Soyinka's poetry. Much of Soyinka's writing bristles with Yoruba gods (see also his other works, Soyinka 1976a, 1976b). Chinua Achebe (1958) also refers to Ibo gods such as Ani, the Earth goddess, and Amadiora, god of thunder and lightning, in his writing.

Among the Urhobo people of the Niger Delta, gods are constantly invoked by devotees to help in difficult situations. Of these gods, four have always fascinated me and entered my writing. They are: *Uhaghwa*, god of songs; *Umalokun* or Mammy Water (called *Olokun* by others); *Aridon*, god of memory; and *Abadi/Ivwri*, god of war. Other Niger Delta groups like the Ijo and the Itsekiri also revere *Umalokun*, goddess of the waters and wealth. To a large extent, a people's gods help to define their spiritual concerns and worldview. In much of traditional Africa, gods are the apotheosization of a people's values, beliefs, and desires. The mystery of the large expanse of the sea instills a certain awe among the Urhobo to worship its spirit. This spirit is the goddess of beauty and wealth that lives in a skyscraper of needles underwater. Such is the impact of the native god/dess that at my first physical contact with the Pacific in the San Francisco-Sausalito Bay Area, I had to invoke *Umalokun*.

Gods have their homes but the efficacy of their influence, blessing, and power goes beyond their places of origin. In other words, there are no barriers to their power over their devotees. That is why a god's totem pet like the iguana will always be treated with reverence by the Orogun clan people of the Niger Delta in whatever part of the world they find one. *Uhaghwa* and *Aridon* are sometimes used interchangeably by Urhobo people and I have made *Aridon* assume the role of *Uhaghwa* and vice versa. I started with having *Uhaghwa* as my mentor god, hence the frequent invocation in my two early collections, *Children of Iroko and Other Poems and Labyrinths of the Delta* (see Ojaide 1973, 1986). I needed the inspiration of the god of songs then to fire me up. Later as I have grown older, memory has become more important to me and I have come to have *Aridon* as my other mentor. It is *Aridon* that I invoke in "The Fate of Vultures" to "blaze an ash-trail to the hands / that buried crates of cash in their bowels. . ." Ojaide 1990:11). I now relate to the two gods as twin-gods and my mentors because I need inspiration and I need the memory to ground my experience.

While the Niger Delta is physical and geographical, it has a mythic dimension whose uniqueness of folklore is tapped by the native artist. Where else than in the riverine area of the Niger Delta will the tortoise/turtle be a major mythic figure? The tortoise has many names in the Urhobo language. It is *orose* (the shell one), *alauke* (the hunch-back), *oroghwuwevwiya* (the one that carries a house along), and *ogbeyin.* The so many attributes of the tortoise in Urhobo folklore involve cunning, greed, selfishness, and meanness. I have transferred the negative attributes of the tortoise to the corrupt Nigerian politicians and military dictators, who are so selfish that they do not care about how the nation suffers from their individual avarice. The Niger Delta myths are sources of allusions to describe the present reality of the Nigerian nation.

There are other examples of the Delta's mythic world. There is the *oko* drumming bird, which comes with the early heavy rains that turn the dry creeks into tumultuous currents that flow into the big rivers that pour themselves into the Atlantic Ocean. "Going to the sea" in Urhobo and Ijo suggests death and entering eternity. There is the belief similar to the Greeks' about the dead being ferried across the sea into the spirit world. A pioneer Niger Delta poet, J.P. Bekederemo-Clark (1964, 1971) uses this image in *A Reed in the Tide.*

The mythic corpus of the Niger Delta infuses poetry and other creative writings with a ready storehouse of allusions which root the poetic vision in a specific culture, locus, and reality. It gives energy and mystical glamor to the creative work.

The Niger Delta as a cultural home has its imprints on languages. By its exposure to the outside world by way of the demarcating Atlantic Ocean, this area has always been in dialogue or conflict over time with other cultures, especially the Western/European culture. This again is testimony that a culture though with a spatial setting is not containable in spatial boundaries. The infusion of European languages and neologisms into Urhobo and other local languages and the emergence of pidgin English are strong indications of the openness of *any* place to foreign influences.

The Urhobo area has its socio-cultural life stamped with early European influence. The Portuguese were the first Europeans to trade with people of the Niger Delta. The Urhobo call them "Potukri" and for a long time called Europeans irrespective of their national origin "Potukri." After slavery, the Europeans were called "*oyibo.*" The "*oyibo*" has a negative connotation because of the slave trade, colonialism, and other forms of European exploitation and domination of Africans. Many Urhobo words today are neologisms or rather Urhoboizing of Portuguese. The following Urhobo words show the Niger Delta's indebtedness to Portuguese: *oro* (gold), *ughojo* (wristwatch/clock), *osete* (plate), *ukujere* (spoon), *meje* (table), *sabato* (shoes), and *isama* (salmon/canned fish).

There is also indebtedness to English. The Urhobo word for sailor is *kruman*, the Urhoboization of "crewman." The Urhobo names of many modern technological items are basically English with a local accent. Words for airplane, radio, television, video, motor car, and many others are transparently English-derived. Other influences of the European incursion include the bringing of the "wrapper" dress which has become a cultural costume of Delta people. The fabric for this dress originated from Goa/India and brought first as a means of exchange by the Portuguese and later by the British in the barter trade between Europeans and Africans. Delta people acted as "middle-men" between the Europeans and the hinterland groups such as the Ibo and Tiv.

Pidgin English in Nigeria was for a long time a Delta monopoly. Sapele and Warri in the present-day Delta State and Port Harcourt in Rivers State are the bastions of pidgin English. Of course, these cities are ports in which there was a lot of exchange between Europeans and Africans. Pidgin English in Warri and Sapele has absorbed Urhobo semantics and syntax for a unique "broken English."

I have a few poems in Urhobo and pidgin English respectively. Part of "The Wrestler" is in Urhobo, a song which begins and ends the poem. However, even when the poems are written in English, the major symbols and rhythms are derived from Urhobo experience. A poem like "The Battle" will make its greatest impact on an Urhobo speaker than on others:

> For fear of exposing its soft body
> the *oghighe* plant covers itself with thorns,
> for fear of bad company
> the *akpobrisi* keeps distant from other trees,
> for fear of falling into the grip of age
> the python yearly casts off its skin,
> for fear of its head
> the tortoise moves inside a fortress.
> For fear of our lives
> we arm in diverse ways
> to fight the same battle.
> (*The Endless Song*, see Ojaide 1989:44).

As I stated elsewhere, many African poets put English/foreign language words over native rhythmic patterns. Thus in "Labyrinths of the Delta," the title poem of the collection, when I write about the turtle/tortoise, I am in fact building a poem on an Urhobo folktale's song. Here's the folksong:

> *Uro bio ogbeyin rhe/Currents, bring back the turtle*
> Tue tue/Steadily, steadily
> Uro bio ogbeyin rhe/Currents,bring back the turtle
> Tue tue/Steadily, steadily
> Ogbeyin ruvwe/Turtle has hurt me
> Oru vwa abo vwirhin/it broke my hands
> Tue tue/Steadily, steadily
> Ogbeyin ruvwe/Turtle has hurt me
> Oru vwa awo vwirhin/It broke my legs
> Tue tue/Steadily, steadily
> Uro bio ogbeyin rhe/Currents, bring back the turtle
> Tue tue/Steadily, steadily
> *Uro bio ogbeyin rhe /Currents, bring back the turtle*
> *Tue tue/Steadily, steadily*

Here is the rendition in a part of my poem:

> Turn the tortoise back, O Waters
> Bring him back
> Spare him mishap on the way
> Bring him back to me;
> He broke not only my hands
> But also my legs and ribs;
> Bring him back to me
> Spare him mishap on the way here
> And let the villain taste
> What he inflicted on me
> From my own hands
> (see Ojaide 1986:26).

Here the Urhobo characterization of the turtle becomes the symbol of exploitation and oppression for which the speaker seeks revenge and restoration.

In my only published pidgin English poem, "I Be Somebody," I try to use the common people's lingua franca to articulate and assert the dignity of the common person. Here's the poem:

I fit shine your shoe like new one from supermarket,
so I know something you no know for your life.
I fit carry load for head from Lagos go Abuja,
so I get power you think na only you get.
If you enter my room, my children reach Nigerian Army;
so I rich pass you, whether your naira full bank or house.
You no know kindness, big man: na me de help
push your car from gutter for rain, not for money at all;
and you de splash poto-poto for my body when you de pass.
To tell the truth, I get nothing; but
you no fit get anything without poor man—
na me be salt for the soup you de chop every day;
I be nobody and I be somebody.
(*The Eagle's Vision*, see Ojaide 1987:69).

With the examples of my writing in Urhobo, imbibing Urhobo folklore and rhythms, and use of pidgin English, the writer could be seen as the socio-cultural product of his or her birthplace. The quality of the product depends on the individual talent of the writer, which is quite another matter.

The interplay of spatiality and time which brings transformations in culture and society shows in the material resources of a writer. The change from the Niger Delta of my youth in the 1950s to the Delta of the 1990s exacerbates the tension in my poetry. There is the image of the past which is drastically different from that of today, an idyllic past opposed to the ecologically tainted Westernized present. The opposition of the traditional Niger Delta and the modern Delta gives rise to two seemingly different "spaces." Mudimbe (1988) poses the questions: "In which sense does the so-called traditional arrangement define itself as an autonomous field outside of modernity and vice-versa? In which mode of being are the concepts of tradition and modernity expressed and formulated within a cultural area" (189)? He gives no answers but suggests that local customs can be transformed by modern systems for the better.

I have nostalgia for the Niger Delta of my youth. I spent all my formative years in my native Delta home. Living with my maternal grandmother, my guardian angel Amreghe, I followed my grandpa and uncles to fish before I started to go with my own age-mates Iboyi and Godwin to fish with hooks. I followed adults in the family to "harvest" ponds. From these activities, I knew about the earthworm used as a bait as being like a woman that likes only soft spots. I knew the mudfish that enters the cone-shaped net as the figurative language for sex. I saw the beautiful *erhuvwudjayorho* fish, so beautiful but denied growing big, a sort of mystical law of compensation. In the creeks and rivers, there was a parade of fishes. There was the *onyenye* with an inimitable beauty. The sword-fish, electric fish, snake-fish (*ogbene*), *okpogun, obo*, and a variety of fresh and salt-water fishes.

There were also the water lilies (*tetebe*) that grew on water, so delicate and so the metaphor for the resilience of a fragile being. Of course, gourds stood on top of fierce currents. By the later 1950s we heard of Gamalin 20 with greedy fishers who poisoned the fish to pick. Some cocoa farmers in Urhobo had converted the chemical from being sprayed on cocoa plants to protect them from being destroyed by diseases to poisoning fishes in ponds. The local bye-laws banning fishing and palm-nut collecting at certain times of the year were still in place.

I followed the men to clear the farms and start planting and watched the rituals before the planting. Every year brought its own demands, but the images of increase and fertility were always invoked. I heard the *apiapia* bird ushering in a new planting season with its song:

> *Ukpe tere/Another year has come*
> Udu ko bruvwe/And my heart beats
> *Kpe kpe/In fear of the unknown.*

I discovered that the python slept deeply and even when decapitated did not die immediately but only after noon when it would have its death jerks. No wonder my Grandma sometimes called me a python when I overslept and risked getting to school late. In the forest there was the man-like anthill (*orato*) with a helmet-like head. What of the civet cat (*aghwaghwa*) crying at night, the fear of the gorilla then said to rape beautiful women who went to farm alone? Even animals, one *udje* dance song states, know the difference between beautiful and ugly women! Thus the waters and the land of the Niger Delta were invaluable resources that sustained the population.

The great change came with the arrival of Shell-BP, the oil-drilling multinational, in the Niger Delta about 1958. In the Urhobo area we heard of Shell's simultaneous presence in Oloibiri, Bonny, and other eastern parts of Ijoland. My childhood memoir, *Great Boys:An African Childhood,* and a collection of poems on the impact of modern Western technology on traditional African life, *Daydreams of Ants,* both deal with the post-Shell presence with its increasing ecological degradation of the Niger Delta. Oil pipes broke and the waters once teeming with fish were polluted and many turned into dead creeks and rivers, which sent fishermen and women out of work. In many areas, including Kokori and Ughelli, Shell flared gas. The staple crops such as yams and cassava wilted. The heat killed the fauna and flora and possibly gave diseases to people who met untimely deaths. The catalogue of Shell's destruction of the environment with its adverse effects on inhabitants of the Niger Delta is endless.

The Niger Delta I once knew as home has changed drastically. The demise of the pristine environment has driven people from rural areas to the cities of Warri and Port Harcourt. The traditional occupations of farming, fishing, and hunting that used to sustain rural dwellers have been wiped out by oil drilling. Shell-BP and other oil corporations in Warri and Port Harcourt have become leading employers in the Niger Delta.

The new wealth brought by these oil companies have changed the socio-cultural lives of the people. The cramping of people in the cities brings its loosening of the traditional values that once governed the people's lives. Now modern urban lifestyles are prevalent: robbery, adultery, greed, and exploitation of others for personal gain.

The oil-boom of Nigeria in the late 1960s and 1970s exacerbated another aspect of the Niger Delta people. As a minority in the Nigerian federation, they feel cheated not only by the oil corporations but also by the Federal Government dominated by majority groups who are united in their exploitation and oppression of minority groups. Many Delta people believe that the Nigerian nation still stands as one only because of the abundance of oil in their area. The story of Nigeria would be different today if the oil was located in one of the three ethnic group areas of Hausa, Yoruba, and Ibo. In any case, the revenue allocation formula which favors other groups at the expense of the Niger Delta people is cause of deep-rooted resentment. The personal enrichment of leaders and the development of other areas as the Delta deteriorated have made the minority Delta people more activist in both drawing attention to their sore plight and calling for compensation. It is in light of this unconscionable anomaly that I wrote "Ughelli" in the late 1970s. The poem reads:

> To see her dry-skinned when her oil rejuvenates hags
> to leave her in darkness when her fuel lights the universe
> to starve her despite all her produce
> to let her dehydrate before the wells bored into her heart
> to have her naked despite her innate industry
> to keep her without roads when her sweat tars the outside
> world
> to make her homeless when her idle neighbours inhabit sky
> scrapers
> to see her lonely when sterile ones use her offspring as ser-
> vants
> to regard the artisan as a non-person when drones celebrate
> with her sweat,
> for the palm's oil to be called the fig tree's
> for the goddess of wealth not to be complimented for her gifts

but spat upon by raiders of her bosom
for one to earn so much and be denied all except life—
robbery wears a thousand masks in official bills—
and for her to be sucked anaemic by an army of leeches,
it is a big shame(74).

Ughelli in the 1960s and 1970s had no electricity (and pipe-borne water) while it supplied the rest of the country immense revenue and power. The same Ughelli whose gas is said to be about the best in the world!

Today the Niger Delta as space/place of oil and minority status in the Nigerian nation has generated ideas of struggle and survival among its people. In Rivers State, Isaac Adaka Boro struggled against regional and national exploitation before his death. The Nigerian civil war was fought for the soul of the Niger Delta because of its huge oil reserves as both parties had their eyes on the "prize," oil. The problems of Boro's time have been made worse by the alliance of multinational corporations and military dictatorship. Ken Saro-Wiwa's struggle for the Ogoni and other minority groups of the Niger Delta is consequent upon the pollution, deprivation, exploitation and neglect of the oil-producing area, synonymous with the Niger Delta. Saro-Wiwa's struggle was for the just compensation of the people for the wealth taken away by Shell and the Nigerian Government, while their birthplace was being destroyed irrevocably by oil spillage, gas flaring, and other forms of pollution. Saro-Wiwa called for investment in the area to correct the ecological destruction suffered over decades because of oil exploration. The Movement for the Survival of the Ogoni People (MOSOP) represents the temperament of the Niger Delta people.

The Niger Delta gives identity to its natives. The inhabitants of this watery land of lush vegetation are a minority in the Nigerian federation with a very strong center that has access to all resources within its frontiers. The status of these minorities is that of an exploited people. It is for this reason that one of the Delta writer's orientation is to signify the Delta, showing its paradox of sitting on oil and yet remaining impoverished.

Different as the Niger Delta is, it is connected with others. I have already discussed the impact of the European connection on Urhobo language and culture. But even earlier and after the European incursion, there has always been a strong African connection. The Urhobo people trace their roots to Benin and Ife, more inland. The Itsekiri whose language is very close to a Yoruba dialect trace their royalty to Ife. The Ijo appear to be the only group that has always been there, since they have no myths or legends of coming from elsewhere to their present abode and other groups like the Urhobo and Itsekiri met them there. Ibo and Edo words appear in Urhobo language and this suggests influence and contact. In the case of Edo, the

Urhobo, Bini, Ishan, and some other groups might have once lived in an eponymous place, Aka, before dispersing to their present locations. In modern times, Warri and Port Harcourt, the two major Delta cities, have become very cosmopolitan in absorbing people of different groups from different places into the Delta community. Apart from Lagos, Warri and Port Harcourt could boast of having the largest population of Europeans and Americans in Nigeria.

The Niger Delta is not just physical space but a spiritual, mystical, and psychological setting. It evokes ideas of public and private space in me: the physical and the psychic Delta which are fused in my individual being. I foreground the Delta both consciously and unconsciously; consciously because it is the place I know best and I am most familiar with and unconsciously because I have so imbibed its spirit that it speaks in me even when I am not aware of it. It is the backcloth, so to say, of my experiences as a writer. It is the context of the text of my writing. The Delta provides me different types of refuge, defense, and guard. This only means that nativity of a place can run deep in one's psyche and perspective. Arguably, it can also be a constraint if not mitigated by a readiness to accept what will nourish and reinforce from other cultures. The Niger Delta is unique in its rootedness but also has by its position as the marine gateway to much of Nigeria absorbed European and African influences. Nativity brings into tension *ours* and *theirs* in values and interests as an exploited minority in the majority-dominated Nigerian polity. However, the Delta area has shown how Sameness does not preclude the Other.

From my discussion so far it is apparent that space and time are interrelated. The Niger Delta has history, an indication of a common experience of a people over time. If "history is a relation to values and sets itself on mechanisms of intellectual valorization" (Mudimbe 1988:192), my vision is colored by the history of the Niger Delta. There have been changes from a traditional idyllic place to a modern area rifled with oil-drilling businesses. The historical inter-relationship between space as place, culture, and society poses challenges of nativity to me as a writer. There is a psychic transference onto Urhobo and the Niger Delta of the past into the present. With the pivotal role of memory in the creative process of writing poetry, nativity is a continuous presence that keeps the flame of associations burning. I see much of the world and life through the eyes of a Niger Delta indigene. My vision emanates from where I *stand*.

The minority people have moved from natural contentment to political agitation against exploitation. The demand by the old Delta Province to become a state of its own without Anioma is another indication of the politicization of nativity. In Delta State, the inhabitants of the old Delta

Province see themselves as the true Delta people! If this coincides with a shift from a poetry of nature invocation to that of political activism, it only means that nativity has so much power on the writer.

There is an accumulation of forces deriving from the particular nature and condition of the Delta. The Delta is a body of place and a spirit. I am not an airplant. I may travel the world and live elsewhere but I am physically and psychically anchored to the Delta. It is the driving spirit of the Delta that shapes the vision and provides the images in my writing.

In conclusion, and to borrow Wall (1985) on Hurston, wherever I journey, I am able to draw on the Urhobo Niger Delta heritage and find strength to remain myself (27). My sense of home is based on a multiplicity of factors, my persona rooted in the Niger Delta of the 1950s to the present. Whether I am physically displaced from home, I am intuitively linked to my home which I can reclaim effortlessly. In other words, place is not only physical but mental, spiritual, and psychic. My experience outside stretches the parameters of my homeland intellectually. The Niger Delta is my identity at home and outside, as in many ways I am one with its people. Nostalgia for this land of evergreen rainforests persists in me. I can always image an inner space filled with pieces from everywhere but dominated and colored by the Niger Delta which strengthens my bond with humanity.

COMING HOME

I might disembark at more ports than
the moon can cope with in a full phase.
I might bring new mirrors to elders,
that breed of tenacious roots who prefer
an interpreter of two languages to recast
their own son's tales of his recent sojourn.
I might be the migrant bird that
shores up the seasons in the calendar.
I might be current finding my way
from mountain to sea, not the river's bed.
I would not be the ship mocking the rock
because it has freedom of movement,
nor would I be the rock mocking the ship
because it does not yield to anybody's craft.

At home every proverb becomes a tonic
that fortifies through jungle cities abroad,
every bird or animal proffers tales of
how to move in the minefield of America;
every native cherry flavours the tongue
with straightface smiles of my childhood—

erased, the aftertaste of not just Diet Coke
but also the toxic breath of smokers.
Every face home, brother or sister;
my gods worship their devotees!

Now silent from the last summons,
Ishaka never breached the clan's walls;
yet spun stories of faraway places—
glass towers, beauties, and monsters;
details gave truth to the scatterbrain.
But who, reeling with laughter and longing
for England, cared about his running mad?
His stories of London launched me on
the fountain-pen trail to meet the Queen.
I might be Odysseus' son in another life,
lost more than one love to absence
and gained one away to take home;
still I would love to be a home fellow
powered by the draughts I imbibe.

Elders talk of "Two mouths, one stomach."
I have not yet encountered the strange one
but have given it a place in memory-yard,
the only charming monster in the world.
Coming home we exchange gifts and tales,
each more fond of the other's special fortune—
alliance of *iroko* and eagle in a divine bond.
And two firm hands lift the calabash
from the ground to the mouth
to slake the parched body!

(May 25, 1994)

REFERENCES

Achebe, Chinua. *Things Fall Apart.* London: Heinemann, 1958.
Bekederemo-Clark, John Pepper. *A Reed in the Tide.* London: Longman, 1964.
Bekederemo-Clark, John Pepper. *Casualties.* London: Longman. Hall, 1971.
Mandelstam, Nadezhda. *Hope Against Hope.* New York: Atheneum, 1970.
Mandelstam, Nadezhda. *Hope Abandoned.* New York: Atheneum, 1974.
McKay, Claude. *A Long Way from Home.* New York: L. Furman, inc., 1937.
Mudimbe, V. Y. *The Invention of Africa: Gnosis, Philosophy, and the Order of Knowledge.* Bloomington and Indianapolis: Indiana University Press, 1988.
Ngugi, wa Thiongo. *Weep Not, Child.* London: Heinemann, 1964.
Ojaide, Tanure. *Children of Iroko and Other Poems.* New York: Greenfield Review Press, 1973.

Ojaide, Tanure. *Great Boys: An African Childhood.* Trenton, N.J.: Africa World Press, 1998.
Ojaide, Tanure. *Labyrinths of the Delta.* New York: Greenfield Review Press, 1986.
Ojaide, Tanure. *The Eagle's Vision.* Detroit: Lotus Press, 1987.
Ojaide, Tanure. *The Endless Song.* Lagos: Malthouse Press, 1989.
Ojaide, Tanure. *The Fate of Vultures.* Lagos: Malthouse Press, 1990.
Ojaide, Tanure. *The Blood of Peace.* Oxford: Heinemann, 1991.
Soyinka, Wole. *Idanre and Other Poems.* London: Methuen, 1965.
Soyinka, Wole. *A Shuttle in the Crypt.* London: Eyre Methuen, 1976a.
Soyinka, Wole. *Ogun Abibiman.* London: Rex Collings, 1976b.
Soyinka, Wole. *Myth, Literature and the African World.* Cambridge: Cambridge University Press, 1976c.
Wall, Cheryl A. *Women of the Harlem Renaissance.* Bloomington/Indianapolis: Indiana University Press, 1985.

IV

THE SPACIALITY OF NATIONS, COMMUNITIES, AND IDENTITIES

cultural project(ion) or narrativity. The latter will be a historical "excavation" that brings the African nation to light in the spatial ordering of its constituent parts. Doing an integrated "spatial history"—integrated because it accounts for the timeline of historical narrativity within the ambience of spatial relations—I hope concurrently to (a) show the basis of the nation in a conjuncture of *uneven* forces; and to (b) derive the nation's character in the measure of this unevenness of forces to generate the element of (human) desire, the desire to alter and realign, the aspiration to "make even," the relation of forces differentially structuring a given space. In those terms we will see the character of the African nation emerge as an articulation or collocation of different (spatial) elements by a historical agency—an African middle class—whose desire is structured socially and politically in the unevenness of the relations between itself and its nativity, on the one hand, and between itself and the coloniality and modernity impinging on its native space, on the other.

To clarify these relations: nativity, as I present it, refers to the domesticity or local(ized) domain of the indigenous African people. As cultural space, it is characterized by ethno-cultural variety, although an endogenous cultural imaginary has emerged in historically recent times that abstracts a transcendent African essence from this native variety and upholds it as a geo-cultural project of collective (continental) self-recovery. This new project(ion) emerges out of and challenges earlier projections by Europeans—of both a speculative and literal kind—mapped onto nativity. The latter arise out of the colonial encounter and have had profound material and cultural consequences on nativity, introducing qualitatively new modes of alienation—more or less negative in some cases, more or less positive in others—within it. The aforementioned African middle class is one of the consequences of this alienation. It is a class that comes to see itself as a potentially transforming agency in relation to nativity (Korang 1995).

The African middle class, as I present it, refers to a fraction of the native people which, as a result of colonial domination of nativity, comes to occupy within the altered social configuration an uncertain, if privileged, location in-between: in between nativity and coloniality/modernity, and thus finds itself entering into complex relations with all three. What privileges this class is access to the modern conveniences put in place by the colonial encounter: European education, western modes of thought, language and professionalization, easy access to the cosmopolitan metropolises of the imperial centers, and so on. Within the spatial confines of coloniality, in short, we find a native fraction at an interface, between "the white man on the one side and [its] untutored [native] brethren on the other" (Sarbah 1906: 250), a fraction that is able to relate to the modern and therefore participate in its cultural-political imaginary.

Yet this is a class whose situation in coloniality is contradictory. As a fraction, a middle class is (culturally) raised "above" and made to feel different from a bigger group of natives, dominated *as such*; but nonetheless it is objectively treated as belonging to this native group. To the extent that it could apprehend its privileged cultural constitution as taking place in a native space usurped by European colonial power, nativity returns to this class as the objective image of its intrinsic powerlessness. In the uneven situation of this fraction then is to be found a predicament that generates a class-desire for self-sufficient or sovereign power, cast as (a) a realpolitical objective within colonized native space; and, (b) an authentication of its modernist (cultural) status, in a way that brings a *local* or endogenous mediation to the modern. Both will be gathered into the cultural-narrative and political definition of the African nation in what we might render as a thematic of African modernity, a thematic locally-defined and serving local ends (Africanus Horton 1868, 1870; Attoh Ahuma 1911; de Graft Johnson 1928; James 1962; Kaunda 1962; Lumumba 1962; Luthuli 1962).

Generally speaking, then, that which provides the grounds for intervention in coloniality by a middle class, and hence accounts in significant measure for the historical agency of the anti-colonial struggle, is a homegrown vision of the modern (mediated, as we shall see, in a *nativism* or its reformed aftermath, *étatisme*). This is a vision imbricated in power and culture: in it a middle class imagines itself in what is, to a greater or lesser degree, a revolutionary conception of power transforming and transformed by culture—which, as we shall see, is notionally connected with "a people"—within post-colonial native space. It is in this regard that the nationalist J. B. Danquah (1943) could demand: "We must have power, and must adequately fill in that power to give us *world* citizenship." If world citizenship is at hand for the nationalist, it is dreamed through a *power base* at home, in nativity.

Danquah was a Gold Coast—later Ghana—nationalist. As empirically located in the Gold Coast as his rhetorical "we" of 1943 is, it nevertheless provides an opportunity for establishing a commonality with other calls beyond this location. Whence the following observation: throughout this essay I make use of an abstraction: the African nation. The task of exemplifying this abstraction, however, falls more or less disproportionately on one particular location: the Gold Coast/Ghana. How to justify this theoretically without recourse to metaphysics, to an African essence somehow magically embodied in this one national location among many—some fifty or so—on the continent?

In the annals of African nationalism, the Gold Coast/Ghana has perhaps produced more than its fair share of significant figures. If a name like J. E.

Casely Hayford stands out among the pioneers of continental nationalism so does the legendary Kwame Nkrumah who, in 1957, oversaw the transformation of the Gold Coast from British colony to independent Ghana, the first nation to achieve this status in sub-Saharan Africa. Be that as it may, this essay is conceived not in congratulation. Indeed, in the final section, in keeping with our opening question "what went wrong?," we will have occasion to interrogate the envisioning of the African nation by Nkrumah—"the symbol of emergent Africa" (Awoonor 1972; Davidson 1973)—by setting it against the farreaching revisionist thinking of Amilcar Cabral, the liberator of Guinea Bissau.

What is of essence in choosing examples from the Gold Coast/Ghanaian record, therefore, is identifying and elaborating an African commonality through the particular example. In that case although, objectively, Africa is comprised of varied nation-spaces, taking the nation as object of study allows us to bring a "unity" to this variety by apprehending this imaginary space in a commonality of its articulation, across the continent, by a colonially-created intermediate native fraction. On the basis of the structural and formal sameness of its imaginary, there is theoretical justification for naming an *African* middle class—and through its modernist instrumentality an *African nation*—even if contingent spatio-historical location makes for pragmatic differentiation of its concrete nationalist tasks.

Hence the (theoretical) necessity of reading Danquah's "we" beyond the Gold Coast moment of its utterance towards an African generality. And, in his anti-colonial call for "world citizenship," if Danquah aligns this "we"— a middle class with an African generality—with a notion of worldliness still beyond its grasp, the time has come to take up the question of the world and its place in the modernist/nationalist imaginary of this native fraction. We will try to locate this worldliness through the modes in which a middle class gauges its, and nativity's, relation to colonial and modern space.

Coloniality is one portion of the dyad imperialism/colonialism which refers to the historic realignment of power that saw western Europeans come to dominate more than three-quarters of the world, including the greater portion of the African continent. The modern and the colonial may be seen as fellow travellers, borne on the militaristic back of European imperialism, and to be understood objectively in terms of a geo-political and political-economic configuration whose space (or areal extent), to the extent that it is able to subjugate local spaces under and subsume them into itself, is global. What is more, this objectivity itself generates a (global) cultural-political imaginary in which the colonial and the modern come to occupy, and to be assigned the spatial normativity of the "world-historical" (Hegel 1822; Weber 1930; Said 1993).

Especially in relation to the non-European world, it is always a difficult affair disentangling modernity from coloniality. However, we may still try to differentiate the one from the other by noting that the former inaugurates new possibilities for nativity that seem to come from, and/or are sanctioned by, a (humanistic) *beyond*—possibilities that therefore elude anything like a genuine erasure or containment by coloniality (Horton 1868, 1870; Attoh Ahuma 1897, 1911). However, since the modern and the colonial arrive in native space at the same time, we should see the latter, by its very nature, acting as a check on the former, "postponing" the full realization of its enlightened promise. Hence, in relation to colonized nativity, modernity reads in terms of a space which exists *in potentia*, a space (whose promise is) yet to come, and which therefore acts on coloniality as a pressure from "beyond," but also active *within* its space, and occupying a narrative timeline of a future-present.

The modern can thus be read as a structure of demand in coloniality, operating within a liminal outside-inside of its space. What comes to see itself incarnating this modern-as-demand in the colony is the native fraction of a middle class. It is a fraction, therefore, that assumes the burden of representing itself to a nativity of the people, and the colonial adversary as well, as bearing in itself the potential beyond that is within (reach in) colonial space. The class fraction casts itself in the image of the intermediate "outside-inside"—that liminal character of the modern in coloniality—which, given struggle over time, will become a fully inducted "inside." Effectively, then, in native locality, the circumstances of colonial domination compel an African middle class to project a narrative in which it salutarily assumes, as central character, the promise, the still-to-come, of the modern (Korang 1995). And, as we have seen in Danquah's representative demand for "world citizenship," this promise borne by the class fraction also contains within itself a world-historical premise of normativity: of norming native space in keeping with the demand of a "modern world" where "everyone can, will, should 'have' a nation as he or she has a gender" (Anderson 1983).

THE NATIVE/AFRICAN PEOPLE:
IMAGINARY CONSTITUTION AND DEBATE

In the outline above, the disposition of elements in which the nation appears has been presented by and large in terms of objective spatial relations. However, room has also been made tentatively for a conception of "imaginative space," for what, in relation to this objectivity, is a reconstitutive "imaginary." This imaginary is to be thought as standing, as it were, "over and above" the impersonal structuring and constraining forces that give definite location and definition to human agents. Hence, in this mode, I have named a general (world) imaginary of the modern, on the one hand, as well as an (African) middle class imaginary, on the other, the former precipitated out of the global realignments occasioned by European imperialism, the latter precipitated out of this imperialism's more or less specific colonial reconfiguration of native space in Africa.

But what is this imaginary that stands "over and above"? The question takes us to Marx's observation about the objectivity of history at large and the important qualification of cultural subjectivity or human agency he works into this objectivity. As he points out, looked at in the (objective) last instance, although men (sic) do not make history *as they please*, they nevertheless *do* make their own history, and do so in the first, and at their own, instance (Marx 1852). If by history in the last instance, we understand the impersonal forces that have conspired, in concrete ways, to dispose elements and the collocations between them in objective space, then history in the first instance accounts for the extent to which human agency, understood in a cultural dimension of originality, makes and remakes the world more or less in its own human image, creating cultural space, that is, out of the otherwise aloof impersonality of time.

The imaginary then is that concept which allows us to posit a shaping human force—a force of origination and calculation—over and above, but also reciprocally implicated in, other forces of a more or less impersonal nature that go into the configuration of any space. There is no pure space outside history, a free, unconstrained space, where the imaginary operates. In that sense the imaginary is not about free-floating fancy, fantasy, daydream, or illusion (Castoriadis 1993). On the contrary, an account of it is incomplete which does not see its grounding in material realities—material realities which give rise to it and to which it gives rise in a more or less uneven reciprocity. The domain of the imaginary, in other words, is shaped both by and within reactive effect and proactive cause: things cause it to happen; it causes things to happen. To the extent that it subsists within spatial and material constraints that compel the imagining of a way out, we have to see the imaginary as constrained to imagine this way out only as a way *through* these givens.

Then, again, the imaginary is not an individual affair, although we may see its symbolic incarnation in special individuals. On the contrary, it is a space of origination, creation and aspiration *collectively* "dreamed" into being and which, as such, lies between individuals as the articulation of a vision shared in common by them. This is a commonality that then confers on such individuals, who would otherwise exist in an aggregate, the conglomerate or corporate character of a group identity. Such is the way we need to situate the native fraction of a middle class. The point is worth

emphatic repetition that this fraction acquires an *African* corporate character to the extent that, beyond the living variety and experientially different
circumstances of the continent, its imaginary, as reactive effect, is given in
the formal sameness of its uncertain location within the colonial conjuncture; and, as proactive cause, is articulated around nation—a nation (to be)
wrested by itself from coloniality—as a common (narrative) vision.[1] This
vision—for some a vision of a pan-African nation, for others pleading prag-
matism, a making do with the boundaries offered by colonial statehood—is
one that imagines a reworking of the ethno-cultural variety of African nativity, translating the Many (native peoples) into a presumed higher rationality
of the One (people).

What we see in all this is the imaginary as a norm-positing domain, a
space of collective self-accounting in terms of both existing and projected
norms. Who are we? On what basis is our being? What are our realistic
possibilities, especially given our circumstantial relations with others, relations that press down on us, in some ways, and open up opportunities for us,
to a greater or lesser degree, in still other ways? All of these are questions
inscribed in the imaginary. They are about the positing and projection of
norms of collective life (Castoriadis 1993); about collective agency gauging
its ability-potential to transform given structures and relations in order to
recast them in what it sees and posits as a normative (self-)image. They are,
finally, about a group metaphysics, that place where questions of essence
and destiny loom large, but also where ideological disagreement and revi-
sionism, regarding means and ends, intervene.

How, in these structuring terms of the imaginary, does a native middle
class fraction gauge its relation with a nativity in general, that colonized
space over which it gives inscription to the potential nation? What does this
fraction posit and project as the norms of the nation? What sorts of "metaphysical" debates emerge that divide a middle class ideologically within
itself even as, in some profound sense, the debates unite this class to the
extent that they settle on the same logic: putting the character of the African
nation on a proper footing? What follows will explore these questions through
a summary discussion that centres Casely Hayford and Nkrumah in the
thought of African middle class nationalism. Another outstanding middle
class nationalist figure, Cabral, will also be introduced briefly in the last
section of the essay. If it is Cabral who has done some of the best thinking
trying to reorder the priorities organizing the nationalist imaginary, he takes
off at that point where the middle class nation in Africa, as embodied centrally by a figure like Nkrumah, arrives at its historic impasse.

The preoccupation energizing much of early African nationalism was
where to find, and how to define (or found), the character of the nation. For

a native fraction standing in an uncertain middle, the question of the nation gave itself as a question (a) of its orientation as to its source and its direction; and (b) of its representativeness. These find their way as central themes into Casely Hayford's 1911 quasi-fictional autobiography, a classic work with the anti-colonialist title *Ethiopia Unbound*. The author's modernist self-definition, as exemplified by his fictional alter ego, is not in doubt. He belongs to a class of "cultured" natives, qualified as such to "lead the masses" of their "unsophisticated" and "less privileged brethren" in a messianic struggle to wrest the nation from the colonial state, a state clearly out of place on the soil of nativity (Casely Hayford 1911: 172, 183, 194).

The decidedly modernist idealization of a middle class as a "cultured" element in native space, to the extent that it hierarchically opposes this fraction to the native generality, also confirms the former as embodying the world-historical normativity alluded to above. But mention of a "cultured" class is also calculated to make the anti-colonial struggle initiated by this native fraction a legitimate struggle. As such it reads as a struggle between members of this fraction and white competitors to whom they are potentially equal, on account of a shared worldliness, but which potential is denied by the fact that colonial domination gives the whites the relative upper hand. We find in the colony, then, that worldliness as norm is split between two factions. On the one hand are the wielders of modern culture without the competitive advantage of power: a less-than-sovereign middle class; on the other, the wielders of modern-state power without the (initial) advantage of local culture: the sovereign functionaries of the colonial state.

Given this circumstance, the native fraction of a middle class could come to imagine itself rediscovering (*re*discovering, since cultural alienation of class members was a reality in coloniality) the advantage of inhabiting native culture and utilizing it to found sovereign power. This is the problematic of nativism read politically: the turning of a cultural people in nativity to middle class advantage.[2] The twin themes of finding (i.e., rediscovering) and founding a national character that recur in Casely Hayford's anti-colonial polemics in *Ethiopia Unbound*, then, turn around the question of how a middle class might best politicize cultural advantage. To this end, early African nationalism, of the kind typified by Casely Hayford, proposes to hegemonically enlist the native people on the side of the anticolonial struggle (a). by making them see their cultural image—i.e., Tradition—*conservatively* reflected in the middle class; and, (b). by making them see in a "cultured" fraction a reflection of their *progressive* pathway upward to the world (see also Blyden 1881, 1908; Sarbah 1897, 1906; Plaatje 1916; Kenyatta 1953).

These are problematic propositions in more ways than one. In the main it can be said that in colonial space, Casely Hayford fails to define the political properly by miscasting the founding terms of the national character, nativity and a native people, in an ahistorical metaphysical essence. Since his rhetoric relies on an absolute opposition between nation and colony, the former's presumed purity is compelled to find its guarantee in a native essence beyond historical contamination.[3] However, this singular, otherworldly construct—a construct that comes also with a primordial guarantee—elides the real ethno-cultural differences making up colonized nativity. Casely Hayford's move — and the historical record all over colonial Africa attests to it—is one that the very colonial power he was contesting would historically take advantage of. For if essence was brought to the centre of contested power and legitimacy, the native peoples, in their variety, stood to be legitimately articulated in their essential *differences*, not sameness. Thus, prompted by its own imperative of survival, colonial power politicizes the very essence claimed by the nationalist by using it to tribalize and administratively compartmentalize the native peoples, a tactic of divide and rule. Essence is shifted from Hayford's pure and wrongheaded metaphysics to pure historical expedient, and holding this expedient captive to its design, colonial power conducts culture-as-legitimation—"Tradition"—into the domain of state formation (Robertson 1975; Hobsbawm and Ranger 1983; Mamdani 1996). Nativism's enlisting of the people into a politics of culture is condemned to remain a gestural, not substantive, politics.

Moving quickly forward from the era of Casely Hayford, we come to a major revisionist phase of the anti-colonial struggle in post-World War II Africa. Here we find a middle class able to face up to the defeat of its sovereign aspirations with colonial power's hegemonic appropriation of nativism into its conservative political order. If the moment required an (imaginary) redefinition of a cultural people, one able to move away from a gestural to a substantive politics, then the politicking of Nkrumah in the Gold Coast allows us to read the lineaments of this significant shift. The key issue was this: in its political deformation, culture, or the domain of the people, had come to serve the colony and not the potential nation—i.e., the structure in which the middle class invests its sovereign self-image. How, then, to rescue a culture in colonial captivity and bring it on the side of the nation-in-waiting? In what terms and to what ends could this rescue be imagined and given a narrative projection to the native people as a process of cultural and political normalization?

In the pursuit of its own advantage, coloniality had proposed the people *as native by descent.* To the extent that it reifies distinctions in ethno-cultural lineage, instituting policies of separate development therewith, colonial power persists in the fracturing of the space of nativity into politically manageable fragments. Picking its anti-colonial cue from this, the post-war project of normalization, as exemplified centrally by the career of Nkrumah, comes to posit the nation beyond colonially-induced cultural atomization. The nation is newly envisioned in a giving back to the native people a representation of themselves as *native by consent*. Hence the project of the nation is quickened within a definition of a native people who spatially are (to be articulated into) one people, differences in ethno-cultural descent notwithstanding. Where a colonial thesis of *lineal* continuity imposes on, and enforces discontinuities within, native space, a middle class rediscovers its proper role as a mending of this fractured socioscape into a *lateral* continuity (Korang 1995).

In this regard the question of essence shifts its ground. From the past perfect, the given, of a metaphysical absolute it is translated to a historical metaphysics: the (re-)making of an essential people, a possible future perfect. In the new nationalist imaginary, the essence of culture is thus repositioned as a coming together, a melding of the colonial peoples: culture awaits restructuring towards a domain where it underwrites political consensus (Nkrumah 1957, 1964; Abraham 1962; Senghor 1964; Nyerere 1966; Cabral 1979).

But where was this domain in which a future-oriented consensus was to receive its backing, the force of its legitimacy? Here, contrary to the nativist refusal characterizing Casely Hayford's earlier stance, we find nationalists like Nkrumah implicating the power of political coloniality, as represented by the State, fully in the cultural logic of the nation. For this power, by gathering different spaces into its one sphere, has always already created the One out of the Many, in which case its maintenance and policing of differences in the colony represented an abnormal case of bad faith. The post-war anti-colonial struggle, then, reads as a recuperation, a normalizing, of the logic of the always already: middle class African nationalism stands poised to find and found the popular guarantee of the nation in the fact of—and not in spite of—the colonial State. Far from an elimination of this exogenous imposition, the new logic demanded its capture. Nkrumah, and we understand him to speak for middle class nationalism generally, would confidently declare: "Seek ye first the political kingdom and the rest shall be added unto you" (1957: 164). The political kingdom of the State is the space where the narrative of the nation wills the finding of its culmination.

Thus in the aftermath of the compromise of the nativist conservatism of its beginnings, we find a middle class whose world-historical mission of norming native space is constrained to identify its ideological prerogatives in the very order whose overthrow it seeks. If this represents a revolutionary shift that relocates the otherworldly metaphysics of the earlier formation—nativism—to a this-worldly one—a post-nativist *étatisme*—African Independence and its heritage today are deeply invested in the cultural-political logic of the latter. It follows, therefore, that it is in terms of this logic that we must render an accounting for the historic compromises—spectacular failures in some cases—of the African nation. To pick up once more, then, the questions with which we began: Where did the nation go wrong?; Where might it recover ground?

ÉTATISME IN THEORY AND PRACTICE: A LEGACY AND ITS CRITIQUE

This section opens with the still-resonant words of "the strategist of genius in the struggle against classical colonialism" (Cabral 1979: 115), Nkrumah, regarding the capture of the political kingdom. The ironic point of course is that they resonate in our time not in terms of a fulfillment of their confident promise but in their disconfirmation: events in an unruly post-independence era have conspired to deny the vision Nkrumah and others sought to realize. In the assertion itself, Nkrumah borrows a Christian formulation ("seek ye first the *kingdom of God* and the rest shall be added unto you") and transfers its *metaphysical* meaning—the kingdom of God as the be-all and end-all—to the political State. If, therefore, in securing the political kingdom, Nkrumah and others of his ilk envision the African struggle for an independent national-social order reaching a moment of culmination—a final moment of coherence, that is—this moment coheres as such in, and is firmly underwritten by, a more or less *étatiste* absolutism. And this absolute places the meaning of culmination by and large within its own logic, or sense, of an *ending* (i.e., as the be-all and end-all).[4] In that sense, a more or less absolute State, a State which has a central, autonomous and directing function (Chatterjee 1986), remains an article of faith with Nkrumah. The culmination of a national people is unimaginable without this postulate.

What does this envision in theory, if not in fact, for the daily practice of culture in the post-independence nation? It means that culture, the proper domain of nation-formation, is subordinated to politics.[5] Appearing from above, it is the *force* of the State, it would seem, that "legitimates" the nation; and not the force of the nation, from a popular below, that confers on the State its true legitimacy. To the extent that the former holds true, the native people, it would seem, become a mere object of politics, as such to be emptied or abstracted into the nationalistic pretensions and requirements of the political kingdom.

The thesis of *étatiste* absolutism advanced here as part of the legacy of middle class African nationalism generally is not the creation of a subjective whim. On the contrary, it bears repeating that its cultural-political logic is imposed by objective circumstances. The anti-colonial struggle, given the ethno-cultural plurality of the colonial countries, and to the extent that its purposes had to terminate in what Gramsci refers to as "passive" or "re-form-revolution" (Gramsci 1971; Chatterjee 1986), had no choice but to begin by positing an antithesis, the exogenous State in this case and position it as prior to a thesis it had then to seek out: what African middle class nationalists imagined as an endogenous principle of modern popular selfhood whose definition, beyond the merely ethnic and ethnocentric, would be national. In the progressive middle class nationalist imaginary, the modernity of the nation, then, points hopefully in the direction of a dialectical entry into a "higher" synthesis of antithesis and thesis, of exogenous and endogenous components.

Inasmuch as this *étatiste* vision of culmination is driven by the dialectical priority of the political kingdom, in retrospect its positivism seems, perhaps, too brash. And one speaks here bearing in mind the convulsions, upheavals and setbacks that have beset (and continue to beset) many nation-states on the African continent since Independence. What has transpired after Independence is a political kingdom which, stamped on the continent by colonial imposition, continues to define an imperative alien to the deepest aspiration of the peoples of Africa (Davidson 1992; Soyinka 1996). This historical and cultural antithesis, moreover, has proven durable and too strong, becoming a structure that insinuates itself into and pre-empts the normative constitution of endogenous national selfhood (Armah 1968). This, more or less, sums up the argument of the cultural critic, Abiola Irele (1992), in a recent exercise in direct political critique that brings an impassioned judgement to bear on "The Crisis of Legitimacy in Africa." Irele's piece marks once more the consistency with which, as failed practice, the political as such has featured as a major theme in the critical and creative projects of African cultural modernity in the last thirty or so years.

Yet, in all the critiques of a failed African nationalist practice that have emerged, one value-constant, perhaps, remains implicitly or explicitly upheld. This, as most centrally projected by Nkrumahist nationalism, is the ideal of a consensual nativity as the foundation and goal of African cultural and political modernity. Perhaps, then, it is in the unflinching drive to realize—by any means necessary, as it were—a consensual nativity that we need to locate the enduring legacy of this species of African nationalism. And yet, if this vision bears, as we have seen in Nkrumah's representative example, its own impressive baggage of *étatiste* liability, then we need to register other possibilities beyond its moment. And, perhaps, more than any figure in the front ranks of African nationalism, it is Cabral who, in his difficult reflections on the relations between the political and the cultural in nationalist practice, suggests the modalities of this going beyond.

It is Cabral, then, who attempts to bring the metaphysics tainting Nkrumah's political kingdom to earth by arguing in outstanding fashion the priority of the cultural in the political, the latter as represented by the antithesis of the colonial State against which the struggle for national liberation contends. In an oft-quoted piece, Cabral argues that to the extent that "imperialist domination has a vital need to practice cultural oppression, national liberation is necessarily an *act of culture*" (1979: 143). The point then is that the political act of liberation begins and ends in culture. Cabral thus redefines liberation or independence as a culmination whose logic is— which must be posited in a sense of—a *beginning*. And in this beginning the cultural and the political, people and power, are seen as elements that must negotiate their way, without the grand political preconception, towards their mutual reconciliation in practice.

This proposition shifts from the étatiste positivism—the grand political preconception, that is—that sees the people as a singular political *object*, an abstraction emptying into the political kingdom, to the people, in their variety, as cultural *subjects*. As such, from below, their variety—and Cabral could appreciate the ethno-cultural variety of the popular component of his own struggle—is radically formative of, rather than waiting to be singularly reformed from above by, the politics of national liberation. For Cabral, then, what I have referred to as the foundation and goal of African cultural and political modernity, a consensual nativity, reads as a datum of gradualism, reached at a "confluence of the levels of culture of different social groups..."[6] But the reality is that such convergence is never "reached," in the sense of arriving at an ideal equilibrium; on the contrary it is a vanishing point which, for this reason, enjoins a nationalist practice able, with the beacon of democracy before it, to renew its goals in, and adapt its means to, the ever changing demands of cultural, political and economic life.

These brief reflections on Cabral must remain at this stage a simplified interpretation of the by no means simple thought of the late Guinéan leader. His necessarily difficult insights into the cultural-political logic of the African nation are in themselves a critical reflection on the fragility, the hollowness even, of the grand constructs of nationalist legitimation of the middle class founders—the world-historically mediated State, representing the ulterior Reason towards which the grand narratives of the nation must strive— when tested against the ground realities of everyday practice in the postcolonial African nation (Korouma 1968; Mbembe 1992; Olaniyan 1992).

And yet the assertion that "the way out is the way through—attributed to the American cultural critic Kenneth Burke (Lentricchia 1983)—is one that

Cabral would appreciate. If so what he leaves us Africans is the insight that we must be prepared to revisit constantly what it is we are going through (and cannot help but go through), treating it not as a process once understood but responding to it as one responds to a protean challenge. In that sense, then, what is required in the imaginary and practice of the nation is not the "metaphysical" sense of ends so much as a radical sense of beginning that, regarding ends as vanishing points, places the emphasis on continually renewed effort—in theory as in practice.

In his *After the Last Sky* (1986), Edward Said has occasion to interrogate a Palestinian identity, *qua* a national identity, in the following terms: "When did we become 'a people'? When did we top being one? Or are we in the process of becoming one? What do these big questions have to do with our intimate relationships with each other as well as with others?" Said's is a call to bring a self-consciously interdisciplinary reading to history, a history able to account for a popular national identity within the force-field of its spatial determinations. Today as we read our situation(s) of crisis in Africa, the critic's self-interrogations hold a relevance for our interpretative methodology. Where have we failed in becoming a people? Accounting for this all-important question must take us beyond the easy consolation of reconciling *nation, people, identity* within a metaphysical principle that is eternally self-begetting, its identicalness with itself thus rendering it immune to engaged spatio-historical analysis. As other pieces in this volume indicate, the time to critically locate African subjects and objects within, and derive their socio-historical significances from a spatial frame is on us.

NOTES

1. Proclaiming "WE ARE A NATION" in the colonial heyday of the British Gold Coast, Rev. S. R. B. Attoh Ahuma goes on to ask: "But if we are a nation are we self-conscious?" The question is directed at an aspirant "rising generation," comprised of the European-educated native fraction. On this fraction, according to the author, has fallen the "birthright, privilege, duty, destiny and honor" of seeking the effective bases for conceiving and birthing nation out of colony (1911: vii, 1). Nation in the nationalist's wake-up call to the rising generation, is the projection of a class destiny. And it assumes the shape of a narrative burden such that the national destiny is borne, of a necessity, on the back of a collective middle-class character. On nativism, see, among others, p'Bitek 1973; Chinweizu *et al* 1983; Appiah 1992; Korang and Slemon 1997.

2. The 2nd December 1915 edition of the newspaper *The Gold Coast Independent* reported the formation by Casely Hayford of the Gold Coast National Research Association. The objectives of the Association were to eliminate

the "white man's standpoint from the black man's outlook"; to restore "national respect and self-confidence" by adhering strictly to native customs unadulterated by European elements; and finally to reconstruct "on paper" the native State "before the disintegrating foreign element intruded, or insinuated itself into it" (Kimble 1963: 525).

3. The phenomenon of one-party States that in quick succession became the norm in post-independence Africa generally supports this interpretation. In Ghana, the slogan was: "the C.P.P. is Ghana and Ghana is the C.P.P." -- making Nkrumah's ruling Party indistinguishable from the nation whose totality it erroneously imagined itself as exhausting.

4. In this regard, the fate of the late Kéita Fodéba, cultural worker and Minister of State executed in 1969 by Guinea-Conakry's Sékou Touré, is emblematic (Miller 1990: 31-60). For a sustained reflection on the State-People, power-culture problem in post-colonial Africa, see the later works of Ngugi wa Thiong'o (himself detained by the Kenyan State for his consciousness-raising populist theatre).

5. The wording I reproduce here is from the translation that appears in *Return to Source: Selected Speeches of Amilcar Cabral* (excerpted in Williams and Chrisman 1994: 59; see also Cabral 1979: 147).

REFERENCES

Abraham, W. E. *The Mind of Africa*. London: Weidenfeld and Nicholson, 1962.

Abrahams, Peter. *A Wreath for Udomo*. London: Faber, 1956.

Achebe, Chinua. *The Trouble with Nigeria*. London: Heinemann, 1984.

Achebe, Chinua. *Hopes and Impediments: Selected Essays*. New York: Anchor-Doubleday, 1989.

Amselle, Jean-Loup and Elikia M'bokolo. *Au coeur de l'ethnie: Ethnies, tribalisme et état en Afrique*. Paris: La Découverte, 1985.

Anderson, Benedict. *Imagined Communities: Reflections on the Origin and Spread of Nationalism*. London: Verso, 1983.

Appiah, Kwame Anthony. *In My Father's House: Africa in the Philosophy of Culture*. New York: Oxford University Press, 1992.

Armah, Ayi Kwei. "An African Fable." *Présence Africaine* 68(1968): 193-196.

Armah, Ayi Kwei. *The Beautyful Ones Are Not Yet Born*. London: Heinemann, 1969.

Attoh Ahuma, Rev. S[amuel] R[ichard] B[rew]. "Colony or Protectorate: Thoughts on the Present Discontent." Addressed to the Gold Coast Aborigines' Rights Protection Society, Cape Coast Castle. *The Gold Coast Methodist Times* April 30, 1897. Rpt. in J. E. Casely Hayford, *Gold Coast Native Institutions* (see below).

Attoh Ahuma. *The Gold Coast Nation and National Consciousness*. 1971. London: Frank Cass, [First published in 1911].

Awolowo, Obafemi. 1960. *Awo: The Autobiography of Chief Obafemi Awolowo*. Cambridge: Cambridge University Press, 1911.

Awoonor, Kofi. "Kwame Nkrumah: Symbol of Emergent Africa." *Africa Report* (June 1972): 22-25.

Azikiwe, Nnamdi. *My Odyssey: An Autobiography.* New York: Praeger, 1970.

Bhabha, Homi K., ed. *Nation and Narration.* London and New York: Routledge, 1990.

Blyden, E. W. 1862. *Liberia's Offering.* New York: J. A. Gray, 1862.

Blyden, E. W. *Christianity, Islam and the Negro Race.* 1967. Introd. Christopher Fyfe. Edinburgh: Edinburgh University Press, [First Published in 1887].

Blyden, E. W. *African Life and Customs.* London: Phillips, 1908.

Boahen, A. Adu. *General History of Africa,* Vol. 7. *Africa Under Colonial Domination 1880-1935.* London: Heinemann/UNESCO, 1985.

Breytenbach, Breyten. *Return to Paradise.* New York: Harcourt Brace, 1993.

Brown, David. "Who Are the Tribalists?: Social Pluralism and Political Ideology in Ghana." *African Affairs* 81, 322(1982):37-69.

Cabral, Amilcar. *Unity and Struggle.* New York: Monthly Review Press, 1979.

Cartey, Wilfred and Martin Kilson. *The Africa Reader: Independent Africa.* New York: Vintage-Random, 1970.

Casely Hayford, J[oseph] E[phraim]. *Gold Coast Native Institutions.* London: Frank Cass, 1903.

Casely Hayford, J[oseph] E[phraim] *Ethiopia Unbound: Studies in Race Emancipation.* London: Phillips, 1911.

Castoriadis, Cornelius. "The Greek and the Modern Political Imaginary." *Salmagundi* 100 (Fall 1993):102-129 .

Chatterjee, Partha. *Nationalist Thought and the Colonial World: A Derivative Discourse.* London: Zed Books, 1986.

Chazan, Naomi. *Politics and Society in Contemporary Africa.* Boulder, Colo.: L. Rienner Publishers, 1988.

Chinweizu, Jemie and Madubuike. *Towards the Decolonization of African Literature.* Washington, D.C.: Howard University Press, 1983.

Danquah, J[oseph] B[oakye]. *Self-Help and Expansion: A Review of the Work and Aims of the Youth Conference, with a Statement of its Policy for 1943, and the Action Consequent upon that Policy.* Accra: Gold Coast Youth Conference, 1943.

Davidson, Basil. *Black Star of Africa: The Life and Times of Kwame Nkrumah.* London: Allen Lane, 1973.

Davidson, Basil. "On revolutionary nationalism: the legacy of Cabral." *Race and Class* 27, 3(1986):21-45.

Davidson, Basil. *Black Man's Burden: Africa and the Curse of the Nation-State.* New York: Times Books, 1992.

de Graft Johnson, J. W. *Towards Nationhood in West Africa: Thoughts of Young Africa Addressed to Young Britain.* 1971. 2nd ed. New Introd. F. K. Drah. London: Frank Cass, [First published in 1928].

Eluwa, G. I. C. "Casely Hayford and African Emancipation." *Pan-African Journal* 7, 2(1974):111-118.

Emerson, Rupert and Martin Kilson, eds. *The Political Awakening of Africa.* Englewood Cliffs, N.J.: Prentice-Hall, 1965.

Fanon, Frantz. *Toward the African Revolution: Political Essays.* Trans. Haakon Chevalier. New York: Monthly Review Press, 1967.

Fanon, Frantz. *The Wretched of the Earth.* Trans. Constance Farrington. New York: Grove Weidenfeld, 1967, 1969.

Farah, Nuruddin *Maps.* New York: Pantheon, 1986.

Franco, Jean. "The Nation as Imagined Community." *The New Historicism,* ed. H. Aram Veeser. New York and London: Routledge, 1989.

Gellner, Ernest. *Nations and Nationalism.* Oxford: Basil Blackwell, 1983.

Giddens, Anthony. *The Consequences of Modernity.* Cambridge: Polity Press, 1990.

Gikandi, Simon. "The Politics and Poetics of the National Formation: Recent African Writing." In *From Commonwealth to Post-Colonial,* ed. Anna Rutherford. Sydney: Dangaroo, 1992.

Gramsci, Antonio. *Selections from the Prison Notebooks.* Trans. and ed. Quintin Hoare and Geoffrey Nowell Smith. New York: International Publishers, 1971.

Gutkind, P. and P. Waterman, eds. *African Social Studies: A Radical Reader.* New York and London: Monthly Review Press, 1977.

Hegel, G. W. F. *The Philosophy of History.* Trans. J. Sibree. Buffalo: Prometheus Books, 1991.

Hobsbawm, Eric J. *Nations and Nationalism Since 1870: Programme, Myth, Reality.* Cambridge: Canto, 1991, [First published in 1822].

Hobsbawm, Eric J. and Terence Ranger, eds. *The Invention of Tradition.* Cambridge: Cambridge University Press, 1983.

Hodgkin, Thomas L. *Nationalism in Colonial Africa.* New York: New York University Press, 1957.

Horton, James Africanus Beale. *West African Countries and Peoples and a Vindication of the African Race.* Edinburgh: Edinburgh University Press, 1969 [First published in 1868].

Horton, James Africanus Beale. *Letters on the Political Condition of the Gold Coast.* London: Frank Cass, 1970, [First published in 1870].

Irele, Abiola. "The Crisis of Legitimacy in Africa." *Dissent* 39 (Summer 1992):296-302.

James, C. L. R. *Nkrumah and the Ghana Revolution.* London: Allison and Busby, 1977, [First published in 1962].

Jameson, Fredric. "Third World Literature in the Era of Multinational Capital." *Social Text* 15 (Fall 1986):65-88.

Jeyifo, Biodun. "Literature in Postcolonial Africa: Repression, Resistance, and Reconfigurations." *Dissent* (Summer 1992):353-360.

July, Robert. *The Origins of Modern African Thought.* New York: Praeger, 1967.

Kaunda, Kenneth. *Zambia Shall Be Free: An Autobiography.* New York: Praeger, 1962.

Kenyatta, Jomo. *Facing Mount Kenya: The Traditional Life of Gikuyu.* London: Heinemann, 1979, [First published in 1959].

Kimble, David. *A Political History of Ghana: The Rise of Gold Coast Nationalism 1850-1928*. Oxford: The Clarendon Press, 1963.

Korang, Kwaku Larbi. "The Writing of Ghana: Nation and the Shaping of African Modernity." Unpublished Ph.D dissertation, University of Alberta, 1995.

Korang, Kwaku Larbi and Stephen Slemon. "Post-colonialism and Language." In *Writing and Africa*, eds. Mpalive Hangson-Msiska and Paul Hyland. London: Longman, 1997.

Kourouma, Ahmadou. *The Suns of Independence*. Trans. Adrian Adams. London: Heinemann, 1981, [First published in 1968].

Lentricchia, Frank. *Criticism and Social Change*. Chicago and London: University of Chicago Press, 1983.

Lumumba, Patrice. *Congo, My Country*. New York: Praeger, 1962.

Lumumba, Patrice. *Lumumba Speaks: The Speeches and Writings of Patrice Lumumba 1958-1961*. Ed. Jean Lierde. Trans. Helen R. Lane. Introd. Jean-Paul Sartre. Boston: Little, Brown, 1972.

Luthuli, Albert J. *Let My People Go: An Autobiography*. Johannesburg: Collins, 1962.

Lynch, Hollis R., ed. *Black Spokesman: Selected Published Writings of Edward Wilmot Blyden*. New York: Humanities Press, 1971.

Maja-Pearce, Adewale. "The Press in Africa: Expression and Repression." In *Writing and Africa*, eds. Mpalive-Hangson Msiska and Paul Hyland. London: Longman, 1997.

Mbembe, Achille. "The Banality of Power and the Aesthetics of Vulgarity in the Postcolony." *Public Culture* 4, 2(1992):1-30.

Mamdani, Mahmood. *Citizen and Subject: Contemporary Africa and the Legacy of Late Colonialism*. Princeton: Princeton University Press, 1996.

Marx, Karl. *The Eighteenth Brumaire of Louis Bonaparte*. New York: International Publishers, 1963, [First published in 1852].

Meer, Fatima. *Higher Than Hope: A Biography of Nelson Mandela*. Harmondsworth: Penguin, 1990.

Miller, Christopher. *Theories of Africans: Francophone Literature and Anthropology in Africa*. Chicago and London: The University of Chicago Press, 1990.

Mudimbe, V. Y. *The Invention of Africa: Gnosis, Philosophy, and the Order of Knowledge*. Bloomington and Indianapolis: Indiana University Press, 1988.

Ngugi wa Thiong'o. *Petals of Blood*. New York: Penguin, 1977.

Ngugi wa Thiong'o. *Detained: A Writer's Prison Diary*. Oxford: Heinemann, 1981.

Ngugi wa Thiong'o. *Devil on the Cross*. London: Heinemann, 1983.

Ngugi wa Thiong'o. *From the Barrel of a Pen*. Trenton, N.J.: Africa World Press, 1983.

Ngugi wa Thiong'o. *Decolonizing the Mind: The Politics of Language in Africa Literature*. London: James Currey, 1986.

Ngugi wa Thiong'o. *Matigari*. London: Heinemann, 1987.

Ngugi wa Thiong'o. *Moving the Center: The Struggle for Cultural Freedoms.* London: James Currey. Portsmouth, N.H.: Heinemann, 1993.

Nkrumah, Kwame. *Consciencism.* London: Heinemann, 1964.

Nkrumah, Kwame. *Africa Must Unite.* New York: International Publishers, 1970, [First published in 1963].

Nkrumah, Kwame. *I Speak of Freedom: A Statement of African Ideology.* New York: Frederick Praeger, 1962.

Nkrumah, Kwame. *Ghana: The Autobiography of Kwame Nkrumah.* New York: International Publishers, 1971, [First published in 1957].

Nyerere, Julius. *Freedom and Unity.* Dar es Salaam, Tanzania: Oxford University Press, 1966.

Olaniyan, Tejumola. "Narrativizing Postcoloniality: Responsibilities." *Public Culture* 5, 1(1992):47-55.

p'Bitek, Okot. *Africa's Cultural Revolution.* Nairobi: Macmillan, 1973.

Public Culture 5, 1(1992).

Robertson, A. F. "Anthropology and Government in Ghana." *African Affairs* 74, 294(1975):51-59.

Said, Edward. *After the Last Sky.* London: Faber, 1986.

Said, Edward. *Culture and Imperialism.* New York: Vintage-Random, 1993.

Sarbah, John Mensah. *Fanti Customary Laws.* 3rd ed. New Introd. Hollis Lynch. London: Frank Cass, 1968, [First published in 1897].

Sarbah, John Mensah. *Fanti National Constitution.* 2nd ed. Introd. Hollis Lynch. London: Frank Cass, 1968, [First published in 1906].

Senghor, L[éopold] S[édar]. *On African Socialism.* New York: Praeger, 1964.

Soyinka, Wole. *The Man Died: Prison Notes of Wole Soyinka.* London: Rex Collings, 1972.

Soyinka, Wole. *Art, Dialogue, Outrage.* Ibadan: New Horn Press, 1988.

Soyinka, Wole. *The Open Sore of a Continent: A Personal Narrative of the Nigerian Crisis.* New York: Oxford University Press, 1996.

Weber, Max. *The Protestant Ethic and the the Spirit of Capitalism.* Trans. Talcott Parsons. London: Unwin, 1968, [First published in 1930].

Williams, Patrick and Laura Chrisman, eds. *Colonial Discourse and Post-Colonial Theory: A Reader.* New York: Columbia University Press, 1994.

Wilson, Henry S. *Origins of West African Nationalism.* London: Macmillan, 1969.

Zeleza, Paul Tiyambe. "The Democratic Transition in Africa and the Anglophone Writer." *Canadian Journal of African Studies* 28, 3(1994):472-497.

Zeleza, Paul Tiyambe. *Smouldering Charcoal.* Oxford: Heinemann, 1992.

12

COMMUNITY, CITIZENSHIP, AND THE POLITICS OF ETHNICITY IN POST-COLONIAL AFRICA

DICKSON EYOH

INTRODUCTION

THE RELATIVE WEIGHTS TO BE ASSIGNED SOCIOECONOMIC interests and ethnic identity as determining variables of political mobilization is, if not the most contested issue in Africanist social science, certainly among its most resilient controversies. Indeed, differences in the thrust of analysis of politics in postcolonial Africa of the dominant postwar paradigms of development (modernization and dependency) have turned on valuations of the factors behind the salience of ethnicity as an element of political mobilization (Mafeje 1971; Saul 1979; Shaw 1986, and Young 1994a:73-78). For the modernization paradigm, the preeminence of ethnicity in the structuration of political relations owed to the inherent backwardness of preindustrial societies, that was doubly reflected by a paucity of social class divisions and the vitality of "primordial" affiliations. The advance of modernization, through industrialization, urbanism and the growth of secular consciousness, would lead to the displacement of loyalties to ascriptive groups by civic loyalties of individual citizen-subjects to the nation-state. For dependency theory and the host of neo-Marxian perspectives ranged against the modernization paradigm, the politicization of ethnicity was a phenomenon manipulated by aspirant ruling classes in their rivalries for control of state power and resources. Despite their theoretical and normative disagreements, both paradigms have shared a proclivity for the denigration of ethnicity. They have ensured that, as Young (1993:23) put it, "Africa stands out in the degree to which, in both state doctrine and most intellectual discourse, ethnicity is thoroughly stigmatized...Usually characterized as 'tribalism', ethnic self-assertion is pejoratively viewed as subversive, juvenile, and backward" (cf., Esman 1994:11-12).

The close of the 1980s witnessed a wave of popular movements of opposition to authoritarian rule, that have set into motion processes of political liberalization in most countries. The heady euphoria with which this development was greeted is now on the ebb. Many regimes that emerged from multiparty elections quickly reverted to the authoritarian styles of their predecessors, while most incumbent regimes have proven to be particularly adapt at managing pressures for political reform without conceding much power (Bratton and Van de Walle 1994; Ihonvbere 1995; and Sandbrook 1995). The celebration of the "rebirth of democracy" (Joseph 1992) was, from the onset, regularly punctuated by fears of the spectre of ethnic conflict. For the Africanist community, hostile economic environments made ethnic and communal conflicts a serious threat to projects of political liberalization that were imperative to redress the impasse in African development. The intense competition over declining pools of resources made it easier for incumbent political barons and opposition politicians to appeal to ethnic solidarities to defend their hold on or compete for power. With these types of reservations, it seems most unlikely that the denigration of politicized ethnicity will soon wane as African societies continue with their struggles to fashion more legitimate forms of governance.

An agreed upon definition of ethnicity continues to evade the social sciences, for "like family, everyone knows what it means but nobody can define it" (Smith, quoted in Alonso 1994:379). Broadly understood, ethnicity represents a sense of collective identity that rests on claims of common decent, shared attributes such as language and cultural traditions, territoriality and political organization. Like other social identities, ethnic identities are relational, markers of differences between groups. As scholars, particularly those attracted to the constructionist explanations, suggest, ethnic identities are neither given or static (see Amselle 1985; Vail 1989:10ff; also Young 1994a:77-81 and Levin 1995 for syntheses of dominant perspectives). Products of human agency, they are valorized and transformed in the context of struggles over structures of power that underpin relations between states and components of civil society and are ordered by hierarchies of race, class, gender, religion etc. Thus, as a force of collective political action, ethnicity is part of the complex web of factors that are implicated in and regulate struggles over arrangements of economic, political, and symbolic power in multiethnic societies.

This, at once cryptic and catholic, definition of ethnic identity and the context of its politicization will suffice to guide the broad discussion of the dynamics of ethnic-based politics in postcolonial Africa which follows. The discussion will profit from randomly drawn examples, without pretending to offer an inventory of the most salient characteristics of intra and interethnic relations and their bearings on patterns of ethnic political competition and conflict. The main purpose is to reveal and interrogate the conceptual, substantive and ideological premises of the stigmatization of ethnicity in both intellectual discourse and official practices. The transcendence of this bias is a crucial step to freeing analysis of ethnic politics from easy vulnerability to being constituted as the main prop in morality plays about the conduct of politics in African states.

The inclination to denigrate ethnic-based politics stems from intellectual sympathy with the aspirations of nationalist discourses and is sustained by progressively bleaker assessments of the fate of these aspirations under the nation-building projects of postcolonial ruling elites. With these burdens, the analysis of ethnic politics easily becomes enmeshed in ambivalences about how to reconcile loyalties to culturally-differentiated communities and the nation-state. Put differently, the ambivalences reflect the abiding tensions of competing conceptualizations of the connections between space, community and the meaning of citizenship that "frames the internal contradiction that is at the heart of the modern nation-state" (Smith 1995:98). A universalized construct of liberal discourse, the modern nation-state is based on the presumption that it is a community of homogeneous people with a standardized package of rights and obligations to the state. But the "people" within its territorial referents are multiply fragmented; their conceptions of the "people" is particularistic, reflecting allegiances to sub-national communities into which they were born or elect to identify with. In Africanist social science, the ambivalences which imbricate the analysis of political ethnicity and organize its stigmatization are fructified by the resort to distinctions between forms of ethnicity. The distinctions - "ethnicity from below" and "ethnicity from above" or what Randrijarian (1996:30) dubs as ethnicity in the "private" versus "public" domain—are based on the numerical size of groups and spatial referents of ethnic identity and consciousness.[1]

Few would gainsay the observation that for Africans, bearing an ethnic identity or belonging to a "tribe" (a term that not too many, regardless of levels of formal schooling, are averse to using) is an ordinary aspect of selfhood and a basic social relation. Seen from this perspective, that is, as "ethnicity from below", ethnicity designates the collective identity of small-scale groups in rural and regional spaces with shared cultures and histories, and its building blocs are the vertical solidarities of kinship. This form of ethnicity is potentially a libratory force; it can be deployed in the struggles for survival by cultural groups that are besieged by the homogenizing impulses of state expansion and commodification. "Ethnicity from above" is the type which is realized outside the spatial boundaries of small-scale kinship groups, and rests on horizontal linkages. The valorization of translocal ethnicities is orchestrated by cultural and political entrepreneurs, who are involved in competition for power and resources at the institutional level of the state. By definition this form of ethnic identity and consciousness is with an inherent potential as a force of oppression and political instability. Its mobilization by elites engenders and sustains sectarian political conflicts, and subordinate strata are the main casualties (Ake 1987; 1993:2-5; Nnoli 1989; 1994:12-15 and Randrijarian 1996:33-36.).

This distinction is certainly with heuristic merit to explorations of the dynamics of ethnic social relations at different levels of society. However, both forms of ethnicity cannot be separated in a substantive sense. As most would readily admit, the valorization of translocal ethnicities is contingent on the manipulation of the cultural and symbolic properties of localized kin-based groups. The real value, or cost of this distinction, is that it allows for the representation of ethnicity as an enigmatic form of identity, and through this, highly subjective evaluations of the positive and negative political expressions of ethnic identity and consciousness. In effect, the distinction encourages the "overideologizing" of analysis of ethnic politics in postcolonial Africa. In order to contain this tendency, it is important to admit to the basic fact that the production and renegotiation of ethnic identity and consciousness are shaped by and in turn shape the responses of groups in different spaces to shifts in power relations and conditions of material life that are associated with state expansion and commodification of economic relations. This requires an understanding of the reciprocal dynamics involved in the production and transformation of local and translocal ethnicities. The starting point of such analysis is necessarily the genesis of the modern African state in colonialism and its postcolonial trajectory. More specifically, the manners in which nation-state formation in Africa, as elsewhere, courses on two contradictory tendencies: The efforts of their architects to, on the one hand, obliterate differences through standardization of social and spatial relations, and the other hand, through the differential incorporation of groups into economy and polity, ensure the reproduction of all types of social divisions, including hierarchies of ethnicities (Appaduria 1996:46-47).

ETHNIC DIFFERENTIATION AND COLONIAL STATE FORMATION

Present-day African nation-states are in every sense European inventions, as hardly any of them can boost a credible lineage to a precolonial political entity. Their territorial referents are coincident with administrative borders of colonial states, which invariably incorporated societies of differing scale as well as sociocultural and political arrangements. Although ethnic formations predated colonialism, contemporary ethnicities are largely the outcome of negotiations and renegotiations of group identities in response to the structures of political domination and transformations in economic and cultural organization under colonialism.[2] As Mudimbe (1988:2-3) reminds us, colonialism was a radical project of transformation that aspired to no less than the total reorganization of African space and social relations into fundamentally European construct. The state which managed this project was a quintessentially hybrid structure, whose political-administrative organization and discourse of domination reposed on a simultaneous insistence of the "sameness" and "alterity" of Africans. A transplantation of juridical norms and bureaucratic systems of the modern-state in Europe, it was autocratic and militarized system of rule that conceived and treated all indigenous populations as subjects of domination, rather than citizens with rights and obligations to the state. Yet, the management of the colonial enterprise called for reliance on indigenous political forces and institutions.

A commonly invoked distinction in approaches to colonial political administration is that between "indirect rule" as a minimalist strategy favoured by the British whereby imperial authority was exercised through indigenous traditional rulers, and "direct rule" of the French and Portuguese who preferred the concentration of administrative authority and its radiation downwards from the imperial centre (Apter and Rotberg 1994:7-12; and Young 1994b:147-54). This distinction has some purchase on explanations of *certain* variations in colonial political styles. However, in so far as political relations between colonial states and their subject populations are concerned, the distinction announces differences of nuance rather than the substance of colonial governance. A governing principle in the fashioning of structures of political intermediation was the denial of space for African participation at higher institutional levels of the colonial state; in a word, the policing of the political marginalization of their minuscule indigenous urban-based europhone elites. Formed in the image of Europe's middle and professional classes, via education in European institutions or their local approximations, these elites were a vexing reminder of the vulgarities of the "mystique of whiteness" (Fyfe 1992:16), that served as the masterly trope for the legitimation of colonial domination.

In the racialized imagination of colonialism, the "tribe" was the primordial unit of African social and political organization. It doubled as the emblem of a universal African backwardness and as a vestibule of traditions which defined and differentiated African societies from one another. The "tribe" emerged as the key to reordering the social and political cartography of colonized society and the design of structures of intermediation of a state form that Mamdani (1996:36-61) aptly labels as "decentralized despotism". Along with other recent reevaluations of colonial state formation and political practices, Mamdani maintains that this "decentralized despotism" was premised the territorial and institutional segregation of colonial state and society. Africans were defined as rural peoples, who were best governed according to customary law and traditions, and to brought into civilization as communities rather than individuals. Europeans and "detribalized" (urban) Africans were to be subject to (European) criminal and civil law. Through this double segregation, the colonial state assumed its cardinal role in shaping ethnic boundaries and the reinforcement of ethnic pluralism. Since tribes were supposed to be lodged within demarcated spaces, reliance on them as discrete units for the political management of native populations would encourage the territorialization of once fluid and mobile cultural identities (Eyoh 1995:43-44; Young 1994b:114-117, 147-54). While the manner of localization of colonial states was conditioned by the particularities of political forms encountered, everywhere hierarchies of chieftaincy were the linchpin of structures of political intermediation. Due to the intermingling of groups that owed to the preponderance of itinerant agriculture as a mode of economic organization and oral traditions which allowed for enormous flexibility in cultural representations, cultural and political boundaries in pre-colonial societies were often non-coterminous (Kopytoff 1989). The delineation of "tribal" boundaries and reorganization of political power in local and regional spaces was informed by administrative convenience and entailed a high degree of arbitrariness. The result was the imposition of collective identities and political boundaries of peoples who previously may never have considered themselves as belonging to such cultural and political entities. An example will suffice to illustrate the consequences of this essential point.

At the beginning of the colonial interregnum, the Lafia region in what is today Plateau State in Nigeria contained over thirty-five related and unrelated acephalus communities in settlements that overlapped. The region was proclaimed an Emirate in 1903, and the "leader" of the *Kamberi* of Lafia Town, who were among the region's smallest groups, was declared the Emir with the official designation of a "second class" chief. In the self-serving reasoning of colonial authorities, which was applied to other Middle-Belt localities with pockets of muslim populations, the Kamberi were the nucleus of an emirate that had gone into decline. The new political arrangements represented a return of the region to its past political history. For the rest of the region, the demarcation of ethnic boundaries and hierarchies of chiefs was based on contested narratives of the sequence of group settlement of the region as well as official catalogues of the social, cultural, political and linguistic characteristics of groups. Groups in which these characteristics were pronounced were taken to be the nucleus of contiguous communities, and together with those who were deemed to be "original settlers" of particular localities, were designated as repositories of state-sanctioned political authority and placed under the supervision of Kamberi Emir of Lafia. The large-scale and politically centralized societies, such as the Emirates of Northern Nigeria, contained majority and minority communities. Here, the institutionalization of hierarchies of chieftaincy meant bringing the Hausa-Fulani ruling oligarchies of these theocracies under colonial supervision, while intensifying their domination over non-Muslim minority communities. In either case, the reconfiguration of local power served as a mechanism for the differential incorporation of groups into the colonial state, and authoring, through juridically-backed gradations of local citizenship (that is, between "original settlers" and "strangers" or ruling and subordinate lineages), of ethnic hierarchies within local society (Eyoh [forthcoming]).

It is still common, in certain quarters, to explain the growth of ethnic pluralism as the result of African acquiesence to the divide-and-rule tactics of colonialism. But the thrust of current scholarship, whether of constructionist and instrumentalist persuasion, sustains the view that the valorization of ethnic identity and consciousness during colonialism is better understood as the outcome individual and collective cultural adaptations in face of new political-economic orders. The significance of African agency to the growth of ethnic pluralism is evidenced by the nature of African adjustments to and uses of the local state. For example, while colonial officials were the final arbiters of politically-relevant aspects of customary law and tradition, local structures of political intermediation afforded latitude for all manner of Africans to engage (re)inventions and manipulations of cultural identities for economic and political reasons. With expanding commercialization of agriculture, chiefly power bore important economic advantages in the form of official stipends, income schemed from tax revenues as well as greater control over labour and communal land. Chiefs became vested with interests in expanding the demographic bases of cultural groups that were the reference points of their political power. With the restriction of African political participation to local arenas, members of emergent translocal elite of school teachers, preachers, clerks etc. with political ambitions could best pursue these by becoming spokespersons for ethnic communities. For "commoners", "tribal" political boundaries provided platforms for reconfiguring conceptions of local citizenship, around the "indigens" and "strangers" distinctions. These distinctions were used to assert differential rights to agricultural resources and political representation. Lastly, in the profoundly patriarchal colonial state, the exercise of political power and the interpretation of customary law and tradition was the prerogative of European and African men, albeit unequally positioned. Through control of native administrations, customary courts, and traditional institutions of power, African men acquired new means to enhance their control over female labour and the commercialization of female sexuality that attended the monetization of bridewealth (Lovett 1990; Mamdani 1996:52-61; Ranger 1983).

The territorialization of ethnic identity and consciousness was not confined to rural society. For one, the classification and entombment of subjects (through tax, school and health records, birth and death certificates, identification papers, business licences etc) in the institutional memory of colonialism according to alleged ethnic identity assured that Africans within and outside rural society could not escape bearing invented or reconstituted identities, even if they mobilized them in ways unintended by managers of colonialism. Economic, social and cultural convulsions of colonialism drove the elaboration of translocal ethnicities, and gave form to the complex horizontal linkages by which they were bound to the vertical solidarities of localized kin-based communities. Of especial significance were the spread of vernacular education, migration, urbanization, spatial variations in the patterns and intensity of commodification in rural societies, and labour market segmentation.

Vernacular education was largely underwritten by Christian missionaries as an instrument for evangelization. In some instances, for example, Nigeria, the colonial state helped finance the formal teaching of indigenous languages (Okedara 1992). The transformation of oral linguistic forms into written (print) languages was inherently discriminatory as only a minority of languages benefitted from this process. The process depended on an evolutionist model of the origins of and changes in linguistic forms, wherein language was posited as the dictionary of a peoples culture and rationality. As conveyed in the interesting account of the emergence of *Gwanda* as "national" language in southeast Africa by Harris (1988), in the case of polyglot communities, the strategy involved the mapping of the spatial boundaries of languages and the construction of hierarchical schemes of languages for within these boundaries. What were assumed to be original languages, through tracing backwards the historical roots of families within language schemes, emerged as print languages which were standardized, through the production of grammars and dictionaries. Besides use for evangelization and political administration, the shift from orality to written languages gave rise to (print) vernacular literatures and ethnic histories. The production of ethnic histories commonly involved the rendering into linear form, based on legends and myths of supposedly original settlers or language speakers, of once contested narratives and histories of intergroup relations in culturally heterogenous communities. This new languages became the medium of communication for the *interlocuteurs valables* of colonialism—translocal elites of school teachers, preachers, clerks, local interpreters, etc.—who relied on ethnohistories and the vernacular press to propagate consciousness of territorially-bound ethnic identity. Indeed, as Berman (1991:201-202) notes, in his analysis of the contributions of the vernacular press to the growth of Gikuyu ethnic consciousness and anticolonial nationalism in Kenya, many of the classics of African nationalist histories produced before the second world war were in fact ethnic charters. They drew heavily from "colonial ethnographic libraries" (Mudimbe 1988:2) of fabricated histories and cultural inventories.

The importance of migration and urbanization (processes that involve redefinitions of social and spatial relations) as vectors of cultural and identity changes are well documented. The colonial city was a city of rural migrants—places in which people had to assume new roles and construct new patterns of social interactions. To cope with life in polyglot cities, migrants, who tended to gravitate towards neighbourhoods with people from their region of origin, created elaborate ethnic networks (cultural clubs, providence societies, etc.) for solidarity. In the city, as well as through interactions in large-scale production sites, peoples drawn from different localities and for whom kinship ties may have been primary in rural society, acquired new (pan-ethnic) identities that they, in turn, transported back to the "ancestral" homes. The official hand was directly complicit in the construction of ethnicity in especially large-scale work places. Along with the overarching racial division of labour (white managers and African labourers), the recruitment of labour, the organization of work parties, housing arrangements and the pursuit of leisure in mining-dependent economies was informed by attention to ethnic differences. The same applied to large-scale agricultural estates. For example, the recruitment of labour for the plantation economy of colonial Southern Cameroons, initially from Nigeria and latter from the more densely populated northern grassfields, served as an engine for the growth of more polyglot communities (Konings 1994:65-70). The disproportional manning of colonial armies with recruits from groups that were designated as "martial races" stands out as one of the clearest instances of how officially-sponsored labour market segmentation encouraged ethnic differentiation and stereotypes (Kirk-Greene 1980:392-414).

While varying from colony to colony, many of the key factors that underwrote new patterns of socioeconomic differentiation encouraged the overlap of these patterns with ethnic divisions. The more dynamic regions of commodity production such as the cocoa-producing areas in southern Ghana (Hill 1963), western Nigeria (Galletti et al. 1956) and Ivory Coast (Amin 1967) were magnets for labour from region's which functioned as labor reserves for colonial economies. The greater availability and use of incomes from agricultural production to finance the education of offspring gave a decisive advantage to members of communities in more dynamic agricultural zones in the struggles to join the circles of emergent middle and professional classes. In the case of western Africa, these conditions of class differentiation compounded the extant advantages of coastal communities with much longer histories of contact with the West and access to western education. In many cases, colonial state policies reinforced the imbalance of opportunities. For fear of undermining the cultural foundations of the power of indigenous ruling oligarchies, colonial states constrained missionary activity and thus the availability of educational establishments in predominantly Muslim regions (Tibenderana 1983). The result was the underrepresentation of members of these communities within the ranks of the social groups destined to inherit colonial states.

The preceding exegesis of the colonial origins of contemporary ethnicity should be sufficient to sustain a number of points that are important to challenging the conceptual and substantive premises of the denigration of ethic politics in the postcolonial era. First, the production and reproduction of local and translocal ethnicities were not separate but conjoined processes. Second, the concatenated forces and interests implicated in the multiple dramas of cultural inventions and (re) appropriations by agents at all levels of colonial society ensured the deep fragmentation of colonial political landscapes. Third, as a result of this fragmentation, African political interests under colonialism were, for the most part, oriented towards the local level and hued by cultural differences. Fourth, consciousness of citizenship in ethnic communities preceded the emergence of national consciousness, which was class-based and driven by the westernized elites who lay claim to colonial states. The salience of ethnicity in postcolonial politics is ultimately modulated by the complex manners in which these two inherited modes of consciousness have interpenetrated and the tensions played out in different spaces since the moment of decolonization.

IMAGINING NATIONS: IDENTITY, CULTURAL DIFFERENCE AND NATIONAL DISCOURSE

The debate about the origins of modern nationalism and the specificity of nationalism in the postimperial nation-states of this century, continues. While it is commonly agreed that modern citizenship is coterminous with the modern state (see Waters 1989:159-61), some, like Smith (1995:38-39) argue for a distinction between nation and state-building processes. In this view, although states can and do promote nation-building processes, either through the incorporation or resistance of communities, state-construction is about the elaboration of technologies of governance. Nation-construction, on the other hand, involves the "forging of a national culture and identity amongst often culturally heterogenous peoples" (38). Although nationalist discourses aspire to homogenous and linear ethnic pasts, the stock of symbols, cultural traditions, historical memories etc. with which national mythologies and public ideological cultures are sculpted are commonly supplied by the dominant *ethnie* within multiethnic nations. This distinction is certainly useful to understanding sequential variations in nation-construction in the modern world. However, it remains the case, as Smith (1983) elaborated previously that nation and state-building have been inseparable processes in the postimperial states of African and Asia for the simple reason that the elites who inherited colonial states have been the lead agents of nation-building projects.

Native intelligentsias, whose privileged position in colonized society and claims on colonial states were predicated on mastery of the western knowledge order, were the main articulators of anticolonial nationalist discourses and leaders of nationalist movements. For native intelligentsias, nationalism, as Anderson (1991:114-116) elegantly argues, represented a pilgrimage—an expansion of consciousness beyond the confines of small kin-based communities in which they may have began their lives towards a larger universe of national communities framed by the territorial boundaries of colonial states. Their imaginings of prospective communities were predicated on imported and internalized European ideas of "nation", "nationness" and "nationality". While Anderson's perspective has justifiably gained widespread admiration as to constitute a point of departure for contemporary discussions of nationalism and nation-invention, it is not without critics. Even as they concede the power of his insights, critics like Chatterjee (1994:5-6; also 1986:19-22) argue that, intentional or not, Anderson tends to reduce African and Asian nationalisms to mere imitations of a (modular) European nationalism. This is due in part to a seeming presumption of an unrestrained enchantment with (western) modernity by native intelligentsias. According to Chatterjee, the unique creativity of African and Asian variants of nationalism was the concession by the colonized of Europe's economic and technological superiority, but the defense of their "cultural sovereignty", that is, a determination to preserve cultural identities that marked their "difference" from Europe. Their ambition was to "fashion a "modern" national community that (was) nonetheless not western" (1994:5).[3] The admonition that the cultural dimensions of anticolonial nationalisms warrant more that cursory attention is pertinent to locating the genesis of intellectual and official hostility towards the political assertion of ethnicity in postcolonial Africa.

The racial denigration of Africans formed the core of colonialist ideology. Not surprisingly, native intelligentsias could not countenance an uncritical embrace of western modernity; to do so would be tantamount to conceding colonialist negative representations of African "otherness". Nationalist claims to the right to self-determination therefore combined a critique of colonial economic exploitation and political subjugation with an insistence on the cultural specificity of Africans. In the language of cultural nationalism, articulated through ideologies of negritude, pan-Africanism, and african personality, race functioned as the key marker of African cultural identity defined in opposition to Europe's cultural identity (see Appiah 1992:1-46; Irele 1990; 1992). The presumption of a coincidence of racial divisions and the stock of attributes that fixed a peoples cultural identity articulated the nationalist dream of prospective nations as communities that would be shaped by the best aspects of Europe's technologies of economic and political organization but whose framework would be a revitalized African cultural heritage. This "syncretic model of development" betrayed the salience of developmentalism (Pieterse 1991)—the presumption of the eminence and desirability of social change in accordance with the western experience—and the assumption of the centrality of state power and westernized elites as agencies of development in nationalist discourse.

But the use of race to situate the *differentia specifica* of Africanness, which is understandable given the racial violence of slavery and colonialism, promoted the falsehood of the cultural homogeneity of African societies. It also masked a profoundly ambivalent and critical attitude towards indigenous cultural traditions. For, as Mudimbe (1994:133) argues, the colonial "economy of cultural conversion—education, christianization, new material cultures, and state disciplinary practices—that produced native intelligentsias amounted to a massive "assault on and trivialization of indigenous cultures" (Mudimbe 1988, cited in Doornbos 1991:63). The implications of the ambivalent stance towards indigenous cultures with regards to the role of ethnic differences in postcolonial politics will be revealed as nationalist discourses that negotiated the shift from ideological criticisms and struggles against colonialism to concrete design of and definition of relations between nations and states. For it meant that westernized elites were given to a ready willingness and arrogated to themselves the right to distinguish between negative and positive features of traditional cultures, based on judgements of whether they impeded or facilitated modernization. Conversely, they denied to the "bearers" of tradition right to make similar distinctions about (western) modernity. In this way, ethnicity emerged as paradox in nationalist conceptualizations of the cultural foundations of their imagined communities. On the one hand, ethnicity would remain a taken-for-granted identity and social relation that underscored the cultural diversity of their prospective nations. On the other hand, the internalization of the European nation-state as the epitome of political modernity and colonialist representation of "tribes" as emblematic of political backwardness predisposed nationalists to hostility towards the mobilization of ethnic identity in political competition.

ETHNICITY AND THE POLITICS OF DECOLONIZATION
Current analysis and debate on politics in Africa pivots on the causes and conditions of the transcendence of the multiple crisis of states and societies. The starting postulate of much of this analysis is the indictment of postcolonial ruling elites as primary culprits of the crises. While the protocols of this indictment vary, its ordering premise is that ruling elites' attachment to what has been labelled the ideology of "nation-statism" (Davidson 1992)—assumption of the centrality of states and their managers as agency of nation-building and the resultant authoritarian rule—is the root of the crises. With this mode of organization of state power, ethnicity, which was denigrated in nationalist discourse, emerged as dominant idiom of political mobilization in the postcolonial era. Although ethnicities reflect the genuine cultural diversity of African societies, ethnic political competition and conflict in the postcolonial era has little to do with defense of cultural autonomy of groups confronted by the homogenizing impulses of state incorporation and economic modernization (Scarritt 1993:261-62). Ethnic politics has and remains, in the evocative characterization of Bayart (1993:51) the postcolonial era's "shadow theatre of accumulation"—the perverse manipulation of indigenous culture by self-serving elites in the form of clientelistic and 'tribalistic' politics.

I have elsewhere queried the foundations of the popular consensus of the roots of the crisis of legitimacy (Eyoh 1996). What is of immediate relevance is that sensibilities behind this consensus are particularly convivial to continued stigmatization of politicized ethnicity. The consensus represents the cresting of intellectual sentiment from the heady optimism of the early years that independence from colonialism marked the beginnings of Africa's political renaissance to increasing pessimism over the nation-building strategies of postcolonial elites. In liberal, and in clearer degrees, radical intellectual opinion, the consensus tends to conflate liberation from colonialism with revolution. The conflation is predicated on the view that nationalist struggles turned on two conflicts—a "social" and "political" to borrow the categories of Davidson (1992: chapter 6). The former represented the desires of the popular masses who were drawn to nationalist struggles on the belief that the termination of colonial rule signaled an expansion of material opportunities, social equality and democracy. The latter mirrored the ambitions of modern elites whose main interest was the conquest of state power. The success of nationalist movements owed to the abilities of their leaders to mobilize rural society in struggle against colonialism. Ethnic-based institutions of urban and rural civil society (cultural clubs, providence societies, agricultural cooperatives, etc.), that were under the tutelage by petit-bourgeoisies, were the main institutional vehicles for the mobilization of rural populations and the institutional muscles of nationalist movements. According to this perspective, then, ethnicity was a positive force in struggles against colonialism and for democracy (cf. Ake 1993; Nyong'o 1995 ; Nnoli 1995:7-8; and Davidson 1992:chapter 6:).

As is typical of populist movements, nationalist movements were alliances of groups with diverse interests that were temporarily bound together by a common objective. The unexceptional claim that anticolonial struggles were structured by a disjunct set of desires succeeds in highlighting the contradictory interests involved in these struggles. At the same time, the supposition that the decolonization moment marked the apogee of ethnicity as a weapon of emancipatory politics manages to obscure appreciation of how the salience of ethnicity in postcolonial politics was mandated by the nature of the colonial political inheritance, while allowing for easy condemnation of ruling elites as prime agents of its politicization. In contrast to this reasoning, it is more productive to regard the salience of ethnicity in postcolonial politics as manifestation of the "fatal dialectic" (Young 1994b:239) of the double fragmentation of societies inherited from colonialism. First, the fragmentation of colonial political landscapes, due to the territorialization of ethnic identity. For societies that were and remain predominantly rural, this assured that political constituencies would, for the most part, be coterminous with ethnic boundaries. Second, the multiple dislocations that impressed a cultural gulf between those who would inherit colonial states and the mass of populations over whom they were destined to rule. Given this cultural gulf, Europhone elites could not escape reliance on cultural relations and symbolic repertoires that were "ethnic" to build political followings. For the mass of their non-Europhone compatriots, bonds of kinship and community had to be of premium in mediating their everyday encounters with the state and for participation in public life. [4]

The manners in which this double fragmentation would engrave the salience of ethnicity in postcolonial politics was rehearsed in the politics of decolonization. Much has been made of the inconsequentiality of the lofty ideals of nation-invention propagated by native intelligentsias to the mass campaigns against colonialism. For the popular masses, independence beckoned higher commodity prices, the death of racial barriers to business aspirations, expansion of opportunities for education, improved healthcare, more and better roads, electricity etc. These common grievances—the ingredients of the "social conflict"—attested to a universal enchantment with the material dimensions of (western) modernity, of not the political vestments. More importantly, the package of material expectations of independence comprised "goods" whose possession stood to improve the standing of whole communities, and no doubt, of the politicians who facilitated their acquisition. In effect, because of the overlap of political constituencies and communal boundaries, the reliance on ethnic networks and political brokers for nationalist mobilization ensured that ethnic affiliation was being inscribed as leading element in claims of the ability for effective representation of communities within the emerging political dispensations.

Colonial regimes everywhere hurriedly assembled liberal constitutions and mandated multiparty electoral competition as the condition for determining the transfer of power. The message of nationalists was nowhere met by a universal enthusiasm. In many cases, for example, Ghana and Nigeria, chiefs and other traditional elites, suspicious of an impending diminution of their powers and privileges as intermediaries of colonial rule, were lukewarm to or actively opposed nationalists. In a variation to this theme, alliances of traditional rulers and the new professional middle classes in the northern regions of both colonies, fearful of the consequences of their underrepresentation within modern class systems, sought delays in timing of independence (see Austin 1964; Crook 1988; Sklar 1963). Furthermore, nationalist mobilization in the post World War 2 period was the responsibility of multiple organizations. While these organizations deferred in ideology and range of territorial appeal, they derived their core support from particular ethnoregional communities. For example, the National Congress of Nigeria and Cameroons was identified with by the Ibos of the eastern region, the Action Party with the Yorubas of western region, and Northern Peoples Congress with Hausa-Fulani groups of the northern region. In Cameroon, the bulk of support for the radical UPC was supplied by Bamilike and southern Bassa groups, while the Ahidjo-led UC that emerged victorious was an officially-sponsored alliance of the elites of northern and southern groups (Joseph 1977). Befitting their superior numerical standing among Kenya's ethnoregional communities as well as the new professional middle classes, the leading nationalist party the Kenyatta-led KANU, was dominated by the Gikuyus while KADU drew the bulk of its support from Luo and other minority groups (Gretzel 1970 and Nyong'o 1988). In general, as decolonization processes drew to a close and "nationalist movements...had to become electoral machines" (Young 1994b:240), electoral success was contingent on the building of alliances between ethnoregional parties. The various compromises needed to placate traditional elites and groups that wanted independence timetables prolonged as well as to cement electoral alliances ensured the differential incorporation of ethnoregional groups within the emergent structures of state power. Moreover, these factors guaranteed that the first post-independence regimes were multiethnic coalitions of elites— a pattern which will endure as the defining characteristic of postcolonial regimes. These coalitions were destined to be fragile, in part because they reflected and sustained hierarchies of representation of ethnoregional communities (Chabal 1992:136-42; Rothchild and Foley 1988).

ETHNICITY AND THE POSTCOLONIAL POLITICAL TRAJECTORY
The broad contours of the postcolonial political trajectory and modalities of the construction of ruling class hegemony have been well-rehearsed to permit a focus on the aspects deemed most relevant to this discussion. The circumstances of the ascent of ruling elites to state power exposed the fragility of early postcolonial regimes. Political elites who perceived themselves as disadvantaged in the distribution of power appealed to a sense of communal injustice to challenge the legitimacy of extant regimes. Conversely, those favoured in the distribution of power emphasized the collective benefits to their communities as evidence of the wisdom of their political support. In response to these centrifugal forces, new regimes, in rapid succession, jettisoned the liberal constitutions bequeathed them, and embarked on the consolidation and centralization of political power around the state. The single-party, fused with the state, became the norm as opposition groups were coopted into the ruling party or repressed into oblivion, and the autonomous organizations of civil society (labour unions, women's organizations, youth organizations etc.) absorbed as auxiliaries of the state party. With the increasing frequency of military seizures of power by the mid-1960s, states like Nigeria, Burkina Faso, Mali, and Ghana, began the pattern of oscillating between no-party rule and brief interludes of civilian rule.

The descent into, or more appropriately the return to, authoritarian rule represented an actualization of presumptions of nationalist discourses of the primacy of states and westernized elites in nation-state building and development. It nonetheless called for a re-scripting of ideologies of nation-invention, through a resort to what Ake (1985) described as "defensive radicalism". The newly-minted ruling elites posited development as a priority, and liberal democracy as a hindrance to its rapid realization. Under different rubrics (African socialism for Tanzania's Nyerere and many more; planned liberalism for Cameroon's Ahidjo, authenticity for Zaire's Mobutu, Humanism for Zambia's Kaunda etc.) they propounded ideologies that denied the existence of cleavages in African societies, or when they admitted them, explained them as perversions of colonialism.[5] Political organization in pre-colonial Africa was based on consensus, and superior to liberal democracy which functioned on conflicts of interests between social groups. As if intended to affect sardonic irony, one-party rule, the institutional pillar of authoritarian rule, was presented as a recovery of Africa's political history in search for new utopias. By the close of the 1960s, the centralization of power was furthered by the elaboration of state control of economies. Self-styled socialist regimes such as Tanzania's embarked on radical programmes of nationalization of foreign and locally-owned enterprises in their bid to frustrate the development of indigenous capitalist classes. Indigenization of economies—the encouragement of local capital through state-mediated alliances between it and foreign capital—became the preferred policy of states like Ivory Coast, Nigeria, Cameroon and Kenya that were committed to capitalist development (see Adedeji 1981).

In downplaying or denying the existence of social and cultural differences as an excuse for the monopolization of political power by state managers, the reconstituted ideologies of nation-invention buttressed official hostility to the use of ethnicity in formal political organization. But authoritarian rule did debase the value of ethnicity as political currency; it simply made state institutions the main arenas of its expression. With the growth of economic etatism, access to state-controlled resources became the primary vehicle for socioeconomic mobility and accumulation, be it in the form of state employment, the procurement of public contracts and other forms of support for private sector accumulation. This made it mandatory for political barons, aspiring politicians and others seeking access to state resources to position themselves as leaders of ethnoregional constituencies, or at least to convey the impression that they commanded the loyalties of such constituencies.

This representation of the forces of the construction of the economic and political foundations of postcolonial state power augurs well with the view that the politicization of ethnicity is primarily orchestrated by intra and inter-elite competition for control of and access to state resources. As previously maintained, this is a partial perspective, as it tends to grossly undervalue the contributions of subordinate social groups in maintaining the salience of ethnic identity as idiom of political mobilization and competition. Bayart (1993) and Chabal (1992), in closely related analysis of the African postcolonial political trajectory, offer suggestive conceptual means for moving towards a better appreciation of how the valorization of ethnic political consciousness is the joint undertaking of social agent across spatial locations and within different positions of political-economic hierarchies.[6]

Of particular importance is their emphasis on the hybrid character of postcolonial political systems - that is, systems that are shaped and continually reshaped by the interaction of attributes of modern-state and indigenous forms of political organization and representation. In Chabal's terms, postcolonial states combine two competing systems of power, conceptions of political community and logics of political representation—a *pays legal* (the constitutional order of new states) and *pays reel* (realities of postcolonial societies) (1992:138). Nationalist discourse and postcolonial elites took for granted the concept of nation as a republican political community of individual citizens-subjects with rights and obligations to the state that was imposed on African societies by colonialism. This conception of political community assumes that the "meaning of representation is the representation of specific, objectively defined, and universal interests (146). Through formal constitutional arrangements (elections, political parties, etc.), the purpose of political representation is, respectively for liberals and marxists, to "give voice" to the interests of individual citizens or members of particular social classes (149). The premises and institutional arrangements of the formal system of representation of the modern nation-state contrasts with the pre-existing, albeit modified, "traditional" conceptions of political community and the meaning of political representation. In the traditional constructions, kinship ties and shared cultural attributes define the boundaries of political community, and the measure of effectiveness of political representation is the ability of political leaders to promote the interests of communities so demarcated rather than ideologies and policies that articulate universal interests. Postcolonial political machines, or what Bayart (1993:chapter 8) defines as "rhizomic" systems of power that are based on dense networks of patronage that cut across class and kinship boundaries, have allowed for the fusion of both constructs of political community and their logics of representation. In other words, trapped in culturally-heterogeneous nation-states and hierarchical relations of power, subordinate social categories are as adept as ruling elites in the manipulation of tropes of kinship to negotiate the conditions of political representation and participation within the wider political system. In this way, they partake in the valorization of ethnic political consciousness at all levels of society, even if they are ultimately the losers in the flow of resources through patronage networks and elite-driven ethic political rivalries.

This admittedly oversimplified summary of what are highly textured arguments accents the pursuit of material interests as the prime determinant of the use of ethnicity in the fashioning of political networks and patterns for political competition.[7] However, the emphasis on the syncretic nature of postcolonial political orders allows for the appreciation of the relative autonomy of ethnic identity and consciousness as part of the ensemble of cultural relations and symbolic codes which shape individual and collective political practices. To concede the relative autonomy of ethnic attachment need not imply subscription to primordialist explanations that regard ethnicity as a given, immutable social relation. It is simply to reiterate that ethnic identity and consciousness, however constructed and malleable, are rooted in the shared cultural experiences of groups. The memories through which these experiences are transmitted as well as contested serve as templates for the articulation and policing of notions of moral obligation of members to their communities. As Chatterjee (1994:232) reminds us, "human beings do not exist as "individuals" before they are born, and when they are born, they are already ascribed as particular members of society." Ascriptive identities are not conflict-free for their bearers; for this reason, individuals may choose to discard such identities or discount their significance as a basis of social and political action. Such choices, for the most part, register discomfort with cultural-embedded notions of moral obligations of community membership. But most people cannot shed easily their ethnic or other ascribed identities. Given current social, economic, political and cultural realities, few Africans can enjoy the "luxury" of non-conflicted escapes from the moral obligations of ethnic attachments that they regard basic to the constitution of selfhood and community belonging. The "post-modernist mirage of a free-market place of identities" (Cheryl Hendricks, personal communication) wherein individuals are able to choose and mix identities willy-nilly is not much of an option for Africans.

To appreciate how the moral solidarities of kinship underscore the relative autonomy of ethnic attachment as a force of politics calls for understanding of the complicated manners in which "ideologies of home"—the ways in which people conceptualize the connections between space, place, and community—are deployed in response to the pressures of modernization. In the context of state incorporation and commodification, ideologies of home regulate the manners in which idioms of kinship and community are revamped and mobilized in in struggles to make concrete what people imagine as development in the changing and unpredictable worlds in which they live. Their contributions to the valorization of ethnic political consciousness are as real as they are nuanced. These contributions cannot be adequately accounted for by instrumentalist explanations that tend to reduce the dynamics of ethnic politics to elite-driven competition for political power and public resources, and do so because they turn on ideologized distinctions between forms and levels of expressions of ethnic identity and consciousness.[8]

At an elementary level, state incorporative processes in the postcolonial era have succeeded in implanting the idea of national identity in Africa societies, even if its meaning and value are regularly contested by individuals and communities (Miles and Rochefort 1991:393-403). Yet the Europe-derived organizational technologies, ideologies and languages of postcolonial state power in and of themselves place a premium on ethnic attachment in everyday encounters with the state system. Even when their fabled inefficiency and corruption is discounted, for the mass of citizens who are not literate in or are with a poor command of official languages, routine activities involving state bureaucracies—processing of identification papers, transactions with state treasuries, contact with the police or judiciary, etc.—require the assistance of intermediaries. This need for intermediaries makes recourse to real or invented kinship ties indispensable for their dealings with state apparatuses. Regular requests for such assistance may be a source of irritation for those called upon to act as intermediaries as they often entail unplanned financial outlays; but a sense of moral obligation to members of one's community elicit, if not acquiescence to such requests, their denial with face-saving gestures.

The apartheid regime of South Africa's homeland policy, which denied blacks citizenship rights in urban spaces by insisting that they belonged to territorially-demarcated tribal enclaves, attests to the demonic excesses of a state whose reproduction, like that of colonial states, depended on the institutionalization of racial privilege and manipulation of ethnic divisions. Yet for Africans, like other peoples, the concept of "home" is fragmented and complicated. It signifies more than one's house and locality of current residence. In everyday language, and even when in reality persons are born and have spent most of their lives outside such localities, home also normally designates an ancestral locality—a village or town that is named as one's natal community. Home in this sense is an "ethnic space", a culturally-demarcated fragment of the nation-space. Although individuals differ in degrees of emotional commitment to this construct of home, the extent to which it is expressive of the relative autonomy of ethnic attachment is easily appreciated. It is most common, for example, to find members of urban-based middle and professional classes who invest in opulent residences in their ancestral homes while living in rented accommodation in the location of their work and to return "home" after retirement. Most telling is perhaps the moment of death, as the normal expectation is that a person's ancestral home will be the final destination in life.

What Bayart (1993:chapter 7) has labelled as the process of the "reciprocal assimilation of elites" and has convincingly demonstrated to be a key pillar of postcolonial hegemonic orders is illustrative of the manners in which ideologies of home mediate the use of ethnic cultural relations and symbolic repertoires by individuals and communities to satisfy needs of a material and non-material nature. Educational credentials have been and remain the primary avenue into the circles of ruling elites. But the expansion of the ranks of modern elites has devalued educational credentials and professional accomplishment as markers of social status. The craze with the acquisition of traditional titles by modern elites in western African societies and elsewhere indicates that, rather than diminishing their utility, modernization increases modern elites need for traditional symbols of status differentiation, even as their meanings are transformed (see Vaughan 1992; Fisiy 1994). For elites, the acquisition of traditional titles, often their outright purchase, is part of the quest for recognition of their social standing. For some, these titles satisfy a personal need for public grandeur. For others, they represent social capital that can be expended in the pursuit of objectives within and beyond the domain of their titles, for example, access to land for commercial farming and mobilization of political support. The grant of traditional titles to modern elites is hardly a benign exercise of recognition of individual accomplishment; it is a mechanism of ensuring that modern elites live-up to their moral obligations to advance the development of their communities.

The ubiquitous "home town" associations are another example of the efficacy of ideologies of homes in ordering communal responses to modernization. These associations bind together individuals from across socioeconomic stations and in spaces far away from their ancestral communities. They serve as powerful vehicles for the mobilization of resources, through levies on their members or prying of access to state resources, in order to promote the "development" of their home villages or towns (Barkan 1994; Thomas-Slayter 1991; Woods 1994). To elites, who are their patrons and whose financial and other contributions are judged in accordance to their social rank, they offer platforms for accumulating social capital that can be expended in the pursuit of political objectives. Along with the commodification of traditional titles, "home town" associations allow for some downward redistribution of wealth. However, their ubiquity and vitality derives from the application of moral pressures on individuals to advance the collective interests (development) of their ethnic spaces. Refusal or unwillingness to be involved in these associations and their quests invites the labelling of recalcitrants as community outcasts or persons whose claims to community membership are to be doubted.

In a word, ideologies of home underwrite the moral solidarities of ethnic attachment in the context of societal change. Because they help to reinforce the territorialization of ethnic identities, and thereby the tensions of competing loyalties to sub-national communities and nation-states, they contribute to the generation of all manner of intra- and interethnic conflicts. For example, the commercialization of traditional titles encourages the debasement of institutions of communal solidarity and to factional struggles in local societies. The same is the case with "home town" associations which, by serving as mechanisms for linking local societies to state-centred networks of power, freight elite conflicts for power in external arenas into local spaces. In multiethnic communities, attempts to assert hierarchies of local citizenship, through distinctions between "indigens" and "strangers", provide fodder for communal conflicts. As a strategy for contesting power, political entrepreneurs can and do fasten onto claims of the natural right of communities to be controlled by "sons of the soil."[9] Appeals of this nature understandably invite similar responses from leaders of groups that are threatened by demands for differential rights to political representation. Conflicts over conceptions of local citizenship are perhaps the most salient factor in ethnic tensions in rural society. As ecological stress, demographic pressures, politically induced population displacements and commercialization combine to intensify struggles for control of agricultural resources and power, groups that regard themselves as original settlers are prone to defining citizenship as autochthonous and to deploy this as the moral basis of their arguments for greater control over agricultural resources and political power. Members of communities whose rights are thus challenged typically resort to universalist definitions of citizenship, by placing the emphasis on settlement and ownership of property (see Mustapha [n.d.]).

The gerrymandering of administrative boundaries by regimes interested in buttressing local structures of hegemony often courses on the manipulation of ethnic hierarchies. A good example of this is the recent and growing politicization of cultural differences in Northern Cameroon. It is driven by contests over a system of ethnic stratification that is structured on religious differences between the Muslim-Fulbe groups and numerically preponderant cultural minorities (Schilder 1995). The precolonial Fulbe theocracies (*Lamidates*) incorporated multiplicities of minorities in loose vassal arrangements. These minorities were derogatorily stereotyped as "pagans" (*haabe*)—peoples whose religious beliefs were inferior to Islam and who judged by the standards of Fulbe cultural practices were "uncivilized". The colonial state institutionalized this religious-based ethnic hierarchy as the foundation of the administration of northern communities. In the postcolonial era, Ahidjo and his northern potentates, who invoked the region's population size to justify their dominance of state power, crafted and maintained an illusion of the region as a culturally monolithic entity. Despite some recruitment of members of northern minority groups into the national political establishment and as local intermediaries of the regime, they remained trapped in a subordinate political position. For members of minority communities, upward mobility within the state system of power often meant suppression of their ethnic identities, through conversion to Islam and adoption of muslim-Fulbe cultural codes. In reaction to what it perceived as a challenge to its hegemonic pretensions by Muslim-Fulbe political barons, the successor regime of Biya split the region into three administrative provinces, and turned to a greater reliance on minority politicians as its support base in these provinces. Elites of minority communities with local and national political ambitions have been the main beneficiaries of this exercise in political engineering. Nonetheless, the change has been conducive to the politicization of ethnicity for reasons that go beyond the increase of political opportunities for elites. It has shaped a context in which collective memories of historical injustices and legacies of cultural denigration can be effectively mobilized by minority group politicians to challenge long entrenched inequalities in the distribution of power between cultural groups, and forced Muslim-Fulbe elites to defend, through appeals to communal solidarities, their privileged position in the region. In effect, the Biya regime, continuing in the tradition of colonial and postcolonial regimes, simply rearranged, for its own purposes, historically constructed cultural divisions with their particular geographies and histories of conflict and placed them on a trajectory whose end cannot be easily foretold.

CONCLUSION

Anxiety over the dangers of ethnic political mobilization is not confined to analysis of politics in Africa; in fact, it is currently one of the major preoccupations in comparative and international politics. The globalization of capitalist production, intensification of international cultural flows and population movements that are expanding diaspora communities in the advanced centres of capitalism and elsewhere have encouraged *fin de siecle* images of a "postnational" world—a world in which the nation-state is being deconstructed as the primary territorial referent of civic loyalties of individuals whose allegiances are increasingly to different, and often times, multiple localities. This supposed trend towards the "deterritorialization of identities" is paralleled by a seeming rise in ethnonationalist agitation. The implosion of the authoritarian states of the former communist bloc, rising demands of minorities groups for equitable representation and reactions of "nativist" groups bent on preserving their privileged positions in advanced capitalist societies, and the struggles of sub-national communities to redefine of state-society relations in African and Asian postimperial states are among the forces fanning this phenomenon (Appaduria 1996). The contradictory processes of the current global conjuncture confirm the truism that processes of nation-invention are never complete and are always subject to reversal. For nation-state building projects, whose essential impulse is the standardization of social and spatial relations, like the forces for globalization of economic relations and cultural practices, provoke reassertions of the particularities of identity, space and community.

The effective management of social pluralism has been, and is destined to remain for awhile, the central task of Africa's postcolonial leaders. The focus of this chapter was the interrogation of the intellectual and ideological foundations of the stigmatization of ethnicity as a force of organized politics. This proclivity, in part, mirrors an easily appreciated concern with the fragility of postcolonial states. It is hardly surprising that the crises of economy and political legitimacy in which African societies are enveloped would fuel an increase in ethnic mobilization and sectional conflicts. This phenomenon, whose intensify and political ramifications vary from state to state, is anchored in the histories of differential incorporation of ethnoregional communities into colonial states, and the continuation of this process in the design of postcolonial hegemonic orders. In the current political conjuncture, then, ethnic-based political mobilization is driven by the ambitions of groups to challenge or defend ways in which inequalities in communal representation have been institutionalized as part of the postcolonial structures of power as well as invocations of the moral solidarities of kinship and community in response to the challenges of modernity. It is a valid temptation to pass judgement about the legitimacy or illegitimacy of ethnic-based political movements and conflicts. Whether they are offered by academic observers or their lead agents, such judgements are bound to subjective. For social scientific analysis to have greater relevance to the management of social pluralism in African societies, it is obligatory to shy away from the inclination to overideologize the discussion of ethnic politics by conceding the modernity of ethnic identities and political consciousness. To do so will require taking as a point of departure the fact that at the heart of ethnic politics in Africa's incipient nation-states are yet to be resolved, if ever completely resolvable, conflicts over the meaning of citizenship, the moral basis of state power and categories of rights (communal versus individual) of representation.

NOTES

1. These distinctions are often related to levels of analysis of ethnicity by different disciplines. Commonly, political scientists, concerned with macrosocietal relations and processes, tend to focus on ethnic politics at the institutional level of the state (ethnicity from above), while anthropologists, psychologists, sociologists, etc. concerned with the dynamics of interpersonal relations usually focus on small-scale societies (i.e., ethnicity from below) (see Esman 1995:21-23).

2. Ekeh (1990:673-83) maintains that the origins of ethnicity in Africa reside in the search for security by kin-based groups from slave-raiding states in precolonial times, and reinforced by the need to defend against the predatory practices of colonial states and their successors.

3. This argument is echoed by many who take exception to the currently fashionable exercise in postcolonial studies to denigrate third world nationalist discourses; cf., Ahmad 1995; Lazarus 1995; McClintock 1995; Parry 1995.

4. To insist on this is not to excuse the complicity of ruling elites in the accentuation of ethnic divisions and sectional conflicts. It is simply to note the that appeals to communal and class interests are both legitimate and non-exclusive motivators of political engagement by groups and individuals, and that in culturally heterogeneous societies popular evaluations of the relation of the distribution of power and the material and symbolic gains of political competition are commonly based on perceptions of relative advantage or disadvantage in both class and communal terms.

5. As Jewsiewicki and Mudimbe (1993) suggest, official ideologies of nation-building shared with African nationalist historiography the inclination to project colonialism as a rude, easily forgotten interlude in Africa's history.

6. Despite substantive and theoretical differences, the thrust of Mamdani's analysis of the legacies of colonialism on postcolonial state construction, concurs with this interpretation of the dynamics of ethnic politics (1996:1-26, 285-301); see also Young (1994a, 1994b:chapter 9).

7. The earlier quoted statement of Bayart that ethnicity is the "post-independence shadow theatre of accumulation," which implies ethnic politics is but cover for pursuit of class interests, is at odds with his sophisticated analysis of culture and political practice in Africa.

8. See Ekeh (1975; 1990) for insightful discussions of the contrast in the normative anchors of ethnic groups and the nation-community.

9. The following statement by a politician in town in Cameroon, whose population is predominantly comprised of immigrants, in response to my questions of why he insisted on labelling persons who were born or had grown-up this town as "strangers" and his anxieties about "strangers" control of political power in the town, illustrates the force of the emotions I wish to convey here: "Well, they cannot contribute to the development of our town because it is not their home. You claim it does not matter because they are born here, make their living here and even married our women. If you want to know what their home is, wait till they die, and see where they will be buried. They

will not be buried here. They will be taken back to their real homes, where most of them prefer to pay their taxes. We cannot rely on them to develop this town, because it is not theirs."

REFERENCES

Ahmad, A. "The Politics of Literary Postcoloniality." *Race and Class* 36, 3(1995):1-20.

Ake, C. "What is the Problem with Ethnicity in Africa." *Transformation* 22, 2(1993):2-18

Ake, C. "The African Context of Human Rights." *Africa Today* 3(1987):1-2:

Ake, C. "The Congruence of Ideologies and Political Economies." In *The Political Economy of Contemporary Africa*, eds. Gutkind, and I. Wallerstein. 2nd edition. Beverly Hills and London: Sage Publications, 1985.

Adedeji, A. "Introduction." In *Indigenization of African Economies*, [by] A. Adedeji. London: Hutchinson, 1981.

Alonso, M."The Politics of Space, Time and Substance: State Formation, Nationalism and Ethnicity." *Annual Review of Anthropology* 23(1994):379-405.

Amin, S. *Le Developpement du Capitalism en Cote d'Ivoire*. Paris: Les Editions de Minute, 1967.

Amselle, J-L. "Ethnies et espaces: pour une anthropologie topologique." In *Au Coeur de l'ethnie: Ethnie, Tribalisme, et l'etat en Afrique*, eds. J-L. Amselle and E. M'bokolo. Paris: Editions la Decouverte, 1985.

Anderson, B. *Imagined Communities: Reflections on the Origins of Nationalism.* London: Verso, 1991.

Appadurai, A. "Sovereignty without Territory." In *The Geography of Identity*, ed. P. Yeager. Ann Arbor, Mich.: University of Michigan Press, 1996.

Appiah, A. *In My Father's House: Africa in the Philosophy of Culture.* New York: Oxford University Press, 1992.

Apter, D. and C. Rotberg. "Changing African Perspectives." In *Political Development and the New Realism in Africa*, eds. D. Apter and C. Rotberg. Charlottesville, Virginia: University Press of Virginia, 1994.

Austin, D. *Politics in Ghana.* London: Oxford University Press, 1964.

Barkan, J. "Resurrecting Modernization Theory and the Emergence of Civil Society in Kenya and Nigeria." *Political Development and the New Realism in Africa*, eds. D. Apter and C. Rotberg. Charlottesville, Virginia: University Press of Virginia, 1994.

Bayart, J-F. *The State in Africa: The Politics of the Belly.* London: Longmans, 1993.

Berman, B. "Nationalism, Ethnicity and Modernity: The Paradox of the Mau Mau. " *Canadian Journal of African Studies* 25, 2(1991):181-206.

Bienen, H. "The State and Ethnicity: Integrative Formulas in Africa." In *States versus Ethnic Claims: African Policy Dilemmas*, eds. D. Rothchild and V. Olorunsola. Boulder, Colo.: Westview Press, 1983.

Bratton, M. and N. Van de Walle. "Neo-Patrimonial Regimes and Political Transitions in Africa." *World Politics* 46, 4(1994):453-489.

Chabal, P. *Power in Africa: An Essay in Political Interpretation.* New York: St. Martin's Press, 1992.

Chatterjee, P. *The Nation and its Fragments: Colonial and Postcolonial Histories.* Princeton: Princeton Univ. Press, 1994.

Chatterjee, P. *Nationalist Thought and the Colonial World: A Derivative Discourse?.* Minneapolis: University of Minnesota Press, 1986.

Crook, R. "Decolonization, the Colonial State and Chieftaincy in the Gold Coast." *African Affairs* 85(1988):75-105.

Davidson, B. *The Black Man's Burden: Africa and the Curse of the Nation-State.* New York: Times Books, 1992.

Doornbos, M. "Linking the Future to the Past: Ethnicity and Pluralism." *Review of African Political Economy* 52(1991):53-65.

Ekeh, P. "Social Anthropology and the Two Uses of Tribalism in Africa." *Comparative Studies in Society and History* 32, 4(1990):660-700.

Ekeh, P."Colonialism and the Two Publics: A Theoretical Statement." *Comparative Studies in Society and History* 17, 1(1975):91-117.

Esman, M. *Ethnic Politics.* Ithaca, N.Y.: Cornell Univ. Press, 1994.

Eyoh, D. "Differentiating Communities in Colonial Central Nigeria: Political and Economic Change in Lafia, Plateau State 1900-1940. " *International Journal of African Historical Studies* [forthcoming].

Eyoh, D. "From Economic Crisis to Political Liberalization: Pitfalls of the New Political Sociology for Africa." *African Studies Review* 39, 3(1996):43-80.

Eyoh, D. "From the Belly to the Ballot: Ethnic and Politics in Africa." *Queen's Quarterly* 102, 1(1995):39-51.

Fisiy, C. "Power and the Quest for Political Recognition: Pseudo-Traditional Titles Among the New Elite in Nso, North-West Cameroon." Paper Presented at the 37th Annual Meeting of the African Studies Association 3-6 November, Toronto, Canada, 1994.

Fyfe, C. "Race, Empire and Historians." *Race and Class.* 33, 4(1992):15-30.

Galletti, R. et al. *Nigerian Cocoa Farmers.* London: Oxford Univ. Press, 1956.

Harries, P. "The Roots of Ethnicity: Discourse and the Politics of Language Construction in South East Africa." *African Affairs* 87, 346(1988):25-52.

Hill, P. *Migrant Cocoa Farmers of Southern Ghana.* Cambridge: The University Press, 1963.

Ihonvbere, J. "From Movement to Government: The Movement to Multi-party Democracy and the Crisis of Democratic Consolidation in Zambia." *Canadian Journal of African Studies* 29, (1995)1:1-25.

Irele, A. "In Praise of Alienation." In *Surreptitious Speech: Presence Africaine and the Politics of Otherness,* ed. V. Mudimbe. Chicago: University of Chicago Press, 1992.

Irele, A."Negritude and African Personality." In *The African Experience in Literature and Ideology.* Bloomington: Indiana Univ. Press, 1990.

Jewsiewick, B. and V. Mudimbe. "Africans' Memories and Contemporary History in Africa." *History and Theory* 32, 2(1993):1-11.

Joseph, R. "Africa: The Rebirth of Freedom." *Journal of Democracy* 2, 4(1992):11-24.

Joseph, R. *Radical Nationalism in Cameroon.* Oxford: Clarendon Press, 1977.

Kirk-Greene, A. "Damnisa Hereditas: Ethnic Ranking and the Martial Race Imperative in Africa." *Ethnic and Racial Studies* 34, (1980):392-414.

Koning, P. *Labour Resistance in Cameroon: Managerial Strategies and Labour Resistance in the Agro-Industrial Plantations of the Cameroon Development Corporation.* London: James Curry, 1992.

Kopytoff, I. "The Internal African Frontier: The Making of African Political Culture." In *The African Frontier: The Reproduction of Traditional African Societies*, ed. I. Kopytoff. Bloomington: Indiana Univ. Press, 1987.

Lazarus, N. "National Consciousness and the Specificity of (Post) Colonial Intellectualism." In *Colonial Discourse/Postcolonial Theory*, eds. F. Barker, P. Hulme, and M. Iversen. Manchester: Manchester Univ. Press, 1994.

Levin, M. "Understanding Ethnicity." *Queen's Quarterly* 102, 1(1995):71-84.

Lovett, M. "Gender Relations, Class Formation and the Colonial State." In *Women and the State in Africa*, eds. J. Parpart and K.Staudt. Boulder, Colo.: Westview, 1990.

Mafeji, A. "The Ideology of Tribalism." *Journal of Modern African Studies* 9, 3(1971):253-261.

Mamdani, M. *Citizens and Subjects: Contemporary Africa and the Legacy of Late Colonialism.* Princeton: Princeton Univ. Press, 1996.

McClintock, A. "The Angel of Progress: Pitfalls of the Term 'Postcolonialism'." In *Colonial Discourse/Postcolonial Theory*, eds. F. Barker, P. Hulme, and M. Iversen. Manchester: Manchester Univ. Press, 1995.

Miles, W. and D. Rochefort. "Nationalism versus Ethnic Identity in Sub-Saharan Africa." *American Political Science Review* 85, 2(199):393-403

Mudimbe, V. *The Idea of Africa.* Bloomington: Indiana Univ. Press, 1994.

Mudimbe, V. *The Invention of Africa.* Bloomington: Indiana Univ. Press, 1988.

Mustapha, R. "Ethnicity and Democratization in Nigeria: A Case Study of Zangon Kataf." Research Report for Codesria Network on Expanding Nigerian Democratic Space, Zaria, Nigeria, n.d.

Nnoli, O. "Ethnic Conflicts and Democratization in Africa." Paper Presented at the Eight General Assembly of Codesria, 26 June - 2 July, Dakar, Senegal, 1995.

Nnoli, O. *Ethnicity and Democracy in Africa: Intervening Variables.* Oxford: Malthouse Press, 1995.

Nnoli, O. "Ethnic Conflict in Africa." Working Paper, Dakar, Senegal: Codesria, 1995.

Nyong'o, P. "State and Society in Kenya: The Disintegration of Nationalist Coalitions and the Rise of Presidential Authoritarianism 1963-78." *African Affairs* 85(1988):229-51.

Okedara, J. T. "Mother-Tongue Literacy in Nigeria." *Annals of the American Academy of Political and Social Science* 520, 1(1992):91-102.

Parry, B. "Resistance Theory/Theorising Resistance, or Two Cheers for Nativism." In *Colonial Discourse/Postcolonial Theory*, eds. F. Barker, P. Hulme, and M. Iversen. Manchester: Manchester Univ. Press, 1994.

Pieterse, J. "The Dilemmas of Development Discourse." *Development and Change* 21, 1(1991):5-29.

Randrajarian, S. "Nationalism, Ethnicity and Democracy." In *Africa Now: People, Policies, Institutions*, ed. S. Ellis. London: James Curry/Portsmouth, N.H.: Heineman, 1996.

Ranger, T. "The Invention of Tradition: The Case of Colonial Africa." In *The Invention of Tradition*, eds. E. Hobsbawn and T. Ranger. Cambridge: Cambridge Univ. Press, 1983.

Rothchild, D. and M. Foley. " In *The Precarious Balance: State and Society in Africa*, eds. D. Rothchild and N. Chazan. Boulder, Colo.: Westview Press, 1988.

Saul, J. "The Dialectics of Class and Tribe." *Studies in Political Economy* 1, 1(1979):1-42.

Scarritt, J. "Communal Conflict and Contention for Power in Africa South of the Sahara." In *Minorities at Risk: A Global Survey of Ethnopolitical Conflict*, ed. T. Gurr. Washington, D. C.: US Institute of Peace Press, 1993.

Schilder, K. "Regional Imbalance in Northern Cameroon." Paper Presented at Conference on Regional Imbalance and National Integration in Cameroon: Lessons Learnt and the Future, Yaounde, Cameroon, October 16-18, 1995.

Shaw, T. "Ethnicity as the Resilient Paradigm in Africa: From the 1960s to the 1980s." *Development and Change* 17, 4(1986):587-605.

Sklar, R. *Nigerian Political Parties*. Princeton: Princeton Univ. Press, 1963.

Smith, A. *Nations and Nationalisms in the Modern World*. Cambridge: Polity Press, 1995.

Smith, A. *State and Nation in the Third World: The Western State and African Nationalism*. Sussex: Wheatsheaf Books Ltd., 1995.

Thomas-Slayter, B. "Class, Ethnicity, and the Kenyan State: Community Mobilization in the Context of Global Politics." *International Journal of Politics, Culture and Society* 4, 3(1991):301-321.

Tibenderana, Peter. "The Emirs and the Spread of Western Education in Northern Nigeria 1910-46." *Journal of African History* 24, 4(1983):517-34.

Vail, L. "Introduction." In *The Creation of Tribalism in Southern Africa*, ed. L. Vail. Berkeley: Univ. of California Press, 1989..

Vaughan, O."The Myth of Modernization: Chieftaincy Politics and Social Relations in Nigeria." Paper Presented at the Canadian Association of African Studies Conference, Toronto, Canada, May 1992.

Waters, M. "Citizenship and Constitutional Structural Social Inequality." *International Journal of Comparative Sociology* 30, 3-4(1989):159-80.

Woods, D. "Elites, Ethnicity and 'Home Town' Associations in Cote d'Ivoire: An Historical Analysis of State-Society Links." *Africa* 64, 4(1994):465-83.

Young, C. "Evolving Modes of Consciousness and Ideology: Nationalism and Ethnicity." In *Political Development and the New Realism in Africa.* Charlottesville, Virginia: Univ. Press of Virginia, 1994a.

Young, C. *The African Colonial State in Comparative Perspective.* New Haven: Yale Univ. Press, 1994b.

Young, C. "The Dialectics of Cultural Pluralism." In *The Rising Tide of Cultural Pluralism: The Nation-State at Bay?*, ed. C. Young. Madison, Wis.: Univ. of Wisconsin Press, 1993.

13

SOUTHERN AFRICA'S LAND DILEMMA: BALANCING RESOURCE INEQUITIES

TIYANJANA MALUWA*

INTRODUCTION

A proper understanding of the notion of property is critical to our understanding of the relationship between law, the state, societal organization and governance. The property debate in Southern Africa, as in East and Central Africa, has largely been about land, the most traditional and archetypal form of property. The reason for this is obvious. As many commentators have noted, this is partly because land continues to be the most valuable form of wealth around in more than one sense. Thus, for those who cannot be fully absorbed by other sectors of the economy, land or land-based resources continue to provide the only, or the most assured, means of obtaining or sustaining livelihood; for governments and political rulers, control over land and its diminishing resources also continues to provide the most effective leverage in the governance of people (Ng'ong'ola 1996a; Shipton and Goheen 1992). Put simply, land is the most important form of property. Indeed, in the popular imagination, and sometimes in legal parlance as well, references to "property" and "property rights" are synonymous with "land" and "land rights." In this discussion, these terms will be used interchangeably.

This paper sets out to provide a general overview of the land question in Southern Africa. As such, I do not aim to present detailed analyses of the land issue in all countries of the region. Such a study would require more space and a more empirically-oriented approach, with appropriate case studies. Rather, the objective here is to present a general survey of some of the conceptual and common policy issues and problems that arise in relation to this question. This chapter, therefore, only proposes to offer a summary discussion of some of the common themes and dilemmas that constitute the land problem in the region. The reader longing for more specific detail will be better served by the specific case studies presented in the other chapters below.

Land underpins the economic, social and political lives of the great majority of people in the world. This is especially true of those societies which have a particular dependency on agriculture and natural resources for their social reproduction and survival. As has been observed by some commentators, land is fundamental to the reproduction of capital and in defining spaces within which other markets and distributional processes operate (Nagan 1993; Gutto 1995; Moyo 1995a). It also provides the basis for political and spiritual territories which configure local and national power structures (Moyo 1995a:13). Access to land, then, determines the boundaries of most people's social and political spaces and, in particular, economic empowerment. Property rights, including questions of access and affordability, tenurial regimes and land reform, are thus located within the political economy of space and territoriality. Not surprisingly, the complex array of use and exchange values located within these spaces has tended to breed conflict and competition among various classes, races, nationalities, genders and other social groupings which struggle for control over land.

The colonial experience in Africa, especially, demonstrates the extent to which the unequal ownership of, and control over, property—such as land, capital, and other forms which constitute the major means of production—determined (and continues to determine) social differentiation along class, gender and racial lines. The struggle for self-determination in Africa was intimately related to the struggle to reclaim the land from which the native populations in the colonized polities had been evicted by the European immigrants and the colonial state. The history of the independence movement and liberation struggles in, say, Kenya, Zimbabwe and South Africa clearly demonstrates that the articulation of the land problem was a central motivating factor on the part of the peasantry in their support for these struggles (Ranger 1985; Gutto 1987).

One of the common themes which runs through the history of land tenure and agrarian reforms in the former colonial territories in Southern Africa is the notion of dual land tenure systems and structures. The broadly similar historical experience of these countries brought about broadly similar issues of concern. In particular, the arrival of settler communities and the imposition of colonial rule towards the end of the last century brought about legal dualism in tenurial practices (Ng'ong'ola 1995:2). There was, on the one hand, land appropriated by the colonial settlers, under "received" forms of tenure governed by the "received" colonial law and legal procedures. On the other hand, land occupied by the indigenous populations fell under "customary" tenure or other forms evolved by the colonial authorities. The distribution of land within these two broad categories was of course skewed and inequitable, since the settler community was invariably allocated disproportionate amounts of the most productive land. It was in this context of inequities and inequalities that nationalist leaders were easily able to marshall up widespread support around the "land issue" as the focal point of the anticolonial struggles. But it has also been observed that despite the overarching importance of the grievances against colonial agrarian and land distribution policies in the nationalist struggles, independence was secured on terms requiring severe compromises in post-colonial land policies. The British government, for one, succeeded in imposing legal and constitutional constraints on acquisition and distribution of settler land (Allott 1968:7). It has further been argued that the lure of immediate political independence, and the mistaken belief that these constraints could always be revisited after independence, provided the explanation for the retreat of the nationalist politicians on the land issue (Ng'ong'ola 1992:118). The reality is that the land question has continued to provide a terrain for contestation in post-independence politics in most parts of Africa, including Southern Africa. A lot of space in the literature on land and agrarian reform in Africa has been given to a consideration of this issue (Downs & Reyna 1988; Bekker 1991; Bassett & Crumney 1992). I do not propose to engage in the debate on this particular issue as such. As stated above, my aim is, rather, to re-focus attention on some of the major conceptual and policy dilemmas that have not often been highlighted in the somewhat fragmented discussions on the problem.

In considering the land policies of Southern African countries, one overriding consideration should be to examine the similarities in the policies of these countries, and thus to draw some lessons concerning post-independence reforms in the region. Although, of course, one must bear in mind the many differences in population growth and demographic spread, urbanization patterns, availability of land, wealth, infrastructure, and so on, among the various countries, some common challenges and problems can be identified within the region as a whole. Ultimately, the problems posed by unequal access to landed property and the challenge of balancing resource inequities in the interests of greater social justice and substantive political and economic equality for all citizens afflict the entire region. Some of these problems will be highlighted here.

Two of the major similarities in matters of access to, control over, and management of land use in the region can quickly be noted. A common major characteristic is the existence of two parallel and separate systems of agriculture—commercial and subsistence—with white large scale farmers (and a tiny minority of blacks) dominating the former sector. This is accompanied by structural inequalities in access to agricultural land in both quality and quantity, and to infrastructural facilities and services, between whites and blacks (at least in Namibia, South Africa and Zimbabwe). One predictable consequence of this in all the former settler colonies of Southern Africa has largely been the accompanying land hunger, overpopulation and low productivity in the subsistence sector, as opposed to under-utilisation of land in the commercial sector. Another common characteristic concerns the gender-discriminatory nature of land policies, and the consequent denial of equal access to, and ownership of, land that women generally suffer. I shall address this problem in some detail below, as part of the discussion of some of the dilemmas faced by the countries of Southern Africa, and the questions and challenges thrown up by the land issue for these countries. Not all these questions are answered here, but they need to be posed as critical issues for further reflection in the discourse on land rights.

SELECTED ISSUES IN LAND REFORM POLICIES: COMMON CHALLENGES AND SHARED DILEMMAS

There are a number of critical issues that must be articulated in any discussion of the contemporary land dilemma in Southern Africa. Only the major ones will be addressed here: land privatization, customary land tenure, land restitution and restoration, women's access to land, and the question of ethnicity and indigenous peoples' claims to land.

Land Privatization

One of the results of the external pressures brought to bear upon African states by donor organizations is the liberalization of land tenure arrangements under structural adjustment programs and the transition towards market economies. This raises a number of questions for consideration. For example, can there be a trade-off —ought there be one?—between security and productivity, on the one hand, and equity and traditional notions of land tenure on the other? The problem would appear to be that while international financial institutions advocate such reforms, apparently in the interests of greater agricultural productivity, and exaggerated free-market illusions of modernization, they would most probably lead to even more rural poverty and landlessness (Plant 1993:14). Clearly, therefore, one of the issues which needs to be borne in mind here has to do with the kind of alternative guarantees that can be devised for land security for the rural poor while accommodating structural changes.

Land Restitution and Restoration

The second dilemma relates to the principle of land restitution. South Africa provides us with not only the most obvious but also the most challenging context for a consideration of the issue of land restitution in the region. It is necessary to discuss its situation, and to interrogate some of the attendant assumptions, in some detail.

Apartheid policies denied millions of South Africans access to land and rendered untold numbers homeless. But even before the imposition of state-sponsored apartheid, with the coming to power of the National Party government in 1948, land dispossession in South Africa had already been in place for almost three centuries. For the history of the European occupation and colonization of the country, going back to the arrival of the first Dutch settlers in the Cape in 1652, was also, largely, a history of land dispossession. The legislation which was to be put in place later, starting with the Native (Black) Land Act of 1913, represented only the starting point of a systematic process of legally sanctioned land discrimination and dispossession. And, although the history of land dispossession is shared with other countries elsewhere in Africa, it was in South Africa that the process lasted for so long, was so complex and vicious, and led to the denationalization of the indigenous populations. The massive forced removals that became the symbol of apartheid were a central plank of this process. According to Platzky and Walker (1985), 3.5 million people were forcibly removed between 1960 and 1983 alone. In 1960 39.8% (4.4 million people) of the black population were crammed into the formal "tribal" reserves. By 1980 forced removals had raised the proportion to 53.1% (11 million people) (Letsoalo 1994:208). Not surprisingly, by 1991 it was generally accepted that about 10% of the South African population owned more than 80% of the 122 million hectares of land in use in South Africa.

Given this historical context, it came as little surprise to most observers in South Africa when the negotiations for a new democratic constitution yielded a special sub-chapter in the interim Constitution (Sections 121-123) devoted to the restitution of land rights to persons deprived of them by apartheid legislation. Towards the end of 1994, the South African Parliament took up this constitutional commitment by enacting the Restitution of Land Rights Act of 1994. The Act establishes a Land Claims Commission and a Land Claims Court to deal with land restitution claims. Some commentators have hailed this as a radical innovation; as a recognition of what the struggle was all about, what people went to jail or into exile for, and what many more had died for. Others have criticized the constitutional provisions as not going far enough because, it is argued, the broader issue of redistribution is ignored and the rights of restitution are subjected to and weakened by existing property rights and an administrative process of ministerial certification (Roux 1995:5). For yet other observers, it is perhaps too early to judge the merits and demerits of the process; one must wait and see how the post-apartheid government will go about delivering and implementing land reform, especially in the area of land restitution and redistribution (Murphy 1995:1). But a number of issues need to be briefly considered here.

The first consideration is this: demands for restitution are based on the fact that the land in question was acquired forcibly, unjustly and in contravention of the rights of the original owners and claimants to the land. Should land restitution now be conceived of solely as a symbolic redress for apartheid wrongs? Clearly not. It has been argued that land restitution should be employed as a developmental tool to re-establish communities deprived of land; that to succeed as a means of social and economic security, the process must be accompanied by mechanisms of developmental and infrastructural support, not to mention financial resources.

Secondly, it is also argued that land claims should not be based exclusively on a narrow, doctrinal positive law of ownership (Van der Walt 1992:431). But, rather, that land claims should be seen as claims of equity, social justice and inherent human rights. Therefore, any restitution process, apart from restoring legitimate rights in land to those unjustly deprived of them, has to take account of the need to redress the denial of rights of ownership by apartheid land laws to the majority of South African citizens and to give recognition to the informal tenures which emerged in response to that prohibition (Murphy 1995:3). The argument here is that land claims cannot, and should not, be based selectively on title deeds or lease agreements for the simple reason that the claims of the greater majority of black people are going to be founded on length of occupation, customary notions of birthright and expectations of secure tenure based on tradition and consensual practices (Swanson 1992:336). In other words, as Murphy aptly notes, "a land claims court ideally should be a court of equity reaching its decisions by balancing a variety of factors of which title is only one amongst many" (Murphy 1995:4). We can only wait to see whether the Land Claims Court, which became operational only recently, will adopt just this approach.

The final issue concerns the imposition of time limits for claims for restitution. This was one area of contestation between the various political parties and others engaged in the debate. In the case of South Africa, how far back can we go in time—1913, when the first major piece of legislation denying Africans equal access to and ownership of land was enacted? Or

1652, which marks the historical starting point in this long process of land dispossession, as some political parties and formations in South Africa, principally the Pan Africanist Congress, have argued? The interim Constitution and the newly enacted legislation settled for 1913 as the cut-off date. This is regarded as a pragmatic compromise which reflects the consensus that the doctrine of aboriginal title should not form the basis of restitution claims in the new South Africa (Bennett 1993:443).

Customary Land Tenure

The third dilemma common to Southern African countries arises out of the process of counter-balancing customary land rights and statutory land rights. The tension between customary law and statutory law is quite pervasive in African societies. This tension is most noticeable in the area of land rights. The issue deserves a fair amount of treatment. As observed earlier, in this era of externally imposed structural adjustment programmes in most African countries, there has arisen a corresponding pressure to replace customary land tenure systems with private and registered forms of ownership. The claim is that private land ownership and land registration programs are mechanisms for promoting security of tenure, inducing more investment in agriculture, and thereby increasing agricultural productivity. This claim is, of course, premised on the rather familiar, but thoroughly debunked, argument that traditional land tenure systems are a constraint upon agricultural development (Bruce 1993).

It has already been indicated that colonial land ownership policies and models almost invariably provided for dual systems of ownership whereby the colonial settlers enjoyed private and alienable rights to the land, while the majority of the indigenous Africans were limited to the enjoyment of communal land rights under the traditional systems of allocation. The colonial ideology purposively promoted the notion that Africans did not "own" property in land, at least not as individuals. This became received orthodoxy, not only among colonial lawyers, anthropologists, missionaries, and so on, but also among most commentators in the post-colonial era. This orthodoxy has recently been challenged as a thinly disguised strategy to distort, indeed deny, ownership of land and property relations among African people precisely in order to provide a justification for the colonial takeover and dispossession of these lands (Chanock 1992:287; Ranger 1993; Gutto 1995:16).

In any event, most African countries have retained the distinction between communal (or traditional) and private (or freehold) land, with varying degrees of the relative responsibilities of central government, local and traditional political authorities. And, indeed, the point needs to be made that customary land tenure systems have remained resilient in the face of attempts by colonial and post-colonial authorities in Southern Africa to facilitate and effect transformation processes. But, as has been rightly argued by some commentators (Ng'ong'ola 1995), since customary law is never static, reforms and changes are inevitable; however, what is more important is the manner in which state organs interfere with this on-going process of transformation. It has been suggested that the political outlook in each country influences the nature and manner of interference with the process, but the coalition of political views and systems in the region also seems to be leading to a coalition of views as regards patterns of customary land transformation. The issues relating to modernization of customary systems are, therefore, common to all countries of the region.

States and governments in Southern Africa are themselves part of the dilemma or problem under examination here. As was intimated earlier, given the centrality of land and land-related resources to the economies of Africa, state control of land is perceived as of paramount importance in the economic and political management of communities. This theme pervades and has continually informed land policies in Africa.

Historically, governments in Africa have never been neutral arbiters of conflicts over land, be they conflicts between customary and European or "modernized" sectors. The interests of Government, or those who influence government, have always lurked beneath, for example, "land privatization" or "tenure modernization" programmes, or, in the case of Zimbabwe, the fitful land restoration campaign (Ng'ong'ola 1995).

The moves towards greater land privatization must be seen against this background. But critical questions remain. Even if it is accepted that increased land privatization ensures better security and access to credit, does it not also lead to more landlessness and land dispossession? How does land privatization impact upon traditional authority, especially in respect of the powers of land allocation which chiefs in most traditional communities still claim for themselves? As regards this last question, a number of approaches have been engaged in some of the Southern African countries. In Zimbabwe, the Communal Land Act of 1982 recognized the concept of communal tenure but vested land allocation powers to elected rather than traditional chiefs. By contrast, traditional chiefs in post-independence Namibia have continued to enjoy the power to allocate land within their recognized "communal areas". In Botswana, the system of land board administration provides a half-way house: the land boards are empowered to allocate land under both customary and common law for traditional and other uses. Their membership used to include both chiefs (or "tribal" authorities) and government-appointed functionaries. Under the current legal arrangements, chiefs and traditional authorities are no longer automatic members of these boards. According to the Tribal Land (Amendment of Schedule) Order, S.I. No. 63 of 1994, promulgated as a result of changes introduced by the Tribal Land (Amendment) Act No. 14 of 1993, the composition of the land boards comprises state-appointed authorities and representatives of communities served by the particular board. Chiefs and traditional authorities are now members of Land Board Committees responsible for the selection of the community representatives. In all these cases, there have been some conflicts between the traditional and the new state-appointed authorities, with the former demanding a restoration of their exclusive powers over land allocation. Similar conflicts are currently playing themselves out in post-apartheid South Africa.

Women and Land Rights:
A Gendered Perspective of the Land Question

The fourth dilemma concerns women's property rights and access to land. It is indisputable that men have traditionally dominated not only the major forms of property, including land, but also the institutions of governance and political power which in turn determine access to, and control over, property. This has remained the case even where constitutions have set out to provide for apparently gender-neutral provisions guaranteeing equality and non-discrimination for both men and women. In all the Southern African countries, and particularly those with entrenched bills of rights, there are constitutional provisions which prohibit sex and gender discrimination. Some of these countries are also parties to the U.N. Convention on the Elimination of All Forms of Discrimination Against Women (CEDAW) which, in its key general provision, obligates state parties "to take all appropriate measures, including legislation, to modify or abolish existing laws, regulations, customs and practices which constitute discrimination against women" (Article 2(f)). The Convention further enjoins state parties to ensure equal treatment for both men and women, especially rural women, in land and agrarian reform as well as in land resettlement schemes (Article 14(2)(g)). Yet, the reality is that there is rampant evidence of continued exclusion of, and discrimination against, women by both officials and institutions with power to allocate and distribute land. Formal equality as guaranteed in constitutional provisions and other relevant legislation is hardly matched by social and political action. Women constitute the largest group of vulnerable persons whose entitlement to land rights and security is not guaranteed in prevailing land policies in Southern Africa. Although it is generally agreed that women play an especially important role in rural agriculture, accounting for the larger share of subsistence food production in Africa (Davison

1988), past agrarian reforms have been largely prejudicial to women's land security. Where traditional customary tenures may have provided some kind of security to women, land reform tenures since independence have tended to discriminate against them. Land registration programs have favoured men, by putting newly registered land in men's names and ignoring women's traditional rights to land use (Jacobs 1988: 26). The legal position as it affects married women in Botswana is particularly instructive in this regard.

In Botswana "state land" is allocated by authorized persons or agencies acting on behalf of the President. This is a category very distinct from "tribal land," which is allocated by or placed under the jurisdiction of the land boards mentioned earlier. State land includes land in some urban areas and the game reserves, national parks and fauna and flora conservation or preservation areas. Under Botswana law, where land is susceptible to individual allocation, it may be allocated to both men and women, and such allocation is made irrespective of whether one is married or not. On the basis of this policy, women not only ought to have access to, but have every right to own, such land. Yet, when it comes to registration of title, Batswana women cannot register such land because, according to Section 18 of the Deeds Registry Act, the relevant piece of legislation in this regard, women married in community of property, or those married out of community but not having excluded the marital power of the husband, cannot register land title in their own names (Qunta 1987; Mathuba 1992). However, this limitation only affects women married to Batswana citizens; women married to non-citizens, in or out of community, can have deeds registered in their names and can deal with their properties without the consent of their husbands.

And here arises the practical problem: for those women who are unable to register title in their own names, the possibility of obtaining loans to develop the land is simply closed off, since banks and other financial institutions insist that borrowers register their leases with the Registrar of Deeds. In fact, Section 18 further requires that such women be assisted by their husbands in the execution of any deeds registered with the Deeds Registry, irrespective of whether they are married in or out of community of property. It is not difficult to see the disadvantaged position of women falling within this category. Such women may not fully and adequately enjoy and exercise real control over a resource that properly belongs to them, rather than to their husbands. The many problems arising out of this legal situation have been well documented by researchers (Mathuba 1989:35). Thus, to mention only one example, a married woman who happens to be the bread winner in the family is effectively denied the opportunity to both own and develop property, since she cannot use it as security to obtain loans from financial institutions unless she complies with the requirements of Section 18; and compliance with this provision compels her to be assisted by the husband in registering or executing the relevant title deeds. In the final analysis, the law simply discriminates against women and has the effect of perpetuating their economic dependency on men, since the latter are not subjected to similar strictures in their access to, and control over, similar property. All this despite the existence of provisions in Sections 3 and 15 of the Botswana Constitution guaranteeing sex and gender equality for all Batswana citizens.

This experience points to the interrelated nature of certain legal issues concerning the position of women—legal capacity, status, marital rights—which have a direct bearing on the question of access to and ownership of land. The formal equality guaranteed by the constitutions is not always borne out in the daily application of some of the legislation and the unwritten Roman-Dutch or English common law which underlie the majority of the legal systems of the Southern African countries.

Women and other concerned interest groups in Botswana have recently begun to organize themselves around the issue of equal access to, and control over, land and other property. Demands for the revision of Section 18 of the Deeds Registry Act, in particular, have intensified following the *Unity Dow* case (see *Attorney General of Botswana v Unity Dow*, Court of Appeal of Botswana, Civil Appeal 4/91, unreported). One consequence of this decision, which declared unconstitutional a gender-discriminatory provision in the Citizenship Act of Botswana, has been to galvanize women's rights campaigners and activists in Botswana to fight for reform of all legislation which contains discriminatory elements that cannot be reconciled with the guarantee of gender or sex equality embodied in the country's constitution. Two such organizations may be briefly mentioned here.

First, Emang Basadi, a women's activist organization formed in the wake of the *Unity Dow* case and dedicated to campaigning for gender equality, in general, and equal participation in the political process, in particular. The other body, Women and the Law in Southern Africa Research Trust (WLSA), is a regional network of researchers, with national chapters in various countries in Southern Africa. WLSA, which predicates its work on a combination of academic and activist approaches, states as one of its principal objectives "providing data on the legal status of women to be used by [organizations], [and] governments attempting to improve the status of women" (WLSA [n.d.]). It thus undertakes research on the legal situation of women under existing laws with a view to identifying ways in which the law can be used to empower women, in both the public and private domains. It also engages in human rights education and advocacy, as well as undertaking or supporting public interest litigation on women's rights issues (the *Unity Dow* case being, in part, an instance of such action). Among the activities that the

Botswana chapter of the organization has undertaken is a law reform study aimed at identifying those aspects of Botswana's legislation that require amendment so as to bring them into conformity with the constitutional guarantee of equality and non-discrimination. The inequities and inequality attending women's access to land and other resources is reportedly part of WLSA's research agenda. But in the view of some legal commentators in Botswana, the most likely reform that can be envisaged, as far as the land issue is concerned, would be to provide for joint execution and registration of community of property titles. It has also been observed that a perusal of the Register of Marriage Instruments at the Deeds Registry reveals, rather interestingly, that Batswana women, by far, prefer to marry in community of property, the proprietary implications notwithstanding. Thus, it is possible to postulate that even the long awaited amendment to Section 18 is unlikely to change societal perceptions about this form of marriage or perceptions about the role of the husband in the disposal of matrimonial property, especially land, in Botswana. This probably reflects the desperate position of women - given the poor economic situation of most women, a joint matrimonial estate is the only way to access some kind of property. Thus, it is important to acknowledge that although women are increasingly working to eliminate these inequities and to find strategies of guaranteeing their rights, what may be required is a social revolution of some proportions before some sort of gender equality in matrimonial relations emerges (Dingake and Lesetedi 1995). But this pessimistic conclusion is equally true of all the other countries in the region.

Now, the need for a gendered perspective arises partly in recognition of the fact that most of the discourse on land has focused on the land rights of the landless as aggregated groups. Often, no regard is paid to the internal divisions or social strata amongst such groups. The emphasis usually placed on efficiency and commercial viability of land use, tenurial regimes, productivity, and so on, rarely takes as much account of differentiations based on gender as it does of race and class, for example. It is argued that this aggregation of land users has obscured the differential interests, inputs, rights and obligations relating to land, especially in the rural areas. Gaidzanwa's observation, in relation to Zimbabwe, that "this trend in analysis is predicated on the evolution and support of [ideologies] that increasingly mute or phase out the entitlement of individual women, especially those in marriage relationships, to unmediated access to land" (Gaidzanwa 1995:2) is equally true of all the other countries in Southern Africa. Indeed, it ought to be obvious that the linkage of women to land only through marriage at a time when land is increasingly becoming a privatised and registerable resource, given the pressures of structural adjustment alluded to earlier, only undermines women's livelihoods and economic rights. Attempts to engender research on land control and access must thus be seen in the light of the increasing struggles by scholars and writers to deconstruct the gendered basis of power relations. But, in a recent critique of studies on the land question in Zimbabwe, Moyo has identified a number of problems with some of the attempts to identify the gendered basis of iniquitous land control and relations: first, that such research tends not to address the key interrelated variables of gender, class, race and ethnicity, or to treat these aspects individually and in isolation. Second, that the land problem also tends to be treated in a narrow functionalist sense, which sees only agricultural and housing land issues as the pivotal locus of a gendered analysis of the land question. And, finally, that existing studies with a gendered perspective often lack an introspective approach, which could critically examine women's local and national scale agency for more equitable land reform (Moyo 1995a: 14).

What is advocated, instead, is the examination of gender relations alongside the examination of such processes as the evolution and role of class formation in differentiating access to land and related resources (Cousins et al. 1990; Moyo 1995a). Similarly, the role of capital, land market processes and private institutional processes which govern land distribution also needs to be interrogated. Some of the emerging body of literature on these issues in the Southern African region has begun to address some of these concerns. Studies on Botswana (Mathuba 1989, 1992, 1993), Swaziland (Rose 1988), South Africa (Letsoalo 1994), Zambia (Himonga and Munachonga 1991), and Zimbabwe (Gaidzanwa 1988, 1995; Moyo 1986, 1995a; Pankhurst and Jacobs 1988) seem to incline towards a common conclusion: that land reform policies have on balance tended to increase women's dependence upon men, despite some benefits. Until women obtain land rights on the same basis as men, this will necessarily remain the case. However, it has also been forcefully argued that land rights alone cannot fully liberate women. Women, unlike men, are constrained by marital regimes and other legal disabilities. The law may constrain them as subordinates to their husbands; where they are not married, they may still be subjected to the legal powers and domination of their fathers and brothers.

What all this suggests is that the disadvantaged position of women cannot be improved dramatically simply by changing the law without some accompanying far-reaching economic, institutional and cultural changes (Jacobs 1992:27). After all, as was noted earlier, the guarantee of formal equality between men and women in constitutions and property legislation has not always ensured equal rights of ownership or access to land for both men and women in Africa. Thus, for example, although Himonga and Munachonga quite rightly observe that the law and procedure relating to the acquisition and allocation of land in Zambia is substantially gender-neutral, they go on to identify and catalogue a number of factors which, in fact, have ensured that women do not enjoy equal access to ownership and control of land: for example, high rates of illiteracy among women, negative attitudes of officials, the subordination of women within marriage, kinship and succession systems, and the lack of economic power of women. The conclusion they draw for Zambia is equally relevant for all the other countries in the region: that the solution to the problem of rural women's access to agricultural land does not lie in the letter of the law and official policy but, rather, that much more must be done outside these regimes to increase women's actual access to agricultural land (Himonga and Munachonga 1993: 70).

Indeed, this calls for new forms of struggle, of resistance and power relationships not only between men and women, but also between women and the state. This is one area which provides a great challenge to all states in the region engaged in the process of restructuring and balancing the resource inequities posed by the land question.

Class, Ethnicity and Indigenous Claims to Land: A Brief Comment

In addition to race, class and, to a lesser extent, ethnicity have also been prominent factors in the land question in Southern Africa. A significant portion of the literature on this subject has, by and large, focused on the role of race and class in determining access to, and control of, land (De Klerk 1991). This is only to be expected, for the colonial construction of land tenure systems was essentially about the entrenchment of racial and class advantage of the colonial settler over the dispossessed colonial subject. As was noted at the outset of this discussion, race is one theme that runs through the history of land ownership and property relations in the former settler colonies of Southern Africa. Intertwined with this has been the question of class: historically, property, especially as understood as the process of appropriating and privatizing land and its resources and products, has always denoted social relationships around economic goods and services. And, as has been argued by some, no single factor is as determinative of social differentiation, especially social class differentiation, as the unequal distribution or the control and ownership of property (Cousins et al. 1990; Marcus 1991). The roles of race and class cannot be overemphasized in this debate.

But there are also at least two other issues that stand to be considered as aspects of the land dilemma in Southern Africa: the relevance of ethnicity and the peculiar land dilemma posed by indigenous communities. Ethnicity is one of the issues at the center of the Mmaboi land claim in South Africa discussed by Richard Levin in this volume. Ethnicity and the related issue of chieftainship also presented one of the first problems for the newly inaugurated post-apartheid government of President Nelson Mandela in 1994. In a sense, the issue raised the question of how land tenure is to be linked to the administrative powers of traditional authorities in the new democratic order. Former State President de Klerk had, literally in the dying minutes of the apartheid regime, assented to a secretly crafted piece of legislation, the KwaZulu Ingonyama Trust Act, which placed approximately three million hectares of land under the administration of the Zulu King Goodwill Zwelithini as the sole trustee, with administrative expenses to be borne by the new Kwazulu-Natal provincial government (*Weekly Mail & Guardian*, Johannesburg, May 20-26, 1994:2). Revelation of this arrangement provoked incredulous and indignant reactions, at least from some sections of the newly established Government of National Unity and from political groups outside the Zulu king's own ethnic and political support base. A cabinet committee was subsequently able to resolve the initial crisis. More recently, the National Assembly adopted a draft law intended to reverse the king's unlimited power of control over these resources. At the time of writing, the proposed law is pending approval in the upper house of Parliament, the Senate.

It has been noted that the short-lived debacle over the Ingonyama Trust showed how constitutional recognition of customary law will require the new government to disentangle customary or indigenous land rights from the colonial legacy of indirect rule, under which political sovereignty and land ownership were intertwined (Klug 1995:120). Now, it is said that indirect rule, in fact, cast the allocation of plots of land within a community as an official administrative act of the traditional leadership (Bennett 1995:133) and that this imposed a system of patronage and political expediency, simultaneously undermining community governance and reshaping the role of traditional authorities in the political process (Klug 1995:120). It could also be argued that the Ingonyama Trust debate demonstrated how this system of patronage by traditional authorities and monarchy can be used as a defining factor in the modern reconstructions of ethnicity and ethnic identities. The Ingonyama grant was not some kind of rational post-apartheid tenurial arrangement aimed at creating a legitimate system of customary tenure and liberating traditional leadership from the domination of administrative processes. Rather, it was meant as part of the attempt to strengthen King Zwelithini's imperial hand the in the battle for the reconstruction of a modern Zulu nation and identity in the province of Kwazulu-Natal. As history has shown, claims to separate ethnic identities that are not backed up by a territorial base rarely ever succeed.

The second issue arises from the complexities relating to indigenous claims to land. To be sure, this is not a problem that affects all the Southern African countries that fall within the scope of this discussion. Botswana is, at the moment, the most directly affected. But, potentially, the problem could resonate in both Namibia and South Africa, the other countries in the region with significant numbers of indigenous or marginalized populations, such as the Khoi and the San.

The last decade and a half has witnessed a tremendous resurgence of indigenous peoples' movements around the world, with claims for land rights featuring high on the agenda of indigenous peoples' concerns. As Plant (1993:16) correctly puts it, there is now a new and evolving body of international law concerning indigenous peoples and their land rights. Examples of this so-called soft law are the International Labour Organization's Convention No. 169 of 1989 and the draft United Nations Declaration on Indigenous Rights. Accordingly, a number of countries have taken up the issue and addressed it within their constitutions or in special legislation designed to recognize the notion of "special" rights for indigenous communities over their traditional lands and territories based either on past immemorial possession, or on written legal title to the land embodied and recognized in treaties or other arrangements predating the emergence of the modern "nation-state," or on the relationship between indigenous peoples and their lands and related environmental resources (Plant 1993:16). In countries, such as Colombia or the Philippines, where special legislation has been enacted, the protection of indigenous land rights has often been attended with restrictions on the right to alienate or mortgage these lands. In other countries, landmark court rulings have recognized the notion of aboriginal title as a basis for the land claims of indigenous peoples. This was most recently acknowledged in the notable Australian case of *Mabo and others v The State of Queensland* (see (1992) 175 CLR 1). But, as was indicated above, as far as South Africa is concerned, the new constitutional arrangements as well as the recently enacted legislation on land restoration deliberately rule out the doctrine of aboriginal title as a basis for restitution claims. But this is not to say that a case cannot be made for recognition of the special rights of certain indigenous and marginalized communities.

The problem of indigenous land rights has recently entered the political debate in Botswana, as some human rights activists and non-governmental organizations have taken up the issue of the marginalization of minority indigenous groups such as the Basarwa. As Ng'ong'ola has argued, the Basarwa and other minority ethnic groups were completely ignored when 'tribal' territories were being demarcated and so-called Crown lands appropriated in pre-independence Botswana. The failure to recognize and accommodate titles and land use rights of these indigenous communities during the long years of colonial rule in Botswana has not been rectified by the post-colonial state, and the problem has continued to confound land policy thirty years after independence. The notion of aboriginal title is still not recognized under Botswana law. The issue has become particularly sensitive as more complaints keep surfacing suggesting that territories which should have been preserved for the least protected communities under the law have been exposed to land grabbing by the more powerful and politically connected. (Ng'ong'ola 1996b; Wily 1994:6-9). A more equitable solution to this century-old problem of the recognition and protection of indigenous titles to land in Botswana ought to be at the top of any future land reform agenda.

At the same time, however, another attendant dilemma ought to be acknowledged in this regard. The recent resurgence of world-wide interest in environmental protection and common property resource management has a bearing on demands for the protection of the land rights of indigenous communities and other special groups. To what extent, for example, do state policies relating to forest management take account of the land rights of traditional forest-dwellers? Or how do policies designed to contain the problem of desertification and other environmental threats accommodate the needs and land rights of nomadic and pastoral communities? Although these specific problems may not, as such, be of current concern to Southern African countries, the questions are not without relevance. In Botswana, for example, the problem of indigenous land rights briefly indicated above is opposed by state interests and policies which favour protection of territories demarcated as game reserves, national parks, and fauna and flora conservation areas. As was stated earlier, these territories form part of what is designated as "state land." And yet, these are also the areas that have traditionally been claimed by the Basarwa and other indigenous and marginalized communities as the last vestiges of their ancestral lands (Ng'ong'ola 1996b).

A CONCLUDING OBSERVATION

So many years after independence, the land question remains as hotly contested in all Southern African countries as it was during the years of struggle for political liberation. A number of issues still lie at the heart of this question, for example: the quality and quantity of land available for redistribution, the procedures and financial costs of land acquisition and redistribution, the efficiency of land use, the economic and social impact of land reform, and so on. The popular perception, in the more recently independent countries such as Namibia and Zimbabwe, for example, is that the expectations for egalitarianism raised during the bitter liberation struggles have not been fulfilled, and that it is capitalist farming elites, predominantly white, who continue to reap most of the benefits of post-independence land reforms (Moyo 1995b:1). It is argued that land reform will remain critical in Southern Africa because of the specific historical experience of settler land expropriation, the culturally specific demands for land, the history of the struggle for land and the contemporary economic hardships facing both rural and urban people, especially in this era of structural adjustment. However, recent state responses to the land question do not generate any confidence and optimism.

There is now an increasing acceptance of the centrality of land allocation in schemes designed to combat poverty and social-economic deprivations in general, and also a recognition that the land interest is deeply interwoven with the public interest and the common interest of the nation as a whole (Nagan 1993:151; Plant 1993:20). Two developments since the early 1980s have been of particular relevance to the debate on land rights in Africa. First, the emergence of the idea of the right to development as a human right. Second, the greater emphasis given to economic and social rights necessarily linked to the issues of land rights, access and affordability, and the recognition of the social function of property. As regards the connection between land rights and the right to development, it has been correctly argued that as land allocation, land use and planning are intimately bound up with the prospects for freezing or enhancing a community's capacity for development, land should not be looked at as some kind of reified, abstract juridical construct, but as a fundamental and important resource implicating an unfolding array of entitlements and interests (Nagan 1993:151). The right to development, much championed by the developing world, stresses the indivisibility of all human rights, and the inter-linkages between civil and political rights, on the one hand, and economic, social and cultural rights on the other.

From a functional point of view, land as a resource that facilitates individual and communal development becomes an important base for economic, social and political power. For land is, in this sense, central to a number of such issues as housing and shelter, communications, food security, environmental management and use, access to credit, finance and security, cultural identity, and so on. All these concerns are related to the issues of economic justice and equity, especially for landless rural communities. The right to development, therefore, underpins the demands by the landless individuals and communities in Southern Africa to a dispensation which respects and guarantees their rights to social and economic development, economic empowerment and human dignity. But the realization of these rights requires, *inter alia*, state intervention to protect not only private land rights, but also, more importantly, group and collective rights. Furthermore, the state must intervene to resolve the dilemmas and problems which have been identified in this discussion. Until then, the imbalances in access to, and control over, land and related resources will persist. Such imbalances, as has been argued in this paper, represent an unmistakable denial of social justice and equity, especially for the millions of the rural poor spread around in the entire Southern African sub-continent.

*   I am grateful to my colleague Dr. Chuma Himonga, of the Department of Private Law, University of Cape Town, for her comments on an earlier draft of this paper. My grateful thanks also go to the participants at the Symposium, and especially the discussant, who kindly enriched the paper with their comments and criticisms. My former colleague Dr. Clement Ng'ong'ola, of the Department of Law, University of Botswana, was, as usual, extremely generous with his invaluable suggestions, conveyed over many electronic and telephonic conversations.

REFERENCES

Allott, A. "Constitutional Change and Political Pressures in Some New Commonwealth African States: Some Random Reflections." In *Collected Seminar Papers on Post-Independence Constitutional Changes (Oct. 1967 - Mar. 1968)*. London: Institute of Commonwealth Studies, University of London, 1968.

Bassett, T. J., and D. E. Crummey. *Land in African Agrarian Systems*. Madison, Wis: Univ. of Wisconsin Press, 1993.

Bekker, J. C. "Land Reform in African Countries." *SAIPA* 3(1991):26.

Bennett, T. "Redistribution of Land and the Doctrine of Aboriginal Title in South Africa." *South African Journal of Human Rights* 9(1993):443.

Bennett, T. *Human Rights and African Customary Law*. Cape Town: Juta, 1995.

Bruce, J. "Do Indigenous Tenure Systems Constrain Agricultural Development?" In *Land in African Agrarian Systems*, eds. T. J. Bassett and D. E. Crumney, 35-56. Madison: University of Wisconsin Press, 1993.

Chanock, M. "Paradigms, Policies and Property: A Review of the Customary Law of Land Tenure." In *Law in Colonial Africa*, eds Kristin Mann and Richard Roberts. London: James Currey, 1991.

Chanock, M. "The Law Market: The Legal Encounter in British East and Central Africa." In *European Expansion and the Law*, eds. W. Mommsen and J. De Moor. Oxford: Berg, 1992.

Cousins, B. et al. *The Dynamics of Social Differentiation in the Communal Lands of Zimbabwe*. Harare: University of Zimbabwe, 1990.

Davison, J., ed. *Agriculture, Women, and Land: The African Experience*. Boulder & London: Westview Press, 1988.

De Klerk, M., ed. *A Harvest of Discontent: the Land Question in South Africa*. Cape Town: IDASA, 1991.

Dingake, O. K. and Lesetedi, G. *A Pilot Study Report on Women's Access to and Control of Resources in Selebi-Phikwe District, Botswana*. Unpublished mimeo, Gaborone, Botswana, 1995.

Gaidzanwa, R. *Women's Land Rights in Zimbabwe*. Unpublished mimeo, Department of Rural and Urban Planning, Univ. of Zimbabwe, Harare, 1988.

Gaidzanwa, R. "Land and the Economic Empowerment of Women: A Gendered Analysis." *Southern African Feminist Review* 1, 1(1995):1-12.

Gutto, S. B. O. "Political Mobilization Through the Land Question." (Ttranscription of an oral presentation). *Journal of African Marxists* 10(1987):43.

Gutto, S. B. O. *Property and Land Reform: Constitutional and Jurisprudential Perspectives*. Durban: Butterworths, 1995.

Himonga, C., and Munachonga, M. "Rural Women's Access to Agricultural Land in Settlement Schemes in Zambia: Law, Practice and Socio-Economic Constraints." *Third World Legal Studies* 1991:59-74.

Jacobs, S."Gender and Land Reform: Zimbabwe and Some Comparisons. *International Sociology* 7, 1(1992):5-34.

Klug, H. "Defining the Property Rights of Others: Political Power, Indigenous Tenure and the Construction of Customary Land Law." *Journal of Legal Pluralism* 35(1995):119.

Letsoalo, E. "Restoration of Land: Problems and Prospects." In *South Africa: The Challenge of Change*, ed. V. Maphai. Harare: Sapes Books, 1994.

Marcus, T. "National, Class and Gender Issue in Land Reform." In *A Harvest of Discontent: the Land Question in South Africa*, ed. M. De Klerk. Cape Town: IDASA, 1991.

Mathuba, B. *Report on The Review of the Tribal Land Act, Land Policies and Related Issues*. Gaborone: Government Printers, 1989.

Mathuba, B."Land Policy in Botswana." Paper presented at the Workshop on Land Policy in Eastern and Southern Africa, Maputo, Mozambique, February 1992.

Mathuba, B. "Land Institutions and Land Distribution in Botswana." Paper presented at Conference on Land Redistribution Options, Johannesburg, South Africa, 12 - 15 October, 1993.

Moyo, S. "The Land Question in Zimbabwe." In *The Political Economy of Transition, 1980-1986,* ed. I. Mandaza. Dakar: Codesria, 1986.

Moyo, S. "A Gendered Perspective of the Land Question." *Southern African Feminist Review* 1, 1(1995a):13-31.

Moyo, S. *The Land Question in Zimbabwe*. Harare: Sapes Books, 1995b.

Murphy, J. "The Restitution of Land After Apartheid: The Constitutional and Legislative Framework." In *Reparations After Apartheid*, ed. M. Rwelamira, 1995 [Forthcoming].

Nagan, W. "Resource Allocation: Land and Human Rights in a New South Africa." In *Land, Property Rights and the New Constitution*, eds. M. Venter and M. Anderson.Cape Town: CLC, Univ. of the Western Cape, 1993.

Ng'ong'ola, C.H. S. "The Post-Colonial Era in Relations to Land Expropriation Laws in Botswana, Malawi, Zambia and Zimbabwe." *ICLQ* 41(1992):117.

Ng'ong'ola, C. H. S."Customary Law, Land Tenure and Policy in Some of African Countries at the Threshold of the Twenty-First Century." Paper presented at the International Colloquium on Property Law at the Threshold of the 21st Century, Maastricht, The Netherlands, 28-30 August, 1995.

Ng'ong'ola, C. H. S. "Land Tenure Reform in Botswana: Post Colonial Developments and Future Prospects." *SA Public Law* (forthcoming), 1996a.

Ng'ong'ola, C. H. S. "Land Rights for Marginalized Ethnic Groups in Botswana, with Special Reference to Basarwa." *Journal of African Law* (forthcoming), 1996b.

Pankhurst, D., and S. Jacobs. "Land Tenure, Gender Relations, and Agricultural Production: The Case of Zimbabwe's Peasantry." In *Agriculture, Women, and Land: The African Experience*, ed. J. Davison. Boulder & London: Westview Press, 1988.

Plant, R. "Land Rights in Human Rights and Development." *ICJ Review* 10, 51(1993): 10-31.

Platzky, L., and Walker, C. *The Surplus People: Forced Removals in South Africa.* Johannesburg: Ravan, 1985.

Qunta, C. *Women in Southern Africa.* Johannesburg: Stokaville, 1987.

Ranger, T. *Peasant Consciousness and Guerilla War in Zimbabwe: A Comparative Study.* Harare: Zimbabwe Publishing House, 1985.

Ranger, T. "The Communal Areas of Zimbabwe." In *Land in African Agrarian Systems*, eds. T. J. Bassett and D. E. Crumney. Madison, Wis.: Univ.of Wisconsin Press, 1993, pp. 35-56.

Rose, L. "'A Woman is Like a Field': Women's Strategies for Land Access in Swaziland," In *Agriculture, Women, and Land: The African Experience*, ed. J. Davison. Boulder & London: Westview Press, 1988.

Roux, T. "Property, Land as Property, and the Interim Constitution." Unpublished paper, 1995.

Swanson, E. "A Land Claims Court for South Africa." *South African J Human Rights* 8, 431(1992):332-343.

Shipton, G., and M. Goheen. "Understanding African Land Holding," *Africa* 62, 307(1992):307-326.

Van der Walt, A. "Fragmentation of Land Rights." *South African J Human Rights* 8, 431(1992):431-450.

Wily, E. "Hunter-Gatherers and the Land Issue in Botswana." *Indigenous Affairs* 2, 6(1994).

Women and Law in Southern Africa Research Project (WLSA). *Organization Pamphlet.* Harare: Women and Law in Southern Africa Research Project, n.d.

Cases Cited

Attorney General of Botswana v Unity Dow, Court of Appeal of Botswana, Civil Appeal 4/91 (unreported).

Mabo and others v The State of Queensland (1992) 175 CLR 1.

14

LAND RESTITUTION, ETHNICITY,

AND TERRITORIALITY:

THE CASE OF THE MMABOI LAND CLAIM IN

SOUTH AFRICA'S NORTHERN PROVINCE

RICHARD LEVIN

INTRODUCTION

THE LAND QUESTION AND NATIONAL DEMOCRATIC TRANSFOR-mation are closely interrelated issues in South Africa. Colonialism, capitalism and apartheid all developed on the foundation of land dispossession and land partition. Private property and associated understandings of social relations were deeply inscribed within the political economic history of the development of racial discrimination in South Africa. Now, in the new South Africa, the search is on for a reconstruction and development path which will overcome the historical inequities of a racially divided society. The restructuring of land relations must be located at the core of such a project.

The ANC-led government has evolved a three-pronged approach to land reform involving land restitution, land redistribution through the market, and land tenure reform (Department of Land Affairs 1996). This paper is concerned with land restitution, and the problems associated with this mechanism of land reform as manifest within a particular land claim lodged in the Northern Province. Land reform is understood as being central to reconstruction and development, not simply in terms of it being a prerequisite of national democratic transformation, but also in terms of the pursuit of a developmentalist vision for South Africa. The miracle of the "East Asian Tigers" is increasingly a reference point for debates around developmental growth paths for the new South Africa (Levine and Weiner 1993:29). Nevertheless, little reference is made to the fact that South Korean and Taiwanese development was predicated on fundamental land reform which stimulated the growth of an internal market, paving the way for rapid industrialization, and leading ultimately to a relative narrowing of rural and urban differentials (Jenkins 1994:78; Edwards 1992:106).

Land restitution through a land claims procedure was the first clear land reform mechanism emerging out of the ANC policy-making process following its unbanning in 1990.[1] *The Restitution of Land Rights Act* (1994) was also arguably the most significant piece of legislation promulgated by the new democratic Parliament in South Africa during its first year of business, following the country's first democratic elections held in April 1994. Minister Hannekom pointed to the huge symbolic significance of the legislation after receiving a standing ovation in Parliament, while President Mandela assured white landowners that the Act did not signify that they were all about to have their land expropriated from them. The new legislation has raised the hopes of South Africa's dispossessed masses, but weaknesses in the legislation itself, as well as changing political dynamics could well see the new legislation producing outcomes which differ widely from the original intentions of establishing a land claims procedure to drive the land reform process. In particular, the resuscitation of the chieftaincy as a key emerging institution in the land claims process, poses a threat to the democratization of land relations in extensive parts of the countryside while raising the specter of new spatial conflicts. It also undermines political and constitutional commitments to restructuring gender relations.

This paper will examine a particular land claim, lodged by the Mojapelo people now resident in the village of Mmaboi in the Northern Province. The claim highlights several issues. It demonstrates that the land claims process, grounded as it is in bourgeois legal discourse undermines formal commitments to popular participatory reconstruction and development processes. It also shows how land claims are themselves contested by other dispossessed communities, and how this contestation is rooted in the institutions of the chieftaincy and territoriality. The claim also reveals shortcomings in the legislation itself, as well as the need for the South African legal fraternity to engage seriously in debates around redefining historical bourgeois understandings of property, rights and tenure relations.

FORCED REMOVALS AND PRIVATE PROPERTY RELATIONS IN SOUTH AFRICA

Forced removals, land dispossession and the creation of private property were at the center of racially-based oppression in South Africa. Six years after the first white settlers landed in the country in 1652, Jan Van Riebeeck notified indigenous Khoi communities that they could no longer dwell to the west of the Salt and Liesbeck rivers. This was effectively, the first formal act of forced relocation since white settlement in the country's history (Platzky and Walker 1985:71). The process continued through colonial wars of dispossession and colonial government policy into the twentieth century and the promulgation of the 1913 Land Act. The act continued an ongoing settler onslaught against African squatters, lessees or sharers on white settled land, and transformed them into a dependent wage-earning class (Bundy 1979:134). The offensive intensified during the final decade of the nineteenth century, and was in large part a response to the emergence of a vibrant African peasantry which had responded positively to market opportunities created by the rapid development of capitalism following the mineral discoveries in the latter half of the nineteenth century. A major objective of the 1913 Land Act, was the eradication of independent black tenant farmers (Keegan 1986:183). The act thus outlawed any:

> agreement or arrangement whereby a (black) person, in consideration of his being permitted to occupy land, renders or promises to render to any person a share of the produce thereof, or any valuable consideration of any kind whatever other than his own labor or services or the labor services of any of his family.[2]

This meant that the only legal rent payment by black tenants to white landlords was the provision of labor service (Keegan 1986:183). This meant that the only legal rent payment by black tenants to white landlords was the provision of labor service (Keegan 1986:183). This established labor tenancy as the dominant social relation of production on land designated for white occupation and use, and in many cases converted *de facto* black occupants and land users into labor tenants. The act also prohibited land purchases by blacks outside of scheduled reserve territory, making these the only places where Africans could occupy land. Within the reserves, the state encouraged the Natal practice of indigenous or customary forms of land tenure rather than the Cape-based strategy of encouraging individual forms of tenure (Platzky and Walker 1985). One consequence was the reproduction and reshaping of the chieftaincy as the institution through which "communal" forms of tenure could be guaranteed, as well as the redefinition of customary land law.

Land scheduled for African occupation was essentially land reserved for Africans in the four provinces which collectively were amalgamated under the Union of South Africa in 1910. It amounted to about 9 million ha or 7% of all land in South Africa (Platzky and Walker 1985). This meant that large expanses of African freehold land and unsurveyed state land, long viewed as African areas were omitted from the schedule. In 1936, steps were taken to allocate more land for African occupation, through the passage of the 1936 Development Trust and Land Act. This legislation added 6.2 million ha of land to the reserves and created the South African Native Trust to acquire and administer that land. The Trust became the registered owner of most reserve land (Platzky and Walker 1985:89). This legislation also created the framework within which the post World War II apartheid policies of the Afrikaner National Party were developed, and laid the basis for further forced removals of Africans from their land.

Forced removals were intensified by apartheid, but must be understood broadly in the context of colonial dispossession, and land partition implemented by the Union government as well. They took a variety of historical forms, including "black spot" removals of Africans who acquired freehold land; "betterment planning" removals to make way for "rational" land use in the reserves; bantustan consolidation removals to join fragments black territory; farmworker and labor tenant retrenchments and evictions; and the privatization of state-owned land.[3]

The full extent of colonial land dispossession or even post-1913 forced removals has not been quantified. Most observers quote a figure of 3.5 million, emanating from the path-breaking study undertaken by the Surplus People's Project (SPP) in the early 1980s. This figure was likely an underestimation, and excluded victims of betterment planning removals in the bantustans, while it also was confined to forced removals implemented between 1960 and 1980 through apartheid policies. At the time of writing, the SPP estimated that a further 1.9 million people were under threat of removal. More recently, de Wet, estimated that there were at least 7 million victims of forced removals since 1913 (de Wet 1994:359), but this may also be an underestimate. While it may not be possible to accurately quantify the extent of land dispossession, numbers are important in assessing whether the judicial process which has been inaugurated by the GNU through *The Restitution of Land Rights Act* will be able to cope with the problem it aims to solve within the time-frames set.

LAND RESTITUTION AND PROPERTY RIGHTS
IN THE NEW SOUTH AFRICA

The *Constitution of the Republic of South Africa Act* of 1994, included property in its Fundamental Rights Chapter, but also facilitated the establishment of a statutory land claims court. Section 8 of the Fundamental Rights chapter included a provision that:

> Every person or community dispossessed of rights in land before the commencement of this Constitution under any law inconsistent with subsection 2 (which outlaws discrimination on the basis of race, gender, sex, ethnic origin etc.) had that subsection been in operation at the time of the dispossession, shall be entitled to claim restitution of such rights.... (Republic of South Africa 1994a:10)

Chapter 8, Sections 121-123, includes a section on Land Rights making provisions for restitution of rights in land through the establishment of a "Commission on Restitution of Land Rights" which could investigate land claims, mediate or settle such disputes as may arise out of land claims and draw up submissions which could be used as evidence in the courts. This clause has been put into effect by *The Restitution of Land Rights Act* of November 1994.

The Restitution of Land Rights Act aims to "provide for the restitution of rights in land" of communities whose land was dispossessed "for the purpose of furthering the objects of any racially based discriminatory law" (Republic of South Africa 1994b). This will be achieved through the establishment of a Commission on Restitution of Land Rights and a Land Claims Court. In order for claims to be processed, they must be lodged within three years of a date fixed by the Minister of Land Affairs.[4] Claims may be lodged if claimants were prevented from obtaining or retaining land on account of racially-based legislation. The central institution for the processing of claims is the Commission on Restitution, established early in 1995. It consists of a Chief Land Claims Commissioner, a Deputy and a number of regional commissioners who were appointed after inviting nominations from the public. The Commission, which is independent from government, is charged with the responsibility of receiving claims and assisting claimants in the preparation and submission of claims. If the claim is undisputed, the Commission can make a ruling, whereas if there is an objection or counterclaim, the claim can be referred for mediation. If this fails, then the claim must be referred by the Commission to the Land Claims Court.

The Land Claims Court is empowered to determine cases of restitution as well as the payment of compensation, taking a number of key factors into account. These include the desirability of: providing for restitution of rights or payment of compensation to the victims of forced removals; remedying historical violations of human rights; meeting the requirements of equity and justice; avoiding major social disruption. (Republic of South Africa 1994b)

The court is empowered to determine the form of land title under which restituted land will be held, and to "adjust the nature of the right previously held by the claimant" (Republic of South Africa 1994b). It may also order the state to expropriate land to restore land rights to a claimant. In such cases, the owner of such land will be "entitled to the payment of just and equitable compensation, determined either by agreement or by the Court according to the principles laid down" (Republic of South Africa 1994b) in the Constitution.

There is little doubt that the act opens up possibilities for communities to reclaim land from which they were forcibly removed. Nevertheless, a number of questions emerge around the practicalities of land claims, including the potential for their rapid resolution. Claims must be lodged within three years of May 1 1995; five years have been set aside for the Commission and the Court to finalize all claims, while all Court orders should be implemented within a ten tear period (Department of Land Affairs 1996:35). On the ground, expectations are very high; people expect their land demands to be realized immediately. Real questions arise as to how rapidly and effectively, a "Commission on Restitution of Land Rights" will be able to deal with specific cases. Communities will require assistance in formulating clear and realizable land claims, while the capacity of the newly formed Land Claims Commission is limited. Complicated legal procedures and rules make it difficult for a people-led land claims procedure to be realized in line with Reconstruction and Development Programme (RDP) commitments.[5] The most serious questions, however, center on the constraints which property rights clauses in the new constitution will impose on the restitution process.

During the later stages of negotiations, concerns were expressed about entrenching property rights in a new Constitution as well as payment of compensation to current landowners in the event of successful land claims. The conceptions which rural people have of land ownership and property rights show how problematic the interim constitution's property rights clause is. Payment of compensation, is rejected by most rural black people. This is clearly illustrated in the resolution on land restoration taken at the National Community Land Conference held in Bloemfontein in February 1994: "Communities who were forcibly removed should have their land and mineral rights returned immediately, unconditionally and at no cost to the community."[6]

The process by which land rights are restored is crucial to democratization and development in South Africa. Legal land claims procedures have been developed with specific communities in mind. The legislation was in many respects shaped by the experiences of victims of apartheid black spot removals where communities held title deeds to land, although it also attempts to provide some opportunities for victims of other forms of removal to lodge claims. Nevertheless, the legislation assumes that homogenous and identifiable communities will, as victims of apartheid, be claiming unitary pieces of land. It is important to consider whether the communities suit the process, but it is also necessary to ask whether the process suits the communities. The potential for participation is restricted by criteria such as cut off date and types of claims, as well as the complicated legal discourse contained within a judicial process. If viewed from the perspective of the land needs of rural communities, then the process may well prove inadequate in terms of handling millions of dispossessed South Africans. The 1994 act does allow the President of the Court to provide for circumstances under which oral evidence may be submitted to the Court, and to conduct parts of the proceedings in an informal way. This is fortunate, since many claimants require a process that does not demand written evidence.

More problematic is the question of *who* will lodge a claim since the process is biased towards the submission of unitary claims from homogenous communities. "Who is the community" and "who decides" are crucial questions that will emerge in the land claims process. Some bantustan villages which have been constituted by forced removals, comprise people with different historical origins. The scattering of labor tenants over vast areas in the former Transvaal provinces, for example, could lead to competing and overlapping claims from communities in different localities. Historical rivalries between different chieftaincies over territory and followership, could similarly lead to competing and overlapping claims. The process clearly favors communities who can be represented by a single institution or organization. The chieftaincy is likely to emerge as the key institution for filing successful claims, since alternatives like the civics are far too tentatively organized in most areas. The act stipulates that:

> If a claim is lodged on behalf of a community the basis on which it is contended that the person submitting the form represents such a community, shall be declared in full and any appropriate resolution or document supporting such contention shall accompany the form at the time of lodgement. (Republic of South Africa 1994b)

Against this background, the paper now turns to a case study of the Mojapelo Land Claim, and attempts to analyze the extent to which government restitution polices and legislation will meet the land aspirations of this community, as well as the contradictions to which the restitution process is giving rise.

THE MOJAPELO LAND CLAIM

Origins and History of the Mojapelo

The Mojapelo ethnic group originates from the Ndebele, through Nkumane, the eldest son of Chief Kekana. Nkumane ate *phohu*, the heart of an eland, which is only supposed to be eaten by a chief. Having breached tradition, he was humiliated by the people and royal councillors, called "*lehlalerwa*" (a wild dog), and expelled from the community. That is where the Mojapelo genealogy started (Mojapelo [n.d]:8-9). Nkumane is viewed as the grandfather of the group. He settled at a place known as Kgaditse with his followers, and they began to marry and establish kraals. Nkumane's royal name was Ramakanyane, and three kraals were established at GaKadiaka, GaMello and GaMadiba. From Kgaditse, Nkumane and his subjects went on to Mphahlele, where Nkumane fell in love with Sebopa's daughter and wanted to marry her. In order to do so, he had to satisfy a circumcision ritual, which he did (Mojapelo [n.d.]:10). It is not known whether Ramakanyane was asked to marry *Ngwana* WaSebopa as the mother of the tribe or not, but she was barren.[7] Nkumane then married a second wife who eventually gave birth to a son, Ramakanyane I.

Nkumane stayed at Mphahlele in Motsetsamong, the area of his wife from Sebopa, but he remained independent of the Mphahlele's, retaining his own totem of *Bahlalerwa*. Nevertheless, in order to maintain their identity, the Mojapelos left Mphahlele and drove their cattle across the Sego mountains to the Mphogodiba mountains where they made contact with the Molepo people. Following custom, the Mojapelos introduced themselves to the Molepo chief, to whom they were required to pay tribute. They did this for some time, co-existing "uncomfortably" with the Molepos,[8] before they decided to move on.

Ramakanyane I gave birth to a son called Kwena I or Leshalagae, who was responsible for most royal matters during this time. He married at GaRamakalela now known as Mohwelereng-Sebobeng. All kraals were asked to contribute cattle for Kwena I to marry the mother of the tribe (*Ngwana* Ramakalela). She gave birth to Kwena II. The Mojapelos realized that the Ramakalelas were weak in comparison with themselves, and when they left the Molepos, they subordinated the Ramakalelas and established themselves in the area now known as Laastehoop. Ramakanyane I died there and was buried at Teejane. The Mojapelos moved on from there to Sebobeng where they stayed at a place called Meumo.[9] They encountered another ethnic group there, the Kadiakas, but they were weaker than the Mojapelos who established themselves at Mohwelereng.

Contact with White Settlers and Confrontation with Neighboring Tribes

In addition to contact with other ethnic groups, the Mojapelos also made contact with the Voortrekkers during the 1830s. Evidence of this can be found in Louis Trigardt's diaries where Trigardt refers to the "Mapielie" "tribe" who pilfered some of his goats (Le Roux 1964:96). Dicke, writing in 1941, interprets the incident in the following way:

> What tribe was it which had the impertinence to seize the Voortrekkers' goats? The tribe of Mapielie...Who then is this chief "Mapielie"? His correct name is Mojapelo...Mojapelo was a petty chief. He never had more than two hundred and fifty warriors. But the country he occupied was of such difficult nature that he was able to uphold his independence, and he repeatedly defeated raids made by Zulus or Swazis. These raiders hardly ever managed even to drive off some of the Mojapelo livestock. The men, women and children would take refuge on impregnable, fortified koppies, from which boulders and stones would be rolled and thrown down, and the livestock would be secreted in a maze of inaccessible creeks and crevices, in which anybody trying to steal the animals would be ambushed with little hope of escaping. That was the kind of country where Trigardt did not think it wise to press his claim for lifted stock. (Dicke 1941:115)

More importantly, he goes on to state that:

> Mojapelo's territory was small. It covered what later became the farms Matjeskraal (346), Palmietfontein (343), Klipspruit (351), and Kleinfontein (347). These farms form a wild mountain complex that rises out of the surrounding flat. To Mojapelo's territory belonged the slopes which descend from the four farms into the adjoining farms, for example, down to Majebaskraal (145) eastward and Weltervreden (140) north westward...Mojapelo's chief kraal was at Majebaskraal. One of his strongholds was the Matjiani Kop at Matjeskraal. The name Matjieskraal is a corruption of "Matjiana's Kraal"...The Sterkloopspruit is the boundary of the Amandebele (from Maune) and Mojapelo. (Dicke 1941:115-116 & 126)

In the meantime, the Mojapelos interacted with a number of other ethnic groups beside the Molepos and the Ramakalelas, and some of these interactions were confrontational, particularly with the Mothibas. Confrontation was generally generated by pasturage trespassing, whereby cattle from one or the other ethnic group would wander into grazing lands of a neighboring group. During one confrontation with the Mothibas, the Mojapelos killed a Mothiba woman, signifying the beginning of ongoing animosity between the two ethnic groups, when the Mothibas pledged vengeance for their deceased (Dicke 1941:115-116 & 126). The result was that Kwena III was ambushed by the Mothibas on his return from a journey to Matome (Zebediela), and killed at Mmabolepu pass. The animosity between the two groups then reached extreme proportions. The Mojapelos also fought against the various Ndebele groups such as the Maune whom they defeated, as well as against Chief Malebogo who was fighting against the Voortrekkers. The Mojapelos fought on the side of the Voortrekkers (Mojapelo [n.d.]:17).

Griffiths written history of the Mojapelos and oral accounts suggest that the Mojapelos were completely oblivious to the fact that the Boer Colonial Government of the Transvaal Republic, enacted legislation through its Volksraad in 1853 which prohibited Africans from owning land in the Transvaal, while permitting whites to demarcate plots for themselves and declare themselves landowners. Although it has been claimed that "farms were only surveyed and given names after the formation of the old Transvaal Government in 1852,"[10] Trapido has argued that a partial land market existed "from the beginning of white Afrikaner occupation of the territory north of the Vaal River" (Trapido 1980:350). Certainly, one would be painting a false historical picture of the Transvaal in the mid-19th century were one to argue that once the process of land titling began, whites established neat and clearly demarcated farms. Rather land was accumulated and held for speculation purposes by Afrikaner notables and land companies owned by South African-based entrepreneurs with European financial connections (Trapido 1980:350). Indeed, between 1850 and 1876, the period when title deeds were first issued in Mojapelo territories, land was used to secure debts by the Transvaal Volksraad which, in view of its inability to secure revenue, also engaged in financial manipulations involving the provision of land in lieu salaries for administrators and the issuing of exchequer bills secured by government farms. In 1865, paper currency, also secured by government farms was issued, but this was insufficient to match government expenditure, and a 1868 finance commission proposed that additional notes should only be issued against one thousand farms or 3 million morgen (Trapido 1980:352). The upshot of all of this is that land was continually being subdivided and changing hands, in many cases without whites actually occupying the land. This becomes evident when examining the title deeds of the farms surrounding the Mojapelo royal kraal at Mmaboi on Majebaskraal. It also explains why according to Mojapelo oral history, the first white to settle Majebaskraal was Granville Nicholson, despite the fact that the land was originally registered in the name of SJ Marais (Nicholson's father-in-law) in May 1865 (Department of Land Affairs 1995:5).

Tenancy Relations, Evictions, Resistance and the Dispersal of the Mojapelo

Nicholson was issued the title deed in 1893, although Ellen Nicholson (b. 1890) was buried at Mmaboi in February 1892. Freddy Swafo, born ca 1906, remembers having grown up in an era when agriculture was vigorously practiced by the Mojapelos who grew sorghum, millet and maize on unmeasured fields with abundant land at their disposal. According to his testimony, Nicholson arrived on the farm shortly before the Anglo-Boer War. He was not sure whether he negotiated with the chief, but asserted that Nicholson measured out fields for himself and drew the Mojapelos into labor tenancy relations.[11]. The ruling chief at the time was Gilbert Mojapelo, whose relationship with Nicholson was generally cordial. A conflict was precipitated in 1928, however, when a certain individual cut the fence. Nicholson tried to find out who the culprit was, and eventually summoned the chief. Gilbert took responsibility for the incident which was actually perpetrated by his father-in-law Joel's children, as he did not want to expose his in-laws to Nicholson.[12] Nicholson then evicted the chief. Most of Gilbert's subjects elected to follow him, while only a few remained on at Mmaboi. This led to the dispersal of the Mojapelos.

Gilbert and some of his followers went to Kleinfontein. Some went to work for other white farmers, while others went to Pretoria and Johannesburg. Some ended up under the jurisdiction of other chiefs including Molepo, Mphahlele, Mashashane, Moletji, Matome, Maja and Mothiba. A sizeable grouping returned to the Zebediela area where the ethnic group originated and settled at Moletlane. These movements should be understood as forms of "covert" resistance to the practices of labor tenancy and the dominance of certain parts of the countryside by racist white farmers. The history of the Transvaal in South Africa, as elsewhere in Africa, has entailed bitter struggles between rural people and forces committed to extracting surpluses in the form of labor, rent, taxes and food. While Beinart and Bundy's studies of the Transkei and Ciskei provide an analysis of some of these processes in Eastern Cape (Beinart and Bundy 1987), these forms of resistance have not been thoroughly documented in the Transvaal. The cutting of the fence, and the resultant Mojapelo exodus, however, must be cast in this light and seen as acts of resistance to the forces of white domination.

Indeed Mojapelo resistance to and mistrust of white rule took other forms which contributed to their dispossession and landlessness. The Mojapelos did not attend the meeting of chiefs convened by the Union Government in 1910. According to Thomas Mothipa Mojapelo:

> In 1910, chiefs were called to Bloemfontein after the formation of the Union of South Africa to be allocated their chiefdoms and boundaries in order to avoid further tribal wars. Since Mothipa (Gilbert) never went, we were denied our tribal land rights. People did not want Mothipa to go since they feared that he would be ambushed and killed like Kwena III.[13]

Moreover, although Chief Mojapelo did release a handful of his men for service during World War I, he declined an invitation to Pretoria after the war when the Pretoria Government summoned chiefs who had contributed to the war effort in order to be given lands as a gesture of gratitude and compensation (Mojapelo [n.d.]:19). Once again, Chief Mojapelo did not go to Pretoria due to fears on the part of his councillors that he would be ambushed on the way. The failure of the Mojapelos to attend these meetings may well explain why the Union government failed to formally recognize the Mojapelo chieftaincy and allocate them land. The question of the legitimacy of the Mojapelo chieftaincy (as discussed below) has become a major issue for present counter-claimants to Mojapelo territory.

While Gilbert was in Kleinfontein, the Central Government promised him a place to stay. Philip Petja was born at Mmaboi in 1928, but moved to Kleinfontein shortly after his birth following the eviction of the Mojapelos by Nicholson. At the time, the farm was registered under "The South African Townships, Mining and Finance Corporation Limited" (Department of Land Affairs 1995). Petja's testimony reveals how many registered 'landowners' in the Transvaal were absentee landlords. Kleinfontein, was originally registered on 5 July 1886 in the name of Johannes du Preez, and ownership subsequently changed hands several times before the farm was transferred to Jozua Naude on 30 April 1940 (Department of Land Affairs 1995). According to Petja no whites actually occupied the farm before Naude, although the Mojapelo subjects used to pay 1 shilling tax per head of cattle. He described how he grew up and became a labor tenant at Kleinfontein:

> I was born in Mmaboi, but moved to Kleinfontein when I was very young. There was a German man called Makurukuru staying in Pietersburg who administered the various farms.[14]

Kleinfontein was under the Mojapelo chiefs, and old man Mothipa (Gilbert) was the chief at the time. My parents had abundant land and we cultivated sorghum, maize, millet, groundnuts and beans. We kept a lot of cattle, more than was necessary. Mr Naude arrived in 1942. He stayed with us, and made arrangements with the tribal elders at Kleinfontein to do so. Naude cultivated tobacco and he kept dairy cattle. People living at Kleinfontein were compelled to work for him. They worked for "*sommer*". Their parents forced them to accept tenancy relations because they were old and could not do much labor themselves. Naude told us that we must work for him because he had bought the farm from Makurukuru in Pietersburg, and he forced us to become labor tenants. We continued to cultivate our own lands. We stayed with Naude until 1962 before leaving. Between 1942 and 1962, many people left the farm. Naude told them to leave as he did not want overcultivation on his farm, and they should get off his land. This was an ongoing and gradual process. In 1962, 5 families remained on the farm. They told Naude that he had found them there, and that it was their historical place and they were not going to move from there. Naude came with lorries at the end of 1962, and forced the people off the land and dumped them at Klipspruit.[15]

Gilbert moved from Kleinfontein before the arrival of Naude, after the government promised him refuge in Vaalfontein in 1938. Vaalfontein was transferred to the South African Native Trust on 26 July 1937, but was not formally handed over to the Mojapelos. In July 1957, Government Notice No 1102 included the Trust Farm Vaalfontein No. 418 (now 179 KS) in the area of the Molepo Tribal Authority (Department of Land Affairs 1995).

When Gilbert was issued a *trekpas* by Nicholson, not all the Mojapelos moved off. Mac Kgadi Mojapelo born ca. 1914-1918, during the war and the great locust invasion of the area, gave the following account:

> When I was young, we lived in Mmaboi growing sorghum and millet. *Matialla* (literally "hit until they cry") Nicholson was living here. The relationship between us was bad because our people were performing unpaid labor for him...When the fence was cut, I was staying with my brother at Moletje looking after his cattle. I was still young when I returned, but people were still working for nothing. People were still moving away from Nicholson, some because they were fired, others in resistance to the unfair work relation. Between 1938-39, we moved away to Mahuma (Matjeskraal). We found a certain boer called

"Masemola" who allocated us land and allowed us to keep our cattle, but once again the snag was the labor tenancy relation which forced us to work for "*sommer*". Ultimately I was issued with a *trekpas* and moved to Manthoroane (Quayle) where I stayed until we eventually moved back to Mmaboi.[16]

These narratives demonstrate how the Mojapelo's were pressured by the existing status quo (white land ownership and associated social relations) to move around the broad area of the Mojapelo community lands in an attempt to cling to their tenuous access to land rights. They also demonstrate the complex character of forced removals, which in many cases were not a single event, but rather a protracted process. An additional pressure upon them was the failure of both the central government and bantustan government of Lebowa to recognize the Mojapelos as an ethnic grouping with their own sovereign chief.

The Struggle by the Mojapelos for Ethnic Recognition and their "Back to the Land" Campaign

In 1935, the respected Government Ethnologist N.J. Van Warmelo published his *Preliminary Survey of the Bantu Tribes of South Africa*. In this survey, he lists the Mojapelo as an independent tribe ("*baHlalerwa, baxaMojapelo*") with their own chief and own totem ("*lehlalerwa*"), residing in the Pietersburg district (Van Warmelo 1935:115). The dispossession of the Mojapelo land has been associated with the loss of their ethnic identity. It has already been observed that the Mojapelos generally engaged in covert forms of resistance to the undemocratic government regimes of the Transvaal Republic and the Union of South Africa and all associated discriminatory forms of legislation. Thus although they participated minimally in World War I, their suspicion of the existing regime led them to decline an invitation to Pretoria in the aftermath of the war. The decision by the Molepos to participate with government structures explains why the apartheid government and its apparatuses attempted to subordinate the Mojapelos to the Molepos, and the animosity between the two groups to which this gave rise. The case of Vaalfontein, as we shall see provides a good example of this.

The role of the chieftaincy within customary land relations facilitates an understanding of why issues of chieftainship have become embroiled within the Mojapelo's struggle to reclaim their land rights. In 1962, the Mojapelos organized a committee to reclaim their land. This committee consisted of the following members:

Chairman: Schoeman Mojapelo
Secretary: John Mashiane

Organiser: Johannes Mojapelo
Additional: Dace Mojapelo
         Mafeufeu Mojapelo
         Magomatlodi Mojapelo
         Mathena Meekoa (Mojapelo [n.d.]:23)

The community took their land petition to the Native Commissioner in Pietersburg in 1962. He was assisted by a number of chiefs, including Chief Chuene, Chief Tseke, Chief Maboa and Chief Molepo. With no response forthcoming, the committee appealed to the central government in Pretoria in writing. They then sent a delegation directly to Pretoria who met with a Mr Bothma from Native Affairs. Bothma sent his fieldworker, Dr Wiid, to investigate whether the Mojapelo people did indeed constitute a chiefdom recognised by government. His report included a genealogy which recognised the Mojapelos and their claim to a chiefdom.[17]

Any progress which the Mojapelos believed they were making in their negotiations with the apartheid central government, were reversed, however, when Lebowa obtained self-governing status in 1972 under Chief M. M. Matlala. The Lebowa government wrote a letter to the Mojapelos stating:

> With reference to your plea or request for chieftaincy and land, we would like to inform you that we reject and do not recognize your chief and therefore you are not liable to any such piece of land as a sovereign. You are requested to return to the jurisdiction of the Matebeles under Kekana. Those who wish to remain behind must be ruled by Molepo. (Mojapelo [n.d.]:23)

In 1974, the Chief Minister of Lebowa, Chief Phatudi, met with a delegation of the Mojapelos who accounted for their genealogy. Phatudi and his secretary accused the Mojapelos of fabricating their genealogy, although they promised them that they would investigate the whole issue and speak to Chief Kekana. The Lebowa government then agreed to allocate the Mojapelos land if they would elect a leader, but not a chief, instructing them to owe allegiance to either Chief Kekana or Chief Molepo (Mojapelo [n.d.]:26). In 1978, the Lebowa government decided to allocate the Mojapelos a portion of Mothibaskraal (Majebaskraal) while another was allocated to the University of the North for Agricultural Research.[18]

Controversy surrounding the Mojapelo chieftaincy continued, however, and following the implementation of the 1978 decision in 1985, a series of meetings and exchanges between the Mojapelos and the Lebowa government took place. Essentially, these exchanges centered on whether the Mojapelos would be assigned community or ethnic authority status. At a community meeting attended by Mr MF Chuene from the department of the Governor of Lebowa, he told the Mojapelos that:

> Mojapelo wanted *bogoshi* (chieftaincy) even before the existence of the Lebowa government. The Republican Government never gave Mojapelo *bogoshi* and thereafter withdrew *bogoshi* from him. I want to emphasize that the government is not in a position to give Mojapelo *bogoshi* and does not refuse to do so. One can have a rubber stamp and say that he is a *kgoshi* (chief) but he may not have an official appointment. Mojapelo did deserve *bogoshi* but was not given *bogoshi*. I am not here to force the Mojapelo people to accept a community authority but I say the government is prepared to give the Mojapelo people a community authority in order to build up the Mojapelo people.[19]

Nevertheless, the Lebowa Government went ahead, and in August 1988, established the Mojapelo Community Authority, with jurisdiction over Portion 1 of the farm Majebaskraal No 1005 LS (Lebowa Government, Republic of South Africa 1988). The Mojapelos took legal advice and with the assistance of Bell, Dewar & Hall attempted to contest the establishment of the Community Authority. In reply to letters sent by the Mojapelo lawyers, the Lebowa government stated:

> According to our records these people (the Mojapelos) never had any *bogoshi* in the past; a search for it prior to the establishment of the community authority, even in the records of the Department of Development Aid, was all in vain. We could therefore be pleased if we could be supplied with a copy in terms of which the alleged *bogoshi* was established. Whereas it would not be difficult for the government to disband the community authority as requested in the penultimate paragraph of your letter, it would nonetheless take such a step at the express and specific request of the community as a whole and on the express understanding that such a dissolution of the community authority may not in itself result in the institution of *bogoshi* in the place of the community authority.[20]

Further correspondence between the two parties continued, but the matter remained unresolved. It did, however, generate divisions within the Mojapelos between pro- and anti-Lebowa Government groups, divisions which the post-apartheid land claim process seems to have to some extent overcome.[21]

The Mojapelo Land Claim

The Mojapelo's land claim rests on the notion that historical ethnic boundaries should be restored, because racially based discriminatory colonial land law and the 1913 Land Act led to the systematic erosion of their community's land rights and converted them into labor tenants. Moreover, it should be recognised that forced removals in this area, were not an event, but an ongoing process. This process was characterized by the arrival of white settlers who demarcated plots and coerced local villagers into working on their farms as labor tenants and sharecroppers. Some villagers fled the area to avoid "working for *sommer*," while others preferred to stay, but were later removed by farmers who cut down and rationalized their labor force over time, and issued "surplus laborers" with _trekpasse_.

Figure 14.1: Farms Being Claimed by the Mmaboi Community in Pietersburg

Names European	African	Size (ha)	New Num.	Occupation
Matjeskraal	Mamasolo Dithabeng	4,081.6106	1047	White farmer
Mathibaskraal	GaMmaboi Sepobeng	8,998.3445	1002	Partially occupied by the Mojapelos
Klipspruit	Makgobaneng	3,636.3580	178	White farmer, rents out to local villagers
Kleinfontein	Maphosane	3,737.9722	172	White farmer absentee. Land leased to local Farmers.
Palmietfontein	Gakganyago Motokolo	3,407.5352	1049	White small holdings
Kuil/Quayle	Mmatharoane	299.3222	180	State owned, allocated to chief Molepo, semi-occupied by his subjects
Vaalfontein	Dipshiring Mokudutswaneng	602.9985	179	State owned, allocated to chief Molepo, used for grazing

Table 4.1: con'd

Kraalfontein	Konyama	681.6653	181	Semi-occupied by chief Molepo
Laastehoop	Sekuto, Sekgophaneng	5,960.6132	1050	Occupied by Chief Molepo
Kalkfontein	Mahuma	5,654.6132	1001	All 53 portions privately operated
Tweefontein	Tshweung	659.9379	173	White farmer
Grysfontein	Marakudu	291.7605	176	Used by white farmers for pasturage

Table 14.2: Title Deeds of Farms Being Claimed by the Mmaboi
Community

Name of Farm	Current Owner
Matjeskraal 1047	AP Bolon
Matjeskraal (portion 1)	Agsam Pty, Ltd.
Matjeskraal (Portion 2)	Roman Catholic Missions of N Tvl
Mathibaskraal (Majebaskraal)	Gov't. of Lebowa
Klipspruit	HM Van Aswegen JH Van Aswegen
Kleinfontein	Portions 1,2,3,5,6, and 7 owned by white farmers; a subdivision of portion 2, Portion 4 was transfered to the State in 1956, and to Chief Maja in 1994
Palmietfontein	KS Van Eeden
Quayle	Gov't. of Lebowa,* transferred to Chief Molepo
Vaalfontein	Gov't. of Lebowa,* transferred to Chief Molepo
Kraalfontein	Gov't. of Lebowa,* transferred to Chief Molepo
Laastehoop	Gov't. of Lebowa,* transferred to Chief Molepo
Kalkfontein	HH Dales
Tweefontein	Portion 1: JM Van der Walt Remainder: PJ Van Niekerk
Grysfontein	Anton Bothma

*   These farms do not appear to have been transferred from SADT
    to the Lebowa Gov't. They have the same title deeds indicat-
    ing that there must have been an endorsement made on the title
    deeds in terms of statute passed.

Figure 14.3: How the Majapelo Claim Overlaps with
Neighboring Community Claims

Mojapelo Claim	Maja	Mothiba	Mothapo	Molepo
Matjeskraal	* (1 portion)	-	-	-
Majebaskraa	-	*	*	-
Klipspruit	*	-	-	*
Kleinfontein	*	-	-	*
Palmietfontein	*	-	-	-
Quayle	-	-	-	*
Vaalfontein	-	-	-	* occupants
Kraalfontein	-	-	-	* occupants
Laastehoop	-	-	*	* occupants
Kalkfontein	-	*	- occupants	- occupants
Tweefontein	-	-	-	-
Grysfontein	*	-	-	-

* Denotes a land claim by a particular group.

As noted, the 1962 "back to the land" campaign initiated by the Mojapelos under the leadership of Schoeman Mojapelo, culminated in their return to a portion of Mathibaskraal at Mmaboi in 1985. Nevertheless, the Mojapelos are claiming a far more extensive area. Table 14.1 and 14.2 list the names, numbers, size and current occupation of the farms being claimed. From the perspective of the Mojapelos, the Mojapelo chief is reclaiming ethnic land rights, which were expropriated through colonial land legislation, as well as the 1913 Land Act, on behalf of the Mojapelo community. The Land Restitution Act defines "right in land" as

> any right in land whether registered or unregistered, and may include the interest of a labor tenant and sharecropper, a customary law interest, the interest of a beneficiary under a trust arrangement and beneficial occupation for a continuous period of not less than 10 years prior to the dispossession in question. (Republic of South Africa 1994b:3)

The right in land which the Mojapelos are claiming pertains to a customary law interest, and/or the interest of a labor tenant, although the claim itself is framed in the former sense. The drawback here, is the cut-off date in the constitution, because although their removal as labor-tenants took place in 1928 and therefore qualifies for a claim, their communal rights were effectively nullified when the process of land titling began.

A further problem with the claim is that it overlaps with claims of neighboring communities. This became evident in a meeting convened by the Regional Land Claims commission in Pietersburg on 14 December 1995, involving the Mojapelos, the Majas, the Mothibas, the Mothapos and the Molepos. All groups are claiming extensive lands, with particular farms being claimed by two or more communities. Table 14.3 illustrates the extent of the overlapping claims in relation to the Mojapelo Land Claim.

Figure 14.1: The Mojapelo Land Claim

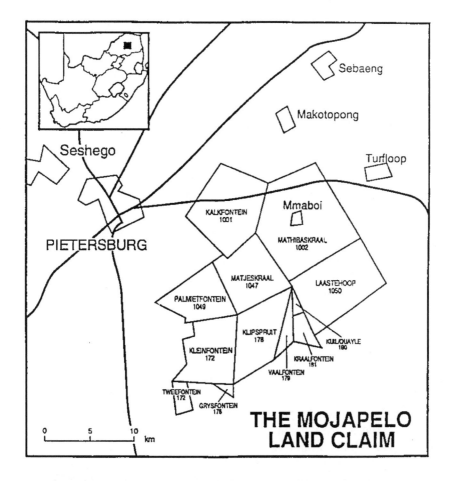

In its attempts to mediate between counter-claiming communities, the Regional Land Claims Commission was able to make some progress in terms of developing a clearer understanding of the Mojapelo claim, a certain amount of progress in clarifying whether or not overlapping claims actually existed, and less progress in terms of facilitating co-operation between different land claiming communities. One solution sought was to attempt to define areas being claimed in terms of their Sotho names, but this line of negotiation yielded little once in the field, where communities themselves ended up deliberating about the farms using the European names, although constant references were made to Sotho names of rivers and mountains.

A major issue which emerged was the status of the Mojapelos, their lack of a recognised chief, and the absence of the Queen Regent in the negotiating process. Chief Molepo made this point very strongly, and during field visits undertaken with the Regional Land Claims Commission to disputed farms, referred to the Mojapelos as his subjects and "children."[22]

The field visits did demonstrate quite clearly, however, very consistent accounts of Mojapelo history by their various informants. In the case of counter-claimants, the historical accounts rendered were generally less coherent, leaving the impression that land was in cases being claimed in order to meet land needs rather than for purposes of restitution. Chief Molepo openly stated that: "We are claiming Kleinfontein and Klipspruit because there are many of us and we need to expand the area of land at our disposal. The farms are vacant and adjacent to our own farms."[23]

When the claim was being prepared, the Mojapelo Development Association was asked whether they want to proceed with claims to particular farms that were allocated to and occupied by other black people, with particular reference to Laastehoop. Patrick Mojapelo replied, saying:

> We want to claim all our land to reassert the Mojapelos rights to the soil. If for example, people under Chief Molepo do not want to accept that authority which our rights will give us, they can leave. If they are happy to owe allegiance to the Mojapelos and accept our authority, they can gladly remain.[24]

The account of Mojapelo history provided above does demonstrate that during the 19th century, the Mojapelos settled on Laastehoop before shifting their headquarters to Mmaboi. At the same time, there is no disputing the fact that the Molepos and the Mothapos were allocated portions of Laastehoop in 1922, and that both portions are now densely populated.

The cases of Quayle, Kraalfontein and Vaalfontein are different, however. All these farms feature in the Mojapelo history, and also represent pieces of state land through which the Mojapelo royal family passed following the eviction of Gilbert and others from Majebaskraal. They also are pieces of land which the Mojapelos were denied secure access to as resisters of the status quo of white domination of land relations, and which the Molepos were ultimately allocated as participants in apartheid structures. This becomes clear from the following Mojapelo account of the history of these lands:

> When the white man came here, he defeated us, but because Schoeman (the initiator of the "back to the land campaign") refused to work on the farms he left. He found Mojapelo subjects tilling the soil and grazing their cattle as far as Vaalfontein. Even these three farms (Vaalfontein, Kraalfontein and Quayle) were later occupied by whites. Later they were turned into trust lands. Gilbert was then in Kleinfontein. Government officials told him to go and stay in Vaalfontein. When we got there, we were not under any chief except our own. Later on we heard that Quayle, Vaalfontein and Kraalfontein were given to Molepo. The government told us that if Molepo is our chief we should obey him; if he is not, we should not. Chief Molepo insisted that we are his subjects and sent his messengers to Vaalfontein. They found the Mojapelo guards there. They told the Molepos not to enter, but to go and fetch their chief. Chief Molepo refused to come. Chief Gilbert never paid his levies to Chief Molepo, and Gilbert himself was a poor man. He rode in a donkey cart. When we lived in Vaalfontein, the place was inaccessible by roads and had no services like schools and clinics. We then left the place for Quayle. It is true that Molepo's subjects the Molemas herded their cattle there, but they did so illegally, as it was not yet a trust farm. No one forced us to leave Quayle, but the government gave us back our original place of chieftainship (Mmaboi). The Molepos are telling the truth when they say that the government allocated these land to them in the 1960s. Now Mojapelo says that he never disappeared, he is still here and is demanding his land, despite the fact that Vaalfontein, Kraalfontein and Quayle have been given to Molepo on a silver platter.[25]

Elaborating on the Mojapelos claims to Vaalfontein and Kraalfontein, Patrick Mojapelo added:

> Because of Betterment Planning, the government wanted to move us from Vaalfontein to Kraalfontein. During those days if you wanted to work in a white area, you needed a permit from the chief. Gilbert was the one issuing those permits, but

after our land at Vaalfontein was given to Molepo, they stopped
Gilbert from issuing permits. We resisted the move from
Vaalfontein, but some of us grew tired of the back to the land
campaign and were prepared to move and live under Chief
Molepo. Kraalfontein was where Schoeman Mojapelo was staying with his followers and we have our burial sites there. That
site is used until today. Today the land belongs to Molepo because the government gave it to him. We are saying, we want
our land back. That is all.[26]

Chief Molepo's response was:

If someone is staying on one chief's land and one of his family
members dies, he will bury him on that land. If he leaves, he
will leave the grave behind. All the graves and ruins were
there when Mojapelo was under Molepo. Where you die, you
are buried. Because we believe in ancestor invoking, if your
ancestors call upon you, you will visit your ancestral lands. We
conclude. We are not claiming Vaalfontein and Kraalfontein.
They are ours.[27]

LAND RESTITUTION, THE CHIEFTAINCY, GENDER RELATIONS AND CUSTOMARY LAND LAW

Historically, chiefs have played a pivotal role in the allocation of land in
South Africa. The search for a new system of land allocation and tenure
will have to reassess the role of chiefs, taking into account their popularity
on the ground. Despite widespread opposition to the institution of the chieftaincy within certain localities during the 1980s, the ANC as leader of the
national liberation movement and leader of the new government has tended
to vacillate on the question of the future role of chiefs. In the interests of
alliance building, this hesitancy ultimately gave way to cautious support for
"progressive chiefs" and their organizations. This conciliatory position can
be traced to liberation struggle alliances forged with the Congress of Traditional Leaders of South Africa (Contralesa), a group formed in the late 1980s
comprising chiefs opposed to apartheid rule. Contralesa aligned itself with
the Mass Democratic Movement and this facilitated the subsequent formation of coalitions between the ANC and Intando Yesizwe of Kwandebele,
Inyandza of Kangwane, the UPP of Lebowa and the bantustan regimes of
Venda and Transkei. The Patriotic Front electoral alliance strengthened the
position of chiefs eager to consolidate their hold over land allocation. As
Mackintosh has observed, "rights of land allocation are certainly a central
basis of power for tribal authorities" (Mackintosh 1990:30).

Control which chiefs exert over land allocation continues to constitute the fundamental material basis of their power, and as Haines and Tapscott point out, is also the "most crucial mechanism for the interplay of corruption and control" (Haines and Tapscott 1989:169). There is widespread recognition of this in rural villages and a growing resentment at the way in which the chieftaincy, through bantustan "tribal" authority structures and its control over the allocation of land has become an increasingly oppressive and corrupt institution. Increasingly, the chieftaincy has employed extra-economic coercion to develop strategies of capital accumulation, as well as accumulation of followership and territory in order to facilitate ongoing reproduction of its hegemony. The process has been contradictory however, since extra-economic coercion has meshed with corruption and ultimately served to delegitimize the chieftaincy.

The main base of opposition to the chieftaincy in areas where it is under threat (in certain parts of the former Transvaal provinces and the Eastern Cape), is the civic movement under the aegis of the South African National Civic Association (SANCO). Nevertheless, in the run-up to local government elections in 1995, the ANC was at pains to effect reconciliation between local civics and chiefs, with President Mandela personally appealing to both sides for restraint and co-operation. This ANC ambivalence around the institutions of the chieftaincy reflects a broader ambivalence on the ground, where a thin line exists between opposition to the chieftaincy, and opposition to individual (often corrupt) chiefs.

While the alliance between the ANC and progressive chiefs has been predicated upon a pragmatic politics of building electoral support, ANC branch and civic structures have clashed with the chiefs in their struggle for the control over political space. In some areas, including within the Northern Province, chiefs treat the land as part of their personal fiefdom, breeding conflict at the grassroots. This poses a major challenge to ANC provincial cadre:

> As the ANC, we do not have a clear position with regards to the chiefs. We are avoiding the issue. It is sensitive in the sense that chiefs regard themselves as the sole owners of the land. This is why SANCO and ANC structures on the ground are in conflict with the chiefs. The chiefs do not want to part with the land. The question often becomes: who is going to allocate the land for development. In one case, Eskom was ready to embark on a project following negotiations with the people. But when Eskom wanted to implement the project, the chief said he did not know anything about it.[28]

Debates around the role of chiefs in local government and land allocation also impinge directly on women's issues, and if the restitution process is likely to reinforce and help restore the institutions of the chieftaincy, then key questions around gender relations and land access emerge. As in the case of the majority of sub-Saharan land tenure systems, women's access to land is tenuous and contingent upon husbands and/or male kin. As noted above, the Land Claims Court is empowered to influence land rights on restituted land and to take steps to ensure that:

> ...all the dispossessed members of the community concerned shall have access to the land or compensation in question, on a basis which is fair and non-discriminatory towards any person, including a woman and a tenant, and which ensures the accountability of the person who holds the land or compensation on behalf of the community to the members of such a community. (Republic of South Africa 1994b)

The RDP itself recognizes the problems of women's land rights. It states:

> Women face specific disabilities in obtaining land. The land redistribution programme must therefore target women. Institutions, practices and laws that discriminate against women's access to land must be reviewed and brought in line with national policy. In particular, tenure and matrimonial laws must be revised appropriately (African National Congress 1994:21).

While legislators and policy makers should be commended for the attention given to women's land rights, the experience of other countries suggests that these cannot be guaranteed through legislation or policy alone. They can only be realized through organization aimed at ending women's oppression.

The lack of land rights is central to an understanding of women's oppression in the South African countryside. The evolution of customary tenure under colonialism to the present, has meant that land is allocated to male household heads through the practice of owing allegiance to a chief, or through inheritance where eldest sons are the major beneficiaries. Customary law must of course be understood as continually being recreated and redefined, and deployed to preserve aspects of existing relations, while serving to legitimize and reproduce relations created under colonialism and apartheid. At the same time, customary law must be seen as highly contested, and in the case of land, an ongoing site of gender conflict. In South Africa, the acute landlessness generated by the process of forced removals has meant that women in black rural areas are particularly hard hit. While in the bantustans, as elsewhere in Africa, women are able to generate strategies at a local level to secure tenuous access to land, this is no solution to the problem. Under conditions of transition, opportunities for a fundamental restructuring of land tenure systems which will be free from gender discrimination are arising.

The Department of Land Affairs has created a joint directorate of Land Restitution, Tenure and Land Administration Reform, so that the institutions are in place to transform tenure relations and restructure gendered relations of land access and control. The foregoing analysis of *The Restitution of Land Rights Act* also suggests that conditions are now present for the judiciary to intersect with customary legal processes around land in order to contest gender discrimination. This cannot, however, be left to the courts on their own. Institutions can only be effective if participation on the ground, within civil society is facilitated. Political mobilization and organization of social forces is a necessary condition for achieving this. The prognosis is not good, however, as demobilization has followed the 1994 general elections in a context where, historically, relatively little emphasis has been placed on rural mobilization by the national liberation movement. Post-liberation, the ANC has been sensitive to women's issues, and guaranteed 30% representation for women on its parliamentary lists. While this has given women significant representation in Parliament, it has also drained the women's movement of some of its most dynamic leadership. Moreover, in keeping with the general trends in South African politics, the women's movement has tended to be stronger in urban than in rural areas. Despite the existence of a plethora of women's rural groupings, these have rarely made an impact on mainstream politics. This is a general problem, identified by South African Communist Party (SACP) Central Committee member and ANC MP, Jenny Schreiner:

> Part of our problem is that we have failed to take gender into the mainstream of politics. (That voice) has been replaced by strong women's lobbies and voices heard at the policy-making level, which means we are empowering each other instead of women at the grassroots. It's elitist. (*Weekly Mail and Guardian* 1995)

Overcoming this elitism will be crucial if spaces opened up by the new political dispensation will lead to an organized onslaught by the women's movement on gendered access to land in South Africa.

The importance of this reaches down to Mmaboi village. Skosana Mongalo is a 42-year-old villager interviewed in February 1995. She said that the ANC had not been active in the village since the April 1994 elections. "The ANC is weak here, it has minimum involvement with people" she said, adding that land "is a central aspiration here. If people had access to land, they could use it for pasturage and cropping". She expressed concern over existing systems of land allocation, complaining that she had approached the chief for agricultural land but heard no response. She also argued that in future, land should be allocated by democratically elected village committees, "since the chief is not responsive to the people's needs", and observed that "women need to be recognised as farmers and should be the first to benefit from land reform since they have been discriminated against in the past."[29]

Interestingly enough, when the Mojapelo community was grappling with the issue of whether to agree to establish a community authority, or to push for their demand of recognition of their *bogoshi*, it was women who swayed the vote: "We have voted twice (for *bogoshi* or a community authority). It was said that we should choose between *bogoshi* and a community authority. Women outnumbered us and they wanted a community authority."[30] The women's vote must be seen in the context of the relationship between the chieftaincy, land rights and gender, where the changing role of the chieftaincy and definitions of customary law under colonial rule and apartheid, precluded the idea of women as landowners. While this denial was absolute, there was, more broadly, an ambivalence surrounding land ownership rights of Africans in general. Martin Chanock argues that:

> There is a profound connection between the use of the chieftaincy as an institution of colonial government and the development of the customary law of land tenure. The development of the concept of a leading customary role for chiefs with regard to the ownership and allocation of land was fundamental to the evolution of the paradigm of customary tenure. (Chanock 1991:64)

With chiefs at the heart of colonial constructions of customary land tenure, rights to land were only secured through political allegiance to the chieftaincy and teritoriality (Chanock 1991:64). In a democratic South Africa, with constitutional recognition of indigenous land rights established, the new government will have to "disentangle indigenous land rights" from this colonial legacy (Klug 1995:4). But this legacy in turn carries with it a double bind: the link between land rights and political allegiance, and the political subjugation of Africans, meant that through colonialism and later apartheid, Africans lost both property and land rights outside of reserve territory. This leads Klug to ask whether "the refusal to recognize a right of indigenous ownership is not merely an extension of the original refusal to recognize any rights at all" (Klug 1995:41).

The need for a redefinition of property rights becomes crucial for South Africa if the *Restitution of Land Rights Act*, is going to succeed as a land reform mechanism, and overcome its fundamental weakness: the 1913 cut-off date. The Mojapelo land claim has been contested by white land owners on the basis that:

> Registered full ownership includes all land rights and it excludes the rights of all other people to the land in question. If the Mojapelos ever had land rights to any of these farms (which is denied) they lost it [sic.] completely between 1864 and 1889. Their alleged dispossession is nowhere near the cut off date of 19 June 1913.[31]

The argument goes further to claim that the eviction of the Mojapelos in 1928 by Granville Nicholson "had nothing whatsoever to do with any discriminating law. The angry Mr Nicholson merely exercised his common law rights as a registered land owner."[32] Within this conception of colonial law and history, Mojapelo territory was "occupied by well established white farmers long before the turn of the century."[33]

This romantic view of settler colonial history contains within it bourgeois conceptions of property and common law, which although sufficiently flexible to incorporate a variety of tenure forms including joint ownership and sectional title, have persistently viewed the land rights of indigenous people as "falling short of ownership" (Klug 1995:41). This means that in order for land restitution to succeed, fierce legal battles will have to be fought over what constitutes a "right in land," in order to ensure that white South Africa's antiquated absolute concepts of ownership of property are turned around to incorporate both registered and unregistered rights in land.[34]

CONCLUSION

During the early 1960s, Chief Molepo attempted to assert his authority over the Mojapelos, who resisted these attempts by refusing to pay their communal levy to him. According to Fixwell Mojapelo, "Chief Molepo then started collecting Mojapelo people's Identity Documents (IDs) because of their refusal to pay the tribal levy. Then the chief threatened to shoot, because people resisted this."[35] Patrick Mojapelo continued the account:

> The day when the chief came to collect the IDs, I found him at Quayle having collected the IDs. Because we approached in numbers, the chief got into his car and left. At some distance

they stopped and the chief got out of the car with a gun in his hand. I was there with women and children and told them to pick up stones. The chief then got into his car and left.[36]

One of the unintended consequences of the *Restitution of Land Rights Act* appears to be the revival of ethnic identities and conflicts through the central role which chiefs are playing in land claims.[37] With the power of chiefs being based on the control of land, territory and followership this is not altogether surprising, but it does not bode well for a democratic land claims process.

This paper has argued that the act is a step forward in providing opportunities for the dispossessed to reclaim their land rights. Nevertheless, the process entailed in the act is problematic, because it does not allow for sufficient participation by the communities involved. When the Mojapelos first sought to pursue their land claim, they were advised by the Regional Director of the Department of Land Affairs to go and put all necessary information together, without being offered any assistance in terms of clarifying what kind of information was required for them to lodge their claim.[38] Without any clear guidelines of how to do this, the community was disempowered, and began to seek the assistance of outside agencies. The claim was submitted to the Regional Land Claims Commission and gazetted, but the notice was later withdrawn, since the Regional Land Claims Commissioner had overlooked certain rules in issuing the notice, and the court required more information. The legal process has proved to be tricky and complicated and has alienated members of the community attempting to pursue the claim. The prospects for community participation in the process are extremely remote.

Land needs of the dispossessed are complex and diverse, but the restitution process is not well suited to individuals lodging their own claims, although this is possible under the act. The question of *who* should claim is in many cases being resolved through chiefs lodging claims on behalf of their communities. This is both strengthening, and in cases resuscitating the chieftaincy, as well as generating the basis for chiefly conflict over land and territory. While restitution seeks to redress the injustices of the past, and implicitly therefore seeks to address land needs, these, in the case study area at least, are being subordinated to the legal requirements of having to prove the validity of the claim. Clearly the village of Mmaboi has land needs: there are currently about 600 households settled in the village, but only 42 of these have agricultural plots of about 1 ha in size. It can also be assumed that villagers under neighboring chiefs competing for land also have genuine land needs. There is no guarantee that a chief-led process will result in land needs being met in a democratic way; rather, as has been argued, given the patriarchal character of the chieftaincy, it is unlikely that these needs will be realized. They will more likely be met through democratic public action entailing a partnership between the state and civil society through participatory sub-regional planning.

Over and above these concerns is the need for a systematic rethinking of property rights in South Africa. Private property rights have historically been seen as absolute, while customary rights have been reformulated by colonialism and apartheid, but only been recognised in territory reserved for African occupation. The failure to recognize customary rights of occupation beyond these territories has been linked to a denial of all rights. With bourgeois property rights firmly entrenched in the constitution, current white land owners have the upper hand in the judicial process. The 1913 cut-off date does not simplify matters, and as has been argued, the history of land law and land partition in the Transvaal means that many communities continued to live on their land, oblivious to the fact that it had been demarcated as private property. Many communities claiming land will therefore find themselves being channeled to the market-led land redistribution process which is now being piloted in all nine provinces. Administrative bottlenecks are currently paralyzing this initiative as the Department of Land Affairs faces problems in transferring land, while post-transfer scenarios will pose major new challenges; but that is another story.

NOTES

1. See for example ANC Position on the Land Question (African National Congress 1991).
2. Union of South Africa, Act 27 of 1913, Section 7(3).
3. These different forms of forced removal are discussed in greater detail in Levin (1995).
4. The date fixed by Minister Hannekom was 1 May 1995.
5. The RDP prioritizes a "people-driven" development process as one of "six basic Principles" which, "linked together make up the political and economic philosophy that underlies the whole RDP" (see African National Congress 1994:5).
6. The Community Land Conference (CLC) was convened by the National Land Committee (NLC), a network of NGOs working on land and rural issues. The conference was attended by representatives from over 350 rural communities from different parts of the country. See Report from the Community Land Conference, 12 and 13 February 1994 at p. 12.
7. Interview, Monica Mojapelo, Gilbert's wife and Griffiths' mother (Previous Chieftainess), Mmaboi, 22 February 1995.
8. Interview, Patrick Mojapelo, Mathibaskraal, 19 January 1996.
9. Interview, Monica Mojapelo, 22 February 1995.

10. P. J. Steytler to Regional Land Claims Commissioner, 27 November 1995.
11. Interview, Freddy Swafo, Mmaboi, 14 February 1995.
12. Interview, Thomas Mothipa Mojapelo, Motamo, 23 February, 1995 and Monica Mojapelo, 22 February 1995.
13. Interview, Zebediela, 23 February 1995.
14. According to the Department of Land Affairs Report (1995): "In 1892 the South Western 1/4, today known as Portion 2 of Kleinfontein was transferred to BJ Vorster (Jnr) and in 1902 the Northern 3/4 (Portion 1) was transferred to WHA Cooper leaving no remainder. Cooper transferred portion 1 to "The African Farms" on 9 June 1902. On 24 January 1920 African Farms (in Liquidation) transferred to the South African Townships, Mining and Finance Corporation Limited who in turn transferred to JF Naude on 30 April 1940".
15. Interview, Mmaboi, 23 February 1995.
16. Interview, Mmaboi, 21 February 1995.
17. Report by Government Ethnologist Dr FGJ Wiid, Hoofbantoesakekomissaris, Noordelike Gebiede, K54/1525/19, 37-22, Pietersburg, 10 May 1974.
18. See Mojapelo (n.d.) who also cites Lebowa Government, Department of Foreign Affairs, D45/1524/450/1, 18/7/1978.
19. Minutes of a Meeting of the Mojapelo Group held on Friday 4 September 1987 at Mathibaskraal.
20. Lebowa Government, Office of the Department of the Chief Minister, to Bell, Dewar and Hall, 23 August 1989.
21. Interview with Barnard Mojapelo, Pietersburg, 14 February 1995.
22. Field Visit to Laastehoop with the Mojapelos, Molepos and Mothapos, 18 January 1996. He also referred to the Mothapos as his "children."
23. Ibid.
24. Group interview with Mojapelo Development Association, Mmaboi, 15 February 1995.
25. Field visit to Quayle, Vaalfontein and Kleinfontein with the Mojapelos and the Molepos, 19 January 1996.
26. Ibid.
27. Ibid.
28. Group interview with ANC Northern Province Provincial Organizers, Pietersburg, 23 February 1995.
29. Interview, Mmaboi, 14 February 1995.
30. Minutes of a Meeting of the Mojapelo Group held on Friday 4 September 1987, with Mr MF Chuene, Representative from the department of His Excellency, the Governor of Lebowa (see Mojapelo, 1987).
31. P. J. Steytler to Regional Land Claims Commissioner, 27 November 1995.
32. Ibid.
33. Ibid.
34. Of course within South Africa there is growing recognition that the ownership of landed property can no longer be understood as absolute, but in order for this to be realized in legal practice, the new legal discourses of the in-

terim and new constitutions will have to be brought to play in order to realize its potential as a powerful tool of interpreting new legislation such as the Restitution of Land Rights Act.

35. Field visit with the Molepos and the Mojapelos, Quayle, 19 January 1996.
36. Ibid.
37. It is too early to quantify this, but it is certainly true in the provinces formerly constitutive of the Transvaal. This point was made by the Regional Land Claims Commissioner for Gauteng, Mpumalanga, North-West and Northern Province, Ms Emma Mashinini, in a meeting with the Chief Land Claims Commissioner, Mr Joe Seremane, Pretoria, 7 February 1996.
38. Interview, Patrick Mojapelo, Mmaboi, 22 February 1995.

REFERENCES

African National Congress. *Position on the Land Question, Discussion Document for the ANC National Conference.* Johannesburg: African National Congress, 1991.

African National Congress. *The Reconstruction and Development Programme.* Johannesburg: Umanyano Publications, 1994.

Beinart, W. and C. Bundy. *Hidden Struggles in Rural South Africa.* Johannesburg: Ravan, 1987.

Bundy, C. *The Rise and Fall of the South African Peasantry.* London: Heinemann, 1979.

Chanock, M. "Paradigms, Policies and Property: A Review of the Customary Law of Land Tenure." In *Law in Colonial Africa,* eds. K. Mann and R. Roberts. London: James Currey, 1991.

de Wet, C. "Resettlement and Land Reform in South Africa." *Review of African Political Economy* 60(1994):359-372.

Department of Land Affairs. *Mmaboi Community (Matjeskraal 1047-LS and 10 Adjacent Farms), District of Pieteresburg, Northern Province, Report No. 66/1995.* Pieteresburg, South Africa: Department of Land Affairs, 1995.

Department of Land Affairs. *Our Land, Green Paper on South African Land Policy.* South Africa: Department of Land Affairs, 1996.

Dicke, B. H. "The Northern Transvaal Voortrekkers." In *Archives Year Book for South, African History.* Cape Town: Cape Times Limited for Government Printer, 1941.

Edwards, C. "Industrialization in South Korea." In *Industrialization and Development,* eds. T. Hewitt, H. Johnson, and D.Wield. Oxford: Oxford University Press, 1992, pp. 106ff.

Haines, R., and Tapscott, C. P. G."The Silence of Poverty: Tribal Administration and Development in Rural Transkei." In *Towards Freehold? Options for Land and Development in Black Rural Areas,* eds. C. R. Cross and R. J. Haines. Cape Town: Juta, 1989.

Jenkins, R. "Capitalist Development in the NICs." In *Capitalism and Development*, ed. L. Sklair. London: Routledge, 1994.

Keegan, T. J. *Rural Transformations in Industrializing South Africa*. Johannesburg: Ravan, 1986.

Klug, H. "Defining the Property Rights of Others: Political Power, Indigenous Tenure and the Construction of Customary Law." *Working Paper 23*. Center for Applied Legal Studies, University of the Witwatersrand, Johannesburg, 1995.

Le Roux, T. H., Die Dagboek Van Louis Trigardt, J. L. Van Schaik, Beperk, Pretoria. "waar wij voor ons vee en gelegentheid heb dat wij alsdan te rug zal keeren na Mapielie..." Unpublished paper, 1964.

Lebowa Government, Republic of South Africa. "Government Notice No R19, 26 August 1988 -- Establishment of the Mojapelo Community Authority: ThabaMoopo District." South Africa: Lebowa Government, Republic of South Africa, 1988.

Levin, R. "Land Restitution and Democracy in South Africa." Paper presented at the 8th General Assembly of CODESRIA, Dakar, June-July, 1995.

Levin, R., and D. Weiner. "The Agrarian Question and Politics in the New South Africa." *Review of African Political Economy* 57(1993):29-45.

Mackintosh, A. "Rethinking Chieftaincy and the Future of Rural Local Government: A Preliminary Investigation." *Transformation* 13(1990).

Mojapelo, Ramakanyane Griffiths. *BaGaMojapelo*. Potgietersrus: Potgietersrus Printers, n.d.

Mojapelo, Daniel. 1987. "Minutes of a Meeting of the Mojapelo Group Held on Friday 4 September 1987." Unpublished minutes, n.d.

Platzky, L. and C. Walker. *The Surplus People: Forced Removals in South Africa*. Johannesburg: Ravan Press, 1985.

Republic of South Africa.*Constitution of Republic of South Africa Act*. Pretoria: Republic of South Africa, 1994a.

Republic of South Africa. *The Restitution of Land Rights Act, Act No 22, 1994*. Pretoria: Republic of South Africa, 1994b.

Trapido, S. "Reflections on Land, Office and Wealth in the South African Republic, 1850-1900." In *Economy and Society in Pre-Industrial South Africa*, eds. S. Marks and A. Atmore. London: Longman, 1980.

Van Warmelo, N. J. *A Preliminary Survey of the Bantu Tribes of South Africa*. Union of South Africa, Department of Native affairs, Ethnological Publications, Vol. V. Pretoria: The Government Printer, 1935.

Weekly Mail and Guardian, May 5 to 11, 1995.

CONTRIBUTORS

Charles Anyinam has taught at several universities in Canada including Trent University, University of Toronto, and most recently was Assistant Professor in the African Studies Program, Founders College, at York University, Ontario. His articles on African medical geography, toxic waste dumping in Africa, and managing biomedical waste in Canada have appeared in Africanist journals and other journals such as *Social Science and Medicine, International Journal of Health Services*, and *Hospital Topics.*

F. Odun Balogun is Professor in the Department of English and Communications, Delaware State University. He has researched widely on modernism and postcoloniality in African and Russian literatures, and is the author of *Ngugi and African Post-Colonial Narrative: The Novel as Oral Narrative in Multi-Genre Performance* (1997); *Adjusted Lives: Stories of Structural Adjustments* (1995); and *Tradition and Modernity in the African Short Story: An Introduction to a Literature in Search of Critics* (1991).

Dickson Eyoh is an Assistant Professor of Political Science and Director of the African Studies Program at the University of Toronto. He is most concerned with Africanist and African discourses on development, and identity politics and nation invention in Africa. he is undertaking a study of Regionalism and Political Change in Cameroon, which is funded by the Social Science and Humanities Research Council of Canada. His recent articles on related issues have appeared in *Queen's Quarterly, African Studies Review, Research in African Literature, International Journal of African Historical Studies*, and *Journal of Contemporary African Studies.*

Wilbert (Wil) Gesler is Professor of Geography at the University of North Carolina at Chapel Hill. He is a health geographer with research interests in the spatial aspects of the delivery of health care services and the cultural geography of health care. His Ph.D. research examined the utilization of a Maternal and Child Health Care Clinic in Calabar, Nigeria, and he spent a year at Fourah Bay College, Freetown, Sierra Leone on a Fulbright scholarship, where he carried out research projects on rural accessibility to health care, utilization of a mental hospital, and patterns of mortality in Freetown. He is the author of *Health Care in Developing Countries* (1984) and *The Cultural Geography of Health Care* (1991). He is currently working on a book titled *Healing Places*. He has authored over 30 refereed journals articles or book chapters on health-related topics and is one of the editors of five health care volumes.

Lynette Jackson is an Assistant Professor of History and Pan-African Studies at Barnard College, Columbia University. She received her B.A. from Wellesley College and her M.A., M. Phil., and Ph.D. degrees from Columbia University. Her current work looks at the history and memory of colonial experience through the prism of medical and public health discourse and practice. She is currently working on a book entitled *Psychiatric Scars: The History/Memory of Ingutsheni Mental Hospital and Social Order in Colonial Zimbabwe.*

Ezekiel Kalipeni is an Assistant Professor of Geography and a member of the core faculty of the Center for African Studies at the University of Illinois at Urbana-Champaign. He holds a Ph.D. degree and a master's degree in Geography from the University of North Carolina at Chapel Hill as well as a bachelor's degree from the University of Malawi. He was recently appointed fellow in the University of Illinois' prestigious Center for Advanced Study. His research interests include the study of population dynamics such as fertility, infant mortality, migration and the interrelationships between population and the environment with special reference to Malawi and Africa in general. Some of his work has explored the spatial and cultural aspects of health care delivery systems in Africa. He has published widely on the dynamics of population change and health care issues in Africa. His most recent books are: *Population Growth and Environmental Degradation in Southern Africa* (1994); *Issues and Perspectives on Health Care in Contemporary Sub-Saharan Africa* (1997, edited with Philip Thiuri); and *AIDS, Health Care Systems and Culture in Sub-Saharan Africa: Rethinking and Re-Appraisal* (special issue of *African Rural and Urban Studies* 1998, edited with Joseph Oppong, forthcoming).

Kwaku Korang is an Assistant Professor of English and African Studies at the University of Illinois, Urbana-Champaign. His research interests cross disciplinary boundaries, taking in the areas of African and world literature, cultural modernity (especially its Pan-African mediations), literary, social and narrative theory, and postcolonial studies. He has published essays with themes that touch on all these areas, most recently "Post-Colonialism and Language," which he co-authored with Stephen Slemon, and appears in an edited collection *Writing and Africa* (1997). Currently he is working on a book on nation and African modernity.

Richard Levin is an Associate Professor in the Department of Sociology at the University of Witwatersrand, South Africa. He has published extensively in the area of agrarian change and land tenure in Southern Africa, particularly in apartheid South Africa. Some of his recent books include *Social Relations in Rural Swaziland: Critical Analyses* (1987); *Land, Food and the Politics of Agrarian Reform in South Africa* (with Daniel Weiner, 1995); *"No More Tears—": Struggles for Land in Mpumalanga, South Africa* (with Daniel Weiner, 1997). He has consulted extensively with the post-apartheid South African Government in resolving land rights issues.

Tiyanjana Maluwa was educated at the Universities of Malawi, Sheffield, and Cambridge and is Professor of Law at the University of Cape Town in South Africa, from where he is on leave while serving as the Chief Legal Counsel of the Organization of African Unity in Addis Ababa, Ethiopia. A leading authority on international law, human rights law, and refugees, he has published widely in African and European law journals. He is also the recipient of numerous awards and fellowships and has served as a consultant for various organizations.

Nkiru Nzegwu, artist, curator and poet, and Associate Professor in the Department of Philosophy and Art History at Binghamton University, is currently Senior Fellow at the Institute for the Study of Gender in Africa, UCLA, where she is completing a manuscript on feminist concepts in African philosophy of culture. She has published widely on gender, family, international development, spirituality, aesthetics, and race, within African and African Diaspora culture and art. Her articles have appeared in *Hypatia: A Journal of Feminist Philosophy*, the *Canadian Journal of Women and the Law*, the *Canadian Journal of Law and Jurisprudence*, *International Review of African American Art*, *Matriart: A Canadian Feminist Art Journal*, and *NKA: Journal of Contemporary African Art*. She has curated major shows on contemporary African art, modern Nigerian art, and the African Diaspora art; and has a forthcoming edited book, *Contemporary Issues in African Art* (1998). Her commissioned manuscript, *The MATCH Model: A 20-Year Study of a North-South Development Partnership*, is being published by MATCH International Canada.

Tanure Ojaide is an Assistant Professor in the Department of African-American and African Studies, University of North Carolina at Charlotte. A renowned poet, Ojaide has published six collections of poetry since 1973. He is also the author of a memoir, *Great Boys: An African Childhood* (1998), and two books of literary criticism, *Poetic Imagination in Black Africa: Essays on African Poetry* (1996) and *The Poetry of Wole Soyinka* (1994). *Invoking the Warrior Spirit: New and Selected Poems* is forthcoming from Africa World Press, Inc, New Jersey.

David Simon is Professor of Development Geography and Director of the Center for Developing Areas Research (CEDAR) at Royal Holloway, University of London. He holds degrees from the Universities of Cape Town, Reading and Oxford, and has published widely on development theory and development issues relating particularly to Africa, and especially southern Africa. He is also a leading specialist on Namibia. His most recent books are *Cities, Capital and Development: African Cities in the World Economy* (1992); *Structurally Adjusted Africa: Poverty, Debt and Basic Needs* (co-edited, 1995); *Transport and Development in the Third World* (London and New York: Routledge, 1996); and *South Africa in Southern Africa: Reconfiguring the Region* (co-edited, 1998)

Paul Tiyambe Zeleza is Professor of History and African Studies, and Director of the Center for African Studies at the University of Illinois, Urbana-Champaign. He is the author of ten books, including three works of fiction, and dozens of scholarly articles published in Africa, Europe, North America, and the Caribbean. He is the recipient of numerous fellowships, research grants, and literary awards, including the 1994 Noma Award for Publishing in Africa, Africa's most prestigious award, for his book *A Modern Economic History of Africa. Volume I: The Nineteenth Century* (1993). His most recent academic book is *Manufacturing African Studies and Crisis* (1997). This book won the 1998 special Commendation by the Noma Award for Publishing in Africa.

INDEX

Abadi 237
Abadi/Ivwri, god of war 237
Abuja 74, 241
Accra 20, 22, 266
Achebe, Chinua
  7, 231, 232, 236, 237
Action Party 285
Addis Ababa 21, 53, 66, 68, 359
African and Asian postimperial states
  294
African cultural identity 282
African freehold land 326
African labourers 279
African middle class 252, 254-255,
  257, 262
African political science 8
African social phenomena 11
African squatters 325
African-American history 228
Africanist social science 45, 271,
  273
Africanization 23
Afrikaner National Party 326
Afropessimism 47, 52
Agbogo mmuo 174, 188, 191
Age-sex structure 95
Agrarian reforms 302, 310
Agricultural cooperatives 284
AIDS/HIV virus 98
Ake 7, 198-199, 202-203, 206, 217-
  223, 226-227, 230-232, 274, 284,
  286, 296
Akunne Uwechia 175, 178
Algeria 22, 60
Alimaunde 93, 99, 100

Amadiora, god of thunder and
  lightning 237
American Literature 232
American literature 232, 233
ANC 11, 323-324, 346-347, 349-
  350, 353, 356
Angola 22, 59
Ani, the Earth goddess 237
Anti-slavery 211
Anticolonial nationalisms 281
Anticolonial struggle 258
Apartheid 3, 10-11, 22, 28-29, 31, 35,
  40, 53, 60, 74-75, 81, 93, 100, 290,
  305-306, 309, 315, 320, 323, 326,
  329, 336-338, 345-346, 348, 350,
  353, 359
Arab-Muslim cultural values 30
Aridon, god of memory 237
Art history 12, 192, 359
Artistic production 3, 5, 188
Asian commercial center 91
Atlantic Ocean 199, 238
Authoritarian developmentalist model
  3
authoritarian states 293
autocratic rule 60

Balancing Resource Inequities 301,
  303
Banda regime 82, 84, 85
Bangui 21
Bantu speakers 76
bantustan consolidation removals
  326
bantustan villages 329

bar girls 98
Bardera 22
Batwa 76
Beira 34
Benin 122, 125, 140, 208, 210-211, 244
Benin Empire 208, 211
Biwi 91
Black intellectuals 212
Black marketeering 98
Black tenant farmers 325
Blantyre 77, 80-86, 94-95, 97, 99, 102-103
Blantyre Supply Company 77
Body-space 5, 171-173, 175-176, 178, 180, 183, 185-188, 191
Boma 76
Booker T. Washington 225, 230
Botswana 51, 67-68, 308, 310-313, 316-317, 319-321
Botswana Constitution 311
Bourgeois legal discourse 324
Bourgeoisie 52, 167
Bread riots 22
Brian Colquhoun and Partners 81
Bridewealth 278
British Economic Commission 81
British government 81, 115, 303
Buguma 189, 190, 191
Buguma Centennial celebrations 190
Bulawayo 18, 149, 154-156, 159-161, 164-165
Burkina Faso 286
Burundi 22, 59

Cabral, Amilcar 9, 254, 265
Cairo: Mother of Megacities 35
Capitalism 23, 45, 65, 114, 124, 142, 153, 269, 293, 296, 323, 325, 356
Capitalist accumulation 44
Capitalist farming elites 317
Capitalist reorganization 44
Casely Hayford 9, 254, 257-259, 264-266

CBD 19, 29, 87, 91
Central Angoniland 76
Chewa 76, 81, 141
Chief Chuene 337
Chief Kekana 330, 337
Chief Land Claims Commissioner 327, 355
Chief M. M. Matlala 337
Chief Maboa 337
Chief Mojapelo 334
Chief Molepo 337, 344-346, 351
Chief Tseke 337
Chimphango 76
Christian culture 200
Christian missionaries 278
Christianizing zeal 23
Ciskei 333
City governance 62
City of death 89
City of superfluity 89
Civil society 47, 52, 59, 61, 65, 272, 284, 286, 296, 349, 353
Class Formation 298, 313
Class Segregation 32
Classic colonial garden city 18
Classical colonialism 261
Collective identity 8, 272, 273
Colombia 316
Colonial agrarian and land distribution policies 303
Colonial District Officer 217, 222
Colonial economic exploitation 282
Colonial government policy 325
Colonial law 303, 351
Colonial settlers 20, 303, 307
Colonial spatial order 60
Colonial state formation 276
Colonial wars of dispossession 325
Colonialist ideology 282
Commercial development 20
Commission on Restitution of Land Rights 327-328
Commodification of economic relations 274

Commodity prices 285
Communal boundaries 285
Communal ethics 221, 222
Communal Land Act of 1982 308
Communal land rights 307
Communist bloc 293
Concentric zone 86, 87, 91
Congo 268
Conservative political order 259
Construction of Landscapes 4, 12
Constructionist explanations 272
Consumption of Leisure 4, 64
Continental nationalism 254
cosmopolitan metropolises 252
counter-urbanization 57
Crisis of Legitimacy in Africa
    262, 267
Cross-cultural comparison 18
Cultural alienation 258
Cultural artefacts 19
Cultural countermovements 23
Cultural ecology 4, 111, 112, 121
Cultural identities 10-11, 276-277,
    281
Cultural oppression 263
Cultural sovereignty 281
Cultural specificity of Africans 282
Cultural subjectivity 256
Cultural theories 11
Cultural-political imaginary 252, 254
Culture in colonial captivity 259
Customary Land Law 320, 326, 346
Customary land tenure 304, 307-
    308, 350

Dakar 28, 34, 36, 64, 68-69, 71, 74,
    114, 298, 320, 356
Dar es Salaam 21, 53, 69, 70, 119,
    125, 269
Death tax 89
Decentralized despotism 276
Decolonization 12, 20, 48, 266, 283-
    285, 297
Deeds Registry 310, 311, 312
Deflationary policies 46, 50

Deindustrialization 49, 50
Delta State 239, 245
Democratic rule 27
Democratization of land relations
    11, 324
Denationalization of the indigenous
    populations 305
Densification 21, 28, 29
Department of Land Affairs 323,
    328, 333-335, 349, 352-355
Desertification 317
Deterritorialization of identities 293
Detroit 88, 248
Development Trust and Land Act
    326
Dhubai 102
discursive formations 2
District Medical Officer 78
Dodoma 74
Douglass, Frederick 212
Dr. Banda 80, 81, 94
Duein fubara 175
Dutch settlers 305

Earth goddess 237
Eastern Cape 333, 347
Ecological knowledge 3, 4
Ecology 4, 59, 62, 63, 68, 111-112,
    114, 121, 124-125, 128-129, 133,
    135, 140, 142-144, 146
Economic liberalization 33, 49
Economic Structural Adjustment
    Programme 19
Economic universalism 46
Ekine Society 191, 192, 194
English common law 311
Enwonwu, Francis 174
Environmental management 4, 136,
    314
Environmental Strategies for African
    Cities 36
Equiano, Oluadah 7, 197, 201, 208
Etatist modernist visions 10
Ethiopia 51, 59, 112, 124-125, 258,
    266, 359

Ethnic pluralism 276, 277
Ethnicity 3, 8-11, 23, 87, 89, 113,
    271-274, 279-280, 282-284, 286-
    289, 293-300, 304, 313-315, 323
Ethnomedicine 127-130, 133-136, 138-
    139, 141-145
ethnoregional communities 285-286,
    294
ethnoregional constituencies 287
Eurocentric views 3
Eurocentrism 18
European American scientific
    knowledge 6
European colonial power 253
European education 252
European exploitation 239
European immigrants 302
European influence 238
European nationalism 281
European philosophy 172
Europhone elites 275, 284
Evangelization 278
Experiential spaces 2
Exploitative model of urban structure
    88
Export processing industries 51
External factors 45

Falls Estate 78
Family spaces 171, 173, 183
Federation of Rhodesia and
    Nyasaland 18
Female headed households 56
female sexuality 278
folk cultures 5, 142
Forced removals 11, 305, 321, 325-
    326, 328, 329, 336, 339, 348,
    356
Formal sector employment 21, 22
Formal sector jobs 97
Fragmentation of colonial political
    landscapes 280, 284
Francophone West Africa 34, 38
Fulbe theocracies 292

Gates, Henry Louis 7, 12, 198
Gauteng Provincial Housing Board
    30
Gender relations 11, 58, 153, 298,
    313, 321, 324, 348
Gender-discriminatory nature of land
    policies 304
Gendered access to land in South
    Africa 349
Gendered analysis of the land
    question 313
Gendered Perspective 11, 309, 312-
    313, 320
genealogy 251, 330, 337
geographic space 234
geographical violence 5
gerrymandering of administrative
    boundaries 292
Ghana 56, 65, 112-113, 122-123,
    134-135, 139, 144, 253-254, 265-
    269, 280, 285-286, 296-297
Gikuyus 285
Global capital 44, 50
Global capitalist crisis 45
Global Plan of Action 27
Global recession 96
Globalization 4, 8, 23, 39, 43-44,
    46-48, 55, 63-65, 67, 293-294
Globalized production 23
Gold Coast 253-254, 259, 264-268,
    297
Government of National Unity 37,
    39, 315
Gramsci 262, 267
Group Areas Act 29
Guinea 65, 210, 254, 265

Habitat II 27, 36
Harare 18-19, 22, 29, 39, 53, 65-
    66, 69, 139, 161, 163, 165-167,
    319-321
Harvard Law School 226
Hausa 164, 167, 243, 277, 285
Hausa-Fulani groups 285

Health care delivery 4, 111-113, 115,
    121, 358
Hegemony 24, 60, 113, 115, 119,
    286, 292, 347
Hierarchies of race 9, 272
Historical geography 45
Historicity 1, 63
History of land dispossession 305
Home ownership scheme 96
House of Commons 210
House of Lords 210
Human agency 9, 63, 256, 272
Human dignity 318
Humanism 121, 286
Humanistic perspective 4, 115
Hurston, Zora Neale 233
Hybrid models 88

Ibadan Government College 221, 223
Ibo 235, 237, 239, 243-244
Ideational space 5, 171, 173
Ideologies of negritude 282
Ife 20, 134, 135, 244
Igbo 7, 187, 194, 197, 201, 205,
    231
IMEX 81, 93
IMF 22, 47, 49, 95
Imperial centers 252
Imperialism 5, 8, 77, 192, 254,
    256, 269
Indigenous social structures 20
Intellectual discourse 9, 192, 272-
    273
Inter-racial dating 224
International financial institutions
    44, 47, 49, 304
International labor migration 57, 82
Interpenetrable spatial spheres 5
Iron smelting 76
Islamic groups 60
Islands of development 74

Johannesburg 29, 36-40, 67-70, 268,
    315, 320-321, 333, 355-356
Joubert Park-Hillbrow-Berea 29

Kabula Stores Ltd. 77
Kalabari-Izhon aesthetics 191
Kalahari Kung 4, 119, 124
Kandodo 77
Kanengo 93, 99-100
Karoi 18
Kasungu District 80
Katsina 20
Kenya 39, 41, 51, 65-66, 68-69,
    74, 114, 116, 125, 135, 138, 145,
    267, 279, 287, 296, 298, 302
Kenyatta-led KANU 285
Keynesian orthodoxy 46
Khoi communities 325
Kigali 22
Kin-based groups 274, 295
Kinshasa 74, 119
Kinship boundaries 288
Knowledge production in Africa 173
Kumasi 20
Kung 4, 111, 119-121, 124
Kwazulu-Natal provincial govern-
    ment 315

Labor tenancy relations 333
Labour market segmentation 278-279
Labour unions 286
Labyrinths of the Delta 237, 240, 248
Lagos 29, 38, 54, 55, 64, 74, 135,
    173, 175, 194-195, 222, 241,
    245, 248
Lake Malawi 77, 85
Land acquisition and redistribution
    317
Land Board Committees 309
Land Claims Commission 305, 328,
    343-344, 352
Land Claims Court 305-306, 321,
    327-328, 348
Land dilemma 301, 304, 314

Land dispossession 11, 305, 307-
    308, 323, 325-326
Land privatization 10, 304, 308
Land registration programs 307, 310
Land resettlement schemes 309
Land Restitution 10-11, 305, 323-
    324, 327, 342, 346, 349, 351,
    356
Land restoration 10, 308, 316, 328
Land rights 10, 301, 304-305, 307,
    309, 312-313, 315-318, 320-321,
    324, 326-329, 334, 336, 339,
    342, 349-352, 356, 359
Land Tenure Reform 11, 321, 323
Land-based resources 301
Later Stone Age 76
Lebowa Government 337-338, 354,
    356
Liberal discourse 273
Liberalization 18, 22, 33, 43, 47-
    49, 66, 69, 272, 297, 304
Liberation struggles 302, 317
Liberia 22, 51, 59
Libya 58
Lilongwe River 77-78, 91
Lilongwe Sanitary Board 78
Literary texts 6, 7, 12
Liwonde 83, 85
Local and national power structures
    302
Location quotients 83
Luanda 21, 23
Lumbadzi Township 93
Lusaka 17-19, 21-22, 53, 70

Machine tax 89
Malambo 76
Malawi 73-74, 76-77, 80-81, 84-85,
    93-97, 101-102, 141, 320, 358-
    359
Malawi Housing Corporation 96
Male youths 51
Mali 286
Mandela 268, 315, 324, 347

Maravi Empire 76
Market-led land redistribution process
    353
Master Plan for Lilongwe 91, 93
Mauritius 51
Mchinji 83, 85, 86, 94
Medical geography 4, 111, 113,
    121-122, 145, 357
Metaphysical meaning 261
Metaphysical, Onitsha scheme 172,
    185
Middle class intelligentsia 9
Middle class residential neighbor-
    hoods 53
Migration and mobility 4
Minister of Land Affairs 327
Mmaboi 11, 314, 323-324, 333-
    336, 339, 341-342, 344-345,
    349, 352-355
Mmaboi Land claim 11, 314, 323
Mmuo ogonogo 6, 183, 186-187,
    193
Modernist Zonal Planning 30
Modernization of customary systems
    308
Modes of representation 10
Mogadishu 21, 22
Mojapelo chieftaincy 334, 337
Mojapelo Development Association
    344, 354
Mojapelo ethnic group 330
Mojapelo exodus 334
Mojapelo Land Claim 330, 339,
    343, 351
Mojapelo people 324, 337, 338
Monkey Bay 83
Monoeconomics 46
Morphology of urban spaces 2-4, 12
Mozambican civil war 83
Multiethnic coalitions of elites 286
Multiple nuclei 86, 87, 89, 93, 94
Muslim-Fulbe cultural codes 293

Namibia 39, 304, 308, 316-317,
    360

National Community Land Confer-
ence 328
National Congress of Nigeria and
Cameroons 285
National democratic transformation
323, 324
National Museum of African Art 174
National Party government 305
National-social order 261
Nationalism 8, 10, 24, 253, 254,
257-258, 260-262, 266, 279-282
296, 298-300
Nchesi 78
Ndi ichie 178
neo-classical economics 10
neo-classical paradigm 45
neo-Marxist 9
New Capital City Planning Area 93
Newtonian physics 183
Niger Delta 6, 7, 233-238, 241-246
Nigerian Women Union 222
Nkrumah, Kwame 9, 254, 266, 269
Nkrumahist nationalism 262

Odinigiwe Ben Enwonwu 6
Oge madu (human-time that encom-
passes body-space) 172
Oge mmuo (spirit-time) 172
Ogolo Metamorphosis 174, 188
Ogolo series 174
Oil-boom of Nigeria 243
Onitsha metaphysical scheme 172,
185
Ontological states 5
over-urbanization 75
overlapping claims 11, 329, 343-
344

Palestinian identity 264
Pan Africanist Congress 307
Pan-Africanism 282
Parastatal bodies 33
Pidgin English 238, 239, 240, 241
Place as Self 206

Plateau State in Nigeria 276
Political economic history 323
Politicization of ethnicity 271, 287,
293
Politics of Ethnicity 271
Port Harcourt 195, 239, 243, 245
Positivist social science 11
Post World War II apartheid policies
326
Post-Banda era 86
Post-Colonial Africa 265, 271
Post-colonial African nation 263
Post-colonial governments 74
Post-colonial land policies 303
Post-colonial native space 253
Post-Fordist global economy 48
Postmodern architectural forms 23
Postmodernism 25, 27, 36, 121,
127
Poststructuralist criticism 6
Postwar paradigms of development
271
Precolonial African towns 31
Preindustrial societies 271
Prescriptive frameworks 49
Pretoria 39, 333-334, 336-337, 355-
356
Primate city 80, 82-84
Pristine environment 243
Private property 323, 325, 353
Private-sector infrastructure 85
Production of identities 10

Racial discrimination 323
Racial segregation 77, 93, 114, 123
Racially divided society 323
Rank-size rule 83
Rebirth of democracy 272
Recolonization by foreign capital 33
Recolonization thesis 48
Reconstruction and Development
Programme 328, 355
Regional disparities 80
Registrar of Deeds 310

Reinventions of primordial ethnic identities 11
Remapping of urban cultural spaces 53, 54
Reorganization of African space 275
Reproduction of capital 302
Reproduction of urban life 3
Residential integration 28, 35
Resource endowments 26
Restitution of Land Rights Act 305, 324, 326-327, 349, 351-352, 355-356
Reverse migration 95
Rivers State 239, 244
Rock paintings 76
Rondavels 32
Rural and urban differentials 324
Rural-urban influx 75
Rural-Urban Interface 54, 64-66, 69-70
Rural-urban interface 54
Rural-Urban Migration 51, 56, 62, 67, 74, 82, 84
Rwanda 22, 59

Sacral objects 5, 171
Saro-Wiwa 244
sector model 87, 91
Self as Place 206
self-determination 61, 282, 302
Settler colonialism 10
Seven Buildings Project 30
sex and gender discrimination 10, 309
Seychelles 51
Shambas 20
Shell-BP 242, 243
Sierra Leone 22, 56, 59, 71, 114, 123, 134, 357
Slave trade 200, 210, 239
Slavery 197, 200, 207, 209-211, 218, 238, 282
Social artefacts 19
Social boundaries 5, 148
Social division of labor 44

Social ecologies 3, 4
Social Integration 32
Social justice 67, 303, 306, 319
Social phenomena 1, 2, 11
Social reproduction 33, 35, 302
Societal organization 301
Socio-cultural change 23
Socio-cultural flux 236
Socio-political reality 198
Sofala province 34
Sokari Douglas Camp 6, 174, 189, 194-195
South African National Civic Association 347
Southern African Development Coordinating Conferen 19
Soyinka 7, 197-198, 202-203, 205, 218-219, 222-223, 232, 237, 248, 251, 262, 269, 360
Spatial division of labor 44
Spatial economy 4, 9, 43, 63
Spatial framework 74
Spatial metaphors 4, 43, 44
spatial relations 252, 255, 274, 279, 294
spatial reorganization of production 4
Spatial Strategies 84
Spatial Structure of Lilongwe 86
Spatialized gender violence 5
Spatio-historical analysis 264
Spatio-temporal frames 173
spatio-temporal notion 171
Spirit-space 5, 171-173, 175-178, 180, 183, 185-187, 191-192
Squatter colonies 75, 96, 100
State doctrine 272
Statutory law 307
Stigmatization of ethnicity 273, 294
Structural adjustment policies 20, 63
Structuration of political relations 271
Struggles for democratization 4, 59
Subsistence sector 304
Sudan 39, 59
Sustainable Cities Programme 27

Sustainable development 25, 26-27, 34, 39, 68, 73
Sustainable urban development 3, 19
Sweatshops of the Third World 50
Symbolic spaces 1

Tambala 76
Technological underdevelopment 6, 179
Temporal-spatial production 4
Tenurial regimes 302, 312
Territorial divisions of labour 44
Territorialization of ethnic identities 9, 292
Things Fall Apart 7, 197, 198, 201-203, 205-206, 211-212, 217, 223, 231-232, 247
Third World oil producers 45
Thope 76
Time-space compression 8, 47
Tiv 239
Town and Country Planning Department 94
Traditional Healing 121, 146
Traditional land tenure systems 307
Traditional rulers 134, 275, 285
Traffic congestion 38, 75
Transforming agency 252
Transkei 333, 346, 355
Transparency 59, 61
Transvaal Government 332
Tunis 22

Uhaghwa, god of songs 237
Ultralow income housing 32
Umalokun 8, 237
Umalokun, goddess of the waters and wealth 237
Umuofia 202, 212-217
UN free-loaders 17
UNCHS 27, 36, 37, 40
UNEP 27
Uneven development of space 44

Union of South Africa 326, 334, 336, 353, 356
United Nations Conference on Environment and Devel 27
United Nations Declaration on Indigenous Rights 316
University of Malawi 102, 358
Upgrading Low-Income Areas 34
Urban Agriculture 53, 62, 64-70, 98
Urban morphology 19, 20, 23, 36, 75, 88, 91, 99
Urban spatial configurations 86
Urban-bias 4, 43, 44
Urban-rural linkages 45
Urbanization 27, 38-40, 68-69
Urbanization 20, 27, 38-40, 56-57, 62-63, 74-75, 81, 94, 278-279, 303
Urhobo concept 235
uwa 171-172

Vaal River 332

W.E.B. DuBois 225
welfarism 199
Western landuse 32
Western modes of thought 252
White cultural bias 199
White land ownership 336
Windhoek 28, 32, 39
Wole Soyinka 7, 237, 269, 360
World Bank 34, 47, 49, 70-71, 97
World citizenship 253-255

Yamoussoukro 74
Yoruba arts and aesthetics 5, 173
Youth organizations 286

Zambia 51, 56, 70, 85, 98, 112, 116, 124-125, 135-136, 141, 146, 267, 297, 313-314, 320
Zimbabwe 5, 18, 38-40, 56, 80-81, 85, 139, 147, 149, 163-167, 302, 304, 308, 312-313, 317, 319-321, 358

Zomba 73, 80-82, 85, 93-95, 99, 103
Zone of transition 87